A Most Remarkable Creature

A MOST REMARKABLE CREATURE

THE HIDDEN LIFE AND EPIC JOURNEY OF THE WORLD'S SMARTEST BIRDS OF PREY

JONATHAN MEIBURG

THORNDIKE PRESS
A part of Gale, a Cengage Company

A Cengage Company

**LIBRARY OF CONGRESS CIP DATA ON FILE.
CATALOGUING IN PUBLICATION FOR THIS BOOK
IS AVAILABLE FROM THE LIBRARY OF CONGRESS.**

ISBN-13: 978-1-4328-8976-0 (hardcover alk. paper)

Published in 2021 by arrangement with Alfred A. Knopf, an imprint of The Knopf Doubleday Publishing Group, a division of Penguin Random House LLC.

Printed in Mexico
Print Number: 01   Print Year: 2021

*To Robin and Anne Woods
and Kay McCallum,
who set me on this path*

Everyone has been more or less a traveler.

— CHARLES BARNARD

CONTENTS

10

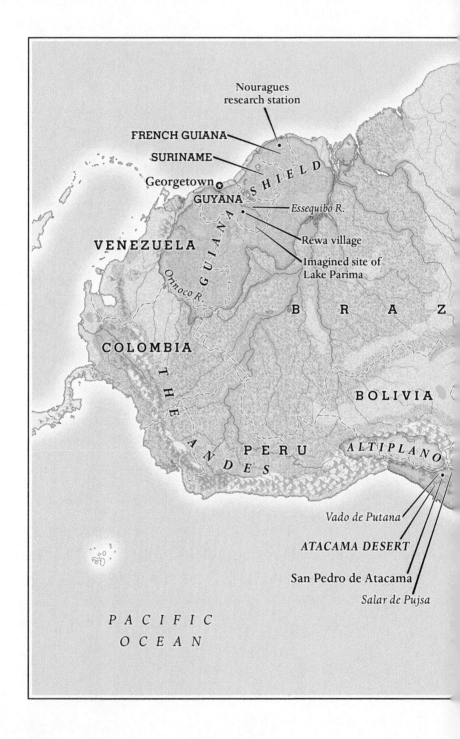

Nouragues
research station

FRENCH GUIANA

SURINAME

Georgetown

GUYANA

GUIANA SHIELD

Essequibo R.

Rewa village

Imagined site of
Lake Parima

VENEZUELA

Orinoco R.

B R A Z ... Z

COLOMBIA

T H E

BOLIVIA

A N D E S

PERU

ALTIPLANO

Vado de Putana

ATACAMA DESERT

San Pedro de Atacama

Salar de Pujsa

P A C I F I C
O C E A N

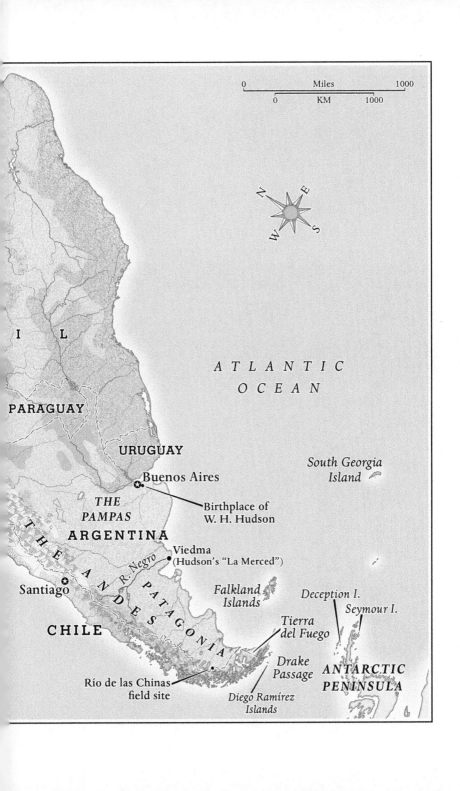

0 Miles 1000

0 KM 1000

ATLANTIC
OCEAN

PARAGUAY

URUGUAY

South Georgia
Island

Buenos Aires

Birthplace of
W. H. Hudson

THE
PAMPAS

ARGENTINA

Viedma
(Hudson's "La Merced")

R. Negro

Santiago

Falkland
Islands

Deception I.

Seymour I.

THE ANDES

PATAGONIA

Tierra
del Fuego

CHILE

Drake
Passage

ANTARCTIC
PENINSULA

Río de las Chinas
field site

Diego Ramírez
Islands

I   L

■ ■ ■ ■

Part I
Flying Monkeys

■ ■ ■ ■

One is astonished at the amount of creative force, if such an expression may be used, displayed on these small, barren, and rocky islands.

— CHARLES DARWIN

The actions of the feathered people have a savour of intelligence in them.

— WILLIAM HENRY HUDSON

1
An Unanswered Question

It's the turning of the Earth that spins the winds around Antarctica. The same force that curls hurricanes into deadly spirals gathers cold gales descending from the South Pole, where ice entombs entire mountain ranges, and launches them into a west-flowing moat of air that piles the seas into waves seven stories tall, shutting out the warmer world to the north. There's nothing to oppose them: sail a boat forever along the sixty-third parallel and you'd never see anything but black-and-white water, the spouts of whales, and the careening shapes of albatrosses skidding down the air on eleven-foot wings, a churning world that's our planet's most enduring scene.

But this endless polar cyclone frays along its northern border, where rogue winds peel off into the great oceanic basins — Indian, Pacific, Atlantic — and Atlantic-bound gusts first strike the green world in the fjords and islands of Tierra del Fuego, where the Andes

17

march into the sea. The winds fling plumes of wet sand against glacially sculpted cliffs and prune dripping forests of evergreen beeches into bizarre shapes — forests that are, in a way, the winds' making, since their fierce chill forces warm air traveling south from the Amazon to drop its hoarded water. Tierra del Fuego's wooded slopes and valleys are carpeted in mosses, ferns, and sundew, its trees draped in pale wisps of old-man's beard; and where its forests meet the sea, flightless sea ducks and giant otters shelter in a labyrinth of coves, inlets, and cobbled beaches that seem freshly carved from the bedrock of the world.

Charles Darwin saw these southernmost forests in the early months of his adventure aboard HMS *Beagle* and thought their grandeur rivaled the tropical woodlands that blew his mind in Brazil. But "in these still solitudes," he noted, "death, instead of life, is the predominant spirit." Without ants or termites to mill them down, Tierra del Fuego's dead trees stand and lie beside the living for years, and crow-sized woodpeckers knock splinters from their trunks with the dull *thunk* of hatchets. Even now, when you can fly the length of Darwin's five-year odyssey in two days, Tierra del Fuego's fog-bound channels are seldom visited, largely inaccessible, and since the demise of the Amerindians who lived there for thousands of years, unpeopled.

Ships occasionally use them to shelter from the mighty Pacific swells, but almost no one lingers.

Nor do the winds. Soaring over the low crests of the southern Andes, they beat north and east to glance off the unclimbed peaks of Isla de los Estados, where Jules Verne imagined a lighthouse at the end of the world, and bend the dry grasses on the plains of Patagonia. Then they go to sea again, dragging a train of whitecaps to soften and die in the tropics. But as they leave the high latitudes, they graze a last spot of land — a cluster of treeless, wasp-waisted islands in the northwest corner of the Falkland archipelago called the Jasons. And it's here, in the lee of fallen boulders and tufts of grass, that a hidden marvel huddles out of the wind's reach: one of the strangest and most wonderful animals on earth.

It didn't stay hidden from Darwin, but it took him by surprise in a place he was impatient to leave. The *Beagle* and its companion, HMS *Adventure,* called in at the Falklands twice before threading through the Strait of Magellan into the Pacific, and Darwin thought the islands' brown, undulating moorlands looked "desolate and wretched," especially compared to the Brazilian forests where it was "not possible to give an adequate idea of the higher feelings of wonder, astonishment, and devotion, which

19

fill and elevate the mind." The Falklands' monotonous landscape, broken only by a few low mountains and ridges of granitic quartz, suggested none of these feelings. "I can very plainly see," he confided in a letter to his sister, "there will not be much pleasure or contentment, till we get out of these detestable latitudes & are carrying on all sail to the land where Bananas grow."

It can be hard to picture Darwin as anything but a white-bearded ancient with a thousand-yard stare, but when the *Beagle* left England he was only twenty-two, a rich kid with an assured future as a country priest. He'd been invited aboard as much to keep the ship's melancholy young captain company as to advance the cause of science, and his unpaid role as a naturalist was incidental to the ship's official mission of mapping the treacherous coasts at the southern tip of South America. Darwin's only real qualification was an undistinguished bachelor's degree from Cambridge, where he often devoted more time to the upper-class pastimes of riding and shooting than to his studies, and even his best reference conceded he was not "finished"; he was simply an amiable and wealthy young man with a growing interest in rocks and insects, a yen for adventure, and a quality his uncle fondly described as an "enlarged curiosity."

The *Beagle*'s five-year voyage, Darwin

knew, would let him indulge this curiosity in places few naturalists had ever seen; and after convincing his reluctant father to pay his way, young Charles resolved to wring all he could from these years of freedom — even on cold, barren islands that left him pining for the tropics. Riding and shooting, as it happened, were useful skills in the Falklands, whose human population consisted of a single British officer and the remnants of a failed Argentine penal colony. Among the former prisoners were a contingent of gauchos, the legendary horsemen of the Pampas, who liked to chase feral cattle across the islands' waterlogged peatlands, and Darwin convinced a pair of them to take him along on one of their excursions.

For five days, they rode at a gallop through blinding squalls of snow and ice, dodging fierce bulls who weren't pleased to see them, sleeping on the bare ground, roasting their suppers of wild beef on fires stoked with bones instead of wood. Darwin's horse slipped and fell in hidden pockets of thick black mud, soaking him through, and by the sixth morning he could hardly wait to get back to his cramped cabin aboard the *Beagle*. But the ride gave him new mysteries to ponder — and chief among them was the astonishing tameness of the Falklands' wildlife. Grazing flocks of native geese barely flinched as Darwin and the gauchos thundered past, and even the legendarily cryptic birds called snipe — seen only in the distance, if at all, in England — let him come almost close enough to touch them. Other animals were bolder still: an inquisitive songbird probed at his shoes with its thin, curved beak, and the wolfish foxes unique to the islands were so tame that the gauchos could kill them by holding out a piece of meat in one hand and a knife in the other. These gullible carnivores, known locally as warrahs, "have been observed to enter a tent," Darwin wrote, "and actually pull some meat from beneath the head of a sleeping seaman." He suspected — correctly — that their fearlessness would soon lead to their extinction.

But a third animal, a handsome bird of prey that resembled a cross between a hawk and a raven, seemed to have an enlarged curiosity of its own. It had an orange face, a silver-gray beak, and glossy black plumage, and it massed in noisy gangs at the islands' only settlement to beg for scraps of kitchen garbage. Unlike the wary hawks and falcons Darwin knew in England, these "mischievous" birds could walk and run with the speed and agility of pheasants, and the crews of the *Beagle* and *Adventure* soon learned that their interests extended beyond food. "A large black glazed hat was carried nearly a mile," Darwin wrote, "as was a pair of the heavy balls used in catching cattle . . . [and]

a small Kater's compass in a red morocco leather case, which was never recovered." The *Adventure,* which surveyed the coasts of the Falklands while the *Beagle* made a circuit of islands in Tierra del Fuego, had to post a lookout to prevent them from flying aboard and tearing the leather from its rigging.

When the two ships met again, the *Adventure*'s crew offered Darwin stories of the "boldness and rapacity of these birds," mirroring the tales of whalers and sealers who'd been using the Falklands as a base for over a century. The sub-Antarctic world was full of strange animals — leopard seals, beaked whales, macaroni penguins — but the hat-stealing birds of the Falklands were unique. "The sailors who visit these islands," wrote one sealer, "being often much vexed at their predatory tricks, have bestowed different names upon them, characteristic of their nature, as flying monkeys, flying devils, etc, etc."

Astonishing as they were, Darwin also knew they weren't entirely singular. He'd just met some of their close relatives on the South American mainland, an odd and distinctive guild of scavengers that were unlike any birds he'd ever seen. The most common was a jay-sized, dusty-brown bird called a chimango, which gathered in flocks at the carcasses of cattle and horses in the grasslands south of Buenos Aires, but the most conspicuous was a larger, more elegant creature now known as a southern crested caracara — a dignified-looking bird with a yellow face and a flattened black crest like a mortarboard cap. Both birds "possess one family air," Darwin wrote, "and agree in habits with the Vultures in the following respects: in living chiefly on the flesh of dead animals, in quickly congregating at any spot, where an animal may have died; in gorging themselves till their craws protrude; in their tameness, or boldness with respect to mankind." The sound of the crested caracaras' weird, rattling call — a dry *karruk-karruk* — lingered in Darwin's mind, along with the contorted pose they struck as they uttered it, throwing their heads back until they nearly touched their tails. Despite their heraldic appearance, their "necrophagous habits" left him feeling uneasy in the deserts of Patagonia, where "they are very evident to any one who has fallen asleep on the desolate plains," he wrote, "for when he wakes, he will see, on each surrounding hillock, one of these birds patiently watching him with an evil eye."

The flying devils of the Falklands, however, puzzled him most of all. They'd been known to science* since 1775, when a naturalist

* Georg Forster, the naturalist who succeeded Joseph Banks as Captain Cook's naturalist during his second voyage on HMS *Resolution,* collected a stri-

traveling with the British explorer James Cook shot one in Tierra del Fuego, but no one had described their unusual behavior. Darwin tried to fill the gap by devoting more ink to their antics in *The Voyage of the Beagle* than he gave any other bird, and his account has the bemusement and mild alarm you'd expect from a young man staring down a predatory bird bent on stealing his hat. Though he didn't speculate about what they planned to do with their loot, Darwin did wonder why they'd chosen these remote islands for their metropolis. Like the giant tortoises and tame mockingbirds he would soon meet in the Galápagos, the Falklands' unique caracaras suggested that larger, unexplained forces — the real objects of his interest — were at work. But he set the mystery of their origins aside, and never took it up again.

Neither did anyone else, which surprised me when I met these birds two centuries later. Scientists have combed through Darwin's notebooks for insights he didn't (or couldn't) pursue: he correctly predicted, for

---

ated caracara at Isla de los Estados (Staten Island) in Tierra del Fuego in 1775. Forster's watercolor of this bird, dated January 2, now resides in the collections of the Natural History Museum in London and appears on the cover of this book.

example, that a species of moth would be discovered whose tongue could sound the depths of a foot-long orchid from Madagascar, and some of his stray thoughts have led to entire fields of scientific inquiry. But the riddle of the feathered thieves at the end of the world — now called striated caracaras — has remained. A few still live on the remote coasts of Tierra del Fuego, and though warrahs and gauchos vanished from the Falklands soon after Darwin's visit, striated caracaras still cling to life on the archipelago's outer islands, where they hunt and scavenge in colonies of penguins, seals, and albatrosses. They are the southernmost birds of prey on Earth, and among the rarest: no more than a few thousand are left, a number only slightly larger than the wild population of giant pandas.

But if you visit them, they refuse to behave like a species on the verge of extinction. They'll pluck the cap from your head, tug at the zippers of your backpack, and meet your eye with a forthright, impish gaze — and it's this earnest, playful quality, not their rarity or remoteness, that caught and held me when I met them twenty-five years ago. Striated caracaras seem disarmingly *conscious,* and they prod at the turf with their bills and feet and crane their necks to peer at everything with keen but slightly dubious interest, as if they've just emerged from the ark and wonder what else the world might have to offer. In the 1920s, the Falklands' official naturalist implored the government to rescind a bounty on their beaks, calling them "an ornament of the local avifauna" and noting that "from their point of view, every unfamiliar object demands immediate investigation." The first ones I saw stared back at me so intensely that I felt slightly abashed, as if I owed them an explanation.

Since then, I've returned to the Falklands every few years to work with the researchers trying to keep these unusual birds from the fate of the warrahs. It takes several days and an array of small planes and boats to reach them, but the thrill of seeing them again never fades: even after I've helped trap them with snares, weighed them in burlap sacks, taken blood samples from their wings, and attached identifying rings to their legs, I've watched them ruffle their feathers and walk right back toward me, as if compelled by a single burning question: *What are you?*

I wish I could tell them that I'm trying to ask them the same thing. The digital age has given us tools for tracking animals into the past that Darwin couldn't have imagined — genetic analysis, Google Earth, even geological maps of the prehistoric world. But piecing together the story of the Falklands' flying monkeys has led me on a long and surprising journey, thousands of miles and millions of years from their homes, and I've emerged with an admiration for them that borders on awe. Calling them odd birds of prey feels like calling the painters of the Italian Renaissance a group of unusually gifted apes.

Unless you live south of the Rio Grande, chances are you've never even heard of caracaras. But if you try to imagine ten separate attempts to build a crow on a falcon chassis, with results falling somewhere between elegant, menacing, and whimsical, you wouldn't be far off. A few species are drab and inconspicuous, but most are boldly patterned in black and white, with red or yellow skin on their faces and legs. Some are nearly as small as magpies; others are as large as ravens. All have broad wings, hooked beaks, and an alert, curious expression, and they live in every part of their supremely varied continent, from the arid peaks of the Andes to the steaming forests of the Amazon basin.

Their most striking qualities, however, are their minds. Unlike most birds of prey, caracaras are social and curious, and they feed with gusto on foods other predators disdain. Darwin wrote that chimango caracaras were "truly omnivorous, and will eat even bread," and in the tropics, the tribal birds called red-throated caracaras thrive on a unique diet of wasps' nests and fruit. In the high Andes, a species whose feathers adorned the heads of

Inca emperors has been seen working in teams to uncover lizards and insects by flipping heavy rocks, and the crested caracaras who unnerved Darwin in Patagonia are said to spread wildfires by dropping burning sticks in dry grass, and feasting on the ensuing stream of refugees.

Despite these remarkable behaviors, scientists and falconers from the northern world have largely ignored the caracaras. Even Darwin called them "false eagles" who "ill become so high a rank," and a sense that there's something unwholesome or disappointing about them has been slow to ebb. The Chilean poet Pablo Neruda spoke with affection when he called chimango caracaras "shiftless wanderers of rubbish pits," but a pair of venerable ornithologists from the United States weren't kidding when they dismissed the entire group as "aberrant falcons" and "a rather unimpressive lot." Joan Morrison, one of few modern scientists to take an interest in caracaras, told me that biologists still suffer from a vague sense that caracaras just aren't what a self-respecting raptor ought to be. "They're dirty birds," she said, with a half smile. "Bad falcons."

There have been a few dissenting voices over the years. In the late eighteenth century, the Spanish naturalist Félix de Azara marveled at the ingenuity of crested caracaras he met near Buenos Aires, writing that "all manner of subsistence is known to this bird; it pries into, takes advantage of, and understands everything." A century later, the writer and natural historian William Henry Hudson had Darwin in his sights when he protested that caracaras had been vilified without good cause; they were a "sub-family of which even grave naturalists have spoken slightingly, calling them vile, cowardly, contemptible birds," he wrote. "Despite this evil reputation, few species are more worthy of careful study."

I daydream about keeping a striated caracara in my apartment. It would be the world's most exasperating roommate, but watching it build a nest of shredded T-shirts, LP jackets, and guitar strings in my bookshelf might be worth it. I can imagine it standing on my kitchen counter in the morning, tearing into a box of cereal with its beak or cracking an egg with a blow from its clenched foot, then stashing a piece of toast under my chair while I boil water for coffee. After breakfast, it might become absorbed in a dirty sock or a roll of paper towels while I try to figure out where it's hidden my keys. All the while, I'd be thinking of Darwin's unanswered questions, and a few of my own: *Why are you like this? Why are there so few of you? How did you come to be?*

Each time I've tugged on these threads, their story has grown larger and wilder than I could have imagined. Striated caracaras and their kin have surprising and important stories to tell us: about the history of life, about the hidden worlds of their grand and mysterious continent, about how evolution can fashion a mind like ours from different materials. They might even offer us some advice about surviving in a world primed for an upheaval.

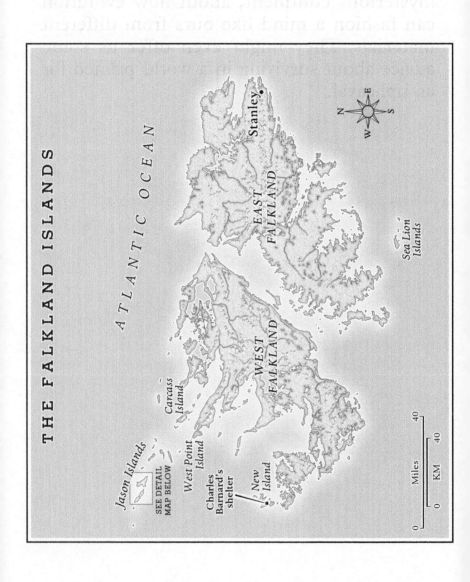

THE FALKLAND ISLANDS

ATLANTIC OCEAN

Stanley

EAST
FALKLAND

Sea Lion
Islands

WEST
FALKLAND

Jason Islands

SEE DETAIL
MAP BELOW

Carcass
Island

West Point
Island

Charles
Barnard's
shelter

New
Island

N
W   E
S

Miles   0   40

KM   0   40

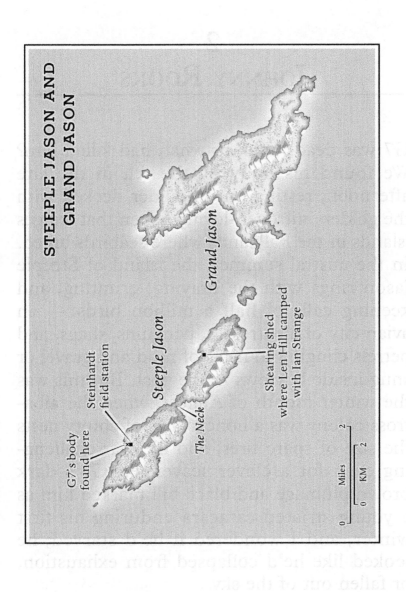

STEEPLE JASON AND
GRAND JASON

Grand Jason

Steeple Jason

Steinhardt
field station

G7's body
found here

The Neck

Shearing shed
where Len Hill camped
with Ian Strange

Miles
0   2

KM
0   2

2
JOHNNY ROOKS

G7 was dead. Who, or what, had killed him? We found his body by the sea in the late afternoon, resting on a boulder decked with the golden, nitrogen-loving lichen that fringes islands in the Falklands where seabirds breed. In the austral summer, the island of Steeple Jason rings with the braying, grunting, and keening calls of half a million birds — an avian city of albatrosses, penguins, shags, and petrels clinging to nests of mud and gravel or snug inside burrows in the peat. But this was the winter month of August, when the albatross colony was a honeycomb of empty nests the size of spare tires, and life was challenging even for a clever scavenger. G7's dark brown plumage and black bill marked him as a young striated caracara enduring his first winter, and I wondered if he'd starved; he looked like he'd collapsed from exhaustion, or fallen out of the sky.

Andy Stanworth, a biologist from Falklands Conservation, stooped to pick him up. G7's long wings fell open, revealing that he'd been half-eaten in a way that seemed oddly fastidious: the muscles of his neck and breast were neatly stripped away, leaving the white keel of his sternum exposed, but the rest of him was untouched — even his wide, glassy eyes. I took off my gloves and held one of his feet against my palm, feeling the reptilian smoothness of its scales and the rounded tips of its talons, blunted from walking on the stony ground. The black plastic ring I'd fastened to his leg a few weeks earlier, with its yellow letter and number, was good as new. I opened my notebook. *3 September 2012,* I wrote. *Found a body.*

The Falklands hold a unique place in the human and animal worlds, but they have a misleading facade. When I first visited the islands in 1997, the capital of Stanley looked like an English seaside village, with narrow streets lined with hedges of Scotch broom and red telephone boxes by the harbor. The whalebone arch in front of the modest cathedral and the flightless ducks milling below the seawall hinted that the UK might, in fact, be very far away — but the rugged hills in the distance could almost have been Dartmoor, and a Union Jack fluttered smartly above the lawn of Government House. Aging Land Rovers trundled through the streets on the left, and English was the only language I heard, spoken with an antipodean twang reminiscent of New Zealand. Hardly anyone mentioned the vast South American continent that lay three hundred miles away.

In the time since Darwin's visit, humans have transformed the Falklands' two largest islands into a patchwork of sheep farms the size of Connecticut, which the world glimpsed during the 1982 war with Argentina that left Stanley's beaches studded with mines. But hundreds of smaller islands — some less than an acre in size — preserve an older, wilder version of the archipelago. Before Europeans brought cattle and sheep to the Falklands, their coasts were blanketed in a forest of giant grass called "tussac" that grew in tall, rounded pedestals, a vaguely Seussian landscape filled with birds. Some were year-round residents like finches, wrens, and geese, but many were seafarers who came ashore to breed in massive colonies like the ones on Steeple Jason. Where farming took hold, this abundance has largely disappeared, but on smaller islands it's still possible to glimpse the Falklands as they were a few centuries ago, innocent of politics or agriculture.

It was a visit to one of these islands, via a two-engine Falkland Islands Government Air Service plane, that introduced me to striated caracaras. Sea Lion Island wasn't the wildest of the outer Falklands, and it didn't look like much from the air: a gently sloping table of rock and pasture ringed with dark cliffs and pale beaches, small enough to walk around in a few hours. Sheep had grazed away most of its tussac, but the island was no longer a farm, and its former residents had begun to reclaim it. Elephant seals lounged on its beaches while penguins played in the surf, and severe-looking seabirds called giant petrels nested at the end of a long, sandy spit. In the center of the island, ruddy-headed geese and red-breasted meadowlarks paced among low shrubs covered in tiny, astringent berries.

I walked Sea Lion's coast all morning and sat down to rest on its southern cliffs, looking down on colonies of rockhopper penguins and cormorant-like birds called imperial shags. The shags turned their slender beaks and bright blue eyes toward me for a moment, then resumed fortifying their nests with beakfuls of mud and seaweed. Their long, curved necks and functional wings distinguished them from the squat, flightless penguins, but they'd been to the same tailor: both species were black above and white below, with whimsically ornamented heads: a curlicue of black feathers and orange nasal wattles for the shags, a spiky yellow crest for the red-eyed rockhoppers. As long as I didn't move, the birds acted as if I wasn't there, and at the base of the cliff, long coils of giant kelp curled and uncurled in the foaming waves.

I was contemplating the blue-black water stretching away toward Antarctica when I heard a rush of wings and a faint clicking of talons on the shale, and turned to face a pair of young striated caracaras — the first I'd ever seen. Unlike the penguins and shags, they were unmistakably interested in me; one took a few steps in my direction and cocked its head like a dog. A gift seemed appropriate, but I didn't have any food, so I fished a pen from my pocket and dropped it on the ground. The two birds gazed at it for a moment, as if deciding what to do, and then one stepped forward to seize the pen with its large, dexterous foot — an almost parrot-like gesture — and looked up at me, as if to say *Is this all you've got?* Then its companion lunged for the pen, flapping its wings and screeching, and the tumbling pair chased each other over the lip of the cliff.

Wait, I thought. *Come back. Explain yourselves.*

Back in Stanley, I asked around about the pen-stealing birds and soon learned two things: that they were called "Johnny rooks" — a rakish nickname from the whaling days — and that they weren't, generally speaking, held in high regard. A few people said they were vicious pests; many simply called them "cheeky." I'd heard New Yorkers call city

38

pigeons winged rats, and Texans muttering darkly about urban invasions of great-tailed grackles, but it seemed especially British to accuse a bird of impertinence. I couldn't help wanting to see them again, and it felt a little like fate when I met a British ornithologist who was bound for the Falklands' wildest edges to study them.

His name was Robin Woods, and we met as guests of a fourth-generation islander named Kay McCallum, who'd turned her compact, century-old house into a B&B by setting out a sign that read KAY'S B&B. Kay's skeptical exterior masked a soft heart, and Robin and I bonded over our mutual fondness for her. She always found a way to house and feed the travelers who appeared at her door, even if it meant sleeping on the floor of her closet-sized kitchen so a guest could have her bed, and she seemed quietly pleased that the world had decided to come to her. The night I turned up, there were tourists from Japan camped in her back garden, an Italian couple on a fold-out couch, a linguist from Oxford on a cot in the living room, and a monkish scientist from the British Antarctic Service in a tiny upstairs bedroom. Among the parade of daily visitors was Kay's spirited six-year-old granddaughter Shanice, who asked Robin if his mother had given him a bird's name on purpose.

Robin said he didn't think so, but she could hardly have picked a better one. He grew up in postwar England but fell in love with the Falklands' birds in 1956, when he accepted a remote posting from the British Meteorological Office in a young man's fit of adventure. Forty years later, he knew as much about the islands' wildlife as anyone alive, and this time he'd come to conduct the first-ever census of striated caracaras in the uninhabited island group called the Jasons. The government was considering new legislation to protect the Johnny rooks, but no one knew how many had survived decades of persecution.

This was an old story for Robin, who'd seen the relationship between Falkland Islanders and wildlife evolve over many years. When he first came to Stanley, its residents lived closer to the nineteenth than the twentieth century; they cut peat from the hills above the town to heat their homes, and communication with England was only possible via telegram or mail boat. Outside Stanley, absentee land-lords hired managers to run vast estates, like Ireland in the days before the great famine, and tenant farmers worked very hard for very little. Though Robin met many people who loved the islands' wildlife, some saw the penguins, albatrosses, and caracaras as a nuisance or an amusement: there were stories of men using rockhopper penguins as foot-balls, and one enterprising landowner turned

40

foxes and skunks loose on islands packed with breeding seabirds, hoping to ignite a fur trade.

By 1997, much had changed. The journey from England no longer required a month at sea, though it was still extraordinary — an eighteen-hour flight that departed from a Royal Air Force base in Oxfordshire, stopped to refuel on a volcano in the middle of the Atlantic Ocean, then carried on to another military base in the Falklands, where civilian passengers took a ninety-minute bus ride to Stanley over a rutted gravel road. Gas stoves had mostly replaced peat, and television had just arrived, but life in the outer farms remained much as Robin remembered it, and on the Jasons he expected to see places that hadn't changed in centuries. I made no secret of my desire to go with him, and after a dinner of shepherd's pie, a few glasses of wine, and an enormous pavlova that Kay had somehow produced from scratch, he agreed to take me on. Like Darwin, I had no meaningful credentials, but I was the same age Robin had been in 1956, which seemed to please him. "I think you'll see things," he said, refilling my glass, "that will make your young eyes pop out of your head."

I didn't know then that I was upholding a tradition. In the winter of 1813, twenty years before Darwin turned up aboard the *Beagle,* another curious young American from New

York had also been surprised by an encounter with striated caracaras. But Captain Charles Barnard was a sealer, not a naturalist, and when he met the Johnny rooks he faced some very pressing problems: his clothes were falling apart, he was running out of food, and he'd been marooned on a desert island.

Only a few months earlier, everything had been going very well. Barnard and his hired crew had sailed from Sandy Hook, New Jersey, hoping to make their fortune from the seals that crowded the Falklands' virgin beaches. They made the six-thousand-mile journey without incident and reached their first stop on schedule — Steeple Jason, as it happened — where they set to work clobbering their quarry with wooden clubs and piling their boat with pelts. But a few days later they met a wilier set of opponents: the surviving crew of a wrecked British frigate. Britain and the United States were newly at war, and when Barnard rescued the surprised Brits in an excess of gallantry, they returned the favor by stealing his ship — leaving him, his dog, and a few fractious shipmates on a crescent-shaped island on the Falklands' western edge. Barnard's companions soon struck out for another island in their only rowboat, leaving him to fend for himself, and he cursed them elaborately in his journal ("Oh, for a whip of scorpions," he raged, "to lash the rascals naked through the world!"). But when his anger cooled he got to work, building a shelter from stones and driftwood and fashioning a jacket and trousers from sealskin. This done, he began to store up food for the coming winter, burying a cache of eggs from a nearby colony of rockhopper penguins beneath a dense stand of tussac.

He was on the verge of feeling pleased with himself when his supplies came under attack. Barnard's buried eggs were discovered, unearthed, and eaten by a curious mob of striated caracaras, who must have been pleasantly surprised to find that their new neighbor had saved them the trouble of forcing penguins off their nests. They began to follow him around the island, watching his every move, and one night he woke to find them trying to pull the shoes off his feet.

Barnard didn't know what to make of these winged marauders, or how to deal with them. He tried waving his arms, shouting, and pelting them with sand, but they wouldn't leave him alone. No matter how carefully he hid his eggs, the birds dug them up as soon as his back was turned, and as he confided in his journal, they seemed to covet everything he had. "I have known these birds to fly away with caps, mittens, stockings, powder horns, knives, steels, tin pots, in fact everything which their great strength is equal to," he wrote. "They compel me to secure my provisions . . . which I fasten down by stones, and then direct the dog to lie down by them to prevent these harpies from hauling off the stones."

There was worse still to come. One afternoon, Barnard misplaced the club he used to bludgeon unsuspecting seals and penguins, a grave loss that sent him into a deep funk. He began to think the island might be haunted by an evil spirit, but a few days later he spotted a group of "piratical rooks" milling around in the air — one of whom, unbelievably, was carrying his club by the iron ring at its base. He spent the day hurling rocks at them, recovering his club and leaving "twelve of their number on the field of battle . . . which instead of diminishing, added to [my] stock." They probably tasted pretty good; twenty years later, Darwin would note that their cooked flesh was "quite white, and very good eating; but bold must be the man who attempts such a meal."

Barnard was bold enough, since they stood between him and starvation, but he also nursed a growing interest, despite himself, in the Johnny rooks. They were "the most mischievous of all the feathered creation," he declared — but he couldn't decide what they were. "From their color, mischievous disposition, and feeding on carrion," he wrote, "they appear to belong to the crow species; while, on the other hand, from their form . . . they appear to be connected with the hawk. I should, from these characteristics, call them the vulture-crow . . . until some ornithologist shall affix to them the proper name."

The Johnny rooks probably didn't know what to make of him either. Charles Barnard was likely the first person they'd ever seen, and no other animal had ever thrown a rock at them, or come equipped with such a fascinating array of accessories. Their meeting was a moment of first contact that had receded into the distant past for most animals on Earth, and the caracaras' "mischievous" behavior, though annoying to a weary castaway, was in fact the key to their survival.

Penguins seem purpose built for life in the sub-Antarctic. They chase glowing shoals of squid in the chilly depths of the southern oceans, insulated by a natural drysuit of fat and feathers, and though they're awkward on land, they're grace itself in the water. During the caracara survey with Robin, I watched them leaping from the waves beside our boat and saw why Francis Drake mistook them for fish: their sleek bodies perfectly matched the demands of their aquatic lives. They suited the wild landscapes of the Jasons, where long summer sunsets magnified the shaggy silhouettes of islands still clad in tussac grass, and gilded the waves with violet and gold.

Against this grand backdrop, the Johnny rooks seemed more like party crashers who'd overstayed their welcome. They couldn't swim or drink salt water, they don't migrate, and their approach to life seemed haphazard. But it was clearly effective: though they weren't the only predatory birds in the outer islands, they were by far the most numerous. Steeple Jason was home to a single pair of peregrine falcons, but we found nearly *three hundred* striated caracaras crammed together on its shores, a shocking number for an island small enough to traverse in two days. Young Johnny rooks massed in loose groups that reminded me of the weasels who ransack Toad Hall in *The Wind in the Willows,* and adult pairs defended slim territories on the edges of seabird colonies. They scurried nimbly among the albatrosses and penguins, trying to snatch their eggs and chicks, and swooped at us when we approached their nests. Unlike peregrines, who eat only fresh meat, striated caracaras seemed prepared to digest almost anything; we watched them pluck fly larvae from mats of rotting kelp, dig in the turf for worms, clean the snotty nostrils of snoozing elephant seals, and tear into seabird burrows with talons they used to dig and grip like hands.

These piecemeal, trial-and-error lives made them seem like survivors of an ancient ship-wreck, determined to wring a living from the island any way they could. When I first saw them running toward me at full tilt, I felt a

46

shiver of cognitive dissonance: *Aren't wild animals supposed to run away?* One yanked the knit cap from my head and landed just out of reach, fixing me with a probing gaze, and as we walked the coasts of the Jasons I often looked down to see a winged shadow merging with my own, then up to find a caracara hovering a foot or two above me. If I stood still, they would descend by inches to tap me on the shoulder and soar away, as if inviting me to play tag.

The Europeans who settled the Falklands in the nineteenth century thought the Johnny rooks had their uses — one woman in Stanley, according to legend, stuffed them down her chimney to clean it — but sheep farmers often took a dim view of the birds, especially when a ewe struggling to give birth became a meal for a group of hungry caracaras. It's hard to blame the birds for taking advantage; it's equally hard to imagine a better mascot for Falkland Islanders than a scrappy, resourceful scavenger whose greatest skill is making the best of what's around. But it's a sheep, not a caracara, that adorns the Falklands' flag, and following a downturn in the price of wool in 1908, the island government placed a bounty on Johnny rook beaks.

The massacre that followed nearly drove the caracaras to extinction, and the government naturalist, James Hamilton, pleaded with officials to stop the slaughter. "There is

47

an irresistible, shambolic clownishness about them that demands attention," he wrote, noting that "one bird, with whom I had a slight acquaintance, would play for a long time with an empty sardine tin." Eventually he prevailed, but by the 1960s the birds survived only on islands people seldom (or never) visited.

Remarkably, decades of persecution haven't frightened the clownishness out of the Johnny rooks. Younger birds will perch on your boots if you sit still long enough, and they've been seen kicking at discarded rubber gloves and playing tug-of-war with scraps of plastic sheeting. All this play serves a purpose: the ocean often coughs up novel items, and you never know what might turn out to be food. But it also carries an undertone of desperation. It takes striated caracaras at least four years to reach sexual maturity — twice as long as peregrine falcons — and like human teenagers with little to lose, young Johnny rooks have to lean into the unknown if they hope to survive. They follow their peers around to see what *they* might be eating, and their bulging crops, which emerge from their breast feathers when they've enjoyed a meal, make it hard for them to conceal good fortune.

Some young birds, however, seem unable to get the hang of living, and wear themselves out begging other birds for food or simply wither away, looking haggard and depressed. The ones that make it to adulthood have mastered the art of finding a meal anywhere they can, and since the larder varies from island to island and season to season, successful Johnny rooks have to maintain an open mind and an ecumenical diet. They catch tiny fish in the shallows at low tide, or fill their bellies with seal shit, and some become seasonally nocturnal to hunt petrels that return to their burrows at night.

Humans have been harder for striated caracaras to understand. James Hamilton lamented that despite the deadly effects of the bounty, the birds "had not learnt that man is dangerous," and Falkland lore includes stories of Johnny rooks stealing underwear from clotheslines and eating tins of engine grease. Though we've come after them with rifles and shotguns, they seem drawn to us all the same: their curiosity, it appears, is stronger than their instinct for self-preservation.

This is a dangerous way to live, but it can be a fruitful one, as you and I know well, since it's also a hallmark of *Homo sapiens*. After we left our hearth in Africa, it took us only a hundred thousand years to colonize the rest of the habitable world, and we advanced along three great fronts: through the Middle East into Europe and Asia; down the coast of India to Southeast Asia and Australia; over the Himalayas into China, Siberia, and the Americas. As we traveled, animals big enough to eat learned to keep their distance, went extinct, or became our companions and slaves. The predators and herbivores of Africa had a distinct advantage, since they'd watched our ancestors learn to hunt and wield fire, and knew to flee or attack when we appeared. But as we pressed on, we met animals who didn't know us at all, and many didn't survive the encounter. The first meeting of a human and a mastodon — or a giant lemur, or a cave bear — must have been an awesome event, but it's easy to forget that for thousands of years, scenes like these were commonplace. Big, edible creatures were always waiting over the next ridge or across the next stretch of water, and they must have been a powerful incentive to keep moving.

Our inborn wanderlust — the way the horizon always beckons — might even be a genetic legacy of this great exodus. Darwin wondered about the obscure but powerful feeling that seized him among the fjords of southern Chile, where the *Beagle*'s crew spent many days climbing through primeval forests in hopes of finding a view, even though they invariably saw more fjords, more mountains, more forests. Nonetheless, he wrote, "there is an indefinite expectation of seeing something very strange."

Maybe we're still looking for animals. Hunting didn't always require stealth, skill, or weapons that kill from far away; it only took a new place whose creatures didn't know us yet, and for thousands of years they were always waiting around the bend. A few "uncontacted" people remain today in the roadless forests of the western Amazon, but uncontacted mammals and birds are just as rare: the whalers and sealers of Barnard's day met the last of them on the islands scattered around Antarctica. The tale of Alexander Selkirk, a British castaway whose adventures inspired *Robinson Crusoe,* was a last glimpse of this world as it receded from memory into legend, and the subject of a popular poem Barnard knew well:

The beasts that roam over the plain
My form with indifference see;
They are so unacquainted with man.
Their tameness is shocking to me.

You and I can feel an echo of these first meetings at a zoo when we're faced with a creature we've never seen — an okapi, say, or a sifaka, or a beady-eyed Surinam toad — and something tingles in the back of our brains. Our eyes still long for new animals, and paintings and carvings in the caves of Europe and the cliffs of the Sahara attest to our long fascination with the creatures who

51

shared our world, and gave us life, in the time when we first became known to them.

The Johnny rooks are among the last outliers. As far as we know, the traveling people who walked across the Bering Strait into the Americas to become Amerindians never learned that the Falklands existed; along with the Galápagos, the Falklands are the only part of the so-called New World that Europeans actually discovered. Barnard's journal describes a group of clever, observant animals taking their first measure of a human being, and there's an irony in their meeting that probably escaped him, since the "vulture-crows" had survived by honing the same talents that had led him there — an opportunism that scraped recklessness, and an irresistible interest in anything new.

I set G7's body in a plastic bucket outside the front door of Steeple Jason's research station, pulled off my boots and coat in the vestibule, and entered its jarringly suburban living room, where a team of scientists and volunteers was transferring data from field notebooks to laptops and cooking an evening meal of mutton from the farm on nearby Carcass Island. We'd all arrived on Steeple by different roads: Andy Stanworth, who spotted G7's body, was a British scientist who'd come to the Falklands to escape the grind of life in the UK; Micky Reeves, a native islander, concealed his deep passion for wildlife behind his wry humor; and Robin Woods had returned with his friend David Galloway, a retired sociology professor who'd taught primary school on West Falkland in the 1950s, when the only mode of travel besides walking was on horseback.

The team's leader was Kalinka Rexer-Huber, a keen and efficient young New Zealander working for the UK's Royal Society for the Protection of Birds. Kalinka had ridden the sub-Antarctic field science circuit for years with her laconic husband, Graham, bouncing from one windy island to another, trying to save threatened seabirds from extinction. In their previous job, they'd spent thirteen months with five other people on Gough Island, a dormant volcano in the South Atlantic draped with the skeletons of albatrosses. The giant birds had been literally gnawed to death by "supermice," oversized descendants of house mice who arrived with shipwrecked sailors centuries ago. Since then, the mice had grown to nearly twice the size of their forebears and developed a taste for flesh, and Kalinka and Graham were studying the possibility of wiping them out with poisoned bait. Their findings weren't encouraging: the island's sharp ridges of eroded lava made it impossible to reach all the places mice might live, and Kalinka showed me a haunting photograph of Graham holding the

53

remains of an albatross, bracing its wing bones against his outstretched arms so they towered above his head. It looked like the skeleton of a pterodactyl.

Mice had also brought Kalinka and Graham to the Falklands. As on Gough, the tenacious little mammals had arrived on Steeple Jason sometime in the past century, and they'd already begun to eat the nestlings and eggs of small songbirds. Conservationists feared for Steeple's colony of black-browed albatrosses — the world's largest, at 140,000 birds — and Kalinka and her team were charged with finding out if the mice could be killed by carpeting the island with poisoned cereal pellets in winter, when the seabirds are away. The first step was making sure Steeple's mice would take the bait, and the team's days were a wearying slog through tall stands of tussac to spread fistfuls of nontoxic test bait laced with fluorescent green dye. After giving the mice a few days to feed, they set and cleared hundreds of traps and brought the dead mice back to the station, where Kalinka shone an ultraviolet light on their viscera to see if they glowed.

It was typical field science grunt work — tough, dull, and faintly absurd — but it had its moments. Steeple Jason's twin peaks give it the stark beauty its Homeric name suggests, and on clear days the cold air streaming in on the southwest wind was so pure that a veil seemed to lift from the world. Giant petrels wheeled above the island's central ridge, and crowds of gentoo penguins emerged from the surf to bask in the sun at its slender neck. Most of the penguins milled and snoozed in a loose colony near their landing beach, but a few followed an obscure yearning and climbed the ridge to gaze at the sea from above.

Even among scenes like these, a dead striated caracara was something special, and after dinner we crowded into the vestibule to watch Kalinka perform a necropsy. Micky consulted his field notes and found that he'd seen G7 that morning, in the company of other young Johnny rooks. Kalinka, opening G7's abdomen with a scalpel, murmured that his insides looked healthy: his stomach was full of the scraps of a penguin's foot, and he wasn't obviously dehydrated, or visibly diseased. Then she turned her attention to his head, pressing up on his lower mandible, and his skull flopped backward.

"There you go," she said. "His neck's broken."

At first this seemed to confirm what we all suspected: that he'd tangled with another caracara and lost. We were wrong, but I only learned that several months later, with the help of a melancholy naturalist whose life and work drew me in with the same curious force as the Johnny rooks. William Henry Hudson was one of the first people to write a kind word about caracaras — and like them, he wasn't what he appeared to be.

3
A HALF-TAMED HAWK

Broadwater Cemetery lies near the center of the coastal English town of Worthing, around the corner from a polytechnic school and a high street. It's unremarkably recent by UK standards — its graves date from the mid-nineteenth to the mid-twentieth century — but its headstones have started to lean, and some of its tallest monuments have collapsed. Moss and wild blackberry grow on plots paved with gravel and sea glass; wood pigeons and magpies boom and chatter in ornamental pines grown large enough to anchor a forest; and two empty bird feeders, patched with duct tape, sway above a newish bench.

A few discreet signs point visitors to Broadwater's three most-visited residents, of whom Mary Hughes, who had a little lamb, is both the most famous and the least known. Around the corner from Mary lies the well-tended grave of Richard Jefferies, a Victorian writer whose fevered autobiography, *The Story of My Heart,* is a talisman for British writers in love with the natural world. ("The air, the sun-light, the night, all that surrounds me seems crowded with inexpressible powers," Jefferies wrote, "so that I walk in the midst of im-mortal things.")

Down a short path from Jefferies lies his friend William Henry Hudson, whose grave looks far less loved: the cross atop it is cracked at the base, and garden spiders have anchored their webs to the headstone. Hudson loved nature as much as Jefferies, if not more, and his many books, with titles like *Afoot in England, A Shepherd's Life,* and *Nature in Downland,* helped spark a surge of interest in Britain's wildlife and landscapes in the early twentieth century. He was a founder of the Royal Society for the Protection of Birds — the same one that sent Kalinka and Graham to Steeple Jason — and the portrait of him that hangs in its headquarters near London shows a pensive, gray-bearded man with dark, deep-set eyes, holding a pair of slim field glasses. A dedicated hill walker, you might imagine, with a country home, and perhaps a seat in the House of Lords.

You'd be wrong. Open one of Hudson's books to any page and a soulful, brilliant, and curiously modern person tumbles out, a man who worked in obscurity for decades but died worthy of his epitaph. "He loved birds and green places and the wind on the heath," it reads, "and saw the brightness of the skirts of God." There are still pockets of Hudson enthusiasts in the world, but like the cemetery where he rests, he seems well along in the process of being forgotten.

He was not at all obscure when he died in 1922, the revered author of a raft of essays, novels, and memoirs that combined a naturalist's eye with a literary mind. Hudson was an early proponent of both *Anna Karenina* and *Moby-Dick,* and his peers envied his ability to inhabit the sensory and mental worlds of animals and people. "You may try for ever to learn how Hudson got his effects," wrote Joseph Conrad, "and you will never know. He writes down his words as the good God makes the green grass to grow, and that is all you will find to say about it." Alfred Russel Wallace, who coauthored the theory of evolution by natural selection with Darwin, gave Hudson's books glowing reviews in *Nature;* Ford Madox Ford, D. H. Lawrence, Ezra Pound, and Rabindranath Tagore were among his friends; Virginia Woolf, Ernest Hemingway, Thomas Hardy, and T. E. Lawrence (of Arabia) admired him. Lawrence and Hudson sat for portraits in an artist's studio on an afternoon in 1919, when the handsome young colonel was at the height of his fame, and Lawrence volunteered that he'd read Hudson's novel *The Purple Land* twelve times. Hudson, for his part, was mostly knocked out by Lawrence's outfit.

I found him arrayed in the most beautiful male dress of the East that I have ever seen, a reddish camel-hair mantle or cloak with gold collar over a white gown reaching to the ground, and a white headpiece with 3 silver cords or ropes wound round it. As he is clean-shaven and has a finely sculptured face the dress was most effective. He said it is worn only in Mecca by persons of importance, and nowhere else but at Mecca . . . I had a grand talk with Col. L. in his remarkable dress and we argued furiously about Science versus Art.

These two worlds — science and art — coexisted uneasily but fruitfully in Hudson's mind. He loved both, but he was as suspicious of the scientist's myopia as he was of the artist's ignorance, and described himself as a "writer and field naturalist." The lives of animals were grievously misunderstood, he thought, and much closer to ours than we imagine, and he often referred to them as people, as in "the rodent people" or "the monkey people."

It's fitting, then, that the most enduring legacy of his writing is a character who straddles this divide: a mysterious girl named Rima, the star of his 1904 novel *Green Mansions: A Romance of the Tropical Forest.* Rima lives in the deep woodlands of southern Guyana, and it's never clear if she's entirely human: she has red irises, speaks a unique musical language, and climbs through the canopy with the ease of a spider monkey. She longs to return to a homeland she calls Rio-lama but learns too late that she's the last of her kind, and dies at the hands of people who believe she is an evil spirit.

Rima lived on, however, in the United States, where *Green Mansions* was eventually adapted into a film starring Audrey Hepburn and a languid Anthony Perkins, and she survives to this day in the pages of DC Comics as Rima the Jungle Girl. In England, a memorial to Hudson in a corner of London's Hyde Park features a likeness of Rima by the controversial sculptor Jacob Epstein, who depicted her bare-breasted and flanked by two birds that could be parrots or eagles. The statue's immodesty caused an uproar when it was unveiled two years after Hudson's death — TAKE THIS HORROR OUT OF THE PARK, crowed the *Daily Mail* — and for an entire summer, crowds trampled the grass around the memorial to hard-beaten earth to see what the fuss was about, seeking, as Epstein wrote, "the obscenities that did not exist." Like Hudson himself, no one knew quite what to think of its jarring combination of refinement and rawness.

"To most of our wild birds," Hudson wrote, "man must appear as a being eccentric and contradictory in his actions. By turns he is hostile, indifferent, friendly towards them, so that they never quite know what to expect." Passionate and ruminative, Hudson makes an interesting contrast with Darwin, who changed scientific thought but rarely tried to inhabit the individual minds — let alone the souls — of animals. (The two men never met, though they once argued in print over the habits of a South American woodpecker.) Darwin had a gift for intuiting the patterns and processes of the natural world, but he occasionally seemed to regard other creatures as complex automatons, and his descriptions of the animals he met during the *Beagle*'s voyage hold them at arm's length, like this one of a shy Andean bird called a tapaculo:

It lives on the ground, sheltered among the thickets which are scattered over the dry and sterile hills. With its tail erect, and stilt-like legs, it may be seen every now and then popping from one bush to another with uncommon quickness. It really requires little imagination to believe that the bird is ashamed of itself, and is aware of its most ridiculous figure. On first seeing it, one is tempted to exclaim, "A vilely stuffed specimen has escaped from some museum, and has come to life again!"

This sense of animals as animated specimens never quite left Darwin, and at moments he appeared to succumb to the tempting idea that human beings are life's crowning achievement — or that we'd somehow earned an exemption from the natural laws his work revealed. Hudson, by contrast, thought that humans were generally overrated, and didn't think it was an insult to be compared to an ass or a cockroach. "A man with the strength of an ant or beetle," he noted, "would be able to place himself under a road engine, and raising it on his back, walk to the Thames Embankment, and throw it into the river."

Hudson also disagreed with Darwin about the origin and purpose of music. Music confounded Darwin, who couldn't imagine its evolutionary function beyond a possible use in attracting mates, and assumed it was peculiar to humans. "As neither the enjoyment nor the capacity of producing musical notes are faculties of the least use to man," Darwin wrote, "they must be ranked among those most mysterious with which he is endowed."

To Hudson, this was plainly ridiculous. Our aesthetic preferences and abilities stemmed from our deepest needs, he argued, which extend far beyond courtship — and he felt this was true not only for us but for all animals. Hudson conceded that "the sex feeling" was an important part of life, but only a fraction of it, and as a childless man who loved music, he might have been stung by Darwin's tone. Our ability to create and appreciate music might be useless, Hudson mused, but in that case, why stop there?

They are just as useless as many other faculties and capacities which are a part of us, and are not concerned with food-getting and so on — and, we may add, just as useful from another point of view. As useless (and as useful) as the instinct of play for example, of running and leaping and climbing and paddling and swimming and diving, and of basking in the sun, and rolling on the grass, and shouting when there's nothing to shout about.

Hudson thought these physical and emotional states — the joy of play, the love of beauty in other beings, the pleasure of making sounds with our bodies — were shared by all animals, and far more than incidental to life or evolution. He was certain that animals' lives felt no less consequential to them than ours do to us, that their intelligence had been vastly underestimated, and that even a grasshopper, observed closely, has its own musical tastes. "You may try him with a variety of sounds," he wrote,

and whistle and sing your sweetest and play the flute and fiddle and he will pay no atten-

64

tion; but try him with a zither, running a finger-nail over the strings, and instantly he is all attention, listening and moving his long antennae about, and presently he will start playing on *his* zither in response to yours. You have come down to his world, his species, and touched a chord in his grasshopper heart.

Above all, Hudson felt scientists hadn't looked at living animals closely enough, or had looked too closely at the wrong things — focusing on anatomy while ignoring behavior, fixating on our differences while playing down our obvious similarities. "All that is in our minds," he insisted, "is also in theirs."

His quest to see the world through animals' eyes reached a pinnacle in his final book, *A Hind in Richmond Park,* an artful exploration of the sensual worlds we share. In an age when people mostly used guns or snares to approach wildlife, Hudson relished the unobtrusive intimacy of binoculars, and in the book's opening pages he trains them on a deer sitting under an oak, chewing her cud, with her long ears turned toward a small patch of forest. "She was not concerned about me," he wrote. "She was wholly occupied with the wood and the sounds that came to her from it, which my less acute hearing failed to catch."

Undoubtedly the sounds she was listening to were important or interesting to her. On putting my binocular on her so as to bring her within a yard of my vision, I could see that there was a constant succession of small movements which told their tale — a sudden suspension of the cud-chewing, a stiffening of the forward-pointing ears, or a slight change in their direction; little tremors that passed over the whole body, alternately lifting and depressing the hairs of the back — which all went to show that she was experiencing a continual succession of little thrills. And the sounds that caused them were no doubt just those which we may hear any summer day in any thick wood with an undergrowth — the snapping of a twig, the rustle of leaves, the pink-pink of a startled chaffinch, the chuckle of a blackbird, or sharp little quivering alarm-notes of robin or wren, and twenty besides.

There's more than a touch of envy in this passage. Later in the book, Hudson imagines debating with the deer about whether humans or the "lower" animals were superior, and she argues him to a draw. It would be "a great quarrel," he wrote, "with many keen thrusts on both sides, also with some laughter."

And all the time the feeling in me, bitter as death, that she had the best of the argument; that it would have been better that animal life had continued until the time of the dying of all life on the earth with no such development as that of the large-brained being who walks erect and smiling looks on heaven.

Even among his friends, Hudson never quite seemed at home. The writer Morley Roberts wrote that he radiated an air of "interested armed detachment," observing other people as if they, too, were wildlife, and compared Hudson to "a half-tamed hawk which at any moment might take to the skies." This was an apt metaphor, since Hudson wasn't as English as he seemed; despite his impeccably British prose, he was from South America, and though he left it as a young man, it haunted and sustained him for the rest of his life.

I learned about Hudson, appropriately enough, through a bird — a rare visitor to Steeple Jason who turned up a few days after G7's death. Robin and I were sitting at the kitchen table in the research station when Micky, suited up for a day of thrashing through tussac grass and clearing mousetraps, stuck his head in the front door and called that he'd just seen a chimango.

Robin got up. This was big news. For years, he'd been compiling a checklist of every bird ever seen in the Falklands, and chimango caracaras — the Johnny rooks' pint-sized mainland cousins — had only been recorded in the islands four times, usually dead. A few years earlier I'd visited Robin at his tidy home in Devon and asked him about other species of caracaras, and he'd handed me his first-edition copy of Hudson's *Birds of La Plata,* published in 1920.

"I think you'll like him," he said. "He's very emotional."

I was soon lost in its pages. *Birds of La Plata* is as much a memoir as a bird guide, a loving portrait of the world Hudson left behind in South America — and he gave chimango caracaras its longest chapter. "However poor our creature may seem," he wrote, "and deserving of strange-sounding epithets from an ethical point of view, I do not know where the naturalist will find a more interesting one." Hudson admired chimangos' ability to find something to eat in almost any situation, and described them in careful, sympathetic terms. "He has probably the largest bill of fare of any bird," Hudson noted, "and has grafted on to his own peculiar manner of life the habits of twenty diverse species.

By turns he is a Falcon, a Vulture, an insect-eater, and a vegetable-eater. On the same day you will see one bird in violent Hawk-like pursuit of its living prey, with all the instincts of rapine hot within it, and another less ambitious individual engaged in laboriously tearing at an old cast-off shoe, uttering mournful notes the while, but more concerned at the tenacity of the material than its indigestibility. . . . He is not a bird who allows dignity to stand between him and his dinner.

It had already been a good day for unusual birds on Steeple Jason. A week of westerly gales and rain had given way to a rare calm, and birds blown over from mainland South America clung to the island like a life raft. Earlier that morning I'd seen a Patagonian sierra-finch, an Andean songbird with a waistcoat of gold feathers around its blue-gray head and wings, and Robin had spotted a pair of tawny-throated dotterels — delicate shorebirds whose wings' bold checkerboard of black-and-white contrasted with the silvered cream of their breasts and a flush of amber at their throats. Seeing these birds was a treat for us but bad news for them: the polar vortex blocked the way back to the continent, and east of us lay thousands of miles of ocean. Robin remembered a tiny mainland bird called an austral negrito he'd once seen on a nearby island — a ball of fluff, he said, tumbling helplessly in the wind.

Chimango caracaras might be rare in the Falklands, but in southern South America they're so common that they're nearly invisible. In Argentina, the word "chimango" is shorthand for anything small, annoying, and worthless, and the saying *no gastes pólvora en chimango* means "don't bother wasting your ammunition on a chimango." In Chile's far south, if you call someone the chimango-derived word "chumango" you're playing with fire — it's like calling someone a Yankee in South Carolina. You might be teasing them or spoiling for a fight, but either way you're calling them part of an unwelcome crowd.

It's true that chimangos seem unremarkable at first, from their drab brown plumage, thin legs, and weak-looking bills (which Hudson called "the merest apology of the falcon's tearing weapon") to their hoarse, complaining calls. But they're unusually social for birds of prey, which aren't known for their love of company. Chimangos often gather in flocks of thirty or forty, like oversized house sparrows; sometimes they even build a little town in a grove of trees, clumping their nests together, as if they can't imagine life without friends and neighbors. Darwin, however, sketched them with an image of solitude and desperation: "It is generally the last which leaves the skeleton of a dead animal," he wrote, "and may often be seen within the ribs of a cow or horse, like a bird in a cage." Decades earlier, Félix de Azara had written that a chimango might have the courage to attack a mouse, but he doubted it.

Hudson disagreed. Chimangos were a constant presence at his family's farm in rural Argentina, and he thought there was far more to these dusky scavengers than met the eye. "A species so cosmopolitan in its tastes," he wrote, "would have had a whole volume to itself in England. Being a poor foreigner, it has had no more than a few unfriendly paragraphs bestowed upon it."

He knew a thing or two about that. Hudson had left Argentina for England in the hope of finding others who shared his passion for wildlife, but ornithologists like John Gould, who cataloged Darwin's specimens, snubbed him as an uncredentialed amateur. He was sometimes reduced to sleeping in Hyde Park, near the site of his present memorial, while he labored in odd jobs: secretarial work for a chronically bankrupt archaeologist, freelance writing for news magazines. After he married Emily Wingrave, a tiny woman fifteen years his senior, Hudson helped run the boarding-house she owned, but times were hard — one week, he recalled, they had only a single loaf of bread and a tin of cocoa to eat. But he always fed the sparrows that came to his window, and he loved walking London from end to end, watching its humans and animals with the same attention he gave the birds of his childhood. He saw London's crows, for

71

instance, as a fellow group of urban commuters:

I should not be surprised to learn that as many as forty crows frequent inner London. But with the exception of two, or perhaps three pairs, they do not now breed in London, but have their nesting-haunts in woods west, north, and east of the metropolis. These breeders on the outskirts bring the young they succeed in rearing to the parks, from which they have themselves in some cases been expelled, and the tradition is thus kept up. Most of the birds appear to fly over London every day, paying long visits on their way to Regent's Park, Holland Park, the central parks, and Battersea Park. As their movements are very regular it would be possible to mark their various routes on a map of the metropolis.

Though it was an ocean away, the wildlife of his birthplace was just as vivid in his mind, including the chimangos that were the crows' equivalent on the farm. Their high, wheezy screeches weren't much like a crow's resonant caw, but they were just as talkative — another atypical quality in a predatory bird — and they seemed to enjoy the sound of their scratchy voices. This was especially true when they were feeding, and he imagined them lecturing each other or complaining about their diet. "The gauchos have a saying comparing a man who grumbles at good fortune to the Chimango crying on a carcase," Hudson wrote, "an extremely expressive saying to those who have listened to the distressful wailings of the bird over its meat."

We caught up with ours in a gully choked with rotting kelp, where a dead sea lion was being devoured by a crowd of young Johnny rooks. The carcass had dried to a leathery husk weeks earlier, but the rain had softened it again, and now there was a heaving scrum of birds jumping on and over each other to tear gobbets of skin from its skeleton. Many were first-year birds like G7, who would surely have been among them if he'd lived; others were closer to adulthood, their legs halfway between gray and pale yellow, their cream-colored faces beginning to shade into yellow-orange. Most were quiet, but one was calling incessantly: shrill, ragged screams that seemed to draw in every Johnny rook in earshot.

As a feeding strategy, this seemed self-defeating. Why call attention to food you want for yourself? But there was a good reason for a young scavenger to throw a party here: the gully lay inside the territory of a sleek adult pair who defended it fiercely against intruders. A gang of hungry teenagers, however, was too much for them to handle, and they settled for perching together on a nearby boulder, looking aggrieved. Every so often, one of the pair charged at a young bird who strayed from the group, then returned to its mate to perform a territorial duet, throwing its head back and screeching in a tone that clearly meant *This is our land, and don't you kids forget it.*

For all the commotion, there wasn't much actual conflict at the carcass. Judging by their sagging crops, nearly all the young birds were eating their fill, and even the ones standing on each other's tails weren't really fighting: they just needed a bellyful of meat, and a bonanza like this could mean the difference between life and death in late winter. I sat on a rock and edged closer until I was near enough to touch them, locking eyes with a bird who kept glancing in my direction. It seemed to be trying to decide whether I was a problem or an opportunity, and I became so fixed on winning our staring contest that I almost failed to notice the chimango standing a few paces away, leaning forward, looking for a way in.

"As a rule," Hudson wrote, "strong healthy birds despise the chimango. . . . His sudden appearance causes no alarm, and they do not take the trouble to persecute him; but when they have eggs or young he is not to be trusted." On the farm in Argentina, chimangos were like small, feathered coyotes: always nearby and mostly harmless, but you might not want to turn your back on them for long. They pounced on sleeping lambs and tore at the saddle sores of horses, and Hudson had often seen "a chafed saddle-horse wildly scouring the plain, closely pursued by a hungry chimango determined to dine on a portion of him." They also shadowed anyone who carried a gun; during Hudson's brief career as a scientific bird collector, they often beat him to a specimen he'd just brought down and carried it away.

Hudson took a long view of these aggravations. "The mind in beast and bird," he wrote, "as in man, is the main thing," and chimangos seemed to have been gifted with a model that exceeded that of most birds he knew. He saw their opportunism as ingenuity, not mischief, and he thought Darwin and Azara had been unfair in painting them as "a sort of poor relation and hanger-on of a family already looked upon as bankrupt and disreputable." Hudson regretted that people were so often repulsed by the animals who understand us best, from rats to city pigeons; every living thing, he believed, had a right to be respected for what he called its "manner of life." Chimangos' improvisational lives might also have struck a chord with him for a more personal reason: he, too, came from a family who'd adapted to a new life in an unpromising place.

4

THE BIRTH OF A NATURALIST

William Henry Hudson was born in 1841, the youngest of five children, in the grassy plains south of Buenos Aires called the Pampas, where he grew up immersed in a world of animals that Darwin only glimpsed. His parents, Daniel and Caroline, had emigrated from the United States to the Argentine province of La Plata in hopes of a freer and healthier life, with mixed results; Hudson later referred to his father, a kind man who was chronically unable to manage his money, as "a man of shining defects." But they were humane and thoughtful people, with a respect for education and literature, and it was through reading that young William came to feel that England, his grandparents' birthplace, was somehow his true home. After his parents' death, Hudson would board a steamer in Buenos Aires in 1874 and sail away forever; but the landscapes and creatures of his home stamped him deeply and permanently, and he saw everything through their lens.

And small wonder. The Pampas in the mid-nineteenth century was a wild, mercurial place, and to Hudson's parents it must have seemed deeply alien. In summer, its level plains were an ocean of grass beneath a huge expanse of sky, but in the fall they became a claustrophobic mass of thistle-like artichokes called cardoons — a European import, run wild in the New World, that towered above riders' heads and turned roads and paths into half-lit tunnels. In the winter, the cardoons' dead stalks fed raging wildfires until spring rains transformed the plains into shimmering wetlands, a waystation for immense flocks of migrating shorebirds and waterfowl.

To young William it was a place of compelling, muted loveliness, even though its peace was often marred by violence. ("Murder," he later wrote, "was a common word in those days.") In the nascent state of Argentina it was the era of the gauchos — dashing, violent cowboys who lived by a capricious and brutal code and loved to drink, fight with knives, recite ballads, and hunt ostrich-like birds called rheas. Darwin, passing through La Plata nine years before Hudson's birth, was impressed by the gauchos' skills and admired their "brightly colored garments, great spurs clanking about their heels, and knives stuck as daggers (and often so used) at their waists," but felt he ought to keep his distance.

"Their politeness is excessive," he wrote, "but whilst making their exceedingly graceful bow, they seem quite as ready, if occasion offered, to cut your throat."

These courtly rogues became heroic figures in Argentina's national mythology, but Hudson's chief memory of the gauchos was the delight they took in the suffering of the cattle (and, sometimes, people) they slaughtered. Their ornate, barbarous lives appalled and fascinated him, and he reflected that the pressures of life in the Pampas had transmuted the gauchos' immigrant ancestors into something much rougher and stranger. He saw an explanation for this change in the dying orchards that surrounded older farmhouses in the Pampas, built by colonists from places "where the people are accustomed to sit in the shade of trees, where corn and wine and oil are supposed to be necessaries, and where there is salad in the garden.

But now the main business of their lives was cattle-raising, and as the cattle roamed at will over the vast plains and were more like wild than domestic animals, it was a life on horseback. They could no longer dig or plough the earth or protect their crops from insects. They gave up their oil and wine and bread and lived on flesh alone. They sat in the shade and ate the fruit of trees planted by their fathers or their great-grandfathers until the trees died of old age, or were blown down or killed by the cattle, and there was no more shade or fruit.

It was a time when endless raids and reprisals between European colonists and Amerindians remained in living memory, an undeclared civil war that roiled the countryside as the armies of General Juan Manuel de Rosas mounted a remorseless campaign against "wild" Amerindians — often conscripting or bribing other Amerindians to do the dirtiest work. Darwin crossed paths with Rosas in the Pampas, where the general's odd combination of civility and insanity unsettled him: Rosas was a brilliant horseman, Darwin wrote, but he had men tortured or killed on a whim, and kept a set of fools on hand to entertain him.

By the time Hudson was born the Argentine frontier had moved south of La Plata and General Rosas had become a reclusive dictator, ensconced in a grand palace outside Buenos Aires. Wars against the Amerindians continued, but in the Pampas they'd largely given way to armed feuds between the rival governments of Argentina, Chile, and Uruguay. William and his five siblings learned to shoot and ride at an early age, and the sight of strange riders approaching the farm always carried a whiff of danger.

In spite of all this, the Hudsons welcomed

visitors. Nothing seemed to make his parents happier, William recalled, "than having strangers and travelers taking their rest with us . . . the poorest, even men who would be labeled tramps in England . . . would be made as welcome as those of a better class." Their guests were fed wild game and pickled peaches in the Hudsons' kitchen, where their stories received sympathetic ears, and the children were allowed to stay up past their usual bedtime. In this, as in many things, Daniel and Caroline didn't begrudge their children's happiness or their freedom, and William later described himself as a "little wild animal running about on its hind legs, amazingly interested in the world in which it found itself." This early curiosity grew into a deep, mystical "feeling for Nature" that sent down deep roots and survived the rigors of farm life, a near-fatal bout of rheumatic fever, and a series of alcoholic schoolmasters. "So powerful it was, so unaccountable," he wrote, "I was actually afraid of it.

Yet I would go out of my way to seek it. At the hour of sunset I would go out a half a mile or so from the house, and sitting on the dry grass with hands clasped at my knees, gaze at the western sky, waiting for it to take me. And I would ask myself: What does it mean?

This profound curiosity — Hudson later called it "animism" — marked him as a bit strange. Caroline Hudson noticed her young son's tendency to wander off on his own, and later told him that she would quietly follow and watch him "standing motionless among the tall weeds or under the trees by the half hour, staring at vacancy." She worried that he might be losing his mind, but finally saw that he was always "watching some living thing, an insect perhaps, but oftener a bird — a pair of little scarlet flycatchers building a nest of lichen on a peach tree, or some such beautiful thing."

As a teenager, William loved to spend days and weeks "idling" — riding his horse far out into the country, observing animals, collecting flowers, visiting distant neighbors, and sleeping under the stars — savoring what Darwin called "the pleasure of living in the open air, with the sky for a roof, and the ground for a table." The countryside of La Plata was a truly wild place, where jaguars and pumas preyed on hairy armadillos, venomous snakes shared their burrows with families of opossums, and rabbit-like rodents called viscachas conducted underground singing contests. On summer nights, rheas that escaped the bolas of the gauchos boomed mournfully to each other in the dusk, a haunting sound that seemed to emanate from the earth itself.

81

When riding late one afternoon in a lowly place on the Pampas, I pulled up my horse again and again to listen to that mysterious noise which is like no other sound on earth. A sound that was like the thin blue summer or dry fog, which partially veils or dims and appears to pervade the entire landscape, producing the effect of a heaven and earth mingled or interfused; a sound that was everywhere in earth and air and sky, but changing in power; at intervals loud as the summer humming of insects, then decreasing and at last so faint as to be scarcely audible, so that listening you came to think it an imaginary sound.

As Hudson grew, his affinity for wildlife matured into a desire to learn all there was to know about it — a difficult thirst to slake on the farm. His family's small library was a century old, and its books mostly concerned the lives of saints and philosophers and the decline of ancient Rome. There was nothing at all about the place where he lived, to say nothing of its nonhuman inhabitants, and he realized that he wanted a different kind of history, "one with animals as well as men in it."

Not finding it anywhere, he set out to write it himself, and his early passion served him well decades later, when his book *The Naturalist in La Plata* (1892), a set of essays about the animals of his home, began to find an audience in England. It was "altogether unique among books on natural history," wrote Alfred Russel Wallace, who thought the book's title undersold its contents. "What renders this work of such extreme value and interest," Wallace continued, "is that it is not written by a traveller or a mere temporary resident, but by one born in the country, to whom its various tribes of beasts, birds, and insects have been familiar from childhood; who is imbued with love and admiration for every form of life, and who for twenty years has observed carefully and recorded accurately everything of interest in the life-histories of the various species with which he has become acquainted." Hudson's gift for rendering his animal companions with empathetic vividness — even the snakes that lived beneath his family's house — was on full display:

In winter they hibernated there, tangled together in a cluster no doubt; and in summer nights when they were at home, coiled at their ease or gliding ghost-like about their subterranean apartments, I would lie awake and listen to them by the hour. . . . Several individuals would hold a conversation together which seemed endless, for I generally fell asleep before it finished . . . a long sibilation would be followed by distinctly heard ticking sounds, as of a husky-ticking clock, and after ten or twenty or thirty ticks another hiss, like a long expiring sigh, sometimes with a tremble in it as of a dry leaf vibrating in the wind. No sooner would one cease than another would begin; and so it would go on, demand and response, strophe and antistrophe, and at intervals several voices would unite in a kind of low mysterious chorus, death-watch and flutter and hiss; while I, lying awake in my bed, listened and trembled.

But of all the creatures Hudson knew in his childhood, birds were the closest to his heart. The Pampas was home to an astonishing variety of what he called "the feathered people," and though its thrushes, swallows, and hawks would have been familiar to European eyes, William's favorites were uniquely South American: quail-like tinamous with glossy purple eggs; buff-breasted ibises with long, curved beaks and metallic cries; and the improbable colors and forms of flamingos and parakeets. Some of these birds came north to escape the Patagonian winter, while others flew south from Brazil and Bolivia to breed in the spring's ephemeral wetlands, and for weeks at a time the country resounded with the voices of millions of sandpipers, plovers, curlews, and gulls. An old red willow at the edge of the farm was William's favorite spot for bird-watching and world-watching, and "whenever I was in the wild arboreal mood," he wrote, "I would climb the willow to find a good stout branch high up on which to spend an hour, with a good view of the wide green plain before me and the sight of grazing flocks and herds, and of houses and poplar groves looking blue in the distance."

It was a good place to imagine another life for himself, in which he had wings instead of arms. He envied the gulls and hawks that spent most of their lives in the air, but the bird he most wished to be was an ungainly creature, endemic to South America, called a crested screamer. Screamers are awkward-looking birds, slightly larger than a turkey, with plump gray bodies, long red legs, and comically small heads. But in the air they transformed, like penguins when they enter the sea:

Here was a bird as big or bigger than a goose, as heavy almost as I was myself, who, when he wished to fly, rose off the ground with tremendous labor, and then as he got higher and higher, flew more and more easily, until he rose so high that he looked no bigger than a lark or pipit, and at that height he would continue floating round and round in vast circles for hours, pouring out those jubilant cries at intervals which sounded to us so far below like clarion notes

85

in the sky. If I could only get off the ground and rise as high, then the blue air would make me buoyant and let me float all day without pain or effort!

The first birds to draw his attention, however, were southern crested caracaras, which Hudson knew as "caranchos." He admired these clever and attractive birds, calling them "lord[s] of the feathered race," though their formal plumage belied a "wonderfully bold and savage spirit" whose eruptions could be shocking. "On one of my early rides on my pony," he recalled, "I had seen a pair of them furiously attacking a weak and sickly ewe; she had refused to lie down to be killed, and they were on her neck, beating and tearing at her face and trying to pull her down." As a young boy he'd discovered the nest of this pair, a bulky fortress in the crown of a peach tree, and it gave him a shiver of fear and delight.

In the convenient hollow formed by the circle of branches the caranchos had built their huge nest, composed of sticks, lumps of turf, dry bones of sheep and other animals, pieces of rope and raw hide, and any other object they could carry. . . . They roosted in it by night and visited it at odd times during the day, usually bringing a bleached bone or thistle-stalk or some such object to add to the pile.

To Hudson's eight-year-old eyes, the nest was a fitting home for birds who seemed "unspeakably savage and fearsome," but he knew it concealed a treasure, since a gaucho had showed him a pair of the caranchos' red-speckled eggs. Coveting one for himself, he gathered up his courage and chose a moment near sunset to make his move. "I managed to swarm up the smooth trunk to the branches," he recalled, "and then with wildly beating heart began the task of trying to get through the close branches and to work my way over the huge rim of the nest.

Just then I heard the harsh grating cry of the bird, and peering through the leaves in the direction it came from I caught sight of the two birds flying furiously towards me, screaming again as they came nearer. Then terror seized me, and down I went through the branches . . . and fled back to the shelter of the house, never looking back.

William never again tried to steal from the lords of the feathered race, and he kept an eye on them with a mixture of admiration and unease. Like the less imposing chimangos, the caranchos were attracted by the slaughter of livestock and gave special attention to animals that were young, sick, injured, or otherwise vulnerable. ("Where anything is wrong with bird or beast," he noted, "they

are very quick to detect it.") Like all caracaras, the caranchos had a gift for finding
partners in their search for food and would
follow pumas, jaguars, and human hunters
while "intelligently keeping at a safe distance
themselves." The gauchos sometimes used
this habit to their advantage, enlisting caranchos as unwitting accomplices to help them
catch tinamous (which Hudson called "partridges").

The snarer has a long slender cane with a
small noose at the extremity, and when he
sights a Partridge he gallops round it in
circles until the bird crouches close in the
grass. . . . He extends the cane and lowers
it gradually over the bewildered bird until
the small noose is dropped over its head
and it is caught. Many Partridges are not
disposed to sit still to be taken in this open,
bare-faced way; but if the snarer keeps a
Carancho hovering about by throwing him
an occasional gizzard, the wariest Partridge
is so stricken with fear that it will sit still and
allow itself to be caught.

Chimango caracaras were also common on
the farm. They were playful, intelligent birds,
Hudson recalled, unusually attuned to the
rhythms of human life, and were "to be found
at every solitary rancho sharing with dogs
and poultry the offal and waste meat thrown

out on the dust-heap." Chimangos didn't seem to hatch with this knowledge, but they were good students of one another — and even, Hudson believed, of other animals. He saw them standing with herons and ibises in shallow lakes, fishing for tadpoles; they gobbled winged termites in midair alongside tiny flycatchers, "undisturbed by any sense of incongruity"; they gnawed at desiccated carcasses with armadillos and foxes; they rooted in ploughed-up fields with pigs. It was as if their greatest skill was their ability to learn from others' successes as well as their own.

But most of all, they were powerfully drawn to people. More than any other bird, chimangos appeared to have grasped that the humans of La Plata would lead them to food, and Hudson noted that they "abound most in settled districts." They were equally attracted to one of our most reliable companions: fire. European colonists and Amerindians alike flushed game by setting the grasslands ablaze, and chimangos knew exactly what that meant. "The moment the smoke of a distant fire is seen," Hudson wrote, "there the Chimangos fly to follow the conflagration. They are at such times strangely animated, dashing through clouds of smoke, feasting among the hot ashes on roasted cavies and other small mammals, and boldly pursuing the scorched fugitives from the flames."

The secret of the chimangos' success, in short, seemed to lie in their minds. They could sense an opportunity when it appeared, even if they'd never seen it before — and it seems only natural that Hudson might have had a soft spot for a bird that resisted categorization, kept a keen and curious eye on the world, and lived by its wits.

The family resemblance between the chimango and the Johnny rooks in the gully on Steeple Jason was clear, though the smaller bird seemed woefully out of his element. He'd been blown out to sea and landed in a world of giants, like the mythical eight-foot people that Europeans once thought lived in his homeland, and the Johnny rooks chased him away whenever he approached the sea lion's carcass. The chimango looked harried and confused, hopping from one rock to another, lifting his chin to give a creaky screech now and again, as if calling for help from friends too far away to hear him.

I wondered what the Johnny rooks thought he was. A competitor? A lost relative? A runt? It was tempting to imagine them as earlier models of the chimango: more heroically decorated and proportioned, but also less worldly. Striated caracaras have mastered the prehistoric landscapes of the outer Falklands, but they're still getting the hang of living with humans: at a farmhouse on an island near the Jasons, I met a man who fed slices of cake to a half-blind caracara he called Frieda. She'd decided, one day, to walk right into his living room.

A few months after the mouse team left Steeple Jason, I opened *Birds of La Plata* again, with G7's death on my mind. Poring over pictures I'd snapped during Kalinka's necropsy hadn't revealed anything special, but I remembered Hudson's warning about underestimating chimangos and went back to his description to look for clues. When they're feeling playful, he wrote, chimangos "sometimes attack birds . . . much too strong and big for them." And then there was this line: "In all times and in all places, the Chimango is ever ready to pounce on the weak, the sickly, and the wounded."

Still, the thought that a chimango could have killed G7 seemed unlikely. It would surely have been too much work, unless G7 was already injured or dying — and Micky had seen him a few hours earlier, looking just fine. Then there was the fact that only G7's pectoral muscles — the equivalent of a chicken's breast meat — had been eaten. That didn't sound like the work of a bird that was the last to abandon a carcass. I flipped back a few pages and glanced at Hudson's brief entry for a more famous bird of prey, the peregrine falcon, and found a sentence that brought me up short.

"The Peregrine," he wrote, "possesses one very curious habit. When a Plover, Pigeon, or Duck is killed, it eats the skin and flesh down to the breast-bone . . . leaving the [rest of the] body untouched."

That was more like it — and there *were* peregrines on Steeple Jason, though I hadn't suspected them because they seemed so devoted to hunting seabirds. They plunged from their cliffside roost to the troughs of waves offshore, where they nabbed delicate birds called prions and diving petrels with the grace of a dragonfly picking midges off the surface of a pond. Once they'd gripped their prey in their long, deadly talons, the peregrines carried them back to shore, beating fiercely against the wind, then plucked and ate them on the beach — leaving only a pile of feathers and a pair of wings still joined at a tiny wishbone. The sheer courage of it was breathtaking; peregrines can't swim, and a false move would put them into the drink forever.

Taking down a striated caracara would also be no picnic. Johnny rooks are larger and heavier than peregrines, strong enough to pin a shag to the ground or dig through heavy masses of rotten kelp. They might lack finesse, but they make up for it in tenacity and versatility. Peregrines, by contrast, are picky and conservative, and their stricter preferences add up to something like a sportsman's code. They almost exclusively hunt living birds, stealing up on their quarry by flying low over the ground, or crashing into them from above in heart-stopping dives that make them the fastest animals on the planet. After they've stunned and gripped their prey, peregrines sever its spinal column with a single, hard bite, using a tooth-like notch in their beak suited for just this purpose.

If I'd thought more carefully about G7's broken neck, I might have fingered the peregrine sooner. G7 was a young bird, and his youth might have been his undoing; young Johnny rooks are especially curious, social, and brave, with many interests and few skills. Maybe the hunting wasn't so good at sea that day for the peregrine. Maybe she just spotted an easy mark on the shore. G7 might have been standing with a group of his friends, digging for grubs or settling a disagreement, when a dark shape the same steely color of the waves came in fast and low from the east. John Alec Baker, an English writer who followed peregrines in the broad estuary near his home in Essex, noted that they often singled out the sick, the old, and the inexperienced — but unlike caracaras, always the living.

I'll never know for certain, but I think I had my man. But if that's the case, the encounter between G7 and his killer reflects a much larger struggle, not just between species but between minds, and an ancient evolutionary argument between generalists and specialists. "In the beginner's mind," wrote the Zen thinker Shunryu Suzuki, "there are many possibilities. In the expert's mind, there are few."

5
THE MOST INTELLIGENT
BIRD IN THE WORLD

Geoff Pearson, seventy-eight years old, wearing a baseball cap and a maroon sweatshirt that reads falconer on the back in gold letters, ducks his head as he opens the door to a walk-in aviary. "Hello, sweetie!" he calls. "Hello, love!" Inside the enclosure, a scruffy young striated caracara named Evita stands on a branch cut from an oak tree, screaming with excitement. *KAOOO! KAOOO! KAOOO!* she bellows, taking a sip of air between each cry. If you'd spent the morning pacing down the mews at the Woodlands Falconry Centre in Totnes, Devonshire, peering in at Eurasian kestrels, Bengal eagle-owls, and North American Harris's hawks, you'd have noticed something unique about Evita, though it might take you a minute to put your finger on it. She seems untidy, with her hunched posture, blackish-brown feathers, hooked beak, and bluish-gray feet that seem a size too big. But it's her eyes that hold you — huge, dark, curious, forthright. She doesn't look past you with vague disinterest, as the other birds do; she looks *into* you, which is charming but also unnerving.

She's also the only bird with a desk in her aviary. Geoff closes the door behind him, and Evita screams even louder, with the insistence and volume of a car alarm. "I *know,* sweetie," he soothes. "Oh, I *know.*" On the chain-link fence that wraps around the front of the enclosure, a sign reads EVITA, STRIATED CARACARA, HATCHED MAY 2014.

Behind his back, Geoff holds an object Evita's never seen: a glass bottle with a day-old chicken's head inside, tied to a green string that sticks out of the bottle's mouth like an unlit fuse. Evita seems to know something's up, but her calls are dropping in volume, like the sobs of a toddler losing interest in a tantrum. She stares at Geoff, tilting and bobbing her head, raising and lowering the short feathers on the nape of her neck, and perches above him as he squeezes into a plastic lawn chair behind the desk. A lesson is about to happen here, but it's not entirely clear who the teacher is.

Geoff produces the bottle with a flourish, placing it on the desk and steadying it with one hand, and Evita falls silent. Then she takes two running steps down the oak limb and leaps to the desk, her talons clattering on the wood, and leans forward to examine the chicken's head in the bottle. She pecks at the glass.

"This is as far as the other birds here would make it," Geoff says. "They'd be, *Oh, food! I'll have that!,* but they'd never get further than this."

Evita draws back and studies the bottle. You can sense her absorption; you can almost see gears turning in her head. She paces around it, peering at it from all sides, and places one of her outsized feet on its smooth surface. Geoff lets the bottle shift in his grip. Then Evita grasps the string and lifts, and the chick's head comes closer. She looks at Geoff. "Go on," he says. Then she leans down, takes the string in her beak, and pulls. Out pops the head, and Evita wolfs it down.

It happens so fast that it's hard to tell if she connected cause to effect, but one thing seems clear: Evita *really* likes this piece of string now. She takes it in her beak, jumps to the ground, and runs around the perimeter of the aviary. She drops the string in the opposite corner from Geoff and studies it, holding one end down with her foot and pulling on the other with her beak, then lifts her head and calls: *I've got it! I've got it! I've got it!* She looks down at the string again. *But what is it I've got?*

In the meantime, Geoff sets three upturned coffee mugs on the desk. "Vita!" he calls, and gives a whistle. Evita looks up at him, then back at the string, as if to say, *You stay here,* and runs back to the desk, launching herself to Geoff's level in a single bound. Geoff places a morsel of chicken on the table, covers it with one of the mugs, and starts to play the shell game, pushing the mugs around and around each other. Evita draws in close to the mugs, swiveling her neck to follow them. She starts calling again. "Tina could do this every time!" Geoff shouts, above her cries.

KAAO! KAAO! KAAO! Evita's calls are louder, tinged with frustration, as if she knows she's supposed to do something, but doesn't know what. She glances back at the string in the corner. *Still there.* Geoff lets go of the mugs. Evita nudges one of them with her head and looks him in the eye, and Geoff lifts the mug with the chicken's leg underneath — not the one she chose. Evita gobbles it up, still calling, and runs back to the string, and when she picks it up again, she goes quiet. In the sudden calm, the vaguely Celtic harp music Geoff pipes into the falconry center comes forward, along with the faint *quark*s of a squadron of English rooks overhead.

Geoff seems slightly embarrassed as Evita stands on the fine gravel of the aviary's floor, absorbed by her new toy. "She's getting better," he says, extricating himself from the desk. "There's still a ways to go." Evita pulls the string this way and that, like a cat toying with a mouse, and Geoff takes advantage of her absorption to lower a net toward her, which she evades at the last instant with a sideways leap to the chain-link fencing of her enclosure, where she clings like a parrot or a monkey. "Oh, no," Geoff mutters. "Don't let her get in the corner."

She gets in the corner. Evita calls again, a cry of alarm and panic, but it's no use — after a brief struggle, Geoff catches her in the net and gently untangles her, drawing loops of mesh from around her clenched talons. Once she's free, he drapes a towel over her head and gathers her in his arms. *KAAAOO! KAAAOO! KAOO!,* protests the towel. Geoff cradles the screaming bundle casually but firmly, like a veteran parent, and carries it back to his office for Evita's weekly weigh-in. "One thing about her I find amazing," he says, "is that she doesn't hold a grudge."

Playing with a string might not seem extraordinary, but it's hard to overstate how surprising this kind of behavior is from a bird of prey. Hawks, falcons, and owls aren't like dogs or monkeys: they're solitary, aloof, and particular, with little interest in games, and spend most of their time conserving their energy for the next kill. Most won't do anything at all if they aren't hungry, and few take kindly to being touched or toyed with.

Falconers, for their part, accept this. They're fond of their birds, but they don't expect their fondness to be returned by creatures who regard them mostly as sources of food or as odd and unsatisfying mates; Geoff once kept a female gyrfalcon who would bow and present herself to him until he pressed at her cloaca with his finger.

And Geoff, as you may have gathered, is not a scientist or a birdwatcher. He's a falconer, which is something quite different, though he can seem more like a retired agent from MI6. He's been many things in life — a factory worker, a sailor, a paratrooper, a sniper, a bodyguard to the Sheikh of Bahrain, a vacuum-cleaner salesman — and he prides himself on his eclectic expertise and his gift of gab. An off-the-cuff lecture about the theory and practice of falconry can veer suddenly into the jungles of Borneo, the deck of a Russian submarine, or an island in the Persian Gulf strewn with human bones. Geoff's soldiering days are long gone, but his pale eyes are quick and piercing, and he admits, over the tot of rum he stirs into his coffee, that he's easily annoyed by jobs or people that fail to interest him.

The problem, Geoff says, is that once he's taken up a new skill or occupation and learned all he can about it, he gets bored, and then he's on to something else. These days, in addition to running the falconry center at Woodlands, he makes jewelry, dances tango, and scours the English coast for Roman coins with a metal detector. Though he's well past retirement age, he can't imagine life as a pensioner; he mimes a doddering version of himself restocking shelves at a supermarket and rolls his eyes in disgust. A series of wives is a source of both pride and chagrin — "Don't ask how many," he says, then bites his lower lip, winces, and holds up four fingers.

Only falconry, it seems, has kept a hold on him. A tattoo of a diving peregrine, blurred with age, covers the back of his right hand, and Geoff's cramped office is bursting with the accoutrements of his art — hoods, tethers, gloves, a radio telemetry set for tracking wayward birds, and a crate of fuzzy yellow corpses: enough defrosted baby chickens to feed his birds for one day. Calipers, pliers, and other tools hang from nails or spill from bins that line the walls, one of which is labeled TINA'S TOYS. Children's drawings of eagles and owls hang below the skull of a roe deer, and a rubber snake, poised to strike, lurks in the crossbeams of the ceiling.

As a boy, Geoff learned the rudiments of falconry from poachers in the English midlands, who also taught him to hypnotize chickens and stun pheasants. Later he tended falcons for the queen's horseman, and during his military days in Malaysia he spent his shore leave befriending local falconers. His skills landed him the bodyguard job in Bahrain by accident when the sheikh learned of his interest in falconry and purchased three years of his contract from the British army. ("Seconded, they call it," Geoff says. "But really he just *bought* me, against my will.") The sheikh had a good eye. Geoff knows and loves birds of prey as much as human beings — and, he admits, maybe more. "Sometimes I see people come through that door and I think, *Oh, God,*" he says, pulling a face. "And then I have to go be *nice* to them."

His misanthropy easily gives way to whimsy. Ask Geoff about Charlie, a crowish hand puppet with an enormous yellow beak that sprawls in a corner of his desk, and he reaches for it with a little boy's delight; a few minutes later, you might find yourself taking Charlie's side when he starts biting Geoff during one of his digressions. "Stop it!" Geoff barks, interrupting himself. "That's naughty!" Charlie continues to gnaw at his shoulder. Geoff softens. "Charlie grabs me," he explains, stroking the puppet's head, "when he doesn't like me." He fixes Charlie with a stare. "Look at me," he says. "You don't want to go back in the box, do you?"

Geoff also takes his work home. A bulletin board in the courtyard outside his office is covered with pictures from his house, and they suggest that although Geoff lives there, it's mostly a nursery for young birds of prey. An indignant snowy owl chick, looking up from the floor of a laundry room, is captioned WHAT DO YOU *MEAN* THAT'S OUT OF BOUNDS?; a kestrel perched on the back of Geoff's bald head, its hunter's eyes boring into a laptop screen, says WATCH OUT FOR THE MONSTERS BEHIND THE ROCKS ON THE RIGHT. Geoff's wife Rita also makes an appearance, lounging on their front lawn with young Mitzi the eagle owl, a fuzzy white puffball with huge yellow eyes.

One photo bears no caption, however, and it's not on public view; it's in a place of honor beside Geoff's desk. It shows a striated caracara standing in a patch of green grass, holding a red ball in its beak, and it definitely isn't Evita. This bird wears the full-dress uniform of an adult, and her tail ends in a smart white band like a chevron. It's Tina. Ask about her and Geoff goes a bit quiet.

Tina entered Geoff's life by accident, when a talented young falconer named Ashley Smith offered her to him in trade for a goshawk. Goshawks are powerful hunters who excel at chasing prey through dense woods, but they're rarely flown for an audience because of their skittish, aggressive temperaments. Geoff, not without affection, calls them "psychotic," and adds that there's a saying among falconers that if you can train a goshawk to hunt for a season without becoming suicidal or getting a divorce, you've mastered the art.

This goshawk, however, played against type. It was utterly relaxed on public display, sitting blithely on its perch and fluffing its feathers even when it was surrounded by strangers. Ashley coveted it for his own collection, and Geoff, who wasn't particularly attached to it, swapped it for Tina out of pure curiosity. He'd never come across a striated caracara in twenty years as a falconer, and had only recently heard of them; it was 1983, the year after the Falklands War, and soldiers were returning from the islands with stories of crow-like birds that peered into their foxholes and perched on the rotors of their helicopters.

Geoff also felt comfortable with the trade because he knew Tina's life story. She was a little more than a year old, the offspring of a pair of captive striated caracaras who'd raised and fledged Tina with minimal help from people. Geoff assumed that Tina would be an interesting but not maddening challenge — but he'll tell you, with a touch of surprise in his voice, that it was Tina who trained him. In their first years together he mostly left her alone, though he indulged her preference for running and walking in demonstrations, which earned chuckles from the audience instead of the gasps of wonder that greeted eagles and owls. After a job took him away for several years, Geoff expected he'd need to slowly rehabituate Tina to his presence, as he did with any captive bird he left for longer than a few months. Instead, Tina gave him the first of many surprises: she leaped onto his shoulder, calling and calling, as if to say, *It's you! It's you!* "She was all over me," Geoff says. "Like a dog."

Shortly after that, Tina let Geoff know she wanted more from their relationship. He dropped his keys one morning while cleaning her aviary, and before he could retrieve them she jumped down from her perch, grabbed the keys in her beak, and ran to the other side of the enclosure, where she turned and looked Geoff squarely in the eye. Geoff was stunned: no bird in his care had ever done anything like this. He took a step toward her, and she leaned forward, poised to run. *This is a game,* he thought. *She wants to play.* For the next few minutes, Tina ran around the perimeter of the aviary with the keys in her beak, deftly evading his grasp, until she finally traded them for food. From then on, this was how each morning began.

As they played together, Tina began to defy nearly all of falconry's conventions. She didn't ignore Geoff or try to mate with him: she simply wanted to *interact* with him, whether she was hungry or not. She loved inedible objects and would study, carry, and manipulate anything Geoff brought her, from plush toys to rubber balls and lengths of rope, and she called for him if he didn't turn up on schedule. On quiet afternoons she sometimes fell asleep on his shoulder.

Months passed, and their daily games evolved: keep-away became fetch, then the shell game, then tasks that seemed to require abstract thought. Geoff built a device out of PVC pipes to test Tina's ability to distinguish objects by color and to associate colors with spoken words — and she could. He also bought a set of rubber balls and blocks to see if she could distinguish between objects by shape — and she did. Then he modified Tina's public performances to reflect her new skills, combining his passions for tinkering and falconry into something approaching behavioral science. Tina went from comic relief to the star of the show, and Geoff began calling her the most intelligent bird in the world.

Flying demonstrations are hard to picture if you haven't seen one. They're part circus act, part educational display, and they always carry an element of risk, since they require giving the birds a moment of freedom. Woodlands' flying arena seats about fifty people, but some larger parks and zoos employ dedicated teams of keepers who fly dozens of birds each day for large audiences;

some displays feature extras like theme music and fog machines.

All this window dressing is meant for the audience, of course, not the birds, whose jobs are as straightforward and predictable as possible. "Demo" birds are usually trained to fly from a perch to a falconer's glove in exchange for a food reward; a well-trained barn owl, for instance, will bounce from one post to another in exchange for bits of chicken, and after the show will pose obligingly for photos, resuming its daily habit of not doing very much. Some falcons can also be trained to show off their hunting techniques, diving to strike at a lure twirled on a line, until the falconer calls the traditional "Ho!" and flings the lure for the bird to catch in the air.

But that's about the extent of it. The performances seldom vary, and demo birds rarely seem to realize they don't have to do what they're told. They seem to like the predictability of the routines, or at least become resigned to them, and they have the comfort of knowing exactly where to find their next meal. From the audience's perspective, birds of prey are so striking and majestic that it's easy to forget their behavior isn't all that exciting: fly in, get food, land on perch, get food, fly out, get food, job done.

Tina's performances at Woodlands were quite different. She became bored and distractible when the same things happened too often, and Geoff found that the best way to keep her attention was to offer her new tasks. She began a typical demonstration by crawling through a pipe to retrieve a hidden morsel, then jumping into a garbage bin and knocking over flower pots to see what might be under them — tasks Geoff's other birds would never attempt. "Most birds," he says, "if they can't see a food item, it's like it doesn't exist."

Then the performance shifted focus from Tina's dexterity to her mind. First she would retrieve, at Geoff's request, a square or round object from a group of blocks. Then she would fetch a red, blue, or green ball — this time at the audience's request. (No matter what color the audience chose, Geoff says, Tina never picked the wrong one.) And then there was the grand finale, in which Geoff threw a handful of miniature stuffed animals — usually Nemo, Piglet, and Donald Duck — over his shoulder while Tina stood watching from a low perch in front of him. Then Geoff would lock eyes with Tina and say, "Go find Nemo," at which Tina would obligingly hop down, run across the arena, pick up Nemo in her beak, and return it to Geoff, dropping the toy in a bucket to receive a food reward. Then Geoff would say, "Now go find Piglet." And she would.

Geoff insists that he wasn't giving Tina secret cues; she actually seemed to understand his intentions and associate his words with specific toys. Sometimes he would tell her, mid-retrieval, that he'd changed his mind and wanted a different character — and she'd drop the toy she was carrying and pick up the one he'd asked for. Finally, Tina would accompany Geoff back to her aviary, riding on his shoulder, and hop back into the enclosure on her own. There was more food in store for her if she entered the cage under her own power, and she'd learned to read Geoff so well that she seemed to anticipate his actions without much effort.

She could also be impatient if things weren't moving fast enough. If Geoff began to digress during a demonstration, she'd nip his earlobe to get him back on track. If an audience member brought any kind of food to the arena, Tina would steal it and eat it on the spot, whether it was a hamburger or an ice cream cone. (Once, to Geoff's horror, she landed on a stroller and snatched a pacifier from a baby's mouth.) It was no use trying to control her with a falconer's traditional tools of jesses and a hood; she only pulled them off and tore them to bits. She performed, it seemed, because she liked to, and she stayed, it seemed, because she didn't want to leave.

There's only one video of Tina in action, working with Geoff's assistant Lyn in 2013, and it's difficult to say who's demonstrating whom. Tina is in an imperious mood, and Lyn, who's nearly Geoff's age but has a less imposing presence, seems a bit cowed. As the clip begins, Tina is perched on Lyn's shoulder, screaming into his ear, and won't quiet down until he gives her a piece of food. "Stop it!" he pleads. "I'm trying to talk!" After Tina retrieves Nemo and Donald Duck, Lyn leads her back to her aviary in some haste, explaining as he walks that if he doesn't give her an extra morsel once she's safely back inside, she'll punish him in the morning. "The trouble with intelligent birds like her," Lyn says, fastening the latch of her cage with palpable relief, "is that they *don't forget,* and if I don't give her that extra tidbit there, in the morning she'll chase me around and bite at my ankles, and I'll tell you what, it bloody hurts!"

This kind of thinking — improvisatory, abstract, several steps ahead — was something Geoff had never seen before from a bird. He couldn't account for the difference between Tina and the other members of his collection, but whatever its source, he was smitten. He even issued a challenge in a local newspaper, daring anyone to produce a smarter bird of any kind. (No one did; but the terms of the challenge, to be fair, weren't very clear.)

When Tina became severely arthritic at the age of thirty-three, Geoff and Lyn were heartbroken. Birds' minds don't usually decline with age, and Tina's seemed keener than ever — but she could barely move without obvious pain, and a hobbled Johnny rook is a picture of misery. A last-ditch surgery failed, and when Geoff made the decision to put her down, he asked Lyn to bury her and not to tell him where.

"I can't —" Geoff says, then corrects himself. "I don't *want* to know." For once, he seems at a loss for words. Then a thought strikes him, and he clears his throat. "You know," he says, "Shakespeare was a very good falconer." A mashed-up verse follows, in a stage-ready baritone, that's part Othello, part Juliet, and part Geoff.

"O, for the voice of a falconer," he begins, "— because they're always shouting 'Ho!' — *To lure my tassel-gentil back again* — tassel, that's a tiercel, a male peregrine — *though her jesses were my dear heart-strings, would I woo her back, and prey her down-wind at fortune.*"

He takes a beat, then another. The harp music creeps forward again, along with the monotonous rasp of a tawny owl's begging call. Geoff seems pleased by the sound of his own voice, but his eyes are far away.

It doesn't seem to have occurred to him to wonder what Tina was doing in England in the first place. In a way, it didn't matter:

111

Geoff was interested in *her,* not the land of her ancestors. But at even a slight remove, the presence of captive striated caracaras in the UK seems improbable, to say the least. The international trade in birds of prey is tightly regulated, and capturing and importing a striated caracara would be nearly impossible today. Even if international treaties weren't an issue, transporting enough Johnny rooks from southern South America to breed them in England would be wildly expensive. Who would have had the means or the inclination to do it — and why?

6
THE COURT OF THE PENGUIN KING

Campbell Murn, a deep-voiced Australian in a khaki uniform, looked a bit weary. As the director of international conservation projects for a handsome wildlife park near Stonehenge called the Hawk Conservancy Trust, Campbell was very often out of the office, and when I met him in the park's café, he'd just returned from Kenya, where he'd been trying to stop elephant and rhino poachers from poisoning vultures. "There are eleven species of African vultures," he said, looking glumly into a mug of tea, "and nine of them are threatened or endangered."

He brightened when I asked about the Johnny rooks. ("Cheeky bastards," he said.) The conservancy was founded by Ashley Smith, the falconer who traded Tina to Geoff for a well-behaved goshawk, and it's still home to Tina's parents, Darwin and Lafonia, who are now well into their forties. They live in a large, open aviary, where they get plenty of food and fresh air, but it's hard not to think they look a little forlorn; they've grown up eight thousand miles from a home they never knew, and they've never seen another member of their species except their own offspring.

Campbell had also never met a striated caracara when he joined the conservancy over a decade ago, and he noticed that Tina's parents were very different from the park's other residents: they were less fearful, more playful, quicker to relax in the presence of new keepers. There was something in their eyes he found inexplicably compelling, almost as if they had a sense of humor, and he was surprised to learn that no one had compiled a studbook for their species — a family tree of captive animals used by zoos and breeders to prevent inbreeding. When he tried to compile one himself, he turned up more striated caracaras in the UK than he'd expected: at least fifty or sixty are scattered throughout zoos and falconry parks in the British Isles, with a few more in continental Europe and at least one in Japan. But when he asked after the birds' origins, his sources often turned vague. Few seemed to know (or wanted to say) exactly where their Johnny rooks had come from.

"Of course," Campbell said, "everyone knew it was the penguin king."

The penguin king, also known as the penguin

millionaire, was a man called Len Hill, a bird enthusiast and tireless self-promoter — an acquaintance called him a "lovable rogue" — who built an extraordinary wildlife park in the Cotswolds called Birdland, where a thousand birds from around the world lived among five acres of ornamental gardens that were once his backyard. Birdland opened in 1957, and by the mid-1970s it was a regional sensation, receiving more than a million visitors a year. Hill's droll, folksy persona made him a favorite of the BBC — a young David Attenborough even devoted an episode of *The World About Us* to him — and Hill wanted as many of his birds as possible to roam freely, with the result that he often spent days chasing after macaws and penguins (and once, a giant Indian hornbill) that set out to explore the countryside.

Inside the park, flightless ducks and purple moorhens swam in artificial ponds while hummingbirds guzzled nectar from tropical plants in a large greenhouse, occasionally plucking strands of visitors' hair to weave into their tiny nests. A pair of hyacinth macaws climbed all over the gift shop, and a loose flock of flamingos and cranes paced across the lawn in front of Hill's house, a restored Tudor manor he called Chardwar. Rows of aviaries housed other colorful specialties, including toucans, cockatoos, and Victoria crowned pigeons from New Guinea —

broiler-sized birds with headdresses of powder-blue feathers.

But Birdland's most famous residents were its penguins. Five different species, from thick-set rockhoppers to tall, elegant kings, waddled through its grounds and swam in a pool fitted with a glass viewing portal, taking their tropical neighbors in stride. "Often, on a dark winter's morning," Hill wrote,

I draw back the bedroom curtains on a scene which would make most people rub their eyes and wonder if they were dreaming: below, on the snow-covered lawn, a silent group of penguins gaze expectantly upwards as if to say, 'Hello, are you getting up today?'. By midday, when the ice has melted, their place will be taken by a gaggle of bright, noisy flamingoes, executing what looks like a tribal dance in slow motion. Finally, as dusk falls, I call out of the study window and in flies Juno, an African grey parrot, who nestles on my shoulder to say goodnight before settling down to sleep in the house.

Juno was a special case. She was ill-tempered and standoffish at first, but she rarely left Hill's side after he nursed her back to health from an infection that clouded her eyes (though she also kept a parrot consort, another African gray named George). Juno

116

enjoyed playing a game with Hill, captured on film by the BBC, in which she lay on her back in his open palm and let him toss her into the air and catch her again, over and over. "Up she comes and down she goes," Hill wrote, "legs in the air, eyes half closed with pleasure, secure in the knowledge that she will land in my hand."

By all accounts, Hill's rapport with his birds was extraordinary. He seemed to have a knack for knowing what they really wanted from life, and his technique for retrieving wayward macaws is a case in point. They were trained to perch on a gnarled wooden stick, and when one of the birds went missing, Hill and his head keeper, the evocatively named John Midwinter, took the stick with them when they loaded up an old station wagon for "Operation Birdlift." Once they'd found their missing bird, Hill and Midwinter attached the stick to the end of a telescoping pole — "rather like those used by old-fashioned chimney sweeps," Hill wrote.

The rods would be wiggled, very carefully, through the foliage, until they came within a yard or so of the macaw. Perched aloft, in an alien landscape, perhaps a bit insecure and certainly somewhat sleepy, the bird would suddenly see a familiar object in front of it, often holding a dainty chocolate morsel. 'Hello, there's my little stick', it would think, then hop on to the wooden 'perch', to be lowered safely and popped into the trap cage.

A veteran presenter of children's wildlife programs insisted that Hill must have been a bird himself in an earlier life, and compared visiting Birdland in Hill's company to "walking into a great children's tea party with Father Christmas." Hill probably liked the comparison. He wanted to believe that his captive birds were enjoying their lives — and what better proof of his success than the fact that given the chance to leave, they usually stayed? A skeptic might point out that his parrots and penguins were as marooned in the Cotswolds as the Johnny rooks were in the Falklands, but birds have ways of showing when they're healthy, if not happy: their feathers are shiny and clean and they seem alert and interested in life, which the general population at Birdland appeared to be. More than most zoos, it felt like a place where humans and animals could imagine they were friends.

Birdland also evoked the aristocratic tradition of keeping private menageries on the grounds of sprawling estates (a baroness near Bristol, for example, once kept a pair of zebras and a gorilla on her squash court). But Hill wasn't a blueblood: he was the son of a groundskeeper and left school at sixteen to become a carpenter's apprentice. "There always seemed to be so many more interesting things going on," he wrote, "outside the classroom."

In some ways Hill bears a passing resemblance to Hudson, who had finally found fame as a writer in London when Len was born in 1912. Like Hudson, Hill's happiest childhood memories came from being outdoors, in the pastures, copses, and streams beside the Windrush River, and though Len's parents didn't share their son's enthusiasm for wildlife, they let him dissect birds on their kitchen table and keep a small menagerie of live snakes and weasels. His best animal friend was a pigeon named Joey, whom he raised from a featherless chick and trained to eat from his open mouth; Joey once interrupted a local christening by flying into the church and landing in the pew next to young Len, who was singing in the choir.

All these furred, scaled, and feathered companions, Hill wrote, "taught me vital lessons in living with animals" in the same way Hudson's childhood in the Pampas gave him a sense of their inner lives. Hill also shared Hudson's talent for sensing opportunities when they appeared: during World War II he made wooden nose caps for bombshells in his carpentry shop, and in the postwar years he prospered by buying, restoring, and reselling dilapidated houses. Hill details his mount-

119

ing fortunes in minute and unabashed detail in his autobiography, *Penguin Millionaire,* and he never seems to have doubted that their best possible use was to create the world of his dreams, where he could own a house like the lords his father worked for and live among birds who adored him.

Hudson, by contrast, was content to build his imaginary worlds on the page and didn't much like zoos, though he might have been seduced by a public garden where he could admire hundreds of free-roaming birds without binoculars. It's easy to picture him standing by one of Birdland's ponds gazing at a Chilean flamingo, a black-necked swan, or a Magellanic penguin — birds of his youth that he'd never have expected to see again. But they might also have seemed painfully out of place, since Hudson thought that animals were only truly themselves in their natural contexts. For him this view was a mixture of common sense, nostalgia, and mysticism, though we'd probably call it "ecological" now, and it was a perspective Len Hill seems to have lacked. He loved his birds, but in his eagerness to gather them around him, he doesn't seem to have given much thought to their far-flung homes.

To be fair, he didn't have much time for reflection; there were no days off at Birdland. Each year its penguins ate their way through seven tons of herring and shrimp, while lorikeets and other nectar feeders consumed thousands of gallons of sugar water and honey imported from New Zealand and Romania. Fruit eaters like toucans and cockatoos required a small army's ration of grapes, apples, bananas, nuts, and sunflower seeds, and insectivores and meat eaters received live mealworms and mice, supplemented with ox hearts; bee eaters required shipments of live bees and wasps; and an emerald-green bird from Central America called a resplendent quetzal had to be hand-fed live locusts. No one in England had kept such a variety of birds at such close quarters before, and Hill and his staff had to invent their protocols and routines through trial and error, coordinating with food suppliers in a time when out-of-season fruit was rare and placing an international call was an ordeal.

But they succeeded as often as not, and as Birdland's popularity grew, Hill's horizons broadened. He began to travel to acquire new birds, which presented him with unusual challenges: how to keep hummingbirds from starving to death on an international flight, for instance (a problem he solved by smuggling them in a cigar box, which he took to the toilet every thirty minutes to feed them sugar water from an eyedropper). Birdland's fame also put Hill in touch with other well-heeled bird enthusiasts, and introduced him to a new strain of thinking about the world's

121

threatened wildlife — one that included concern not just for wild animals, but also for the places they lived.

Among these enthusiasts was Peter Scott, the founder of the World Wildlife Fund. Scott had a special fondness for penguins because of his father, Robert Falcon Scott, who died walking back from the South Pole in the ill-fated British Antarctic expedition of 1910–12. In a final letter to his wife, Scott had implored her to make their newborn son "interested in natural history if you can; it is better than games." Peter Scott wanted to see the frozen continent for himself, and in 1968 he organized a unique cruise to the Antarctic Peninsula, the mountainous tendril of land that uncurls toward South America and supports most of the continent's wildlife.

Scott invited Hill to join a coterie of amateur naturalists and photographers on the trip, and Hill eagerly accepted. A few months later he found himself in an airplane above Tierra del Fuego, whose landscapes looked as forbidding to him as they did to Darwin. "As we flew over Patagonia and saw the black, infertile soil still bearing traces of the Ice Age," he wrote, "it seemed strangely appropriate to hear that the average life expectancy of the remaining native Indians of this wild region is still only thirty years."

As the Antarctic world revealed itself, Hill became even more entranced. He'd kept penguins at Birdland for nearly a decade and knew their temperaments and preferences, but now he saw them resting on jagged black cliffs among calving glaciers and ice floes, or swimming at astonishing speed through the deep blue waves beside Scott's chartered ship, the *Navarino.* They called in briefly at Stanley, where Hill met a priest who'd once arranged a shipment of penguins for him, and the first wandering albatrosses appeared in their wake as the waves of the polar vortex swelled around them.

The scientists, technicians, and soldiers who manned the Russian, British, and American bases scattered along the Antarctic Peninsula were an odd and insular tribe, equipped with helicopters, snow tractors, and cargo planes that landed on skis, but Hill was more interested in the landscapes that surrounded them. "As man diminishes," he noted, "so the wildlife flourishes." Leopard seals gazed at Hill from saucer-shaped floes of pancake ice, pods of orcas patrolled the shore near penguin and seal colonies, and curious humpback whales sometimes approached the ship. It was a mesmerizing and contradictory place, idyllic but inhospitable, and it lulled Hill into a feeling that he'd entered the prehuman past — an illusion that broke down when the *Navarino* steamed into the flooded caldera of the volcano called Deception Island, where a whaling station lay in ruins.

"Here we saw bleached whalebones and the decayed remains of boats," Hill wrote, "reminders of the horrors of the early decades of this century when the whale was slaughtered *en masse,* its oil being processed for soap, the thin plate from its upper jaw for corsets and the ambergris for perfume." It was a sobering monument to human greed, and to an industry that was still thriving: land-based whaling stations were abandoned only because factory ships that could kill and process whales at sea had made them obsolete. Len had heard about the slaughter of Antarctic wildlife from Scott and others, but seeing its traces firsthand shook him.

The legion of penguins nesting on the slopes of Deception's harbor, however, seemed unperturbed by its bloody past. They merely stared at Hill as he walked toward them across a broad beach of steaming black sand, in a moment that must have felt like a waking dream. Seeing the birds living free and unafraid in the ruins of a factory of death was an indelible image, as was an immense flock of little black-and-white seabirds called Wilson's storm-petrels, which hovered over the ocean like a swarm of giant moths. It was one of the most moving sights of his life, Len wrote, a vision of a lost paradise.

Back home, Len had trouble readjusting to life at Birdland, which paled beside the world he'd glimpsed with Scott. He longed to return to the far south, and when a remote pair of islands in the Falklands covered in penguins, albatrosses, and sheep went up for sale a few months later, he couldn't help himself. The asking price was £10,000 — about $400,000 in today's dollars — and Hill offered £5,500, without the sheep. The owners balked, but Hill was the only interested buyer, and the sheep were removed. The deed arrived in his hands in 1970: a formal, antique-looking proclamation, covered in stamps and an embossed seal, that conveyed to him forever, and free of encumbrances, the islands of Grand and Steeple Jason. Leonard Hill, the son of a groundskeeper, had bought one of the largest private nature reserves in the world.

A floatplane carried him to Steeple Jason in the austral summer of the following year. Len had snagged a spot on the weekly mail run from Stanley to the western settlements, and on the flight to his islands he felt like a schoolboy playing postman, dropping padded bags of letters into the outstretched arms of waiting islanders while the pilot flew as low as he dared. But when the plane left him, Hill stood for a moment in awed silence. Steeple Jason's peaks soared above him, imposing and ancient, and a vast throng of nesting albatrosses stretched as far as he could see. As he drank in the scene, two curious striated caracaras came winging in, swooping over and around him, to see what he was about.

An islander named Ian Strange had preceded Hill to the island, and the two of them roughed it on Steeple for about a week, camping in a derelict shearing shed and tramping for hours through the albatross colonies. Removing the sheep had not only saved Len money, it had saved the island's wildlife; healthy stands of tussac still remained on its steepest inclines and edges, sheltering legions of seabirds and seals. He was especially delighted by the hidden colonies of gentoo penguins, artfully concealed behind natural hedges of tussac, in which each penguin sat atop a pyramid of white pebbles they carried from as much as a mile away. "The gentoo nest," Hill wrote, "is certainly just as much a masterpiece of construction as the Egyptian monuments.

So fascinated was I by this avian architecture that when I came across one nest which was 2ft 6in wide and about 9–12in high, I dismantled it and found it to be composed of some 500 pebbles. I then put it together again, I hope to the owner's satisfaction.

Hill sometimes imagined himself as a lord of the manor addressing his grateful avian subjects, a fantasy he'd more or less made a reality at Birdland. But Steeple Jason let him indulge it on an even grander scale. Its multitudes seemed either unconcerned by his presence, like the penguins, or interested in him, like the starling-like tussacbirds that perched on his penny loafers. Most delicious of all was that these birds were *his,* to do with as he pleased, and in the near term they looked like money in the bank: Hill now had a nearly unlimited supply of birds that almost no one in England had ever seen, and a surplus he could trade for other rarities. In their remaining days on the island, Hill and Strange captured birds from their colonies and packed them in specially made shipping crates, and Hill returned to Stanley with a cargo of sixty-six penguins and a few pairs of geese. As he passed through customs, he casually paid export fees of about $25,000 and informed the officer that he was the proud owner of forty million pounds' worth of wildlife. By Len's reckoning, his purchase of two treeless islands in an anonymous corner of the world was one of the greatest real estate deals in history.

Len Hill reigned as the penguin king for another decade, then died of a heart attack in 1981, just shy of his seventieth birthday — and Birdland never really recovered from the loss. He'd held it together in part by sheer force of personality, and gaps he'd papered over with enthusiasm became clear in his absence, including his casual attitude toward record keeping. Successors trying to figure out where and when he'd procured his birds, or to whom he might have traded or sold them, found only a stack of dog-eared papers impaled on a spike, and eventually both Birdland and the Jasons were sold to repay his many debts.

One of Len's legacies, however, was Tina. He returned to the Falklands several more times to collect birds, and on at least one of those trips he returned with several Johnny rook eggs. Hill was never too keen on birds of prey, but striated caracaras probably came in handy when he needed to make a trade, since no one else had them. No one is sure how many he imported — certainly more than two, and probably fewer than ten — but all the captive striated caracaras in the world today can probably be traced to birds Len carried back from Steeple Jason.

Such a small gene pool comes with an existential risk, but for now the descendants of Birdland's Johnny rooks appear to be thriving. One pair ended up at the London Zoo in Regent's Park, where they've bred for many years, and today you can see Tina's brothers, sisters, and cousins at Chessington World of Adventures, Herrings Green Activity Farm and Birds of Prey Centre, Suffolk Owl Sanctuary, Woodside Wildlife Park,

Cotswold Wildlife Park and Gardens, and the JungleBarn at Paradise Park (among others). At the International Centre for Birds of Prey in Newent, Gloucestershire, a young striated caracara named Peebles has her own Instagram feed, and at Eagle Heights Wildlife Foundation, an hour from London by train, you can meet an adult pair named Mr. and Mrs. Butthead. Sometimes it seems that every falconry park in England has a Johnny rook with a funny name lurking in the back somewhere, and a keeper who can't wait to tell you about them.

The behavioral scientists you'd expect to be fascinated by these birds, however, don't seem to know they exist, even though several Johnny rooks live mere miles from Oxford's Behavioural Ecology Research Group, whose members are preoccupied with the mental feats of tool-using crows from New Caledonia. But among falconers the word has spread, and Johnny rooks are increasingly prized for their entertainment value. Though falconers rarely know much about striated caracaras' lives in the wild, they seem to have agreed on a set of activities that Johnny rooks (and visitors) enjoy, which usually involve knocking things over, crawling through PVC pipes, solving puzzles like Kerplunk or Jenga, or jumping into bins and boxes. People often film these displays and post them on the internet, and in one of my favorites, a falconer in Oxfordshire named James Channon shows off a young striated caracara named Boo. Boo stands by James's side, untethered, as James introduces her to a circle of curious visitors and sets three plastic flowerpots on a gravel path.

"This bird," James purrs, "takes intelligence to another level."

As if on cue, Boo charges toward the pots and knocks over the first one, then the second, where there's a morsel of food waiting for her. Then she stops and looks up at James.

"This might seem simple," says James, "but other birds here would never grasp this. She knows there's only one bit of food, so there's no point in knocking over the third one; *there's never anything there.*" He stops, and looks around; Boo is nowhere to be seen. "Boo!" he calls. "Where'd you go?"

The camera tilts above James's head, where Boo pops up on the roof of her aviary. "What are you doing up there?" James asks. Boo blinks.

"Come down here, love," calls an older woman. "We want to have a look at you and take your picture!"

A new Birdland, under different ownership, now occupies a new site in the Cotswolds. It doesn't have the charmed feeling of Len Hill's garden, but some of its inhabitants are descended from his birds; a few of the king penguins may even be original. A pair of striated caracaras who are almost certainly Tina's cousins, if not siblings, live in a small, wedge-shaped aviary with a nest box and a cloudy birdbath, and when I visited in 2015, the female was standing chest-deep in it, looking as if she'd been soaking for a while and planned to stay longer. There wasn't much else for her to do.

I wondered what Len had thought about her species, since striated caracaras would seem to be the kind of birds he liked best: attractive, social, and curious. But he didn't offer them the freedom he gave his macaws and flamingos — perhaps out of concern for his penguins — and he doesn't seem to have considered what someone willing to devote the kind of time and attention he gave to Joey the pigeon or Juno the parrot could have learned from a Johnny rook. He did, however, give them something they'd never had before in the history of their species: a new continent to live on, and an audience of people who might wonder what they were.

He'd also saved the birds of Steeple and Grand Jason. The islands passed from one owner to another for a decade after his death, but no one put sheep on them again, and a financier from the United States eventually bought and donated them to the Wildlife Conservation Society, the owners of the

Bronx Zoo. It's probably safe to say that no one will ever harvest wild animals from Steeple again; conservationists around the world now hold it in the awe Hill felt when he saw it in 1971. The shearing shed where he camped with Ian Strange has been flattened by the wind, but among its ruins a few scattered crates still bear "Birdland" stencils; one has "Hill," "Stanley," and "Falkland Islands" written on it in faded blue ink.

Tina was still alive when G7 died on the shore of Steeple Jason in 2012, and if they'd met, they'd probably have recognized each other, though Tina might have been shocked to realize she wasn't alone in the world. But the very qualities that made her a friend to Geoff and a star at Woodlands — her curiosity, her restlessness, her distractibility — might have been the very ones that made G7 an easy mark for his killer.

Let's go back to the instant of his death, as the peregrine bent to break his neck. It's been only seconds since she crashed into him, and he's probably too stunned to resist. Her bright yellow legs are short compared to his long gray ones, but though he's a larger bird, she has a purposeful, deadly air that he lacks. Notice her long, slender toes, gripping his neck and shoulders. Notice the fine black barring of her pale breast, cool and smart against his mud-brown primaries. Notice her blue-gray wings, spread in an arc above him as she leans in to feed: an ancient pose falconers call mantling. Notice the frozen waves like hills of glass. The shoal of penguins arcing out of them. The blunt snout of a sea lion surfacing to breathe. The puff of steam above its nostrils.

Now zoom out in space and time, and shrink Steeple Jason to a speck in the blue. Larger shapes and patterns appear, invisible at ground level: a range of mountains hugs a seam in the earth's crust. Lakes of oil lie sealed beneath the ocean floor. G7 and the peregrine become abstractions, no longer individuals but members of their species, points along faintly glowing lines that have forked and forked again in response to the forces of geography, time, luck, skill, competition, and accident.

This is the process contained by the word "evolution," and if you follow the branching lineages of G7 and the peregrine back through time, you arrive at a surprising fact: they're members of the same family of birds, the falcons. In evolutionary terms, striated caracaras and peregrines have only been separate for a short while, about the same span of time that lies between chimpanzees and gorillas, and at this remove, the scene of their meeting becomes unnerving, like watching a chimp devour a colobus monkey.

In a way, you might think of G7's death as

a spat in an evolutionary feud that's simmered for millions of years, and like many family arguments, it involves a clash of certainties about the best way to approach life. On one side are generalists like the Johnny rooks — curious learners with a malleable sense of how to make use of the world. Staring them down from across the room are the specialists — experts with specific tastes and little room for error. These professionals might look down their noses at the amateurs: *Sit still for once, you dilettantes.* The generalists, on the other hand, might glare back and mutter, *Try opening your minds for a change.* And right there, in the divergent lives of these two falcons, lie the traces of something that happened to our planet long ago. Something very, very important.

■ ■ ■ ■

PART II
FAR AWAY AND
LONG AGO

■ ■ ■ ■

It is impossible to reflect on the changed state of the American continent without the deepest astonishment. Formerly it must have swarmed with great monsters.

— CHARLES DARWIN

I wanted a different history, one with animals as well as men in it.

— WILLIAM HENRY HUDSON

7

IN THE WAKE
OF THE DINOSAURS

William Henry Hudson was eighteen years old when he woke from a dream so frightening it was vivid for him fifty years later. In the dream, he was standing on the plain outside his family's house in the Pampas, on a sunlit day, under a brilliant blue sky, but something was terribly wrong. "Looking up," he wrote,

I saw a dark object like a cloud at a vast height, but coming swiftly down toward the earth. I then perceived that it was no cloud but something solid, and as it came lower it resolved itself into iron, in bars about twice the thickness round of a hogshead, the bars being a mile or two in length. When the lowest, which were very distinctly seen, were near the earth, I could see that they extended in a stream of bars — tens of thousands or millions of bars — far up into the heavens until they faded from sight. Gazing up at this swift-coming torrent, I said: This is the end of everything; all life will be killed on earth by the shock, and the earth itself will be driven out of its orbit.

The next day, he found he wasn't alone. The Hudsons and their neighbors in the surrounding countryside had all bolted awake at about the same time, and some had heard a sound like an immense thunderclap. In a sense, Hudson's dream was likely correct: a fist-sized meteor had probably exploded overhead, shattering into a cloud of metallic vapor and tiny fragments that rained down on the plains. But the scale of his dream seems eerily prescient now, almost as if a memory embedded in the earth itself had seeped into his sleeping mind. A century later, scientists realized that something very much like Hudson's dream did in fact happen, though not in his lifetime, or any human lifetime.

If we slide Hudson's dream back sixty-six million years, north by about five thousand miles, and out of the dream world into waking life, Hudson would have been gazing into the same sky from a calm, shallow sea — let's give him a rowboat — that covered the eastern half of what's now the Yucatán Peninsula of Mexico. Below him, in the clear blue water, reefs of giant tubular clams and solitary corals sheltered thousands of bony fish, sharks, mollusks, starfish, and crustaceans, many of them not unlike the ones you might see today in the seas off Cozumel, though the long shadow of a giant marine reptile called a mosasaur might also have passed beneath his little boat. As he stared upward, he would have noticed something very beautiful and strange — not a dark spot but a searing pinpoint of light growing rapidly in size: a hunk of metallic rock at least six miles wide. It was traveling so fast that it scraped against Earth's atmosphere like a match head on sandpaper and burst into a roaring corolla of flame. The last thing Hudson would have seen, before its impact vaporized him, was an unbearable brightness spreading across the sky.

When the asteroid struck the sea, it triggered a wave of death so terrible that it seems like Shiva himself in mineral form. It marked the end of the span of ancient time geologists call the Cretaceous period, and the more we learn about this moment, the more dreadful it becomes: the asteroid's destructive power was equal to *ten billion* Hiroshima bombs (the largest volcanic eruption to occur in human history, by contrast, was about a fourth as powerful). It carved a hole in the earth thirty miles deep and 120 miles wide, heaving up a brittle ring of mountains taller than the Himalayas in about ten minutes. As the ocean poured into the gaping pit, a mega-tsunami rolled outward; if an identical object landed in the same place today, it would send a six-hundred-foot wall of water crashing over most of Central America, the north coast of South America, the islands of the Caribbean, the Atlantic coast of Mexico, most of Texas, and all of Louisiana, Mississippi, Alabama, and Florida. Its blast wave would flatten forests and buildings across North America while slower-moving shock waves would ring the earth's lithosphere like a bell, waking sleeping volcanoes on the west coast of North America, rattling floors in Moscow, shattering windows in Mumbai.

The trouble with the past is that it keeps changing. The asteroid's effects on the history of life were so sudden and pervasive that it's easy to forget we didn't even know about it until very recently. Paleontologists knew for more than a century that *something* caused most dinosaurs, along with many other plant and animal species, to vanish suddenly from the fossil record, but it seemed we might never know quite what it was; I remember hearing several explanations for the dinosaurs' demise as a child, when the asteroid was still a new and contentious hypothesis. But evidence for it piled up swiftly through the 1980s, and the site of its buried crater was publicly confirmed in 1991, setting off a wave of disaster films starring giant space rocks as implacable villains.

Even then, scientists remained cautious. A conference of experts didn't officially conclude that the asteroid most likely caused the Cretaceous extinctions until 2010, and there's still a great deal we don't know about the impact and its aftermath. The first attempts to drill into the crater began only a few years ago, and the resulting cylinders of ancient rock, shot through with pink-hued granite forced up from the earth's mantle, continue to reveal surprising facts about a moment when almost everything changed for life on Earth.

One of these surprises is that the asteroid's effects were wildly uneven. It entered our atmosphere at an oblique angle, and its blast launched a flaming cloud of debris and ash north and west, striking at the heart of North America. For anything in its path, this cloud was a waking nightmare: it was thousands of miles wide and moved at hundreds of miles per hour. There was little chance of escape if you stood in its way, and few plants and fewer animals in the Northern Hemisphere survived.

The southern half of the world, by contrast, may have been relatively spared — though we tend not to think about it, since most of our planet's habitable land now lies in the north. The Australian biologist Tim Flannery noted that while North American pollen records reflect a scorched-earth cataclysm in the wake of the impact, samples from southern Australia suggest that forests in the far south barely felt it — though the animals that lived in them didn't fare so well. Plants were better equipped than animals to handle the years of cold darkness that spread around the world in the blast's aftermath, and many vegetable survivors from that time are common enough today to be unremarkable, including pines, palms, ferns, mosses, cycads, and magnolias. Even farther south, the continent of Antarctica — a landmass twice the size of Australia — was thick with plants and animals whose experience of the Cretaceous extinctions is mostly hidden from us, since their fossil traces would lie under miles of ice.

There's little doubt, however, that the blast's effects were planetary in scope. The gypsum-rich seabed of the impact zone, heaved skyward, injected millions of tons of sulfur-bearing minerals into the upper atmosphere, turning blue skies brown and black, shot through with blazing curtains of amber and crimson at dawn and dusk. Heavier particles ejected by the blast fell back to Earth as flaming beads of glass, igniting massive fires; finer ones bonded chemically with water vapor and fell for years as acid rain. The late Cretaceous was already a time of intense volcanic activity in some parts of the world, but the asteroid's debris would have added insult to injury: on the island continent of India, which hadn't yet collided with Asia, two magmatic "hot spots" erupted with great force, shrouding the world with further clouds of dust and ash. The remains of these mighty explosions lingered in the atmosphere as a sulfurous veil that dimmed the skies for decades, plunging our planet into the cool twilight of a polar winter.

Needless to say, this sudden and drastic shift in Earth's climate made life unbearable for many animals, and the largest species suffered most. Even if they lived through the blast waves and forest fires, their food supplies were often so disrupted that they couldn't survive the months that followed, and in the sea the problem was especially acute: without sufficient sunlight, populations of the microscopic plants called phytoplankton collapsed in a few days or weeks, triggering a cascade of starvation that traveled swiftly up the food chain.

On land, some animals were better suited for a dark, cold, caustic new world than others. Judging by their living descendants, mammals, amphibians, and reptiles that lived at least partly underground or spent part of the year hibernating stood a better chance of surviving. (Snapping turtles, for example, spend much of their lives submerged at the bottom of ponds, absorbing oxygen from the water through their skin, and they survived even in fire-ravaged North America.)

The larger dinosaurs did none of these things. They'd thrived for tens of millions of years in a world that was bursting with meat and fresh greens, and they ran their bodies hot. Like us, they were warm-blooded, nimble, and needed to eat frequently — and they also had to manage the energy-expensive chore of incubating giant eggs for months on end. In the wake of the asteroid, dinosaurs who'd survived the initial blast faced a planet that could no longer feed them, and according to one estimate, nearly every animal that weighed more than about fifty pounds seems to have died out in the post-impact world — except in the deep oceans, where ancient scavengers like sleeper sharks still go about their unlit business today. They might even have enjoyed a bonanza as the carcasses of mosasaurs rained from the surface waters into the black depths.

In my lifetime, this version of the Cretaceous extinctions has gone from a hypothesis to history, and we've taken its sobering news in stride, folding it in among other once-controversial facts like the glaciers that spread across the world in the ice ages, or our species' origin in Africa. Dinosaur exhibits are as popular now as when they were first unveiled to the public in the early nineteenth century, but their meaning has changed: since we will almost certainly be visited by another giant meteor, every dinosaur skeleton now comes with a warning label that reads ONE DAY, YOU WILL BE ME.

Before we knew about the meteor, scientific explanations for the big dinosaurs' demise tended to look for a fault in the dinosaurs themselves, arguing that they were too sluggish, too small-brained, too intolerant of heat or cold or disease. But it now appears that the dinosaurs didn't provoke their extinction in any way, and nothing in the fossil record suggests that the late-Cretaceous world had entered some sort of decadent phase. On the contrary: life on Earth was flourishing. At the moment of the asteroid's impact, our planet was about as cozy and hospitable as it's ever been — though you and I would have found it an unnerving place to live. Even in Antarctica, the dinosaurs' planet was a warm, lush place, covered mostly in forests. We can glimpse something like its abundance and diversity today in places like coral reefs and the Amazon jungles, and the more we learn about this vanished time, the more acute the ache of its loss becomes. What child, looking at a picture book of dinosaurs, hasn't shuddered at the grin of a *T. rex* peering from behind a tree fern, or marveled at the wicked spikes of an ankylosaur without also wishing, at least a little, that their world were still here?

But in many ways it is, and not just in the

fossil record; the post-impact world was emphatically *not* a clean slate. Every living thing today has an ancestor that survived the blast, and some, without sufficient pressure to change, have retained their ancient forms, like the ginkgoes that line streets in New York, or the giant marine pill bugs that wander the deep oceans. Others seized the opportunities of the asteroid-addled world by radiating into new and different forms, including us.

The oldest known primate skeleton dates from about fifty-five million years ago, and it wouldn't be anyone's pick for a world conqueror: this furry little grandfather, with its slender toes and long tail, would fit in the palm of your hand. It probably clambered around in trees and ate bugs. But its lineage had a bright future: as the animal world rebuilt itself, a largely nocturnal set of furry creatures that had scurried for millions of years in the shadow of the dinosaurs or sheltered in tunnels and burrows underground emerged to find that they'd inherited the world. This is the reason that the geologic era that contains every moment from the asteroid's impact to now, the Cenozoic, is also called the age of mammals. On the face of it, mammals' claim to this title seems fairly strong — they diversified into thousands of new forms in the post-Cretaceous world, taking over niches the big dinosaurs left open. Some of them, like baleen whales and mammoths, became nearly as large as their saurian predecessors, and their remains have left an unmistakable signature in the earth.

It's important to remember, however, that the mammals weren't the only animals left alive. Since the asteroid's discovery, another controversial hypothesis about the extinction of the dinosaurs has gathered steam and burst into the realm of fact: that it didn't happen. The animals we call birds are direct descendants of dinosaurs who survived the blast, and if you keep this in mind, you can begin to understand what Tina, Evita, G7, and the peregrine really are.

They aren't as easy to explain as you might think. In some ways, they're harder to define than *we* are, because they've been recognizably themselves for so much longer. If I could take you back in a time-traveling spaceship to the morning before the meteor hit, you'd notice many strange things about the world — but the strangest of all might be its similarity to the one you know. From orbit, Earth would have looked much like it does now, if a few shades greener, and most of the continents had arrived at the positions and shapes you'd find on a globe today. But there were subtle differences even at this scale, and if you pressed your nose against a porthole of our spaceship for a few minutes, you'd start to notice them. South America was still joined to Antarctica by a slender land bridge, as was Australia, and Antarctica itself was divided by a narrow sea. India was still riding its tectonic plate toward Asia to create the unborn Himalayas. North America was also divided by an inland sea whose remnants are still evaporating in the basin of the Great Salt Lake. There were no glaciers and few deserts, and Antarctica was covered in forests of southern beech trees, like New Zealand or Tierra del Fuego today.

And if we landed our spaceship, there'd be no mistaking the fact that we'd arrived in an ancient world, especially if we happened across a group of long-necked titanosaurs in Patagonia — each one the length and weight of a passenger jet — or a gaggle of duck-billed, kangaroo-shaped hadrosaurs munching on succulent grasses in the marshes of western North America. (You might linger for a confused moment, however, over some of the hadrosaurs' neighbors: there were plenty of crocodiles around back then, some of which would look so modern to our eyes that they'd seem like visitors from the future, when it's really the other way around.)

You'd also be certain to notice a host of feathered dinosaurs that would look familiar but slightly off, like the half-imaginary animals you sometimes meet in dreams. They ranged in size and shape from something like a blue jay to a giraffe, and many of them could fly. Some had long, bony tails and teeth, and most had grasping claws on their forelimbs; one group even had long flight feathers on their legs as well as their arms, like living biplanes. Paleontologists have unearthed a wide array of winged dinosaurs in the past few decades, mostly from fossil beds in northeastern China, and it's likely that many more discoveries await.

The fossils we've found so far suggest that most feathered dinosaurs were hunters. They seized insects, lizards, mammals, fish, and other dinosaurs with their jaws and feet, running them down or diving on them from above. Even the ones that couldn't fly had stiff plumes or bristles that fanned out from their forelimbs and tails, while others had shaggy coats of down that probably helped their owners stay cool in the day and warm at night. Their longest, most ornate feathers might also have helped them signal to each other or attract mates, and they were brightly patterned in black, white, gray, and brown — even iridescent blues and greens.

The social lives of the feathered dinosaurs are harder to discern. Most were able to provide for themselves from the moment they emerged from their eggs (which may have come in a range of colors); a newly hatched dinosaur found in a chunk of Burmese amber has surprisingly well-developed flight feathers. But a mixed-age group of one species found in a single location in China appear to have died together, suggesting that at least some feathered dinosaurs were social; they might even have gathered and foraged in packs or family units.

Fossils, though, can tell us only so much about an animal's life, and there's a great deal we'll never know about these weird and wonderful creatures. Like the giant sauropods and hadrosaurs, most feathered dinosaurs died in the turmoil that followed the asteroid's impact, and they largely disappear from the fossil record in most of the world. Late-Cretaceous fossils from the western United States, for example, include at least four groups of bird-like feathered dinosaurs (including fish-catching divers), but no fossils of any of these groups appear after the asteroid cleaned North America's clock.

But in the far south, some feathered dinosaurs survived among the forests and grasslands of the Southern Hemisphere — many of them, perhaps, in Antarctica — and they're still with us today. At least a dozen separate lineages appear to have weathered the asteroid's impact, and as the earth recovered, they diversified with abandon beside the mammals. These surviving dinosaurs were smaller than the titans of the Cretaceous, and all of them, it seems, could fly, though some lost that ability again during the age of mammals. A few even regained the titanic proportions of their ancestors: one group of two-legged meat-eating birds grew taller than a man, and a chicken-like Australian herbivore called Stirton's thunderbird stood ten feet tall and weighed more than a thousand pounds. Both of these giants survived into historical time, and prehistoric humans almost certainly met them.

By evolutionary standards, then, the dinosaurs recovered from a crushing defeat with impressive speed. If we took our time-traveling ship forward from the asteroid impact by ten million years — a modest distance in evolutionary time — we'd find a version of Earth that was once again filled with feathered dinosaurs. They'd already evolved into the forty major groups of birds scientists recognize today, and a few more besides, and you'd probably have no trouble spotting the ancestors of ducks, chickens, ostriches, and gulls. But you'd have to travel forward *forty million years* to find an animal that strongly resembles you or me, and you could argue that we're still living in a golden age of dinosaurs. Only about seven hundred dinosaur species have been identified from the Jurassic and Cretaceous periods we regard as their finest hour, but more than ten thousand species of dinosaurs are alive today, outnumbering mammal species by more than two to one. The variety of their sizes, lives, and minds is so staggering that it's tempting to wonder why the Cenozoic isn't called the age of mammals *and dinosaurs.*

The living dinosaurs, of course, are smaller than most of their ancestors, and they've adjusted their diets accordingly. Many have become vegetarians, feeding on grains, fruits, and nectar, while others chow down on bite-sized invertebrates like insects, spiders, and worms. A few even feed on leaves, including the strange hoatzins of South America, spiky-crested birds with bulging red eyes that nest in seasonally flooded forests and exude a strong, earthy odor from their multi-chambered digestive tracts. And some have adapted to live almost exclusively off a new and highly reliable source of food: us. Mynahs, grackles, starlings, and city pigeons are a few of the living dinosaurs that flock to human population centers, like the herring gulls and carrion crows of Hudson's London. This strategy has been such a good bet that the dry *chirrup* of the house sparrows Hudson fed from his window now resounds from the nooks and crannies of nearly every city on Earth. They might not look much like tyrannosaurs, but they're probably the most widespread and numerous dinosaurs that have ever lived.

The dinosaurs we call birds of prey, however, have never abandoned their ancestors' hunting lives. They still prey on animals nearly their own size (or larger), and some exclusively hunt their fellow dinosaurs. Many are famous — in the United States, for example, nearly everyone can picture a bald eagle, a red-tailed hawk, or a great horned owl — but others are obscure, and most people aren't aware they exist.

This isn't because they haven't been identified. Scientists have assembled a fairly exhaustive catalog of the world's birds, and if the discovery of a new bird is a rare and newsworthy event, finding a new bird of prey is even rarer; it last happened in 2002 and may never happen again. Hunting birds were among the first to be described by early naturalists, in part because they're often large and striking, and we've known for a while what they look like and where they live. *How* they live, however, is a very different question. Where the caracaras are concerned, we know very little indeed; they keep unusual company among the hunting birds, and it's worth winnowing them out from their relatives with some care.

First, let's look at what we *do* know. Birds of prey — hawks, owls, falcons, eagles, vultures, and secretary birds — account for only 5 percent of all bird species, but if we pull their bulging file down from the shelf and spread its contents on a table, you might be surprised by how big the table needs to be; 5 percent of ten thousand is still about five hundred species. They live on every continent but Antarctica and include some of the most impressive animals on Earth: Andean condors, the heaviest flying birds, have ten-foot wingspans; twenty-pound harpy eagles prey on monkeys and sloths in the tropics of the Americas; Steller's sea eagles, orange-beaked catchers of full-grown salmon, nest on the remote coasts of the Kamchatka Peninsula and the Sea of Okhotsk; red-eyed Siberian eagle owls, twice the size of their great horned cousins, sneak up on smaller owls in the frosty silences of the taiga; and the unique secretary birds of sub-Saharan Africa are four-foot-tall snake stompers with orange faces and long black crests that stride across the savanna like living griffins. (There isn't room to go on about bearded vultures, honey buzzards, and Blakiston's fish owl, but you get the idea.)

At the other end of the scale from condors and eagles are birds you'd hardly notice if you weren't looking for them. Elf owls, barely four inches tall, eat insects and live in abandoned woodpeckers' nests in giant cacti in the southwestern United States and Mexico. African pygmy falcons are so small that they can live inside the many-chambered nests of sparrow-like songbirds called sociable weavers, and leap out from time to time to feast on their neighbors. A diminutive falconet from the Philippines is smaller than the largest hummingbird.

Size isn't everything, of course, but it

determines what you can hunt, and hunters are defined by two things: their quarry and their style of killing. People who study birds of prey like to call them "raptors," a word that comes from a Latin verb for snatching or grabbing, because they seize their prey with their talons; think of the velociraptors, the nimble villains of *Jurassic Park*, whose name means "fast grabber." But Hollywood's version of these clever, social dinosaurs lacked a crucial detail: in real life, velociraptors were among the many dinosaurs who sported full coats of feathers. (A scientist remarked that if you saw one on your street, your reaction probably wouldn't be *Oh my God, a dinosaur!* but *What is that big, weird bird?*) It doesn't take too much imagination to connect modern birds of prey with velociraptors, and a bird like Evita makes it especially easy: seen at the right angle, she seems like she's stomped right out of the Cretaceous with her giant scaly feet, predatory glare, and sprinter's gait. You can picture a version of her with teeth, but it's not as if she needs them.

T. rex and its contemporaries have thrilled and spooked museum visitors since Darwin's time, but humans were drawn to birds of prey long before we knew their dinosaurian origins. For thousands of years, we've praised and envied their sharp eyes, their grace and speed in flight, and their skill in hunting. (That none are large enough to put us on their menu also helped their case, for the same reason that a tiger is scary but a tabby is adorable.) We're hunters, too, but compared to a hawk or an eagle we're awkward and earthbound, and we like to use them as symbols of power and rank — think of the terrifying sphinxes of the Assyrians, the Egyptian falcon god Horus, or the imperial eagles of Rome, Byzantium, Germany, and the United States.

All this symbolic freight makes it hard to see raptors for what they really are — and in truth, they're not much like us at all. They might look noble and commanding, but they're only masters of themselves, and they usually prefer to work alone. They don't suffer from the need for company that we do, and though a lack of social attachments can seem like a sort of freedom, it's a freedom from nearly everything we care about. Falcons are especially notorious for their single-mindedness; they're known for their skills, not their personalities, and the process of "manning" a hawk or falcon, like breaking a horse, isn't so much about forming a partnership with the bird as forcing it to accept a falconer's presence as an inevitable fact.

This is why Geoff's experience with Tina was such a surprise, and why Barnard and Darwin were so bewildered by her cousins in the wild: though caracaras are birds of prey, they don't follow the same playbook as other raptors. William Henry Hudson might have been less surprised by Tina if he'd met her, since he knew her relatives from his South American childhood, but even his intuitive sympathy couldn't have shed much light on the origins of her curious mind. How had she arrived at a love of play and company, a desire to learn, a piercing aura of *consciousness* that made her so different from her avian colleagues at Woodlands? Was her curiosity an innovation peculiar to her species, or was it an ancient legacy that other hunting birds cast aside?

These questions might sound impossible to answer, but new technologies have revealed that Tina's ancestors have a surprising history that makes her behavior more intelligible. They've also shed light on how the Johnny rooks and the peregrines became so different from each other — and why their family is unique among the living birds of prey.

8
A FAMILY SECRET

On a cold, barren mountaintop in southern Chile, Julia Clarke knelt to peer at the ground through a pair of ski goggles she wore against the wind and the high-latitude sun. Clarke, a tall, raven-haired paleontologist, was looking for the fossilized remains of flying dinosaurs, a skill for which she's nearly legendary, and she'd paused at a place where something caught her eye. To me it looked no different from any other part of the slope we'd been ascending all morning, a confused jumble of reddish-brown boulders and scree, but Julia was unusually still in a way I'd come to associate with the moment she found a fossil.

"I think there's a dinosaur here," she said, carefully turning over a finger-sized fragment of ancient sandstone. "I think these bones are going into the cliff." This seemed impossible to me, but Julia's eye was rarely wrong; she's known not only for finding new fossils but for finding hidden features in well-studied fossils that other paleontologists have

158

overlooked. She'd spent years of her life on fascinating and uncomfortable expeditions to islands at the tip of the Antarctic Peninsula and the scorpion-filled wastes of the Gobi Desert, where she camped beneath a truck for months; among her discoveries is the oldest known syrinx, the unique organ that birds use to produce sound, which she spotted in the fossil of a duck-like bird that lived among its fellow dinosaurs in a warm Antarctica. She'd also helped reveal the colors of dinosaur feathers through microscopic fossil structures called melanophores, and was the first to realize that a mysterious lump of rock languishing in a Chilean museum was the egg of a mosasaur.

I'd imagined that prospecting for dinosaurs would be a slow, painstaking process, but Julia liked to move fast until she spotted something promising, and following her long stride up the mountain made me glad the southern Andes are much shorter than the mightier ranges farther north. We'd already passed up the preserved impressions of geoduck-sized clams and purplish lumps of sauropod bone, the remains of animals as large as a city bus — which amazed me, but failed to move her. "That stuff's way too big," she said. "I'm not carrying that around unless it's a skull."

Below us, two of Julia's students, Sarah Davis and Hector Garza, were pacing deliberately up a Martian-looking slope, their eyes on the ground and their heads in the age of reptiles. To them, the exposed faces of the mountain were animal-rich slices of the deep past, its layered beds of sandstone a time capsule that preserved the versions of life that once thrived here. Sarah had found the curved tooth of a predator who probably looked something like a small *T. rex,* and Hector had turned up the more primitive-looking tooth of a mosasaur, a half-inch cone of shining black rock as straight as a railroad spike.

The remains of these two animals — one terrestrial, one marine — revealed this desolate mountain for what it was: a piece of the ancient coastline, intermittently drowned by the sea, that once joined South America to the Antarctic Peninsula. If Antarctica was indeed a haven for animals while the rest of the world burned, this was the bridge its residents would have crossed to enter (or reenter) South America. After the end-Cretaceous meteor struck the Earth, *thirty million years* would elapse before an undersea tongue of the Pacific plate wedged itself between the two continents. This didn't just isolate them from each other; it removed the last barrier to the ocean's unimpeded flow around Antarctica, and the circumpolar vortex was born. Over the next thirty-five million years, the great southern continent would slowly become the icebound landmass we know today — the coldest, driest, most inhospitable place on earth.

The fossils buried in the mountain where we stood were too old to shed light on the time after the asteroid's impact, but they were a glimpse of the dinosaurs' last years in a very special place: we were about as far south as you could be and still find Cretaceous fossils that aren't buried under thousands of feet of ice.

Julia took a few samples of fossil bone and sealed them in a plastic bag, and after a brief rest we headed back down toward our camp, a cluster of orange and yellow tents in the grassy valley below. We were visiting for only a few days, but the tents housed a team of young Chilean paleontologists who'd been here for weeks, led by a bearded, charismatic paleobotanist named Marcelo Leppe. The stumps of ancient palm trees and the massive femur of a sauropod were among this season's discoveries, but their most exciting find was a tiny molar, smaller than a pea— the tooth of a mammal who'd lived among the dinosaurs. It was the oldest mammal bone ever found this far south.

Julia, however, was hoping to find an ancient bird, and she paused at a bowl-shaped pit of fine gravel and sand blown out by the wind. Places like this, she said, can leave delicate fossils lying on the surface — and within ten minutes she'd found two tiny teeth, along with a few lentil-sized plates of bone that might have been part of a turtle's shell, or the scales of a small, armored lizard. Sarah logged the coordinates in her notebook.

"Let's call this site 'toothyplace,'" Julia said. "We'll remember that."

I sat down at the edge of the pit, hoping to spot another tooth among its multicolored pebbles and slivers of petrified wood, but my eyes soon glazed over. I was about to give up when I noticed an odd impression in the pit's surface, about the size of my hand. Its three slender lobes fanned out from a central point, and each lobe ended in a small, sharp divot, like the imprint of a claw. As I drew back, I saw that it was the deepest of a faint set of dinosaurian footprints, but they looked so fresh that I wondered if someone had etched them in the sand as a joke. I motioned to Sarah, who came over to look and fell silent. Even Julia was flummoxed for an instant, but then she smiled: they were the tracks of an Andean condor.

"Theropod dinosaur," she said, without irony. "Isn't it nice to know they're still around?"

A need to organize the world around us seems to be as basic to our species as language or religion — or, as Hudson said, shouting when there's nothing to shout about. It's an impulse that's given us many gifts, from the cosmologies of religious thought to the table of the elements, though it's also given us the Nazis' racist fantasies and the atomic bomb. Sorting the nonhuman world into types and categories is one of its more benign outgrowths, a project that's consumed shamans, philosophers, and other knowledge hoarders for many centuries before Darwin.

But a faithful Darwinist might note that our obsession with classifying other living things has entered a period of rapid evolution. Taxonomy, the science of naming, began as an attempt to tidy up our knowledge of the living world by grouping like with like, and by standardizing the names of living things so naturalists could be sure they were talking about the same creatures. Students of biology still learn the hierarchical ranks proposed by the eighteenth-century botanist Carl Linnaeus: kingdom (as in "the animal kingdom"), class, order, family, genus, and species. These categories fit inside one another like nested dolls, and Linnaeus thought their distinctions would be fine enough to describe the entire living world.

He was wrong. Elements of Linnaeus's system are still in use, but it's been revised and expanded as scientists try to fit their understanding of life to its own criteria and not the other way around. Natural systems are rarely as straightforward as we'd like, and though most scientists recognize a species as a population of individuals who breed only with one another, even that definition is contested in some circles.

To see what the caracaras really are and where they came from, it's important to understand how ideas about sorting living things began to change in the late nineteenth century, when William Henry Hudson was a young man and Charles Darwin an old one. It was an exciting moment for classifiers of life: the term "scientist" was first coming into vogue, and a taxonomic revolution was in the air. Naturalists who embraced it found their work renewed — and rearranged — by three discoveries that made a finer and truer study of life possible.

The first was the realization that Earth was much older than they'd ever imagined, almost older than we *can* imagine. This knowledge didn't arrive all at once; when Darwin died, in 1882, the best estimates suggested our planet was about one hundred million years old. Its true age was most recently revised in 1953, when radiometric studies of a hunk of extraterrestrial metal called the Canyon Diablo meteorite suggested that our solar system formed about 4.5 *billion* years ago — a number so large it repels understanding.

164

Our response to figures like this is usually to nod in their direction and go about our business. But for the scientists of Darwin and Hudson's day, the realization that Earth's history stretched millions of years into the past was a great relief. It allowed geological and biological processes enough time to give rise to improbable wonders, and helped scientists see that the fossil remains of plants and animals that no longer exist were evidence of former versions of life on our planet. This seems self-evident now, but it was far from clear a few centuries ago, when Western scholars had to square fossil creatures and living animals with a world thought to be a few thousand years old.

One of these scholars was a sober, meticulous Jesuit from Spain named Bernabé Cobo, who labored for decades in the early 1600s to assemble a history of the two continents Europeans called the New World. Cobo spent most of his adult life trying to Christianize Amerindians in Spain's new territories of Mexico and Peru, but he was also a naturalist, and the volumes he finally completed in 1653 are filled with bewildered descriptions of South America's people, landscapes, and creatures. The Jesuits were a newly minted and controversial group of reformers, dedicated not only to the church but to the powers of reason, which Cobo called "the richest jewel that we possess." But it left him on the horns of a dilemma when he tried to account for the unique animals of South America.

"Acknowledging jointly what we know from the Holy Scriptures," he wrote, "that all animals of the land and air perished except for the ones that were saved in Noah's Ark . . . we find ourselves obliged to open the way for them from the place in which the Ark ran aground, and Noah stepped down from his post, to these regions of America, so distant from there." For Cobo, this was mostly a problem of logic. If God had placed different animals in each part of the world and dispatched angels to bring them to Noah, how had they returned to their native lands when the waters of the great flood receded?

He wasn't the first to be troubled by this question, but he felt others had gone astray in devising convoluted escape routes for animals that issued from the ark. Why were there tigers in India but not Africa? Why were there horses in Europe but not South America? How could hummingbirds have survived a trip from the Middle East to the Andes? Answering questions like these seemed to require an untidy profusion of miracles, and Cobo could only set his mind at ease by reducing their number to two. If angels had delivered the world's animals to Noah, he argued, it seemed most reasonable to assume that the same angels returned after the flood and put the animals back where they came from. "If this solution does not meet with approval," he wrote, "I do not know of any other that can be proposed without including in it either special and miraculous intervention by the Lord, or enormous drawbacks and absurdities.

Scholars of note are not lacking who, so as to avoid admitting the Lord's intervention . . . get mixed up and entangled in such an intricate labyrinth, so full of new obscurities and problems, that no matter how many sleepless nights they spend, nor how much they tire themselves trying to hit upon a way out, in the end they are forced to admit effects that go far beyond the style and course that nature usually takes, and that cannot be explained logically without special divine assistance.

It's hard not to feel for Cobo when you read these lines. This careful and intelligent contemporary of Galileo is almost surely describing himself, and you can sense the stirring of thoughts in his writing that would lead to the scientific method less than a century later. But his consternation was inevitable: the authorities he relied upon had built their houses on sand. Two hundred years would elapse before Darwin answered the question of animals' origins by reframing it with a second revolutionary idea — that every living thing descends from a single common ancestor. Or, as he put it, "I should infer from analogy that probably all the organic beings which have ever lived on this earth have descended from some one primordial form, into which life was first breathed."

It's worth lingering for a moment on this leap of logic and imagination. To embrace it is to accept the deeply counterintuitive idea that you share the same kind of relationship with an oak tree or a dung beetle that you do with your grandmother, that the difference between you is only one of degree, and that if you retraced your separate journeys through time, your paths would lead back to each other. This is a lot for any human mind to absorb — and in a way, Darwin provided a rhetorical escape hatch for Cobo. If you think of the great flood as a metaphor for the earliest version of Earth, which was a hostile place pummeled by planet-sized asteroids and crazed with rivers of lava, all life really *did* issue from one place, once things settled down a bit.

But Darwin was also dedicated to extrapolating from what he could directly observe, which ultimately led him to the third idea: the principles we now call the theory of evolution by natural selection. Darwin (and his coauthor Alfred Russel Wallace, who'd arrived at the same theory on his own) argued that life's variety wasn't the product of a master plan; it had sorted *itself,* over time, by passing on the traits of varied individuals to their descendants. Life on Earth, they concluded, will never arrive at a fixed state. It is always changing, and the illusory permanence of species is a side effect of our own short lives.

The furious debate over Darwin and Wallace's theory has been bogged down in theological arguments from the moment it was proposed, but its effects on the way taxonomists organize the living world, though less public, were no less profound. The classifiers of Darwin and Hudson's day couldn't yet observe life at a molecular scale, but the confluence of an ancient Earth, a common ancestor for all life, and an ever-changing world shaped by natural selection suggested a new approach. What if we sorted living things not by likeness but by *relatedness*? If Darwin was right that "descent with modification" — the ability of parents to pass new combinations of traits to their offspring — is the organizing principle of life, then we ought to be able to travel down the branching ancestries of living things into the deep history of the world, connecting everything alive now with the earlier forms of life on our planet. Classifiers would no longer need to invent new categories of beings; their job, instead, would be to reveal them.

"There is grandeur in this view of life,"

Darwin wrote, in his most famous sentence, "with its several powers, having been originally breathed into a few forms or into one; and that, whilst this planet has gone cycling on according to the fixed law of gravity, from so simple a beginning endless forms most beautiful and most wonderful have been, and are being, evolved." The project this sentence began — revealing the family tree of all life — is still under way, and will be for a long time to come. Scientists continue to revise their concept of the tree to reflect new evidence, challenging old arguments about who was related to whom and how closely; and in recent years, new tools for unearthing the relationships between living things in the present have made it possible to ask them directly about the world of the past.

You might think of the tree of life as a huge, spreading oak buried in a dune, with only the tips of its branches sticking out of the sand. These branch tips would represent every species living today — sometimes called crown species, from the crown of a tree — and let's assume, for simplicity's sake, that the branch tips nearest to each other represent species that appear to be most alike. But superficial likeness can be deceptive, and branch tips aren't the whole story of a tree. Most of the tree's forking limbs end before they reach the surface of the dune, and some branches that extend far enough to poke above the sand have swerved and diverged in surprising ways to arrive near their neighbors.

This is where sorting organisms gets tricky: How can you tell if similar species really are closely related? Some crown species look alike because they share a recent ancestor, as you might expect. But some have arrived at similar appearances, behaviors — even minds — by very different roads.

When this happens, it's called convergence. Sharks and dolphins are an obvious example: sharks belong to a lineage that's never left the oceans, while dolphins are the descendants of a lineage that began in the oceans but diversified on land. Some of these land animals eventually became what we call mammals, and some mammals then went back to the sea. A shark's pectoral fin is a slab of cartilage — and always has been — but dolphins' journey from the sea to the land and back is written in their bodies: inside their flippers are the bones of a five-fingered hand. But if you'd decided to classify dolphins and sharks as fast, gray, torpedo-shaped fish eaters that live in the ocean rather than sorting them by their disparate lineages, you might have mistakenly lumped them together.

Birds, as it happens, are one of the most studied groups of animals. They helped steer the thoughts of both Darwin and Wallace, and some scientists might argue that they've

171

received more than their fair share of the limelight, given the small fraction of life they represent. But they're an undeniably handy group of animals: common, conspicuous, attractive, and large enough to see with the naked eye, and their evolutionary history has been scrutinized, sorted, and re-sorted at a fine scale. Taxonomists still debate where to place a few enigmatic species like those weird, stinking hoatzins, but scientists generally agree that the major ancestral relationships among birds have been resolved. So it came as a surprise when a team of researchers recently suggested a major revision to the way we think about birds of prey.

The tool that revealed this was DNA analysis, which allows scientists to identify similarities and differences in the chemical blueprints of living things that are invisible to our eyes; like the hand inside a dolphin's flipper, the history of every organism is hidden in its genome. It's impossible to overstate DNA's importance to scientists working to unearth the tree of life today, since it's the mechanism by which evolution actually works, and it offers physical evidence of the ancient links among living things. Analyzing it is as close as you can come to sitting another being down for an interview about its history. I couldn't tell you anything about my own family more than two or three generations back, but my DNA can; it contains information that hasn't changed since before my ancestors left Africa. Some of it is unchanged since they had gills. And it still bears the chemical fingerprints of diaphanous, single-celled creatures floating in the seas of the young Earth.

It's also revealed places where our sharpest eyes have been fooled. For over a century, all birds of prey were presumed to be closely related to one another and were placed on two neighboring branches of the tree: one for day hunters (hawks, eagles, falcons, vultures, kites, ospreys, and secretary birds) and one for night hunters (owls). This is a nice, clean, intuitive division — but as it happens, it's also wrong. The falcons' genomes indicate that they don't belong with other birds of prey at all; their nearest relatives are parrots, and they've been on a separate evolutionary path from other raptors for as long as seventy million years — possibly even before the Cretaceous extinctions.

On the morning after the storm that blew the chimango to Steeple Jason, I walked out across the stretch of level ground between the field station and the base of the island's central ridge. I was heading for a broad meadow where I'd often found striated caracaras digging in the turf for their breakfast, but I stopped short at a boulder that had tumbled from the cliffs above. A hollow in its lee had filled with fresh water, and two adult Johnny rooks were standing in it.

They eyed me for a moment and returned to their bath, plunging their bodies and rising to shake water from their folded wings. Two more adult birds stood beside the pool, as if waiting their turn, and a third, dripping wet, leapt to the top of the rock to dry in the sun. Then a fourth bird with the awkward gait and head-down posture of a juvenile stepped from behind the rock and began to pace around the pool's edge. He stopped and leaned forward, stretching his head over the water — then drew back and kept pacing, while the bathing adults ignored him. After a half circuit of the pool he tried again, leaning out even farther for a long, anxious moment, then backed away. Everything about him suggested a child working up the courage to jump in the deep end, while his adult companions seemed to be hanging out at a sort of social club, like a Roman bath.

I wondered if this behavior was an echo of the caracaras' shared lineage with parrots, who like nothing more than being with one another. In the wild, most parrots live in large, garrulous flocks or smaller groups of a few pairs and family members, and their innate sociality makes them good companions for dedicated and attentive humans, as Juno was for Len Hill. (In this sense, Tina's fondness for Geoff makes her seem more like a

174

compulsively social parrot than a typically aloof bird of prey.)

But we might also have the wrong idea about parrots. We usually think of them as tropical vegetarians, an image that owes more to their current lifestyle than their ancestral ecology. A closer look reveals signs of their probable origins as carnivores: captive parrots will readily eat meat, and in New Zealand the crow-like alpine parrots called keas sometimes crawl into the burrows of nesting seabirds to eat their helpless chicks, just as Johnny rooks do in the Falklands. Keas belong to the oldest surviving lineage of parrots and live comfortably in a habitat that's often covered in snow; like the Johnny rooks, they're compulsively playful, fond of carrion, and attracted to new objects. They're infamous for stripping windshield wipers from parked cars, and hikers who leave boots outside their tents in kea habitat often find them unlaced in the morning.

It's also possible, of course, that a love of company evolved separately in caracaras and parrots. This seems unlikely for a number of reasons, but there's been enough time for it to happen, since a lineage isn't just a what, it's also a *when* — and exactly when falcons and parrots parted ways is another question their DNA can answer, thanks to a hypothesis called the molecular clock. The more divergent two species' genomes are, the thinking goes, the further they are in time from their nearest common ancestor, and a molecular clock assigns a span of time to a certain amount of genetic difference. Applying this principle to real data is a complex process with wide margins of error, but the most current estimates suggest that falcons' and parrots' last common ancestor lived sometime between fifty-five and sixty-five million years ago — a window that opens, you might notice, at about the time the asteroid struck the Yucatán.

Here's where it gets really interesting. If you know when two lineages diverged, then you can start to think about *where* it happened, and why, by overlaying their journey through time on the history of the Earth. Given the end-Cretaceous asteroid's holocaust of the northern world, it seems most likely that the common ancestor of falcons and parrots survived in the far south — in South America, Africa, India, Australasia, or Antarctica. This is an enormous target area, however — nearly half the globe — and to narrow it down further we have to think about the world as it was. The oldest surviving lineages of parrots live in Australasia, and the oldest surviving lineages of falcons live in South America; and since both Australia and South America were attached by land bridges to a temperate, forested Antarctica when the asteroid hit, it's possible — if not likely —

that the parrot-falcon ancestor survived the Cretaceous extinction there.

We won't know for certain, however, until we can peer under the ice. It takes a lot of educated guessing to follow the geographic trail of a lineage through millions of years, and where fossil evidence is scant or non-existent, as it is for most creatures, it becomes harder still. This problem was so intimidating to poor Bernabé Cobo that he called on the angels for help, but evolutionary theory allows scientists to reconstruct the physical journey of a lineage through time and space by overlaying its family tree on the world's geological and climatic history.

The results of this combination are often surprising. You might plausibly answer Darwin's question about the origin of the Johnny rooks, for instance, by suggesting that maybe they never left the far south — that, like New Zealand's meat-eating parrots, they simply came up a short distance from Antarctica and stayed put while their relatives traveled farther north. Their DNA, however, suggests a far more complex journey: a twenty-million-year odyssey through every part of South America, driven by profound changes in its climate and landscape.

One of the principles of evolutionary biology is that new species can form when a single population of living things is divided by a physical barrier, like a mountain range or an ocean. Natural selection acts on these newly separate populations in different ways, sending them on unique paths that eventually make them distinct from one another — which means that the molecular signature of a diverging lineage often reflects a change in the physical world. A sudden flowering or "radiation" of species — as happened in birds, mammals, and frogs after the end-Cretaceous asteroid — can even signal a major planetary event, like the freezing or thawing of the world, the rise or collapse of a land bridge, or the closure of an oceanic basin. Connecting the biological journeys of living things with the geological history of the earth is sometimes called historical biogeography or phylogeography, but it's really just a new kind of history — the one William Henry Hudson dreamed of, with other living creatures in it.

Just like human history, the stories this discipline produces can be fiendishly complicated. They span enormous swaths of time, and the further back they go, the hazier they become; but this has been an area of intense scientific activity in recent decades, and new combinations of genetic and geographic analysis emerge with every passing year. Some cover millions of years, others merely thousands, but all stem from the same idea: that it's possible to ask the present about the past. And the stories embedded in the cara-caras' DNA shed light not only on their family's distinct journey from other birds of prey, but also on the evolutionary journeys of G7 and the peregrine that struck him down.

Let's go back to our imaginary table piled with the case files of raptors. If we gather up all our owls, hawks, eagles, kites, harriers, vultures, ospreys, and secretary birds and set their files on the floor, the portfolios of sixty-four species — every member of the falcon family — would remain. Within this family, DNA sorts the falcons even further into three distinct subfamilies. The largest and most familiar is the peregrine's group, the so-called true falcons, and if the word "falcon" brings an image to your mind, it's probably one of them. They're remarkably fast, strong, and fierce in their pursuit of living prey, especially in open or partly wooded landscapes like savannas, tundras, and deserts, and their tapered, blade-like wings give them a deadly and purposeful grace. Owning one is a potent status symbol in some parts of the world, and they don't come cheap; legally purchasing a peregrine can set you back $10,000, and a purebred gyrfalcon, the largest of the true falcons, can fetch $250,000 in Qatar, whose annual falconry festival lasts over a month.

Peregrines, whose name means "wanderer," aren't only the fastest birds on Earth; like most true falcons, they're also long-distance migrants. Many peregrines commute season-ally between hemispheres, logging as much as eighteen thousand miles in a single year, and though some of their routes are fairly straightforward (New England to Cuba, for instance, or northern Siberia to Turkey), there are some curious variations. One bird banded in Nome, Alaska, turned up a few months later in Hawaii; another, banded in Arizona, later surfaced in Japan, where it was suspected of hitching a ride on a container ship. Along with these prodigious feats of flight and navigation, true falcons' visual powers nearly defy belief; peregrines have the fastest visual processing speed measured in any animal, and their eyes are so sharp that they could read the headline of a newspaper from a mile away. John Alec Baker noted that a human with eyes in the same proportion to its skull as a peregrine would have eyes that measure three inches across and weigh four pounds each.

The true falcons are so impressive and familiar that scientists from the northern world often treat the remaining eighteen spe-cies in their family, all of whom live in South America, like an afterthought — as if they were somehow "false." But DNA tells us unambiguously that the South American lineages of falcons, including the caracaras, aren't at all aberrant; in fact, they're geneti-cally closer to their family's ancestors than "true" falcons like the peregrine. Fossil evidence is scarce, but the genes and present-day distribution of true falcons suggest that when the peregrine's ancestors left South America, they first made a new home in the open spaces of central and western North America, where they probably refined their hunting skills and evolved their giant eyes and narrow wings. From there they pressed on into Asia, Australia, Africa, and Europe, following the grasslands that spread across the cooling world of the past five million years. Somewhere in Africa, birds from this line would be the first to glimpse our hominid ancestors, who would eventually follow the falcons' journey in reverse.

In the meantime, the falcons who remained in South America followed their own paths. Few of them are migratory, and they're generally less dogmatic in their feeding habits than the true falcons; you might say they seem to have more imagination. Some are barely known, like the forest falcons — secretive birds of tropical jungles who feed on birds, snakes, lizards, and insects. If you catch them in a shaft of sunlight, they're stunning: they have red or yellow faces and boldly patterned blue-gray plumage, finely barred and streaked with white, and their short, paddle-shaped wings are perfect for chasing prey through the forest or floating slowly above it. But they aren't long-distance migrants or speed kings; you won't see them at a falconry center in England, or a convention in the Persian Gulf. And no coat of arms has ever featured a laughing falcon, a unique little snake hunter whose wide eyes, black mask, and pale, tousled crest make it look as if it's just woken up from a nap.

The caracaras, however, seem to be the most adventurous of the South American falcons. Though at least one caracara species has joined the forest falcons in the tropical woodlands, most prefer a wider horizon; some have even found a home in the high Andes. But all of them take a different approach to life from "true" falcons. Instead of specializing in one hunting technique or habitat, most caracaras have kept their options open, pursuing a broad range of food on the ground and in the air, and they've developed — or perhaps maintained — not their eyes, but their minds.

By now, you may be wondering what a peregrine falcon was doing in the Falklands at all if its ancestors left South America long ago. This is a fair question, and its answer is a good example of the role geography can play in creating new species. Though the true falcons stayed away from South America long enough to become distinct from the forest falcons and caracaras, a few species have returned to the continent they once left behind; and peregrines are the newest arrivals of all. Their DNA suggests they reentered South America sometime within the last million years, and perhaps much more recently than that.

I've often imagined the moment that the first one arrived in the Falklands — a moment the Johnny rooks might even have witnessed. Like Charles Barnard, it would have simply *appeared* one day among the crowds of seabirds and sea lions, a strange and threatening visitor the caracaras had never seen before. In this light, G7's death takes on another, slightly sinister meaning: it was a murder of a native resident by a relative who'd been changed by a long journey abroad.

There are risks, however, in making too many assumptions about the deep history of animals that can travel long distances through the air. It's possible that the falcons' origins lie somewhere else — even in the far north, or in a bit of continental crust that's been submerged for millions of years. But the genetic evidence points toward Antarctica, and the fossil record, such as it is, seems to agree. Fossil caracaras have never been found in Africa or Europe, but several have been unearthed in South America, and the oldest falcon bone ever found comes from an island at the northern tip of the Antarctic Peninsula. It's a tarsometatarsus, the bone that joins birds' shins to their feet, and it belonged to a creature that lived about fifty million years ago. It looks very much like the leg bone of a caracara.

9
THE CURIOUS CASE OF
THE MISSING CROWS

You could argue that the evolutionary contest between the peregrine and the Johnny rooks was settled long ago. Peregrines' success is undeniable: they live almost everywhere, from rugged wildernesses to urban centers, and they're the undisputed masters of hunting on the wing. "Everything he is," wrote John Alec Baker, "has been evolved to link the targeting eye with the striking talon.

> The whole retina . . . records a resolution of distant objects that is twice as acute as that of the human retina. . . . Endlessly scanning the landscape with small abrupt turns of his head, [he] will pick up any point of movement; by focussing on it he can immediately make it flare up into larger, clearer view. Aimed at a distant bird, a flutter of white wings, he may feel — as it spreads out beneath him like a stain of white — that he can never fail to strike.

Johnny rooks' skills are harder to define.

They're as large and powerful as gyrfalcons, but they don't have a peregrine's speed or agility, or their giant eyes. No scientist has ever examined the eyes of a striated caracara, but a study of chimangos revealed the worst visual acuity ever measured in a bird of prey, suggesting a mind that doesn't rely only on targeting and striking at speed. Caracaras seem to live in a more nuanced world of family and friends, of individuals and objects known and unknown — and the unknown, for the Johnny rooks, glows with an irresistible luster.

Whether this is an asset or a liability is debatable. The Johnny rooks' tiny range suggests the latter, and their approach to life can seem clumsy when compared to a peregrine's deadly efficiency. But it's easier to see the curiosity and sociality of parrots in caracaras than it is in the "true" falcons, and I wonder sometimes if peregrines gave up society as they pared down their lives and built up their hunting skills.

Striated caracaras' lives seem far more like ours. It's the curious, social animals — cats, dogs, parrots — that we find easiest to love, because we recognize their need for affection, novelty, and play, and some birds are so good at interacting with us that it's easy to forget how distantly related we are. An egg-laying amphibian that lived three hundred million years ago was the most recent ancestor that humans and birds share, but even this yawning evolutionary distance couldn't keep Geoff and Tina from understanding each other well enough to play fetch and keep-away, to remember one another after years of absence, and to be so closely allied that Geoff was inconsolable at Tina's death. What else could you call this but a stunning example of mental convergence?

Geoff and Tina's friendship becomes even more astonishing when you compare the structure of their brains. The first scientists to examine birds' brains, noting their smooth surfaces, assumed that they were unsophisticated, since the tight folds of the human forebrain have long been identified as the seat of our concepts of "self" and "other," our social intelligence, and our ability to project ourselves in time — all the ingredients of what we might call consciousness. From the 1890s to the 1960s, most scientists presumed that birds were purely instinctual creatures, incapable of thought or feeling.

William Henry Hudson held a different opinion, and he'd be relieved to know that in the century since his death, the concept of birds as mindless bundles of pure instinct has been thrown out. We now know that some birds are capable of nearly all — if not all — the attributes of consciousness we once reserved for ourselves, including the ability to plan for the future, abstract notions of time and self, and the need to process daily experiences through dreams.

In the past decade, the fruits of this research have worked their way out of the obscure realms of cognitive science and into popular culture. Videos that demonstrate the flexibility of birds' minds have proliferated on the internet, where a quick search reveals a New Caledonian crow solving puzzles involving levers, weights, ramps, and pulleys; an Indian mynah joking with its owner in English; and a crow-like bird called an Australian magpie wrestling playfully with a dog and swinging from a clothesline. Some birds have even reached levels of fame usually reserved for humans; the death of an African gray parrot named Alex who conversed with researchers at Harvard about concepts like number, shape, and color was mourned around the world. But the video that sticks most in my mind shows a wild raven perched on the deck of a suburban house in Canada. The raven utters a series of remarkable liquid sounds, like water tumbling over rocks, toward a laughing man who holds the camera. The man approaches the raven, extending a finger, and the raven nips at it *and mimics the man's laughter back at him.*

Scientists' admission that there's more than instinct in birds' minds would have pleased Hudson, but he'd probably have chastised them for taking so long to accept the obvious. Birds, he believed, had their own senses of reason and aesthetics, and he used them to argue against the philosopher George Santayana's concept of beauty, just as he did with Darwin's thoughts about music. "When Santayana in his *Sense of Beauty* states that it is a small thing in our lives," Hudson wrote,

And its outcome no more than the wild and pretty herbs that root themselves in granite mountains which represent the realities of our nature, I disagree with him and his simile. Beauty is not a casual growth, the result of a seed fallen from goodness knows where into a man's life; it is inherent in the granite itself. . . . It is in us all from birth to death — from the ant to the race of men: in the lowest and meanest of us. And it is in the animals, as we see from their games and music. All my long, close observation convinces me that such a sense is well developed in the birds — especially in the crow and parrot families.

Though he didn't grow up with crows, Hudson came to know them very well, from the streets of London to the cliffs of Cornwall, and they amazed him with their feats of social organization and memory. But England also gave him more experience than he might have expected with parrots, which were a surprisingly common feature of household life in the Victorian era. This pleased him at first, but it gave him little joy to see them caged and forced to perform tricks, and their plight triggered a private nostalgia. "It is a depressing experience," he confessed, "on a first visit to nice people, to find that a parrot is a member of the family.

When I am compelled to stand in the admiring circle, to look on and to listen while he exhibits his weary accomplishments, it is but lip service that I render: my eyes are turned inward, and a vision of a green forest comes before them resounding with the wild, glad, mad cries of flocks of wild parrots. . . . In his proper place, which is not in a tin cage in the room of a house, he is to be admired above most birds; and I wish I could be where he is living his wild life; that I could have again a swarm of parrots, angry at my presence, hovering over my head and deafening me with their outrageous screams.

There was one parrot, however, for whom he made an exception: a large, green-and-gold bird he met at The Lamb, an inn in the North Wessex Downs. The parrot belonged to the inn's owner, a widow who inherited it from her husband — who, in turn, had bought the bird from a young girl in Mexico half a century earlier and unimaginatively named it Polly. According to the widow, Polly talked up a storm in Spanish when she first arrived in England and "had two favorite songs, which delighted everybody, although no one could understand the words."

But in the succeeding years, Polly's vocabulary changed. She began to pick up and use English words and phrases, and eventually seemed to forget her Spanish altogether. Despite Polly's advanced age, tattered plumage, and a slight tremor, she still had an unmistakable spark about her when she met Hudson, and her eyes were "full of the almost uncanny parrot intelligence." Polly enjoyed the run of the inn and was a regular at evening meals, where she sat at the table on a perch and ate what she liked. "As she was of a social disposition," Hudson wrote, "she preferred taking her meals with the family, and eating the same food" — including meat.

At breakfast she would come to the table and partake of bacon and fried eggs, also toast and butter and jam and marmalade, at dinner it was a cut off the joint with (usually) two vegetables, then pudding or tart with pippins and cheese to follow. Between meals she amused herself with bird seed, but preferred a meaty mutton-bone, which she would hold in one hand or foot and feed on with great satisfaction.

Hudson tried to make friends with Polly by offering her a sweet or a scratch on the top of her head, but she wasn't having it and bit him hard enough to draw blood. Then he began speaking to her in Spanish, "in a sort of caressing falsetto . . . calling her *lorita* instead of Polly, coupled with all the endearing epithets used by the women of the green continent in addressing their green pets." This had an immediate and striking effect.

Polly instantly became attentive. She listened and listened, coming down nearer to listen better, the one eye she fixed on me shining like a fiery gem. But she spoke no word, Spanish or English, only from time to time little low inarticulate sounds . . . it was evident after two or three days that she was powerless to recall the old lore, but to me it also appeared evident that a vague memory of a vanished time had been evoked — that she was conscious of a past and was trying to recall it. At all events the effect of the experiment was that her hostility vanished, and we became friends at once. She would come down to me, step on to my hand, climb to my shoulder, and allow me to walk about with her.

A few months later, Hudson received a letter from the owner of The Lamb: Polly had died on June 2, 1909, at the age of fifty-five.

This was relatively young for a large parrot, but Hudson noted that "half a century of fried eggs and bacon, roast pork, boiled beef and carrots, steak and onions, and stewed rabbit must have put a rather heavy strain on her system." Whether or not she'd been done in by pub meals, Hudson was moved by the thought that he and Polly might have shared a memory of a common home to which neither of them could return, and to him, her curious reaction to his Spanish seemed like proof of not only her intelligence but her ability to access the mysterious and melancholy depths of memory.

Hudson's tales of the natural world were alternately admired and dismissed, but his thoughts about birds' minds now seem more farsighted than wishful. Crows and parrots have especially large brains, and they've been the focus of many studies; researchers have even subjected crows to PET scans to observe the inner electrical workings of their gray matter. But no one has studied the anatomy or function of caracaras' brains, even though we now know they're next door, evolutionarily speaking, to the parrots — possibly because birds of prey still aren't high on the list when scientists think about "brainy" birds.

In the past decade, however, scientists in Argentina have broken the mold by conducting behavioral research with chimango caracaras — the social scavengers Hudson singled out for their ability to study and learn from other birds as well as each other. The biologist Laura Biondi and her colleagues took up this question in a 2010 paper, noting that chimangos are "gregarious raptor[s] showing great ecological plasticity," whose "ability to explore new resources has allowed them to survive in areas with increased human modification." Biondi and her team wondered if chimangos were teaching each other to deal with humans rather than relying solely on trial and error, and decided to test their social skills with an experiment.

First, the researchers captured thirty wild chimangos from the suburbs of Mar del Plata, a coastal town about two hundred and fifty miles from Hudson's birthplace, where they're often seen rooting through garbage bins and tearing open plastic containers. The researchers placed each bird in a separate cage and sorted them into three groups, isolating them from one another with fabric partitions. Members of the first group, the "demonstrators," were taught to open the sliding lid of an opaque plexiglass box containing a morsel of food — a task they mastered quickly. Then the researchers allowed each member of the second group, the "observers," to watch as a demonstrator bird opened the closed box and retrieved the food reward. A third group, the "control," were also shown closed boxes but given no clues about how to open them.

The observer birds became agitated as they watched the demonstrator birds feeding, perhaps because they didn't like being left out; they paced up and down in their cages, fluffed their feathers, and screeched — and the demonstrators called back to their jailed peers. But when the researchers allowed the observers to explore the boxes themselves, nearly all of them retrieved the food quickly and easily, and some even invented different techniques than the demonstrators had used to do it. When birds from the control group investigated the closed boxes, a few of them also found the hidden food, but the observers, following the example of a fellow chimango's success, were far better at it, succeeding in 84 percent of the trials. This might not sound like a big deal, but in the world of animal behavior it's extraordinary — the kind of result you might expect to see from a primate. The observer chimangos had learned, from a single observation, that an object they'd never seen before contained food, and their peers' actions had taught them how to get at it.

After a month in captivity and a series of further experiments, the chimangos were released exactly where they were captured, no worse for wear but surely a bit confused. (I imagine them asking each other *What was all* that *about?* for the rest of their lives, and keeping an eye out for plexiglass boxes.) Biondi and her colleagues were elated; they'd collected evidence of social learning in chimangos, a rarely seen behavior in birds of prey — or any animals, for that matter. Their excitement shines through, if you know where to look, in their paper's conclusion: "The gregarious habits exhibited by [chimangos] along with their ability to acquire novel behaviors via individual learning (Biondi et al. 2008), are likely to influence social learning opportunities in natural conditions. These characteristics allow some adaptive behavioural patterns to be socially transmitted."

Citing your own work in a scientific paper means you think you're onto something, and in this case, that something is pretty significant. If the ability to train your own intuition, rather than waiting on natural selection to do it for you, leads to the process that we might call consciousness, then another name for "socially transmitted adaptive behavioral patterns" — compounding the insights of individual consciousness — is culture.

Chimangos seem so comfortable around us, in fact, that it's almost as if we evolved together over millions of years, like the African wildlife that learned to deal with us in our ancient homeland. But that's not what happened. We're a significant part of the chimangos' world today, but in evolutionary terms we've only just turned up. How, then, did they have eyes to see us for what we are — a reliable, if sometimes inscrutable, food factory — and learn so quickly to take advantage of our wasteful, ever-changing habits?

Earlier scientists were right, in a sense, to conclude that birds' brains are very different from ours. As you grew inside your mother's womb, drawing nutrients through your umbilical cord, your folded neocortex grew from the lower surface of your fetal forebrain. Tina's equivalent structure, a smooth bulb called a pallium, grew from the *upper* surface of hers, as she slowly absorbed the yolk of her hard-shelled egg. But though the structures of the neocortex and the pallium are distinct, their functions are alike: Geoff and Tina, like Hudson and Polly, could understand each other because their parallel journeys had led them to the same place.

Why Geoff's and Tina's minds converged is a question that scientists have been wrestling with, on a larger scale, for decades. If qualities like curiosity, innovation, social learning, and culture can evolve independently in different lineages, then why do they appear in some species but not others? Put another way, why isn't everything "smart" in the way that we are? There's been a long debate over whether the ingredients of intelligence are innate to an organism's lineage, or produced by the challenges and opportunities of its environment.

The answer may be closer to a combination of the two. One factor that seems especially important in the evolution of what we call intelligence is a habitat in which the distribution, type, and availability of food is inherently *unpredictable.* Any animal that finds itself in this situation can't afford to rely on pure routine or rote behaviors; it needs to be observant and curious enough to find new sources of food, even if it's never seen them before. (Charles Barnard, for example, managed to survive for months in the Falklands by eating the tender stems of tussac, a plant he'd certainly never seen in New England.)

This is where social learning is especially helpful. If you can learn from the example of your peers, you can reap the benefits of their successes and failures in your own lifetime, without waiting for natural selection to do its slow work on your gene pool. But keeping track of so many details — the individual personalities and relationships of other members of your social group, the locations of many different food sources, and the places you might have hidden food to eat later — requires a larger, more flexible brain. It's also the kind of life that you'd expect to favor generalists over specialists. Indeed, nearly all the animals we regard as intelligent — baboons, crows, raccoons, caracaras, humans — are big-brained social generalists that thrive in unpredictable environments.

Another side effect of a large brain may be a longer, less stressful life. One study showed lower background levels of a stress hormone in large-brained, long-lived crows and parrots than in smaller-brained, shorter-lived birds like pigeons and quail — suggesting, rather obviously, that living in constant anxiety takes a toll on the body. This isn't to say that pigeons and quail don't have thoughts, but it does make sense that birds whose powers of memory and foresight aren't as acute probably lean harder on the instinctive warnings of reflexive fear to avoid threats.

You might point out that pigeons and quail are social birds, which is true. But some social lifestyles don't require as much curiosity or innovation as others. Penguins, for example, are definitely social, but a penguin researcher once told me, not unkindly, that the only thing dumber than a penguin is a rock. He didn't really mean this as a knock against penguins; by "dumb," he only meant "not like you and me." Penguins perform stunning feats of navigation and endurance but rarely have to solve novel problems: their lives consist of chasing their favorite prey, following other penguins around, avoiding scary aquatic predators, and basking in the sun on the islands where they breed.

The Johnny rooks' problems are the opposite. As scavengers and opportunists, they need to notice and understand everything around them — *especially* if they haven't encountered it before — and if you wanted to test the proposition that an unpredictable environment favors the evolution of curiosity and intelligence, you could hardly design a better laboratory than Steeple Jason, a remote island where the availability and types of food vary from one season to the next, and the ocean reliably coughs up strange new creatures and objects. Striated caracaras in the Falklands have been the subjects of this natural experiment for thousands of years, and the result seems to have favored individuals who were best at spotting and exploiting new opportunities and weren't afraid of anything.

But their small range makes me wonder if there's such a thing as too much curiosity, or too much courage, and it points to an uncomfortable conclusion: the qualities we call intelligence might not guarantee survival. We're proud of our large brains, but they come with troublesome drawbacks — existential doubt, for example — and they consume about a fifth of our bodies' daily metabolic needs. If we didn't need our giant brains, we'd probably start to lose them — just as we long ago lost the ability to breathe under water, which locks us out of three-quarters of the surface of our world.

Another way to think about the waxing and waning of intelligence is to consider the ability we envy most in birds: flight. It took feathered dinosaurs tens of millions of years to evolve it, and it might have helped them escape the worst effects of the asteroid's impact. But the demands of flight place severe constraints on birds' bodies, especially their size and weight, and where they've been able to thrive without it, they've abandoned it many times. Some flightless birds are famously extinct, like the dodo (which was doing fine until we came along), but others are still with us, like penguins, ostriches, and emus. Less well-known flightless birds include Galápagos cormorants, a nocturnal parrot from New Zealand that looks like a big green owl, and the cantankerous sea ducks of the Falklands and Tierra del Fuego. Once there was even a giant, flightless caracara, which probably ran down its prey among coastal grasslands during the cold snaps of the ice ages. (A flightless bird of prey might sound improbable, but it's important to recall that many feathered dinosaurs were flightless, too.)

The differences between the caracaras and the "true" falcons might reflect a similar evolutionary bargain. Judging by their behavior, I'd suspect that if you compared a peregrine's brain to a Johnny rook's, you might find that the peregrine's enormous eyes have crowded out some of its forebrain, especially the parts devoted to keeping track of the details of social life. Peregrines love solitude, crave routine, and avoid mistakes; Johnny rooks love novelty, crave company, hate boredom, and do risky things all the time, investigating anything that catches their curious eyes. Like us, they seem to have an uncontrollable urge for discovery. To have maintained it for thousands — perhaps millions — of years, it must somehow be serving them.

One afternoon on Steeple Jason, Robin Woods walked up to a pair of striated caracaras who were raking for grubs and worms. The birds glanced up at him for a moment, then turned back to their business until he tossed them a mouse-sized scrap of rolled-up cardboard tied with a string. Most birds would have ignored or avoided this humble offering, but for the Johnny rooks it was a big deal: the birds stopped foraging for almost ten minutes to catch it, chase it, steal it from each other, and pull it to shreds, until its remnants blew away in the wind.

This was pretty much what Robin expected, since he'd had plenty of experience with striated caracaras' attraction to unfamiliar objects. In 1995, he'd been digging up prehistoric bird bones from a peat bog on nearby West Point Island — the home of Frieda, the cake-loving caracara — when several young Johnny rooks alighted near his excavation and walked over to check him out. Robin worried that they might make off with the bones, but found he could distract them by tossing a few lumps of peat their way, which they chased, attacked, and prodded as if he'd offered them a football. Robin and his colleague Mark Adams, from the British Natural History Museum, were later surprised to find that most of the bones they retrieved from the bog belonged to striated caracaras that lived five thousand years ago — about the same time that people in ancient Sumeria were inventing written language.

A few years after Robin found the remains of the prehistoric Johnny rooks, I went with him to meet Tina's brother Sirius, who lives at the Hawk Conservancy Trust in Andover. Sirius was two years old, dressed in an adolescent's dark plumage, and had just graduated to a separate aviary from his parents. He stared at us intently as we approached, and Robin took a leafy twig and passed it through the wire mesh of the enclosure, as if slipping him a cigarette. Sirius wasted no time. He yanked the twig out of Robin's hand and ran around his pen, clutching it in his beak, like his older sister with Geoff's keys years earlier. Cavorting with this strange, inedible object seemed to please and excite him, as if it scratched an indefinite but powerful itch in his brain.

"Look there," Robin said. "What's the point of that?"

Charleses Darwin and Barnard, wondering at Johnny rooks' curiosity, had called them "mischievous," an adjective you don't often see attached to birds of prey. Falconers who know striated caracaras today would probably agree. It's as if they *enjoy* testing our limits, seeing what we'll tolerate, like the ravens in Yellowstone who sometimes nip the tails of wolves feeding at the carcasses of buffalo and moose. There's logic in this behavior, since the ravens are angling for a share of the meat, and it makes sense to see how closely you can approach a top predator if you're planning to feed beside it. But who can say how it *feels* to a raven to pull a wolf's tail? Ravens are emotionally sophisticated animals, compelled by the cocktail of experience and instinct we call intuition, and also by a sense of what we might call fun. Think of Tina: Did she grab Geoff's keys, on the first day they played together, because she thought they might be food? Did she think they had some other value? Or was she just bored?

Beyond their curious behavior, Darwin had also wondered why caracaras were unique to South America. Though this mystery ultimately stumped him, he nearly cracked it with an offhand observation — not about something he'd seen, but something he hadn't. Caracaras "well supply the place of our carrion-crows, magpies, and ravens," he wrote, "a tribe of birds widely distributed over the rest of the world, but entirely absent in South America."

Two centuries earlier, Bernabé Cobo had also noticed the continent's puzzling lack of crows. As he piled up evidence for angels offloading Noah's ark, he placed special emphasis on the fact that the animals of Peru differed wildly from the ones he saw in Mexico — and that nearly all of them were different from the animals of Europe. "Who distributed and picked out the types of wild animals, beasts and birds that had to cross over to these Indies," he asked, "and prohibited the rest from coming here?

Who could be persuaded that the animals would take such a long journey on their own volition, traveling over so many extensive regions with such great differences in climate, many contrary to their nature, innumerable plentiful rivers and in not a few places swamps, tidelands, and thick, impenetrable forests and jungles? And if, by their own volition, they traveled through so many lands that they arrived here, where they stopped and took up residence, why, not having changed their nature, did they tire so many centuries ago and stop their roving?

"Not having changed their nature" might be the most significant phrase in this passage. Cobo, like most of his contemporaries, believed that living things were the same now as on the morning God created them, which gave him no end of trouble when he tried to figure out why these supposedly unchanging animals, which had berthed together in the ark, were now lodged so firmly in separate places. "I do not want to mention the vicuñas, a species of animal native to this Kingdom of Peru, which never descend from the high sierras and very frigid *páramos* where they live," he fumed:

I will keep silent about the animals of the tropical *yunca* lands, such as monkeys and others that we never see come out of the hot *montaña* to go up to the cold climate of the sierra. Let the example of the crows suffice; although North America is full of them, they never come here to South America, nor are they ever seen in Peru; and even though they come as far as Nicaragua, they never go beyond its borders.

The missing crows also bothered Darwin. Though he'd only been away from England for a few months when he met the Johnny rooks and their mainland relatives, South America already seemed unaccountably different to him, not only from Europe, but from what he knew of *North* America. It was almost as if there were two New Worlds, not one, despite their connection at the Isthmus of Panama. The two continents were home to different plants, different insects, different mammals, and different birds — and Darwin's travels had added a dramatic new wrinkle to this story. At the *Beagle*'s landings along the coast of Argentina, he'd uncovered an astounding trove of fossil bones that weren't the remains of dinosaurs; they belonged instead to strange, enormous mammals that no one had ever seen.

Darwin shipped these bones back to England, where their size and oddity caused a sensation. Some appeared to belong to sloths the size of grizzly bears; others to an animal like a rhinoceros with the head of a hippo; another was something like a humpless camel with a trunk. To the everlasting envy of paleontologists, Darwin didn't labor for weeks to find the remains of these creatures, or sift through a mountain of sediment; he found most of them in a single eroded bank, beautifully whole, and their discovery ensured him enough fame to save him from life as a country parson.

The timing of Darwin's find was especially fortunate, since a mania for extinct giants had just seized Europe and the United States. Dinosaurs had been revealed to the public for the first time, and Richard Owen, the founder of Britain's Natural History Museum, wrote the official descriptions of Darwin's South American monsters, deducing the huge sloths' mysterious diet from the shape of their teeth. "Professor Owen," Darwin wrote, "believes that, instead of climbing on the trees, they pulled the branches down to them, and tore up the smaller ones by the roots, and so fed on the leaves . . . strongly rooted, indeed, must that tree have been, which could have resisted such force!"

Neither Owen nor Darwin, however, could fathom these animals' origins, or why they'd so recently gone away. Bernabé Cobo might have suggested that they were passed over by the angels as they escorted the world's animals to Noah — and Darwin, too, thought that a great cataclysm was involved in their death: something terrible seemed to have happened to South America, and not very long ago. "It is impossible to reflect on the changed state of the [South] American continent," he wrote, "without the greatest astonishment."

But here he could go no further. The discovery that Earth's crust is a floating mosaic of shifting plates would wait until the mid-twentieth century, and without it the larger patterns of life's distribution would remain inscrutable. If Darwin had known it, he'd have seen immediately that there really *were* two New Worlds, and that the missing crows — and the caracaras that sat in their places — hinted at a much grander story. North and South America might share a hemisphere, but in a geological sense they've only just met. It was a meeting with profound consequences.

10
THE ISLAND OF GIANTS

One night, when I was ten years old, I heard a faint scratching sound on the porch of my family's house in North Carolina. I flicked on the light, expecting to see our cat asking to come in, and was startled instead by the ghostly face of a creature I'd heard of but never seen — an animal with ragged gray fur, a quivering pink nose, five-fingered hands, and a long, bare tail. It was an opossum, and it was mesmerizingly odd; it seemed built from a very different set of blueprints than our neighborhood's squirrels, rabbits, skunks, and raccoons. I'd heard somewhere that opossums were marsupials — but didn't marsupials live in Australia? Why was there one at our back door?

I set these mysteries aside for years, but the answer, when I finally learned it, amazed me: the opossum's ancestors had walked to my house from South America. Virginia opossums are the only marsupials that live north of Mexico, and they thrive in most parts of the United States, where they roam forests, suburbs, and city streets by night in search of carrion, earthworms, insects, and garbage. Their fondness for tipping over trash cans hasn't endeared them to suburbanites; neither does their slight resemblance to giant rats. But they're living evidence of the same fact as the jaguars and vicuñas of Peru that confounded Bernabé Cobo and the missing crows that puzzled Darwin: the two continents Europeans lumped together as a single New World are a recent couple, and they're still getting to know each other.

The Supercontinent of Pangaea, in which all the land on Earth was once united, began to break apart about 180 million years ago. This was a much warmer time in our planet's history, with no ice caps at the poles, and a great desert rolled across Pangaea's heart, while forests of conifers and ginkgoes carpeted its mountains and coastal plains. Its lakes and rivers swarmed with turtles and fish, while feathered dinosaurs and other giant reptiles roamed everywhere on land and sea, and the half-moon silhouettes of pterosaurs filled the skies. It was a beautiful and dangerous world of vast silences, broken only by the cries of animals and the rushing of wind and water — a place where the flow of time would seem to have stopped.

But our planet is never at rest. Beneath the

earth's crust, currents of molten rock were straining to pull Pangaea apart, and in time they succeeded, breaking it into a northern continent geologists call Laurasia and a southern one they call Gondwana. This pair of titans would later divide into the continents we know today, but the fates of the two Americas had already diverged: North America was part of Laurasia, while South America belonged to Gondwana. When a new rift in the earth tore the Americas away from present-day Europe and Africa, the Atlantic Ocean rushed in to fill the gap, and they rode separate plates into the Western Hemisphere, meeting again between three million and five million years ago — a sliver of geologic time compared to the hundred million years they'd spent apart.

During their long separation, the two New Worlds might almost have belonged to different planets, not least because the Cretaceous extinction occurred while they were independent of each other, and they were repopulated by different sets of survivors. These species radiated into new forms as the world recovered, and when the Americas finally joined hands again, their separate casts of living things met for the first time, in a moment one paleontologist called "one of the most extraordinary events in the whole history of life." Ever since, living things from the two New Worlds have been meeting, mingling, competing, and learning to live together, in a process with the cumbersome name of the Great American Biotic Interchange.

Many creatures who took part in the interchange are still with us, and the North American animals who colonized the south are mostly familiar; they include cats (big and small), dogs, otters, deer, horses, camels, bears, mastodons, and mice. North America shared most of these animals with Eurasia thanks to their intermittent connection at the Bering Strait, but South America had been a giant island since its bridge to Antarctica fell away thirty million years earlier. During this long isolation, its animal survivors — including the caracaras — pursued unique evolutionary journeys, and the opossum's strangeness hints at its extraordinary origins.

Darwin was perplexed by the Americas' mismatched faunas because he was missing a crucial piece of the puzzle: he knew geological forces could transform entire continents, but he didn't know that the continents themselves were moving. The theory of plate tectonics, which revealed the earth's crust to be a set of interlocking plates that are always forming, disintegrating, and grinding together like wrestlers locked in a clinch, wouldn't be proposed until 1912 — thirty years after Darwin's death and ten years before Hudson's. Even so, it was regarded as a fringe theory for decades and wasn't widely accepted until a new generation of geologists tested and confirmed it in the 1960s. You and I grew up with this idea as an uncontroversial truth, but it was a scientific revolution that transformed geology as thoroughly as *On the Origin of Species* had changed biology a century earlier.

Biologists also welcomed this geological revolution, not least because it helped unravel the mysteries that drove Bernabé Cobo to call on the angels for help. Some living things had gone along for the ride as their continental plates sailed across the earth's mantle; others wandered into new realms when their worlds collided and radiated into new forms; and some died out in their ancestral homes but survived in places far from their origins. The jumbled distribution of life on Earth is partly the product of the continents' separate journeys, and just as stone tools and fragments of bone reveal the paths of our ancestors, the locations of living things today reflect the tangled history of our planet's geology, ecology, and climate. The opossum on my back porch was no exception: it was part of the same story that produced Darwin's giants, the screamers and rheas that entranced Hudson, and the Johnny rooks that irritated Charles Barnard in the Falklands. I didn't know any of this on that summer night in 1986, but I sensed the presence of something very special, and I watched our peculiar visitor finish its meal, groom its hands and face, and trundle away into the dark.

The twentieth-century paleontologist George Gaylord Simpson called South America's long isolation "splendid," and if you like weird mammals, it's hard to disagree. From the raw materials of creatures who survived the Cretaceous extinctions in the Southern Hemisphere, South America produced some of the strangest animals ever to live on our planet, including a host of the opossum's marsupial relatives. Marsupials, it turns out, don't come from Australia; they're an ancient group of mammals who once lived all over the world, but the asteroid appears to have dealt them such a heavy blow that they survived only in South America. Some of these surviving marsupials then walked across Antarctica into Australia, where they gave rise to its famous kangaroos, koalas, and Tasmanian devils. But some never left South America, where dozens of marsupials you've probably never heard of are still living, from mouse-sized pygmy opossums to an otter-like animal called a yapok, a webbed-footed creature that catches fish and crustaceans in tropical streams. Before the two Americas reconnected, South America was home to an even wider variety of marsupials, including cat-like predators with huge, sickle-shaped teeth — alternate versions of the saber-toothed cats that stalked camels and bison in North America and Asia.

But there were no bison or camels in South America before the great interchange. In their place were the beasts Darwin unearthed in Argentina, and the density of bones in the deposit he excavated suggested a staggering number of them. If you could take a safari through the grasslands of southern South America ten million years ago, you'd be amazed at the profusion of outlandish-looking creatures that grazed and browsed there, including families of bipedal ground sloths, rodents the size of buffalo, and hard-shelled herbivores called glyptodonts — armored lawnmowers that lumbered across the plains wielding clublike tails for defense.

The glyptodonts were well protected for good reason. Along with the meat-eating marsupials, South America's largest predators were a set of flightless, feathered carnivores scientists call terror birds, the largest of which stood nearly ten feet tall. These fearsome birds had long, powerful legs and ax-like beaks with a sharp hook at the tip, and like the big cats of Africa today (or the velociraptors of the Cretaceous), they ambushed their prey by running it down in a sudden burst of speed, then dispatched it with quick, stabbing blows. One look at a terror bird would be enough to convince you that the hunting dinosaurs of the distant past had made a comeback — and, in a way, they had.

But if you've never thought to imagine a terror bird, a glyptodont, or a ground sloth, you're in good company. They've never been as famous as the woolly mammoths and cave bears of North America and Eurasia that prehistoric humans hunted and feared, whose large surviving relatives like grizzlies and elephants make it easier to picture their extinct forebears. The South American giants' surviving descendants, by contrast, are few and small: the largest living sloths are no bigger than a dog, while the glyptodonts' nearest relatives are the comparatively diminutive armadillos. Many of Darwin's fossil discoveries, like the rhino-like creatures called toxodonts or the vaguely giraffeish litopterns, have no living descendants at all.

Caracaras, however, are still with us. Fossil evidence shows them keeping South America's giants company (and, most likely, feeding on their remains) as recently as thirty thousand years ago, when humans had already settled across Africa, Europe, Asia, and Australia. But we hadn't yet reached the two New Worlds, and in southern South America, the glyptodonts and ground sloths were still thriving among a host of animal immigrants who'd arrived during the great biotic interchange. The result was a menagerie unlike anything our world has seen before or since. Big cats, wolves, mammoths, camels, deer, and bears twice the size of modern grizzlies had made it all the way to La Plata, where they grazed and hunted beside their southern counterparts, while ground sloths wandered north as far as present-day California, where workers excavating subway tunnels are still finding their massive bones under Los Angeles. In this meat-rich world, some caracaras attained huge proportions: a fossil bird unearthed in the Pampas, aptly named *Caracara major,* is the largest falcon ever found. It was about the size and weight of a bald eagle, with an eight-foot wingspan.

But mega-caracaras weren't the only winged scavengers in the giants' world, and they certainly weren't the largest. *Caracara major* shared La Plata's broad grasslands and wide skies with an assortment of huge vultures, including the ancestors of today's turkey vultures and condors, and these were dwarfed by even larger scavenging birds called teratorns. One of these, *Argentavis magnificens,* had a wingspan of nearly twenty feet and for many years held the record as the largest flying bird that ever lived. Like Andean condors today, this thunderbird-like creature probably had no trouble dominating other scavengers at a carcass, even if it arrived late to the party.

Giant scavengers, however, need giant meals, and with all those teratorns and condors around, *Caracara major* probably didn't rely on bulk alone to get the food it needed. Like its modern relatives, it might have been social and inquisitive, following and imitating its neighbors and peers, seizing opportunities that others missed. (It could have played a similar role to the one ravens play in the Serengeti, where they feed beside much larger African vultures at the carcasses of zebras and elephants but round out their diets with small mammals, invertebrates, and fruit.)

Huge caracaras might still be gorging themselves on half-eaten glyptodonts today, in fact, if it weren't for a disaster that upended the world of South America's giants. When Darwin wondered at the "changed state" of the southern New World, he was talking about the biggest question his fossil discoveries raised: Where had all these animals gone? Their bones were scattered across southern South America, in deposits that had collected for thousands of years, yet they were inexplicably missing. No litopterns snuffled across the plains of Patagonia; no teratorns blocked the sun with their wings. The landscapes of the far south "can be described only by negative characters," Darwin wrote, "without habitations, without water, without trees, without mountains" — and without the animals that once thronged them.

In the century and a half since Darwin discovered their remains, the timing of the giants' disappearance has become clearer. Fossil evidence suggests that some of South America's largest animals died out during the earlier phases of the interchange, including most terror birds and the sickle-toothed marsupial predators — perhaps due to competition from northern immigrants. But many survived, including the ground sloths and glyptodonts, until a wave of extinctions rolled across the Americas about thirteen thousand years ago. In less than a thousand years, this oddly selective event took down nearly all the largest mammals on both continents, from mammoths and saber-toothed cats to toxodons and litopterns — leaving only bones for Darwin to collect, ponder, and send back to England.

Why, after flourishing for millions of years in varied habitats and climates, did so many animals suddenly vanish? Small asteroid strikes have been suggested, and climate change seems to have played a role; the extinctions took place during a period of global warming, and rising seas inundated coastal plains where the giants were once abundant. But Earth's ice sheets had waxed and waned several times over the previous million years without wiping out the Americas' largest animals, and it's hard to overlook the fact that this moment was special for another reason.

While South America edged toward its

meeting with North America, another group of animals was evolving on the opposite side of the world. Like the caracaras, they were curious, social omnivores, and one species traveled far from its hearth, like the South American marsupials that walked to Australia. As this new animal migrated along the coast or moved inland through grasslands filled with grazing animals, it developed a knack for finding and exploiting new resources.

It's an animal you and I know very well: it's *Homo sapiens.* The first people to reach the Americas, like the first saber-toothed cats to cross the isthmus, were confronted with a world of creatures who'd never seen anything like them, and the element of surprise gave the first Americans a deadly window of opportunity. Though monkeys had arrived in South America long before the great interchange (possibly by rafting over from Africa on floating mats of vegetation), there were no great apes in the Americas when our species walked across the Bering Strait, and the hunting was probably very good for an invasive hominid predator armed with fire, blades, and projectile weapons.

Humans' precise role in driving the Americas' largest mammals to extinction is still debated, but few survived for very long after we turned up. Archaeological evidence suggests that people completed the journey from

Alaska to Tierra del Fuego in only a few thousand years, and the Americas' wealth of large, native animals probably fueled their travels. The Amerindian people Darwin met in Tierra del Fuego seemed incomprehensibly primitive to him, but he didn't give them enough credit: they had walked from Africa to the very end of the habitable world, while Darwin's ancestors had strayed no farther than northern Europe.

This disruption probably had a cascading effect, as the sudden hunting pressure from humans upended the natural balance between the largest herbivores and predators like saber-toothed cats and dire wolves, whose numbers dwindled along with their prey. Amerindian people spent many centuries making up for the loss of the Americas' giants, domesticating smaller animals like llamas and guinea pigs and cultivating plants like corn, potatoes, tomatoes, squash, cassava, and beans. But saber-toothed cats didn't have the option of suddenly changing their diets, and scavengers who depended on these predators to supply them with carcasses would also have felt the pinch. Without enough dead meat lying around to fill its stomach, *Caracara major* followed the glyptodonts and mammoths into extinction.

Darwin didn't see any wild animals larger than a guanaco in South America, but he failed to guess that his own species might be the mysterious catastrophe he was looking for. He also didn't realize that the caranchos and chimangos he saw cleaning the skeletons of foundered livestock were a surviving piece of the vanished world that fascinated him. The caracaras' ancestors had probably made it through the giants' extinctions by doing what their lineage seems to do best: using their brains to make use of every resource at hand, from the chicks and eggs of other birds to the offal human hunters left behind.

It's no surprise, then, that the southern crested caracaras of Patagonia turned an appraising eye on Darwin and his companions. For these birds, the nineteenth century had been a time of unexpected good fortune: they'd weathered ten thousand years without the glyptodonts and ground sloths that fed their ancestors, but their patience had been rewarded with a sudden influx of new animals: Europeans' horses, cattle, and sheep. No place embodied this shift in the caracaras' fortunes better than the infamous slaughterhouses of Buenos Aires called *saladeros,* where livestock from the surrounding countryside were driven to be killed for their hides and fat. The animals' flayed bodies were left to rot where they lay, and Darwin, who visited the site in 1833, called it "horrible and revolting," writing that the ground was "almost made of bones, and the horses and riders are drenched with gore."

A young William Henry Hudson saw the *saladeros* a decade later, and the memory pursued him into the twentieth century. "To this spot were driven endless flocks of sheep, half or wholly wild horses and dangerous-looking, long-horned cattle," he wrote, "each moving in its cloud of dust, with noise of bellowing and bleating and furious shouting of the drovers as they galloped up and down, urging the doomed animals on.

> You could see hundreds of cattle being killed in the open all over the grounds in the old barbarous way the gauchos use, every animal being first lassoed, then hamstrung, then its throat cut . . . with a suitable accompaniment of sounds in the wild shouts of the slaughterers and the awful bellowings of the tortured beasts. Just where the animal was knocked down and killed, it was stripped of its hide and the carcass cut up, a portion of the flesh and the fat being removed and all the rest left on the ground to be devoured by the pariah dogs, the carrion hawks, and a multitude of screaming black-headed gulls always in attendance.

The killing pens were encrusted with a viscous layer of dust and coagulated blood, and their smell, according to Hudson, was "probably the worst ever known on the earth." For the "carrion hawks," however —

crested and chimango caracaras — the slaughterhouses were a smorgasbord. An army of saber-tooths couldn't have produced the carnage these caracaras enjoyed at the *saladeros,* and nearby plantations proclaimed the ascendance of South America's mightiest hunters with a macabre decoration: the low walls that lined their fields and roads were built from thousands of cow skulls, stacked eight or nine deep. They were a grim sight, but to Hudson they also affirmed the stubborn persistence of life. "Some of the old, very long walls," he recalled, "crowned with green grass and with creepers and wild flowers growing from cavities in the bones, had a strangely picturesque but somewhat uncanny appearance."

There's a great deal missing from this sketch of the Great American Biotic Interchange, the arrival of humans, and their effects on the caracaras' world, in part because it's oddly easy to forget that most living things aren't large animals. Giant creatures hold an outsized place in our imaginations, just as they did for our prehistoric ancestors, but focusing on them to the exclusion of smaller ones (to say nothing of invertebrates, plants, fungi, and microbes) has led to a narrative of the interchange that smacks of manifest destiny, in which superior beings from North America supplanted inferior ones in the south. In the logic of this story, South America's long isolation left its animals unprepared for a meeting with a larger world, and the North American fauna were tougher, smarter, and better prepared for conquest by their wider experience and bigger brains.

Where the largest mammals are concerned, this is hard to dispute. Some of South America's unique animals did manage to travel north; glyptodonts, ground sloths, and even terror birds reached the present-day United States and thrived there for a time. But only three small mammals from South America live north of the Rio Grande today — nine-banded armadillos, porcupines, and opossums. In South America, the opposite is true: its largest mammals are mostly North American in origin, and even the vicuñas that confounded Bernabé Cobo in the Andes are immigrants whose ancestors died out in their North American homeland.

What's true at one scale, however, doesn't necessarily hold at another. Throughout South America, many smaller animals, including primates and marsupials, held their own against northern immigrants or adapted to make room for them — and though it's easy to fixate on Darwin's vanished giants, many of South America's most outlandish animals are very much alive and easily seen, if you know where to look.

One of the best places to look is up. South

America might have imported more mammals than its northern neighbor, but it exported more birds. Today it holds nearly a third of the world's bird species, more than any other continent, and many familiar North American birds are the descendants of immigrants from the south, including flycatchers, woodpeckers, hummingbirds, and falcons. But a host of South America's birds still live nowhere else, from the long-legged swamp stalkers called seriemas to the crested screamers that were William Henry Hudson's gawky favorites. Hudson felt sure that the avian wealth of his home continent indicated something important about its past, but his mind might have reeled at the complexity of the truth: South America's birds have an even more tangled history than its mammals. Several of its most prominent bird families arrived long before the great interchange, while some were blown in later from as far away as Europe and Africa. And some early arrivals, like parrots, probably took the reverse route of the marsupials and came across from Australia via the forested coasts of Antarctica, before the big freeze.

Caracaras are some of South America's oldest feathered residents, and like every animal to call it home since the Cretaceous extinctions, they faced a choice between its two basic flavors of habitat: the open plains of its southern cone, or the warm, wet forests of its northern bulge. Both have advantages, but caracaras often gravitate toward open country — perhaps because there aren't as many scavenging opportunities in a closed forest. It's tempting to imagine that the woodlands of the Amazon swarm with cryptic monsters, but tropical forests are such complex and efficient ecosystems that few large herbivores or predators thrive in them; most of their animals spend their lives in the canopy, which doesn't lend itself to thousand-pound behemoths. Grasslands and savannas, by contrast, favor larger grazing animals that don't need to climb trees; and the grinding teeth of Darwin's fossil giants suggested a mostly vegetarian diet.

But it's in the forest, strangely enough, that we can pick up the genetic trail of the Johnny rooks. The last ancestor common to all living caracaras lived about twelve to fourteen million years ago, after which a deep fork appears in their lineage. One side of this split leads to the crested caracaras Darwin met in the Pampas and Patagonia, and you might expect that striated caracaras, since they live even farther south today, would be descended from this group. But their genes tell a different story: the Johnny rooks' ancestry lies along the other genetic path, which appears to have led their forebears into the forest.

We may never know exactly why the ancestors of the caranchos and the Johnny rooks

228

parted company. At the time of their split, the Earth was in a long, slow cooling phase, in which forests shrank while grasslands expanded; and in southern South America, the rain shadow of the rising Andes was drying out the plains of Patagonia. It may be that one population of ancestral caracaras gravitated more toward the grasslands, while another traveled farther afield; but they may have been nudged apart by an inland sea. As the earth warms and cools, the polar ice caps wax and wane, and much of South America lies so low that even a brief period of warming can send the ocean spilling over the lip of the continent, forming long, shallow seaways that race inland for hundreds of miles.

The full extent of these inland seas is unclear, but their effects were dramatic: they left scallop shells and sharks' teeth on the eastern slopes of the Andes, nursed a brackish swamp the size of Texas in what's now the western Amazon, and seeded the rivers and wetlands of the tropics with oceanic species like the stingrays and pink dolphins that still live there today. One of the largest prehistoric seaways descended through the basin that now holds the Orinoco River, submerging much of Amazonia, while another long finger of salt water surged north from the mouth of the Río de la Plata, where Buenos Aires sits today. These two seaways may even have connected for a time, dividing the continent from north to south and carving it into a set of huge islands.

The arrival of an inland sea is exactly the kind of event that can split a lineage in two, and the La Plata seaway might have appeared at the right time to divide the caracaras. If we're reading their DNA correctly, the ancestors of today's Johnny rooks and caranchos appear to have parted ways during a moment when the oceans rose by hundreds of feet, and caracaras on the western side of the seaway might have remained in the drier, cooler south, which it sealed off like a lid. But birds on its eastern shores would have faced a different fate. Unless they chose to travel many miles over open water, they'd have been forced to go north toward the tropics, where their descendants would find new opportunities — and make surprising choices — in a very different version of the world.

■ ■ ■ ■

PART III
GREEN MANSIONS

■ ■ ■ ■

I do not know how to describe it, seeing things as we did that had never been heard of or seen before, not even dreamed about.
— BERNAL DÍAZ DEL CASTILLO

It is not only species of animal that die out, but whole species of feeling.
— JOHN FOWLES

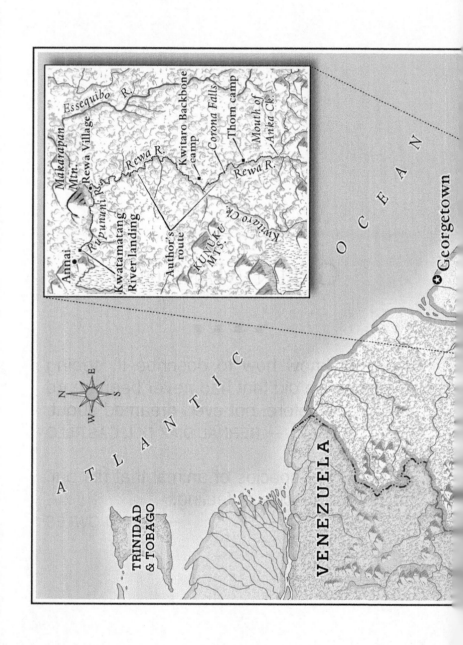

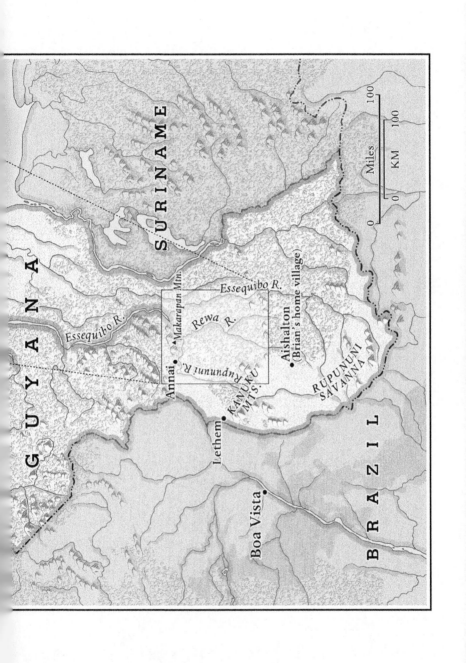

GUYANA

SURINAME

BRAZIL

Essequibo R.

Essequibo R.

Essequibo R.

Rewa R.

Makarapan Mtn.

Annai

Rupununi R.

KANUKU MTS.

Aishalton
(Brian's home village)

RUPUNUNI
SAVANNA

Lethem

Boa Vista

Miles

KM

0

100

100

11
BUSH AUNTIE-MAN

On the banks of the Rewa River, in the deep forests of southern Guyana, three Amerindian men — Brian Duncan, Jose George, and Ramnall "Rambo" Roberts — sat on folding chairs in a circle of light. It was long after sunset, and the sounds of the tropical night surrounded them: a shimmering chorus of trilling frogs, ostinato insects, and the querulous whistles of big-eyed, bug-hunting birds called nightjars. The light came from a single bulb that dangled from a forked stick, rigged to a boat's twelve-volt battery, and from the hammock where I lay behind a scrim of mosquito netting, the broad sandbar where the men sat looked like the floor of a stage. It almost seemed they'd gathered around a ghost light, the lamp in empty theaters that keeps unfriendly spirits at bay. Every few seconds, a bat flicked across its beam.

I'd come to Guyana for two reasons. The first was to follow the Johnny rooks' lineage through its surprising detour into the tropics and meet their relatives who live there today — especially red-throated caracaras, who've become so unlike any other falcon as to be almost unrecognizable. The second was tied to Hudson: I was curious to visit the setting of *Green Mansions: A Romance of the Tropical Forest,* his most popular novel. *Green Mansions* is filled with detailed descriptions of a place Hudson never actually saw, and I wondered how his imagination would square with the real world. Brian, Jose, and Rambo had agreed to take me up the Rewa for a month into one of the wildest places in South America, a place their ancestors first saw at least fifteen thousand years ago; and in the river's upper reaches, we would draw closer to the forest as the caracaras found it, millions of years before humans set foot in their continent.

Brian and Jose (pronounced "Josey") were Wapishana, descendants of the Arawak people who met Columbus, while Rambo belonged to the larger Macushi tribe, who number among the people Europeans dubbed Caribs. Arawaks and Caribs were bitter rivals until a few generations ago, but today they live and work together, and though their languages are mutually unintelligible, Brian, Jose, and Rambo shared Guyana's official language of English — a legacy of colonial Britain, laced with antique words like "vex" (for anger) and

236

"cutlass" (for machete). Guyanese English leans toward the expressive Caribbean English of Trinidad and Jamaica, but it's acquired a gentle, distinctive cadence in the country's thinly populated south, where it's hemmed in by Brazilian Portuguese, Venezuelan Spanish, and Surinamese Dutch, and tempered by the softly spoken languages of South America's first settlers. Around the ghost light, Brian, Jose, and Rambo's conversation was spare and quiet, accompanied by the murmur of a river that had curled through its basin since long before the two Americas met.

Farther along the shore, another light emerged from the forest and bobbled toward my hammock. It was the headlamp of Sean McCann, a young, red-bearded biologist from Canada who'd just earned a PhD by studying red-throated caracaras. He'd been drawn to them by a biological mystery too tempting to resist: How did they survive on a diet of aggressive, venomous wasps?

I'd first seen Sean online, giving a lecture called "Red-Throated Caracaras Are Way Cool Because They Are the Wasp-Murdering Superheroes of the Rain Forest," and got to know him better through his photo blog — a collection of artful close-ups of birds, insects, and spiders adorned with earnest captions and Latin names. In person, he was much like his internet persona: wry, energetic, and delighted to explain the finest details of his work, his cameras, or any other subject for as long as I cared to listen. I'd brought him along to complement our guides' deeply rooted local knowledge, and he'd spent the evening walking slowly along the riverbank, photographing fishing spiders, toads, and other night creatures. He seemed completely unfazed by a cloud of biting flies that swarmed around his light.

The Rewa is a small but powerful river, broken by a series of precipitous waterfalls, that drains a thousand square miles of virgin forest. Unlike most streams in tropical South America, its water isn't bound for the Amazon; it's a tributary of a larger river called the Rupununi, which flows north toward the Caribbean from the ancient granitic highlands of the Guiana Shield, a formation that runs east from southern Venezuela across Guyana, Suriname, and French Guiana. The first two of these small states were colonial footholds of Britain and Holland, respectively; French Guiana is still a *department* of France. They're often glossed over in descriptions of South America, since their combined population of less than two million people speak neither Spanish nor Portuguese and don't fit neatly in the popular concept of Latin America.

Earlier in the day, on a flight south from Guyana's capital of Georgetown, Sean and I had watched the landscape appear to slip backward in time. Below us, the cane fields and rice paddies of the Essequibo River delta gave way to second-growth stands of palms and bamboo. Tar-sealed roads turned to dirt and corduroy, and the lurid gashes of gold mines and clear-cuts finally surrendered to the deep green of mature tropical forest. A pair of pink-faced tourists from Holland shouted to each other over the drone of the plane's single engine, and I thought about the frayed links between Dutch and English — once the same language, now so estranged that they're completely distinct — and the way a single species, divided by choice or accident, can become two. Sean beamed as we descended into a broad savanna on the forest's southern edge, where distant wildfires sent plumes of smoke into a clear sky.

We touched down on a grass airstrip at a hamlet called Annai, where we piled into a pickup truck and rode to the Rupununi through a striking, open landscape that could almost have been east Africa, except for the columns of Amerindian children walking to school in blue-and-white uniforms. At the river we met Brian, Jose, and Rambo, who shyly shook our hands and loaded our packs into two slim aluminum boats, laden with provisions. The boats were flat bottomed and slightly larger than a canoe — the kind, I thought, you might use for an afternoon of fishing on a quiet lake. Ashley Holland, a deeply tanned South African who'd lived in Guyana for decades, pulled up on a motorbike to see us off; he'd organized the trip and offered us a few words of advice. The dry season had been long this year, he said, and the rivers were unusually low, which meant that stingrays would be more concentrated in the channel than normal. He also told us to watch out for the small but deadly *Bothrops* snakes, which sit in a tidy coil, waiting for unsuspecting rodents to pass. The forest was mostly a safe place, he said, but stepping on a *Bothrops* was probably its greatest hazard.

With that, Ashley wished us luck and zoomed away. Sean balanced himself beside me in the first boat while Rambo, stout and baby-faced in a baseball cap and sunglasses, took his place behind us at the outboard. Jose, who wore an open army shirt, wedged himself among waterproof bags and kitchen supplies at the bow, holding a short paddle carved from a single piece of wood. I looked back and gave Rambo a thumbs-up, which he solemnly returned. Brian, with an air of good-natured authority, took the helm of the second boat, which carried a drum of diesel fuel, a cylinder of propane, sacks of cassava meal, and a stack of tarpaulins. As the motors roared to life Sean leaned in to my ear. "WE'RE GOING TO A REALLY EXCEL-LENT FOREST," he shouted. "IT'S WHAT

EVERY OTHER FOREST WANTS TO
BE."

The heat and searing light of our first afternoon on the Rupununi were a shock, but my
mind was buzzing with the high of soaking in
a new landscape, and I didn't notice my
sunburned arms and neck until it was too
late. In the washed-out colors of early afternoon, the river looked like milky tea, and was
so low that it seemed as if someone had
pulled a plug and let most of its water drain
out. Scoured banks of orange-white sand and
clay stood high on either side, pocked with
holes dug by fish in the wet season that now
sheltered birds and bats. Their sheer walls
turned the river into a long, sinuous canyon,
blocking our view of the savanna we'd left
behind. Black caimans as long as our boats
surfaced and sashayed toward the bank, looking pointedly unhurried, while jabiru storks
stood on sandbars like ghostly sentinels, their
wicked-looking beaks slightly agape, their
scarlet throat pouches bulging with fish. Each
time Rambo spotted a new animal he shouted
its name, as if calling the roll.

On a satellite map, the Guiana Shield's
forests look nearly identical to the Amazon
basin, but at a finer scale they're remarkably
different. The domes of purplish granite that
emerge from them like the backs of grazing
dinosaurs are some of the oldest exposed

rocks on earth, and the shield is home to endemic plants and animals that don't live in the basin to the south. Many related pairs of similar species appear in each region, suggesting they were once divided by a natural barrier, such as a shallow sea or a band of grasslands, before reuniting in the fairly recent past.

The shield's interior is also one of very few tropical regions on Earth that's more or less uninhabited by humans. Few of its cascading streams are an easy journey for boats of any size, and the only way to access its farthest reaches is on foot or by helicopter — a marked contrast to the Amazon's dense network of meandering rivers, which have long been a natural highway system for people and animals alike. The first European visitors, finding the Amazon inhospitable in the extreme, assumed that few people had ever lived there, but it's become clear that many thousands — perhaps *millions* — of people lived in the basin when the first immigrants from the Old World turned up, bringing deadly epidemics of smallpox and other diseases with them. Signs of Amerindian civilizations have been found throughout the Amazon basin, where vast pockets of enriched soil, massive earthworks and canals, and fragments of elegant pottery bear witness to thousands of years of human occupation.

In one sense, however, the Europeans were

correct: the forest is unwelcoming to new-comers, who have to elbow for space among established citizens who've been refining their approaches to life for millions of years. Veteran creatures of the forest eat specialized diets, live in razor-thin slices of habitat, and converse on finely tuned chemical, sonic, and visual channels. They're also masters of deception, ambush, and self-defense: there are spiders disguised as ants, flowers disguised as insects, insects disguised as flowers, and trees that strangle and maim other trees. Plants and animals bristle with spines and subtle poisons, and the famous hardness and density of the tallest trees is a defense against unsleeping armies of termites, which pull the forest down almost as fast as it builds itself up. Since its nutrients are so efficiently recycled by insects, microbes, and fungi, the forest's soils are thin and poor; only a few inches of loam lie beneath a thin layer of fallen leaves.

To find a place in this ornate world, the ancestors of today's tropical caracaras faced the challenge of immigrants everywhere: they had to find and seize an opportunity no one else had grasped. As they moved north into the forests, they'd have met their secretive cousins the forest falcons, who'd already found a niche beneath the canopy millions of years earlier as surreptitious hunters. The forest falcons didn't have to worry about competition, however; most tropical caracaras keep to the banks of rivers and streams and avoid the deep forest. No matter how much a river's path shifts over time, there's often something to tempt a scavenging omnivore on its margins, from dead fish to immense swarms of butterflies, and clinging to the river's edge helped two tropical species — black caracaras and yellow-headed caracaras — sidestep the specialization the forest often requires.

Black caracaras prefer wilder stretches of tropical rivers, away from most people, but yellow-headed caracaras — small, pale-breasted, gull-like birds — seem to have taken humans in stride, like the chimangos of the Pampas. They're a familiar sight along rural highways, which they patrol in search of road-kill, and most tropical villages have at least one resident pair of yellow-heads who make sure no edible refuse goes to waste. But they arrived in the South American tropics long before humans did, and a curious note in the *Journal of Raptor Research* offers a glimpse of their lives in the days before we turned up, even before the great biotic interchange.

The authors, ornithologists from the United States, were visiting a university in Caracas, Venezuela, where they were surprised to see two yellow-headed caracaras clinging to the back of a three-toed sloth in a tree on campus. The sloth "showed no sign of defensiveness or aggression toward the caracaras" as the birds gleaned invertebrates from its head and neck, and seemed to welcome the caracaras' attention: it "assumed a relaxed posture, reclining on a branch with its front legs extended behind its head." The Brazilian name for yellow-headed caracaras, *garrapateiro,* means "tick-eater," and they're often photographed feeding from the backs of cattle; another pair of biologists recently described a yellow-head grooming a white-tailed deer in a park in Panama City. "Neither deer nor caracara," they wrote, "seemed to be particularly alert to any potential danger, or to express concern about our unconcealed presence or the presence of traffic close by."

Red-throated caracaras, the strangest of the tropical caracaras, also enjoy a diet rich in invertebrates. But they've made a bolder choice of habitat and prey, and aren't city birds; they prefer the forest's interior, where they feed on the larvae-studded nests of social wasps — a meal that interests few other animals. Like most caracaras, red-throats are vaguely crow-like, but they're so colorful that they slightly resemble toucans (if you subtracted the enormous bill). The bare skin of their faces and throats is scarlet; their eyes are an even deeper shade of red; the tips of their bluish beaks are bright yellow; and their plumage is black except for a spray of white feathers above their red legs. It's an outfit that makes them both striking and slightly ridiculous, like weaponized chickens. No one keeps red-throated caracaras in captivity, and though they live throughout the woodlands of the Guiana Shield and the Amazon basin, they can be surprisingly difficult to find. They seem to prefer large tracts of mature, undisturbed forest; the wilderness of the upper Rewa — I hoped — would be a likely place to meet them.

Near a tiny village Jose called Crash Water, we passed a young family traveling in a dugout canoe. The woman at the bow held a toddler in her arms, while the man at the stern carried a broad-shafted paddle. Behind him, in a plastic bucket, a bundle of thick-shafted arrows were fletched with the black tail feathers of a curassow. Rambo respectfully cut his wake, and they shyly returned my wave; theirs was the only other boat we would see for the next month. A few hours later we hauled out to rest on a sandbar, where Jose handed us bowls of chicken curry doused with a yellow pepper sauce; *dinosaur stew,* I thought, finding a whole foot in my bowl. I ate gratefully, and was rinsing my dishes in the river when I heard an unexpected but familiar sound: a loud, staccato croaking, like a stick dragged across the top of a picket fence.

It was the call of a northern crested caracara — a nearly identical cousin of the black-capped, orange-faced caranchos whose "necrophagous habits" spooked Darwin. It was standing across the river from us, pacing stiffly back and forth on its long yellow legs. Crested caracaras have a dignified, inscrutable expression one old guidebook calls "grandfatherly," and this one seemed in high dudgeon as it called again, *karruk-karruk-KARRRRRUUUUKKK,* tossing its head back in the posture Darwin found hard to believe. ("This fact, which has been doubted, is quite true," he wrote. "I have seen them several times with their heads backwards in a completely inverted position.") This time, the caracara received an answer: a burst of shrill, piping cries from a squadron of southern lapwing plovers bearing down on it in attack formation. Though most birds in their family are timid and flighty, southern lapwings are dapper warriors with red eyes, copper epaulets, and a pair of purple, thorn-like spurs where their dinosaurian thumbs once were. They feinted at the caracara twice, which ducked its head to dodge them, then opened its long wings and retreated over the lip of the riverbank.

Scientists regard northern and southern crested caracaras as separate species, but they're so alike that they're nearly indistinguishable. Their combined range is the largest of any caracara lineage, stretching from southern Tierra del Fuego to southern North

America, but they're always open-country birds, and I hadn't expected to see one this close to a forest — or to see a scene from *Birds of La Plata* reenacted in front of me. William Henry Hudson was riding his horse across the Pampas one afternoon when a southern crested caracara flew past, trailed by a screaming flock of about thirty lapwings. When one of the lapwings came too close, the caracara doubled back to chase it. "The angry hectoring cries of the lapwings instantly changed to piercing screams of terror," Hudson recalled, "which in a very short time brought a crowd numbering between two and three hundred birds to the rescue.

But the Carancho was not to be shaken off; he was never more than a yard behind his quarry, and I was near enough to distinguish the piteous screams of the chased Lapwing amidst all the tumult, as of a bird already captive. At the end of about a minute, it was seized in the Carancho's talons, and, still violently screaming, borne away. The cloud of Lapwings followed for some distance, but presently they all returned to the fatal spot where the contest had taken place; and for an hour afterwards, they continued soaring about in separate bodies, screaming all the time with an unusual note in their voices as of fear or grief, and holding excited conclaves on the ground, to all appearance as greatly disturbed in their minds as an equal number of highly emotional human beings would be in the event of a similar disaster overtaking them.

"My great-grandmother used to tell me stories about the caracara," said Jose, stowing pots under the bow of the boat. "Just little stories, to make us go to sleep." I asked what they were, but he smiled and said he'd tell me later. Instead, he told me about a crested caracara he knew that liked to consort with a group of barnyard hens. Most of the time it scratched peaceably in the dirt with the chickens, Jose said, but one day it seized one of its neighbors and poked her eyes out.

We reached the mouth of the Rewa before sundown, calling in at a nearby village whose Wapishana people are the river's custodians. No one ascends or descends the Rewa without their knowledge and permission, and at the top of a wooden staircase that led up the bank from the landing we met Rudolph Edwards, an elfin, smiling man who managed the village's tourist lodge. A hand-painted sign above its thatched roof read LAUGHING ARAPAIMA BAR, but there were no tourists now; the sport fishing season was over, and the blinding rains of the wet season were only a few weeks away.

"From here on," Rudolph said, "there is no

more civilization." He kindly offered us a beer, which we politely and stupidly declined, since we wouldn't see another for weeks. He also offered us hope that we'd find red-throated caracaras. He'd recently come across a group of them upriver, in the tall forest behind a place called Kwitaro Backbone. "It's like a caracara factory in there," he said.

That Rudolph had seen several birds at once wasn't surprising, since red-throated caracaras pursue a lifestyle that lies farther off a typical raptor's path than even the Johnny rooks have dared to go. Instead of pairs, red-throats form troops of several birds — as few as three and as many as twelve — who jointly patrol a shared territory. These groups gather to scream at anything they consider an intruder, including other red-throats, monkeys, and people, and their alertness and aggression led the colonial British to call them "bulldogs." In French Guiana they were once called *capitaines de gros-becs* — toucan captains — because they frequently travel with a retinue of other loud, colorful birds like macaws, toucans, and oropendolas.

Brian, Jose, and Rambo had another name for them: bush auntie-man. This was a peculiar nickname, to say the least, since "auntie-man" is a derisive pan-Caribbean term for a gay man. Exactly how the caracaras acquired it isn't clear; it probably has something to do with their alarm calls, which don't endear them to hunters. Most foreigners who make the effort to visit the Rewa are bent on hooking its giant fish or seeing iconic animals like jaguars and harpy eagles, and compared to these marvels, our guides seemed to feel the bush auntie-man was a weird object of interest. I wondered if Sean and I seemed like tourists who'd traveled thousands of miles to Central Park and asked to see the pigeons.

Red-throated caracaras have been quietly vanishing, however, from places Brian, Rambo, and Jose had never seen. Though the rain forests of the Guiana Shield and the Amazon basin still cover an area nearly the size of the western United States, they're being eaten away by logging, mining, and industrial agriculture, and the caracaras' range is shrinking with them. At the current pace of deforestation, the Amazon's forests could vanish within a century, and though Guyana's old-growth woodlands aren't being felled at quite the same rate, they stretched unbroken to the Caribbean as recently as the 1950s. They now cover only the country's western and southern highlands, where logging has slowed since Norway began paying Guyana to leave its forests standing.

All these concerns seemed a world away from our serene camp on the Rewa, where the ghost light finally dimmed and I heard Jose's miniature voice say *Yeah, my hammock say she ready.* I lay thinking about what we

251

might see in the weeks ahead while Sean anchored his mosquito net with water bottles and shooed out two large hunting spiders who'd found their way into his rucksack. For him, this trip was a rare luxury: he didn't have to worry about gathering data or disproving a hypothesis, and his only jobs were to talk to me, linger over anything that interested him, and take his fill of pictures. It might also be his last chance to see the redthroats in the wild, since the demands of a scientific career were leading him away from their world.

"Good night," he said, switching off his headlamp. "I hope you dream of the bush auntie-men."

I asked if he'd ever dreamed of them himself. He had, but only once, early in his field research. In the dream, a cloud of redthroats were descending on Vancouver, perching on maples and firs in city parks and speaking fluent English. The birds were regaling passersby with stories about their lives, and dream-Sean rushed downtown to meet them, giddy with excitement and relief. He'd been chasing them through the jungle for years, and they were finally going to tell him what he wanted to know.

12
HYMENOPTERAN DREAMS

In 2006, Sean was a graduate student in the medical entomology program at the University of Florida, and not an especially happy one. He'd gone to college in hopes of becoming a herpetologist, a biologist who specializes in reptiles and amphibians, but he'd switched to insects because it was more likely to lead to a job — and because, after a few semesters of learning about insect societies, he felt they'd been unfairly maligned.

It didn't take many months in Gainesville for him to feel he'd made a serious mistake. Medical entomologists study insects that carry human diseases, and though mosquitoes are a triumph of evolution, they're so instinct-bound that they seem almost mechanical; researchers probably wouldn't pay much attention to them if they didn't affect us. Outside his classes, Sean spent his days as a cog in his supervisor's research, performing experiments on mosquitoes that carry West Nile virus and Japanese encephalitis, with the eventual aim of killing as many of them as possible.

This was a long way from the life he'd imagined, and he decided that if he was going to survive a PhD, he needed to study an animal with a bigger brain. He'd been plotting his escape from medical entomology by reading in the emerging discipline of chemical ecology, the study of how living things perceive the molecular world they can't see or hear — and how they use it to lure, warn, and seduce one another. Despite its esoteric-sounding name, chemical ecology is intimately familiar to everyone: your nose, like a moth's antenna, is a sophisticated chemical detector. The sensations we call smells are our brains' interpretation of the chemical world in the same way that colors are our interpretation of certain wavelengths of light. Smells have an ineffable power: they're immediate, expressive, and impossible to ignore. Some warn us of danger. Others tell us about food. Many are obscurely attractive or evocative, like the musty tang of old books or a lover's sweat.

William Henry Hudson was also fascinated by the causes and effects of smells, despite their status as a nearly taboo subject in Victorian England. The suspicion that people in his adopted country — especially men — seemed to bear toward scents of all kinds exasperated and puzzled him, as he'd never encountered this prejudice in South America. "When I first came to England," he wrote,

I soon discovered that all scents on the male person, natural or artificial, were distasteful and even abhorrent to men. I had been kindly taken in hand by new-found friends who desired to make an Englishman of me — a respectable person. They told me to wear a silk hat and frock coat, tan gloves, and to carry a neatly-folded umbrella in my hand . . . I obeyed them in everything, but when they objected to a little Cologne or lavender on my pocket-handkerchief I revolted. They said I had come from a semi-barbarous country and did not know all that this meant — that an English gentleman with scent about him aroused a strong feeling of hostility in others, and that it was considered very low and indicated a person of an effeminate and nasty mind.

This aversion fascinated Hudson. "Nastiness was not in *my* mind," he noted, knowing that interesting stories often lay beneath uncomfortable subjects. "Intellectually," he wrote, "smell does not rank so highly . . . but it is, on the other hand, more emotional, and stirs the mind more deeply than seeing and hearing," an observation his contemporary Marcel Proust might also have made. Hudson went so far as to make a list of his favorite scents — a capsule sketch of the airborne chemistry of English life.

The heavy greasy smell of sheep, for instance, and of sheep-folds, of cattle and cow-houses and stables, of warehouses filled with goods, and drapers', grocers', cheesemongers', and apothecaries' shops, of leather and iron and wood, of sawpits and carpenters' workshops. Wood-smells are indeed almost as grateful as aromatic and fragrant scents. And many other smells — tanneries, breweries, and all kinds of works, including gasworks. But it is always a pleasing change from the great manufacturing centres to the country and the dusty smell of rain after dry, hot weather; the smell of rain-wet pinewoods, of burning weeds and peat, and above all the smell of the fresh-turned earth — the smell which, as the agricultural laborer believes, gives him his long, healthy life.

Hudson was unashamed to embrace what he called his "smelling hunger." "So far as a smell is not a warning or disgustful one," he declared, "even if acrid or sour or pungent, it is agreeable to me." He took walks through bogs and marshes for the sake of their smells alone, and especially loved patches of the wetland plant called golden withy, or sweet gale. "I can stand knee-deep among its thick-growing shrubs," he wrote, "and rub my hands and face with the crushed leaves and fill my pockets with them so as to wrap myself up in the delicious aroma." Pretending that the world of scents was unimportant seemed like an act of moral cowardice to him, and he felt this prejudice had unjustly infected the sciences. "It is useless to try to 'look up' the subject of smell in the libraries," he wrote. "Those [books] I have consulted say that it is an obscure subject, [and] when you look into it you will find you have got hold of a rather low subject which had better be dropped." This was a great pity, he thought, since smells were clearly so important to the rest of the living world.

He illustrated his point, as usual, with a memory from his childhood. The cattle ranches of European colonists on the Argentine Pampas were open range, and their immense herds were an incredible sight: nothing but "cows and sky" as far as the eye could see. But they were sometimes roiled by stampedes of panicked animals fleeing Amerindian raiders. These stampedes could extend along a front of fifty or sixty miles, and often mysteriously began hours or even days before anyone saw the raiders themselves. This, Hudson wrote, was because the animals could *smell* the coming attack. Rather than approaching from downwind to conceal their scent, Amerindians used it to their advantage, smearing themselves with rancid horse fat and letting the wind drive their scent before them, terrifying the horses of Argentine soldiers who manned forts along the frontier. "With a horse maddened by terror under him," he wrote, "no man could use his carbine," and though the Amerindians were armed only with bamboo lances, they were "victorious as often as not." This was an ingenious use of a chemical weapon, and Hudson admired it; in his view, the Amerindians had sensibly used their understanding of smells to overcome a military disadvantage.

Hudson acknowledged that some scientists had studied the structure of the smelling organs of certain mammals, and advised his readers that there was productive reading to be done on the subject "as long as you are satisfied to study the organ and to know nothing about the function." But he was certain that much remained to be learned about the world of smells, and doubted that the mammals could hold a candle to the "infinitely more subtle" power and resolution of the olfactory sense in "that imperfectly known, fascinating insect realm," whose members organize their lives around it above all else.

Once again, Hudson was ahead of his time. The term "pheromones" was coined in 1959 to describe the chemicals living things use to communicate with one another, and nearly all animals (including you and me) both receive and produce them. Insects, however, have refined their use to an awe-inspiring degree, with a subtlety that can rival spoken language. Sean was especially drawn to the elaborate chemical languages of the insects known as hymenopterans — ants, bees, and wasps — which also have a curious tendency to form complex societies.

As anyone who's battled an infestation knows, ants are social creatures, and their colonies are often compared to single, conglomerate organisms. But they're really more like civilizations, in which thousands of separate individuals, bound by a common language, pursue common goals. Marking the path to a food source with a trail of pheromones is the most famous trick in their arsenal (and the reason that once they've found your honey jar, it might be time to throw it away). But that's only the tip of the iceberg. Peering into the world of ant societies can induce a kind of cognitive vertigo, if not a full-blown identity crisis, since it's hard to find a complex human behavior ants don't pursue with equal or greater vigor — including architecture, farming, division of labor, and warfare. Whatever you might think of their reproductive strategy, in which a minority of fertile females produce thousands of sterile daughters to do their bidding, it's certainly more elaborate than ours. No one's found an example of art, music, or philosophy in social hymenopterans, but no one's really gone looking for them, either — and would we know it when we saw, heard, or smelled it? You'd be laughed out of the room if you asked most scientists if insects have complex emotional lives or a sense of aesthetics, but you'd have received the same treatment if you'd said the same about crows and parrots only a few decades ago.

Sean's hymenopteran dreams didn't extend quite this far, but his initial curiosity became a growing sense of opportunity. Though ant societies have absorbed evolutionary biologists for decades, Sean was drawn to the lesser-known world of social wasps, whose lives preserve an elegant balance of autonomy and collective action. Wasps coordinate the behavior of thousands of flying workers, like ants in a much higher gear, and have the largest brains for their body size in the insect world. Every species of social wasp has its own culture — one, for example, is strictly nocturnal — and they make mental maps of their foraging grounds and maintain complex relationships with their peers; the members of at least one species can tell their sisters apart by their faces.

But it's hard to find funding for research on animals few people care about. Unlike honeybees, social wasps don't produce anything we consume or sell; unlike mosquitoes, they don't spread disease. Scientists who dare to study them face subjects that are hard to observe in the wild or the lab, since some wasps fly as fast as twenty-five miles per hour, and if you're stung too many times by workers defending their homes, you might end up in the hospital, or worse.

Social wasps also share a skill that exceeds the ability of nearly every mammal on earth: they're master builders. Wasp colonies divide themselves into age-class "castes" to construct, supply, and defend the nests that protect their queens and larvae, and the nests' cascading ranks of brood cells are marvels of craft and design. Unlike honeybees, which ooze construction-grade wax from their abdomens, most social wasps fashion their homes from a papier-mâché of chewed-up wood fibers mixed with their own saliva, and each species builds in its own style. Some weave delicate envelopes, thin and weightless as rice paper, which they conceal on the underside of leaves; others erect imposing fortresses armored with stone-hard layers of mud or a felt-like paper shell; and a few, taking no chances, excavate underground chambers and build their homes inside.

Compared to these grand feats of social organization and architecture, the mosquitoes in Sean's lab in Florida seemed distinctly unimaginative, and in 2007 he bid them farewell to pursue a PhD at Simon Fraser University in Vancouver, under the supervision of a chemical ecologist named Gerhard Gries. Gries's students worked mostly with household and agricultural pests like earwigs, houseflies, and cockroaches — species of interest to corporations that funded his lab's research — so Sean expected he'd have to make a case for studying wasps by stressing their threat to human health. But Gries surprised him, in their first conversation, by asking Sean what animals he liked best.

Sean wondered for a moment if he should admit his passion for reptiles to an entomologist, but he told the truth, adding that he also loved birds of prey — and this, to his surprise, got Gries's attention. Gries told Sean that he'd had a project in mind for a while that involved both wasps and raptors and held the potential for a newsworthy discovery. But it would be risky and difficult, and it might easily lead to a dead end.

This kind of talk was catnip for Sean, who listened with growing excitement as Gries told him about the persistent rumor that red-throated caracaras had a chemical in their feathers or skin that could repel wasps. If this was true, such a substance would be unlike anything known to science, and if Sean could find and isolate it, he'd score a scientific coup. A natural wasp repellent might merit publication in a top-tier journal like *Science*

262

or *Nature,* along with a potentially lucrative patent for Gries's lab; it might also save lives, since wasps and bees kill hundreds of people worldwide every year.

Sean told Gries he'd think it over. The quest for a wasp-repellent bird would let him spend months in the field with animals that interested him, and a bird with a protective chemical in its feathers wasn't entirely far-fetched: a group of oriole-like songbirds in New Guinea called pitohuis secrete a poison that's chemically identical to the toxin some South American frogs ooze from their skin. Neither the pitohuis nor the frogs, however, manufacture this complex substance; they somehow harvest it from their insect-rich diets. To Sean, this suggested a possible source of repellent chemicals for the cara-caras: perhaps the birds had somehow evolved a way to use the wasps' chemical languages against them.

But this was all speculation. Red-throated caracaras certainly didn't look well equipped to defend themselves from wasps; the bare skin of their faces and throats was an obvious vulnerability. More tantalizing still was the fact that most details of their lives were unknown, or at least unpublished; no one had ever described their nests or how they feed their young, or measured the ratio of males to females in one of their troops (an especially interesting question, since nearly every mating system imaginable exists among birds, from the strict monogamy of albatrosses to the extreme promiscuity of fairy wrens). After a search of scientific literature going back to the eighteenth century, Sean felt pretty sure he'd found every word ever written about red-throated caracaras, by scientists and amateurs alike. It added up to a single afternoon's reading.

The most vivid description of their behavior came from an article by Alexander Skutch, an American botanist who took a job with the notoriously worker-unfriendly United Fruit Company in Jamaica in the 1930s, fell in love with tropical birds, and moved to Costa Rica to study them. Skutch especially loved chronicling the lives of obscure species, and when a red-throated caracara demolished a wasp nest on a high branch of a tree beside his house, he took careful notes on its methodical and relentless assault.

When the big bird bent far over the side of the stout branch to peck at the side of the wasps' nest, it would slip down and regain its balance with difficulty. But finally it succeeded in making the holes large enough for its purpose. Now clinging back downward below the wasp nest with its toes in the perforations it had made, the caracara began to tear large papery flakes from the upper part of the corrugated envelope of the hive. Soon its head was inside, hidden from my view, but I had no doubt that it was enjoying a feast of tender white larvae and pupae. White belly upward, tail half-spread, wings partly open and hanging in random attitudes, the caracara reminded me of a dead hawk hung up by a gamekeeper to frighten away others of its kind. . . . I was amazed that a carton so thin could sustain in this fashion so large and heavy a bird. From time to time the caracara would shift its position and tear away more of the nest covering, always working downward, then again bury its head in the interior to proceed with the feast. Through my binoculars, I could clearly see the big wasps hovering around the despoiler of their home, but they preserved a slight distance from it, and none alighted on its glossy, blue-black plumage.

Wings partly open? Belly upward? The redthroat in Skutch's backyard didn't sound very concerned about being stung, even as it shoved its undefended throat into a wasp nest, and the last sentence — about the wasps not landing on the caracara — was especially odd. Why didn't they attack their attacker? Sean read on:

When, proceeding in this fashion, the caracara reached the bottom of the nest, it

265

experienced greater difficulty. Its foothold gave way and it fluttered down into the bushes . . . then it flew off to perch in a tree in the neighboring pasture. After a brief rest, it returned to the attack, uttering its raucous war-cry . . . seven times the caracara attempted to cling to the nest, only to have its toehold promptly give way. At last becoming discouraged, the noisy bird flew to the tall trees beside the river to rest and digest its meal. A whole city of wasps had been destroyed to supply one meal for a caracara.

Three decades passed before another ornithologist took up the chase. Jean-Marc Thiollay, a raptor specialist, was working at a research station called Nouragues in the forests of central French Guiana when he noticed a troop of red-throated caracaras whose territory included the station. He couldn't have missed them: they were loud and busy, and called to each other as they passed through the forest on unknown errands. Thiollay decided to follow them for several years, like an anthropologist tailing a band of chimpanzees, which proved a daunting task: the birds moved every fifteen minutes during the day, often by a mile or more, and Thiollay wore himself out trailing them on their daily rounds. When he did spot the birds, they often stayed in the high canopy or stopped what they were doing to scream at him, which didn't tell him much about their lives. It took him almost five years to learn to anticipate their movements — and to make himself nearly invisible.

What he discovered was a bird of prey like no other. The red-throats were remarkably cohesive, and seemed obsessed with their troop's safety; when a bird broke off from the group to forage on the ground, others remained in the trees to sound the alarm if anything seemed amiss. They were also unusually talkative: one account describes their stentorian cry as "an accelerating sequence of *gheh*s . . . turning into a *ka-ka-ka* . . . that resembles cackling of a hen, culminating in full loud cries, *ka-o,* with timbre of a parrot or even a macaw, which are repeated by the flock, even in flight." Thiollay heard all these sounds, but he also heard them calling quietly to each other when they were foraging together — a series of soft, irregular clucks, almost like a private conversation. Most predatory birds have a small vocal repertoire of a few stereotyped calls, but the caracaras cackled, screamed, and cooed to one another as if they'd invented their own language.

Then there was the matter of their diet. Unlike almost every other raptor, the red-throated caracaras Thiollay trailed at Nouragues appeared to have given up chas-

267

ing after things that fled from them, and he watched them carry off caterpillars, millipedes, and small, round fruits, "which the birds scraped laboriously." But wasps were their clear favorite: nearly half the items Thiollay saw them eating were nests whose denizens ranged from "small stingless bees to medium-size or large black or yellow wasps that were extremely aggressive and painful (personal experience)." The caracaras would fly to a perch, holding the nest in one foot like a parrot, and daintily extract the larvae with their beaks. Then they carefully licked the surface of the nest envelopes, as if cleaning frosting from a mixing bowl.

This was all very well for the caracaras, thought Sean, but what about the wasps? Like Skutch, Thiollay had been perplexed at the insects' passive reaction to the birds' attacks. "As soon as one bird reached a nest," Thiollay wrote, "the insects abandoned it and never attacked the raider, nor followed it when it carried the nest away." Thiollay, too, suspected them of producing a repellent — but he also knew how unusual that would be. "As far as I know," he ventured, "a similar adaptation has never been reported in any other vertebrate species."

A light clicked on in Sean's mind when he read this passage: Thiollay might have known his birds, but he clearly didn't know much about wasps. All social wasps produce a chemical signal if their home is under attack, triggering a massive defense; but the large tribe of wasps called swarm founders keep another pheromone in reserve for the awful moment when the nest is no longer defensible. If it's been torn in half by a falling branch, or knocked to the ground, or carried off by a predator, the wasps sound this last-ditch chemical alarm, abandon the nest, and regroup with their queens in a shivering huddle. A handful of scouts fan out to look for likely nest sites, confer with one another, agree on the best candidate, and return to the swarm. Then they lead their mothers and sisters along a scented chemical trail to a new home.

This profound sacrifice — abandoning their home and children so their family can survive — fascinated Sean, and he suspected red-throated caracaras had learned to take advantage of it. If so, the caracaras might only have to disturb the nests enough to make their residents abandon ship, which seemed a more likely strategy than chemical warfare. But Thiollay's work, even if it was wrong, was a godsend: it gave Sean a hypothesis he could test, a trail of tantalizing clues, and a ready-made study site where he could build on Thiollay's work while he searched for a wasp repellent. Even if the work didn't make him famous, it would let him explore the daily life of an obscure animal in a remote area, a kind of research that's usually impossible to fund. And if his hunch was wrong and there really was a wasp repellent — well, so much the better.

Sean kept his doubts to himself when he went back to Gries and agreed to take on the quest for the secret of the red-throats. Six months later, he packed up his equipment for his first field season, including a finely woven bird trap called a mist net, a decoy caracara he sculpted out of Styrofoam, and a beekeeper's helmet and gloves. Before his work was done, he'd also need a gas chromatography machine, a crossbow, a guitar amp, a climbing harness, and a dose of pure doggedness and courage. He would also lose thirty-five pounds.

13
THE LOST WORLD

Sometime after midnight a windstorm rolled through the forest along the Rewa, rattling the tarps above our hammocks and waking me from a surprisingly deep sleep. I'd never heard wind like it: a succession of distinct waves that began as a murmur and grew to a roar. The trees above us trembled and groaned, and I remembered Hudson's description of a private forest near London called Savernake, where he loved to sit among giant copper beeches and listen to the wind in their branches — an experience, he wrote, "worth going far to seek."

That is a mysterious voice which the forest has: it speaks to us, and somehow the life it expresses seems nearer, more intimate, than that of the sea. Doubtless because we are ourselves terrestrial and woodland in our origin; also because the sound is infinitely more varied as well as more human in character. There are sighings and moanings, and wails and shrieks, and wind-blown murmurings, like the distant confused talking of a vast multitude.

England's forests were the first Hudson ever saw, since his only South American travels were confined to the plains that stretch from the Pampas to Tierra del Fuego. He never walked among the Antarctic beeches and monkey-puzzle trees of the southern Andes, or glimpsed the woodlands of the tropical north — an old-growth forest as large as Europe — but he knew it was there, and pictured it every time he saw a flock of migrating parrots in the skies above La Plata. Britain's last primeval forests were long gone, felled a thousand years before he arrived, and its prehistoric lions, bears, hyenas, and woolly rhinos vanished with them. But scattered patches of regrowth, some of them centuries old, became Hudson's favorite parts of his adopted country and let him imagine the South American forests he never knew. In the Pampas the wind had a lonesome flavor, but at Savernake he felt anything but alone. "The suggestion is ever of a vast concourse," he wrote. "Crowds and congregations, tumultuous or orderly, but all swayed by one absorbing impulse, solemn or passionate . . . Their innumerable voices are as one voice, expressing we know not what, but always something wholly strange to us — lament, entreaty, denunciation."

The same was true on the Rewa, where I lay awake through the storm in an anxious mixture of awe and suspense. When the winds finally died away, they left a pure silence in their wake that magnified the smallest sounds. The voices of frogs and crickets slowly reemerged, along with the cautious whinny of a pygmy owl, and I heard Sean's headlamp click on, then off, then on again. Then I heard him thumbing through the pages of a book, and I asked him how long he thought it might take us to walk to his research site in French Guiana, through hundreds of miles of roadless forest.

Sean thought for a moment. "We'd probably die of starvation in a couple weeks," he said. "But if we did everything right, I bet it would take six months."

In 2008, Sean arrived at the Nouragues station after a five-hour boat trip from Cayenne, where he was relieved to find a troop of bush auntie-men in the same place Jean-Marc Thiollay had seen them twenty years earlier. Once he'd learned the reserve's network of trails, Sean put his nets and decoy to work, and soon became the first scientist to capture red-throated caracaras and swab them for chemical weapons. He was surprised at how small and light they were; in his hands, they felt no bigger than an American crow, but in flight their blaring voices and bold colors made them seem twice as large. They stared angrily through their bright red eyes at the pale, bearded ape who was clearly about to kill them — then, inexplicably, let them go.

Sean took his samples back to Canada, where he parsed them into their chemical components and tested them on wasps' nests at Nouragues the following year. But none of the chemicals had any more effect on the wasps than misting their nests with water, and months of intensive work in the lab and the forest led only to the conclusion that if the caracaras were producing a chemical repellent, it was very well hidden indeed. All he needed to rest his case, he thought, was to film the birds attacking a nest and show that the wasps were wisely absconding from an untenable position, not fleeing from a malodorous bird.

This was surprisingly difficult. The caracaras were raiding dozens of wasp nests every day, but guessing where and when they would strike was impossible. After an exhausting season of chasing them around the forest, Sean decided to bring the birds to him. He nailed a pair of two-by-fours to trees near the research station, set up two video cameras to keep an eye on them, and baited them with wasp nests he gathered at night while their inhabitants were sleeping (though he wore his bee helmet, just in case). Once he'd clamped the nests to this unique bird feeder, he recorded the red-throats' calls and broadcast them through a battery-powered guitar amp, hoping to draw them in.

By this time, however, the caracaras had become wary of Sean and his devices. They took several days to approach the feeder, but when they finally arrived their methods of attack were much as he'd expected: they poked and plucked at the nests with their beaks and talons until the wasps fled, then carried away the combs to eat at their leisure. The wasps, for their part, made reasonable choices: the smallest nests put up the least resistance, and their residents absconded almost as soon as the caracaras arrived. But the architects of larger nests, who'd invested more energy in building them, put more effort into their defense. The caracaras flinched and scratched at their faces as the wasps attacked, but they were rarely deterred for long; at one of the largest nests, a caracara who'd been chased away returned a few minutes later with a partner. The two birds attacked the nest in tandem until one of them rammed it with a power dive, knocking it to the ground, and video playback showed a squadron of wasps streaming out from the nest in a doomed but valiant effort to fend off their attacker in mid-air. Just as Sean had thought, red-throated caracaras weren't impervious to the wasps' defenses; they'd simply learned to overcome them with persistence and overwhelming force.

Being proved right was bittersweet. Sean's hopes of riding a wasp-repellent bird to fame had gone up in smoke — there would be no paper in *Nature,* no tenure-track position at a major university. But it was satisfying to see his hunches confirmed, and his efforts to learn more about the red-throats' lives had been amply rewarded. Early in his first field season, he'd discovered one of their nests, which was hidden two hundred feet above the ground in the wide, spiky platform of a tree-dwelling plant called a bromeliad. This was a surprise: bromeliads trap tiny pools of water in their stiff, whorled leaves, providing homes and breeding grounds for frogs and insects, but no bird had ever been found nesting in one. The station's technical director, Philippe Gaucher, helped Sean ascend to it on a line he lobbed into the canopy with a crossbow, and Sean cleared the lip of the bromeliad to find himself eye to eye with a startled young red-throated caracara. It sat in a small clearing in the bromeliad's heart, clad in its first coat of soft black down. Unlike the adults, the chick's bare face and throat were gray, its eyes a mellow hazel. But it wore the same fierce expression as its more colorful parents, and it gaped its beak at him, as if expecting a treat.

Sean was ecstatic. The chance to observe a

nest of red-throated caracaras — a scientific first — was too good to pass up, and Gaucher helped him mount a camera above the bromeliad, connected to a video recorder on the forest floor. To power the recorder, Sean had to lug a thirty-pound battery nearly a mile down a steep hill each day before sunrise, and back up again after dark to recharge it; and in the following weeks he ascended to the nest several more times to adjust the camera's lens, wearing a helmet against the talons of enraged caracaras who screamed and swooped at him. Even so, one still managed to draw blood from his ear.

All this effort yielded images no one had ever seen — an intimate portrait of the red-throats' home lives as they tended their growing chick — and though Sean tried to remain professionally detached, he couldn't help rooting for this fuzzy little dinosaur with wide eyes and a voracious appetite. It appeared to have six parents, who roosted in or near the nest at night and brought food to the chick every thirty minutes during the day. Sometimes as many as three crammed into the nest at once to groom the chick and feed it wasp combs loaded with protein-rich larvae; they also brought small yellow fruits, a snail, and dozens of millipedes, whose curled bodies littered the nest.

This last item was especially intriguing to a chemical ecologist, since millipedes ooze a noxious goo when disturbed and have very few natural predators. The adults held the millipedes up to the chick as if they were food, but the chick didn't show much interest, and Sean wondered if the birds might be using the many-legged arthropods for another purpose. Though the millipedes' strong-smelling secretions didn't have a noticeable effect on wasps (he checked), some monkeys and lemurs have been seen rubbing millipedes on their bodies, possibly to repel or kill skin parasites, and it seemed possible that the red-throats might be using them to protect their vulnerable chick from ticks and mosquitoes. It wasn't a wasp repellent, and it wasn't going to make anyone rich — but if it were true, it was a use of the forest's resources that approached a kind of technology.

There wasn't time, however, to stage the experiments that might prove it, and Sean reached the end of his fieldwork with a mixture of relief and regret. He'd refuted the wasp repellent hypothesis, but there was far more to learn about the birds, and his work had raised as many questions as it answered. DNA analysis would later confirm that the troop contained multiple males and multiple females — an odd social unit for a bird of prey, or any bird at all, and Sean wondered if the red-throats' unusual diet might have led them to a unique family structure. If an adult could eat an entire nest of wasps in one meal, raising even a single chick would require hundreds of additional raids, an effort that might be better suited to a team than a typical pair. Larger troops might also be able to control larger territories — and thus more food — but this meant some group members were giving up a chance to breed to care for someone else's kid. This kind of sacrifice, unusual in nature, pointed to the biggest mystery of all: Who *were* these birds to one another? Were they a nuclear family, with a senior pair assisted by offspring who might one day found troops of their own? Were they a set of pairs who'd banded together to share the burdens of child care? Or were there "pairs" within the group at all, in any conventional sense?

Sean had to let these questions go with great reluctance. He'd chased the red-throats for four summers, and would gladly have returned for more, but he'd collected enough data to finish his degree, and his funds were exhausted; for now, at least, the red-throats would keep the deeper secrets of their communal lives to themselves. Sean felt grateful to have spent so much time with them in a place where creatures he'd never even imagined had become his neighbors: curassows and dog-sized rodents called agoutis often passed him on the reserve's trails, like pedestrians on a city street. Among the privileged crew of European students and scientists at the research station, it was easy to feel he was part of a team exploring another planet — an illusion that was periodically shattered when haggard-looking gold prospectors from up-river appeared on the trails without warning, looking for a way out of the forest. They'd made the desperate choice to walk into the wilderness after running out of food or falling out with other miners, and they seemed very surprised to be alive.

In an emergency, Sean and I would stand a better chance than the lost miners of Nouragues if we headed west from the Rewa, where a narrow range of low mountains separated us from the Rupununi savanna, the golden island of open country we'd passed through on our way to the river. Unlike the clear-cuts that sprout along highways in the Amazon, the savanna is an artifact of geology: its thin, metallic soils, the remnants of ancient lake beds, are so unyielding that they support only grassland, and its gently rolling hills are home to cattle ranches, Amerindian villages, and creatures that are rare or absent in the deep forest. Giant anteaters, yellow-footed tortoises, and lizards the size of house cats roam its fields at dusk, and the feathery topknots of palms that live nowhere else on Earth line seasonal creeks that course through its hills like veins.

Like the Pampas of Hudson's youth, the

Rupununi wears different faces throughout the year, and in the late months of the dry season — the northern world's fall and winter — the smoke of wildfires summons crested caracaras, black vultures, and savanna hawks to feast on roasted insects and rodents. But from April to September, its namesake river swells with rain and overruns its banks, forming a shining wetland that briefly links the watersheds of the Amazon and the Essequibo. Aquatic travelers have used this ephemeral connection to travel between the two rivers for millions of years — including the leviathans called arapaimas, three-hundred-pound fish with flattened snouts and coats of shining red scales, as well as other unusual animals like lungfish, electric eels, and giant otters.

The most recent and consequential travelers to reach the Rupununi, however, are humans. Brian, Jose, and Rambo's ancestors arrived at least ten thousand years ago — about the same time the Sumerians were domesticating cattle in the Middle East — and many of the hill-sized boulders that erupt from the savanna's low hills bear enigmatic clusters of petroglyphs carved in a wild, abstract style. Their descendants live there still, hunting peccaries and agoutis, farming cassava, and fishing in the rivers. Though the forest has many resources for people with eyes to see them, the savanna's milder landscape is easier to live in, and its residents have enjoyed both for millennia, spending days beneath the trees and nights under the stars. Europeans didn't learn about the Rupununi's existence for more than a century after Columbus, but it swiftly colonized their imaginations, and English writers and adventurers have been drawn to it ever since.

One of the first to feel its pull was Walter Raleigh, a sometime favorite of Queen Elizabeth I. Raleigh, a poet and naval commander, believed that the forested uplands of the Guiana Shield concealed an Amerindian empire like the ones the Spanish had plundered in Peru and Mexico, and he proposed an expedition up the Orinoco River to claim its riches for England. The Orinoco empties into the Caribbean at the present-day border between Guyana and Venezuela, and its source, according to a dubious account Raleigh was keen to believe, lay in a mysterious highland lake called Parima.

On the shores of this lake, the tale went, sat a city called Manoa — a place so rich in precious metals that its ruler smeared his body each morning with animal fat and gold dust. Raleigh was sure this gilded king, also known as El Dorado, was a relative of the Inca emperors dethroned by Francisco Pizarro in Peru; the sack of Manoa, he argued, could be the windfall for England that Cuzco had been for Spain. Raleigh convinced his well-heeled patrons to fund an armed party to sail to the New World and attempt this proposed conquest — a wild scheme, in retrospect, that approached insanity. But it was hard to know what to believe about South America. Judging from Spain's improbable successes, it appeared to be overflowing with gold, and with defenseless people from whom it could be easily taken.

Raleigh's expedition was long, expensive, and fruitless. He and his men rowed up four hundred miles of the Orinoco and its tributaries in search of Manoa, wearing themselves to the bone and contending with the river's endemic crocodiles. They would almost certainly have died without the aid of Arawak people living along the river who fed and housed the deluded Englishmen, got them roaring drunk on cassava wine, and were relieved to hear that Raleigh despised the Spanish as much as they did. But they knew nothing about a mysterious lake. Raleigh finally halted at a series of rapids on the western edge of the shield, in a dreamlike landscape where slender waterfalls streamed from flat-topped mountains in long curtains of mist. He was sure that a golden city lay atop these mountains, but his boats could go no farther, and he returned to England with only a sack of mica-laden rocks and a sheaf of florid descriptions to offer his unimpressed creditors. As he faced them he was characteristically unbowed, insisting that his discoveries had equaled Pizarro's, and that gold lay in shining flakes on the riverbanks in the dry season; only bad weather, he said, had kept him from carrying it back as proof. "Guiana is a Countrey that hath yet her Maydenhead," he wrote, "never sackt, turned, nor wrought.

> The face of the earth hath not been torne, nor the vertue and salt of the soyle spent by manurance. The graves have not beene opened for gold, the mines not broken with sledges, nor their Images puld down out of their temples. It hath never been entred by any armie of strength, and never conquered or possesed by any Christian Prince.

He noted, moreover, that Guiana's astonishing wildlife would make it a royal park to end all royal parks. England's nobles liked hunting more than anything, and Raleigh clearly thought he might tempt them with a shooter's paradise. "There is no countrey," he claimed, "which yeeldeth more pleasure to the Inhabitants, either for these common delights of hunting, hawking, fishing, fowling, and the rest, than Guiana doth . . . it hath so many plaines, cleare rivers, and abundance of Pheasants, Partridges, Quailes, Rayles, Cranes, Herons, and all other fowle . . . eyther for chace or foode." He was especially awed by the bewildering variety of many-hued birds, "some carnation, some crimson, orenge tawny, purple, greene, watched, and of all other sorts, both simple and mixt . . . and it was unto us a great good-passing of the time to beholde them."

The gold was a fable, but the wildlife was not, and Guyana kept a peculiar hold on Raleigh for the rest of his life. Twenty years after his initial venture, Raleigh would return to the Orinoco and fail again, and a botched raid on a Spanish garrison in Venezuela during the trip led to a death sentence from Elizabeth's successor, James I, who suspected Raleigh of taking part in a conspiracy to supplant him. The legend of the golden city and its mysterious lake, however, proved much harder to kill, and European adventurers continued Raleigh's search for it for nearly two hundred years. After a while, the weight of many failed efforts almost gave its myth a perverse credence: Why would so many people look so hard, and at such great cost, for a place that didn't exist?

It fell to Alexander von Humboldt, the German polymath who inspired Darwin and other scientifically minded travelers, to finally write Lake Parima's epitaph. The lake continued to appear on maps long after its existence was disproved, and was still popping up as late as 1844 — but it had a tendency to migrate just past the edge of surveyed land. The rumor of it persisted, Humboldt argued, simply because people were loath to give it up, and he saw it as a monument to the power of human desire to resist all reason. Manoa and its golden king were "like a phantom that seemed to flee before the Spaniards, and to call on them unceasingly."

But "all fables," he noted, "have some real foundation," and he wondered if the legend's source might lie in the Rupununi savanna. It sits exactly where Raleigh was trying to go — east of the Orinoco, north of the Amazon — and when it swells with summer rains, it looks enough like a lake that it might have become one in the telling. "It is in the nature of man, wandering on the earth, to figure to himself happiness beyond the region which he knows," Humboldt mused, and El Dorado "disappeared by degrees from the domain of geography, and entered that of mythological fictions."

Mythological fictions have their uses, however. Even after Humboldt banished Manoa and El Dorado from the physical world, the forests and savannas of southern Guyana retained a special allure for British writers for another generation. They were a perfect setting: remote, little known, and full of beautiful and deadly creatures, a stage where Arthur Conan Doyle could place a lost world of flying dinosaurs and giant apes, and Evelyn Waugh could imagine a South American equivalent of Joseph Conrad's Congo.

Waugh's dark satire *A Handful of Dust* takes place in a remote savanna that strongly resembles the Rupununi, where a rich but foolish young Englishman travels up the Essequibo and falls prisoner to a sinister expatriate named Mr. Todd. Todd rescues the young man from certain death and takes him back to his compound, where he's styled himself as a lord among the Macushi and Wapishana like Kurtz in *Heart of Darkness*. At first Todd is a gracious and obliging host, but he slowly tightens his grip, and the young adventurer ends up forced to read the collected works of Charles Dickens aloud for the rest of his life.

Somewhere between Waugh's grim allegory and Conan Doyle's fantasies lies *Green Mansions*, William Henry Hudson's last novel. It's told in the voice of a vain young Venezuelan named Abel, who falls in love with the bird-girl Rima, the last survivor of a tribe of unknown origin. Hudson presents Rima as a sort of terrestrial mermaid: she has a psychic connection to all the forest's creatures and wears a flowing dress of spiders' silk, and though she speaks Spanish, her preferred language is a musical confection of chirps and whistles. Abel is besotted with her from the moment he hears her sing, and his determination to make her his wife leads to her doom.

No book is quite like *Green Mansions*, but

it feels slightly disingenuous to call it a lost classic. Abel is as improbably resourceful as a one-man Swiss Family Robinson — at one point, he whips up a guitar from scratch — and Rima is playful, flirtatious, rude, sulky, valiant, and helpless, depending on the demands of the plot. But the real romance of the book is between Hudson and the forests he would never see, and its atmosphere of unrequited longing gives it an uncanny power. Readers in Britain, where *Green Mansions* was published to middling reviews in 1904, didn't know what to make of it, but the novel was a surprise hit twelve years later in the United States, perhaps because a North American audience was nearer in time and space to the wilder landscapes of their own continent. The book's late success gave Hudson a steady flow of royalties in his last years, and in a grateful letter to his American publisher he compared it to "seeing a dead thing come to life again."

He was in a much darker frame of mind when he wrote it. Hudson's first novel, *The Purple Land,* had been savaged as "a vulgar farrago of repulsive nonsense," and in *Green Mansions* he sketched an unflattering self-portrait in Abel, who dreams of making hay from his misfortunes by writing a memoir. Like Hudson, Abel lives in self-imposed exile, and his narrative opens with his escape from

Caracas, where he'd joined an ill-fated attempt to overthrow the government. Abel flees up the Orinoco to escape among its "countless unmapped rivers and trackless forests," and holes up to write in a mosquito-infested trading post run by an unscrupulous polygamist named Don Panta, who does a brisk business selling liquor to Amerindians. Abel makes steady progress on his manuscript until the rainy season reduces it to a sodden pulp, and Don Panta finds him sitting on the floor of his leaky hut, sunk in gloom.

In answer to his anxious inquiries I pointed to the pulpy mass on the mud floor; he turned it over with his foot, and then, bursting into a loud laugh, kicked it out, remarking that he had mistaken the object for some unknown reptile that had crawled in out of the rain. He affected to be astonished that I should regret its loss. It was all a true narrative, he exclaimed; if I wished to write a book for the stay-at-homes to read, I could easily invent a thousand lies more entertaining than any real experiences.

Don Panta suggests that if Abel wishes to go on living, he should travel upriver to the southern highlands, where he can nurse his melancholy in a country free from politics and malaria. "If you want quinine while you are there," Panta says, "smell the wind when it blows from the south-west, and you will inhale it into your system, fresh from the forest." Abel takes his advice, and after a few weeks in the savanna feels recovered enough to take a long walk through its "scattered tussocks of sere, hair-like grass" for a view of a distant peak called Ytaioa. Atop a stony ridge, he makes a startling discovery: the savanna lies on the doorstep of another world.

The sterile ground extended only about a mile and a quarter on the further side, and was succeeded by a forest . . . extending from the foot of Ytaioa on the north to a low range of rocky hills on the south. From the wooded basin long narrow strips of forest ran out in various directions like the arms of an octopus, one pair embracing the slopes of Ytaioa, another much broader belt extending along a valley which cut through the ridge of hills on the south side at right angles and was lost to sight beyond; far away in the west and south and north distant mountains appeared, not in regular ranges, but in groups or singly, or looking like banked-up clouds on the horizon.

Hudson was almost certainly describing the Rupununi. Ytaioa is nearly identical to a real mountain called Makarapan, visible from every part of the savanna, and though it's been more than a century since Hudson wrote *Green Mansions,* the Rupununi is still much as he pictured it: a bright oculus of grassland embraced by a forest as wide as the sea. It's this forest where Abel meets Rima — and it was this forest I'd entered with Sean, Jose, Rambo, and Brian, hoping to meet the bush auntie-man.

14
SWEET FISHES TO EAT

"Watch he," said Brian. It was midday, and we stood on the shoe-sucking edge of a stinking, mustard-yellow pond, about twenty feet across: all that remained of one of the Rewa's former meanders at the end of the dry season. Brian pointed toward the center of the pond with his cutlass, where a swirl of lurid yellow scum was churning and bubbling — a sign of something big below the surface, maybe a large caiman. Maybe something else.

The rest of the pond's comma-shaped opening in the forest had dried to a cracked mud flat fringed with tall grass and the tracks of wood storks, who'd kept a grim vigil as the dwindling pond starved its residents of oxygen. The storks fled when we emerged from the trees, opening their eight-foot wings and ascending in a stately spiral. I counted twenty-two, and couldn't help feeling we'd arrived at the end of a grand and solemn performance. They were like feathered men in stilts and masks drawn up on invisible strings, and their bald, wizened heads looked almost human.

The pond was a deathly place even without an audience of silent scavengers. It smelled of rot, and the forest around it was utterly still except for an oblivious family of jacanas — gracile, long-toed wading birds who chased and squeaked at one another at the pond's far end. Brian probed thoughtfully in the dirt with a stick, and a shrieking phalanx of blue-and-gold macaws flew above us. Then a huge, green, gulping mouth broke the surface of the pond. It rolled and vanished with a great splash, trailing a long, red-scaled body like a dragon, and it seemed as impossible as it was undeniable: an arapaima, the largest scaled freshwater fish on Earth, was lying before us in a giant puddle. The scum closed over its wake, and Brian gazed after it wistfully.

"Now, that is a sweet fish to eat," he said.

Oddly enough, this was exactly where you'd expect to find one. During the wet season, the Rewa swells and adjusts its channel, seeking the fastest route through shifting banks of mud and sand, undermining trees until they groan and collapse. Traces of its earlier selves lie in a broken chain of oxbow lakes that parallel its present course, and the oldest lie miles from its current banks, filled with black caimans and giant lilies. Younger oxbows reconnect to the river in the rainy season, and arapaimas use these seasonal pools as nurseries, a place to keep their young safe from predators that lurk in the main channel of the river. That a twelve-foot-long fish could live for weeks in a stagnant pond might seem unlikely, but arapaimas can breathe air through lung-like tissues in their swim bladders, and as the ripples of the giant's splash subsided, two smaller green mouths rose, gulped air, and vanished with the same corkscrewing motion, the last survivors of this year's brood. They were probably too big for the storks, but if the pond shrank any further, they'd risk the attention of more fearsome hunters: caimans, jaguars, humans.

Arapaimas were plentiful in the Rewa until a few decades ago, when an armada of trappers came up from Brazil to slaughter them. Along with the fishes' long, flayed bodies, Rewa villagers saw the strangers hauling away braces of macaws, stacks of river turtles, and the man-sized pelts of giant otters — a scene like the ones that attended European fur trappers in North America in the 1700s, or whalers and sealers in the sub-Antarctic a century later. The government of Guyana declared the Rewa off-limits to commercial fishing and imposed a hefty fine for killing arapaimas, but the damage was done: the giant fish are cautious, territorial creatures, and they've been slow to return. In recent decades they've become scarce in most of their former range in the Amazon and Essequibo basins, caught between humans' appetite for their succulent flesh and a black-market value that grows as their numbers decline. For the giant in the shrunken oxbow, this year's gamble was almost up, and its odds didn't look good: if the pond shrank any more, its back and flanks would emerge, and predators would close in.

Sean liked it here. "If you staked this place out at night," he said, "you'd see a *lot* of animals." Caimans and anacondas come up from the river to forage in the oxbows in the dry season, as do jaguars, which look like low-slung leopards but hunt like tigers, stalking their prey along — and sometimes in — tropical rivers. Jaguars can weigh three hundred pounds, and though they're especially fond of the pig-sized rodents called capybaras, they'd happily take a beached arapaima. As the pond settled, I realized that one could very well be watching us from the forest's edge, and on the walk back to the boat I stayed close behind Rambo, who swung his cutlass absently at the tall grass, whistling through his teeth.

It was our second week on the Rewa, and we still hadn't seen a red-throated caracara. Once or twice Sean thought he'd heard them but couldn't be sure — though there'd been more than enough for me to absorb even without them. Every bend of the river revealed something new, from shoals of black piranhas to the loud, playful screams of macaws trying to knock one another off a high branch. Gull-sized terns with huge yellow bills dive-bombed us as we passed the sandbars where they nested, repeating a shrill, two-note cry: *Go away, go away, go away.*

I could hardly blame them. Our roaring boats shattered the peace of the river, and each time Rambo cut the motor my ears rang faintly in the silence. Rambo stood at the outboard for hours on end, hugging the twisting channel while Jose pointed out hidden obstructions from the bow, and the sun swung across the horizon like a pendulum, as if we weren't traveling upstream so much as spiraling inward. In a few places we had to jump out and push the boat over sunken trees; once, climbing back in, I looked down to see the pale disk of a stingray looming up through the water like a death's head.

We hadn't entered the forest yet on foot, but what I could see from the river wasn't the majestic, open gallery of Hudson's imagination. Above the high walls of the banks, the trees were mostly obscured behind curtains of vines and lianas, and even where I could distinguish individual trees I couldn't recognize them: there were no pines, oaks, or cedars. Low shrubs perched atop sandbars that flooded in the summer, and rows of slim, thorn-studded trees called long johns sprouted behind them, their upturned branches draped with the basket-shaped nests of gaudy birds called oropendolas, who sometimes follow troops of bush auntie-men.

Sean pointed out a laughing falcon on a snag above the river, and a bat falcon catching dragonflies looked like a pint-sized peregrine, its white collar glowing in the late sun. But the Rewa's most obvious avian residents were its fishing birds: kingfishers and herons, gull-winged ospreys, black skimmers and swallow-tailed kites, whose parabolic flight was almost absurdly graceful. Strangest of all were the sinuous relatives of cormorants called anhingas or snakebirds, which pace along the river bottom spearing fish on needle-sharp bills. They leaped from low branches into the water at our approach, opening their wings as they dove, and disappeared as if they had never existed. But I also saw them circling high above us, like ravens with long skinny necks, and envied their ability to travel seamlessly between worlds.

Mammals were a different story. At first they were rarely more than a distant shaking of leaves or a line of fresh tracks in the sand, but they grew less wary as we ascended the river. Just upstream of the arapaima's pond we saw a giant otter gripping a catfish in its front paws and devouring it like a burrito, and an hour later we surprised a puma lounging on a sandbar, which raised its head and eyed us coolly. Jose turned to me, beaming; the night before, he'd told me how one had nearly killed his grandfather.

That afternoon we hauled out at Kwitaro Backbone, a sandbank with a commanding view of a wide bend in the river. Brian said that he'd once seen a fishing party here from what he called the "deep south," whose eight dugout canoes carried everything they needed for a monthlong trip, including dogs and children — an ancient scene that still belongs to the present. "Sixty miles," he said, a note of pride in his voice. "With no motor."

We made camp among soaring trees braced by the curved fins of buttress roots while Brian took one of the boats upstream on a mysterious errand, raising a flurry of swallows from the opposite bank. They wheeled and darted above the river while Jose set up a makeshift kitchen, shading his bins of supplies and portable stove with a tarp and slinging his hammock from the low branches of a mango tree. In less than an hour it looked like a place he could live comfortably for weeks. He was lying in the hammock with one leg dangling, snoring lightly, when Brian returned and set a pale, softball-sized object on the table: the skull of a giant river turtle.

"Somebody catch he and eat he," he said.

Jose stirred. "Camoodi hide, Uncle Brian?" he asked.

"Camoodi hide, boy," Brian replied. He sat in a folding chair, took off his cap, and rubbed his face with both hands. "There was an anaconda here," he explained. "A big one. Fifteen, sixteen feet. But I hear someone shot him with an arrow." He paused uncomfortably, as if deciding whether to say more; and I thought about the broken, black-fletched arrow I found just inside the forest, like the ones we saw in the dugout below Crash Water.

"Maybe he is resting," Jose suggested.

"I don't think so," said Brian.

I bent to tie my shoe and saw a large black ant lurching across it with six smaller ants clinging to its legs, biting at its joints while their giant victim flailed. I dislodged them with a twig, then saw I'd been watching a melee in a much bigger battle: all across the bank, hundreds of staggering ants were being mauled by the same tiny assailants.

Cephalotes," said Sean, arriving with his bag. "Turtle ants. Those are the big ones. The little ones are probably spraying them with horrible chemicals." He scooped up one of the ants in his palm and sniffed at it.

"No caracara, Sean?" asked Jose.

"No caracara," said Sean, taking a seat beside me. "But this is a healthy forest. There should be some big spiders in here."

I didn't love the sound of that, but Sean insisted he could teach me to love them. The previous night he'd showed me the gleaming legs of a pink-toed tarantula, hiding in the bark of a fig tree like a crab in a crevice of rock. "There's a lot we don't know about tarantulas," he said, tickling its toes with a blade of grass. "This might even be a new species." The pink-toe didn't budge, but at the base of the tree I found its molted skin, light as air and surprisingly colorful, with an iridescent green patina and a flush of red at the base of its curved fangs. What an ordeal it must be, I thought — and what a relief — to slough off the outside of your body like a scab. What would it feel like, on the first night after a molt, as your new skin hardened in the cool air?

Brian perked up at the mention of spiders. "When you see the *Theraphosa,*" he said, smiling broadly, "now, that is a *beautiful* spider to see."

It wasn't the word I'd have chosen. *Theraphosa blondi,* the Goliath birdeater, is the largest spider on Earth, and a specialty of the Guiana Shield. It doesn't have any stripes, spots, or iridescence, but what it lacks in ornament, it makes up for in bulk: female birdeaters can weigh half a pound, and their legs can span eleven inches or more. Like most tarantulas, birdeaters lead uneventful lives; they spend most of their time hidden in a burrow from which they ambush insects, lizards, rodents, and (rarely) birds that disturb silken tripwires. Females seldom wander, but males go on seasonal walkabouts to find mates, who often kill and eat them after sex. Part of me wanted to see one, in the same way Hudson longed to peer inside the caranchos' nest; another part was quite happy not to.

"You will see him," Brian said. "A few days from here."

Sean, seeing the look on my face, leaped to the spider's defense, urging me to remember that tarantulas are afraid of almost everything, since mammals and birds love to eat them. He started to tell a story about a bird-eater he'd found in a hollow tree in French Guiana but stopped mid-sentence, listening.

"You hear 'em distance?" asked Jose.

"No," said Sean, grabbing his bag. "Close!"

He charged up the bank to a rise with the best view of the river, and I found him a moment later fiddling with a small, battery-powered speaker. He held the speaker up and away from his body and played the calls of red-throated caracaras he recorded at Nouragues: a chorus of thin, descending sirens, building to an explosion of *ka-ka-KAAAAOOO*s. The speaker couldn't muster much volume, but the evening choir of frogs and insects hadn't cranked up yet, and Sean hoped the prospect of a scream-off with rivals might draw the birds in. He stared at the far side of the river, as if willing them to appear,

301

while a solitary cicada whined and subsided. Nothing. He played the call again.

"I heard them," he said, a little sheepishly. "I did."

A black, crow-like bird appeared above the trees on the opposite bank and circled above us. It had a bare yellow face and yellow legs, and everything about it said caracara, from the long fingers of its primaries to the indignant little screams it uttered as it flew. But it wasn't a bush auntie-man. It was a black caracara — a shy relative of yellow-headed caracaras that generally avoids people. It swooped close enough for me to see how the skin of its face shaded to deep orange around its eyes, which were fixed on me, and it struck me that of all the animals we'd seen, it was the first to approach us instead of running or flying away. The caracara soared above Jose's kitchen and careened over the bank, revealing a thick white band across the base of its tail, and a moment later it returned with two more black caracaras in tow. One had a lighter face and streaks of brownish gray in its plumage: a fledgling. Were they a family? They circled above our camp, flapping and screaming, and I had the distinct feeling they were casing the joint. Sean set down his speaker and took up his camera, squeezing off a few shots before the trio vanished behind a screen of trees on the far side of the river.

"That was *awesome,*" he said. He'd never seen one before. Black caracaras are thought to be abundant, but they've attracted even less scientific attention than red-throats; we know they exist, and that's about it. They're usually seen combing the edges of tropical rivers for edible flotsam, like Johnny rooks on the beaches of the Falklands, but there's little written about them beyond a description of a single nest and a few notes about their diet. Besides carrion, black caracaras have been seen eating termites, fish, palm fruits, and the eggs of birds and turtles, and a German ornithologist named Helmut Sick reported a curious alliance with tapirs — chunky, pig-like forest animals with a snuffling proboscis like a stunted version of an elephant's trunk. Tapirs, Sick wrote, give a high-pitched call that seems to attract the caracaras, then roll over like dogs and offer their taut, round bellies for tick removal. It was an unusual pairing, but it fit a familiar pattern: from the caranchos that trailed gauchos across the Pampas to the yellow-heads attending the sloth in Venezuela, caracaras excel at finding partners in their search for food. I told Sean I was surprised that no one had followed up on this story, and he smiled ruefully.

"You should try insects," he said. "They do all kinds of amazing shit, and nobody cares."

We stood listening as shadows lengthened and light yellowed on the tall trees across the river. A pair of red-and-green macaws shooed a black vulture off a high branch with a frenzy of flapping and screaming, then settled to groom each other's neck feathers with their massive bills, shrieking tenderly at half their usual volume. I thought of Len Hill chasing Birdland's macaws around the Cotswolds — a landscape that seemed dull and plain compared to the Rewa — and wondered if these birds' lives were more vivid or enjoyable than the life of Juno, who bounced happily in Len's palm and slept in his manor house. Life in what we call the wild might look like freedom, but it comes with its own constraints; and who can say where animals' desires might lead them, if those constraints were removed?

Even so, it was hard not to envy the macaws. They tended to each other like true friends, a precious thing in a place where intense and deadly competition seemed to be the rule, and they might have been partners for decades. After a few minutes' rest, they flew off to settle in an evening roost, and the trills and whistles of smaller parrots swelled in their absence. Sean tapped me on the shoulder and pointed to the lanky black shape of a spider monkey, swimming through the crowns of trees half the height of the Flatiron Building. She was hooting softly as she went, as if humming to herself, and stuffing her mouth with flowers.

As we watched her, an eerie sound rose from the forest: a deep, resonant roaring, almost like the throat singing of Tibetan monks. It surged and faded, modulating gently in pitch, suggesting scenes beyond the scale of human life: mountains falling into the sea, the Earth spinning in space. I couldn't imagine an animal capable of making it, and it certainly wasn't the wind.

"Howlers," said Sean, shouldering his bag. "When you're close, you can hear all kinds of weird details in their calls."

The chanting of howler monkeys was a sound William Henry Hudson longed to hear, and he gave it a featured role in *Green Mansions*. When Abel enters Rima's forest for the first time, he strolls for hours through its open understory and lies on his back to gaze into its upper branches, as his author loved to do at Savernake, and Hudson gave himself license to combine his reveries with a dash of English cathedrals. "What a roof was that above my head!" Abel exults.

Here Nature is unapproachable with her green, airy canopy, a sun-impregnated cloud — cloud above cloud; and though the highest may be unreached by the eye, the beams yet filter through, illuming the wide spaces beneath — chamber succeeded by chamber, each with its own special lights and shadows.

But the forest's crowning glory is Rima, who beguiles Abel not with sight but sound. He hears her voice for days before he sees her — "a low strain of exquisite bird-melody, wonderfully pure and expressive" — and she leads him on a tour of the forest's sonic wonders before she reveals herself, including the musical chirping of tree frogs, which Abel compares to "a tribe of fairy-like troubadour monkeys," and the cries of birds Hudson would never hear: "the distant wailing calls of maam and duraquara, the quick whistle of cotingas; and strange throbbing and thrilling sounds, as of pygmies beating on metallic drums, of the skulking pitta-thrushes." Most of Hudson's readers would have drawn a blank at the mention of a cotinga or a pitta-thrush, but their names have an incantatory power, and the music of their voices was as vivid a fantasy for him as the hidden vaults of the forest canopy.

As a grand finale, Rima lures Abel to a place where hundreds of howlers break out in chorus at once, and he dives to the ground in fright, expecting to be devoured by "a pack of those swift-footed, unspeakably terrible hunting-leopards, from which every living thing in the forest flies with shrieks of consternation, or else falls paralysed in their path." When Abel discovers that the sound is a choir of monkeys, he salvages what he can of his pride: the howlers, he protests, "would outroar the mightiest lion that ever woke the echoes of an African wilderness."

Red-throated caracaras go to similar lengths to make themselves heard. When Sean caught and banded them in French Guiana, they'd screamed with such force that his ears rang, and their scientific name, *Ibycter americanus,* is a nod to their voices; *Ibycter* is a Cretan word for a soldier who starts a war chant. But we didn't hear any more of their cries at Kwitaro Backbone, even after the howlers' chorus receded, and Sean shrugged helplessly.

The deep greens of afternoon shaded into the blues of early evening, and we found Jose roasting a pumpkin in his kitchen, fresh from his third bath of the day and wearing a sweatshirt emblazoned with the words THE OPRAH WINFREY SHOW. He put a pot of rice on the stove while Rambo sat in a camp chair, contemplating the sky. Brian announced that it was time for us to catch our dinner, and we headed down to the boat to try our hand at fishing in the Rewa.

"First fish, good or bad, gonna be piranha," Rambo warned, as Brian paddled us into the current. Rambo disdained fishing rods, and it was a pleasure to watch him twirl a line above his head and drop a hook anywhere he liked.

Then it was our turn, and Sean's first throw arced out beautifully. Mine was ungraceful but adequate, and my hook had barely landed when I felt a powerful bite. I pulled against a firm, steady pressure, and had just begun to wonder if I'd hooked a branch when a shining black piranha flopped into my lap.

It was larger than I'd imagined, a rhomboid fish about a foot long and almost as tall. It was also very beautiful — not black at all, but a deep blue-gray that shaded through forest green to its silver belly, with eyes as red as the bush auntie-man's. I held its body while Rambo pulled the hook from its jaws, whose rows of triangular teeth were impressive but not sinister. A slight underbite gave it a boxer's pout, and though it clearly meant business, it was hard to take seriously as a man-eating menace.

Brian agreed. "Most people bitten by piranha," he said, "are bitten in the boat." I pitched it overboard, feeling sorry to have bothered it. A few seconds later, Sean felt a bite and pulled harder than I did, his face reddening with the struggle, and when he reached the end of his line he was eye to eye with a gleaming, whiskered fish as long as his arm.

"Tiger catfish!" Rambo announced.

A labyrinth of black and white stripes decorated its coppery skin, and its sloped head was nearly a third of its length, with a mouth like a vacuum nozzle and six-inch barbels. Brian freed Sean's hook and dropped the catfish into the boat, where it lay grunting mournfully until he whacked it with the blunt side of his cutlass. A few minutes later Rambo pulled in a paiara, or vampire fish, which surged out of the water as if spoiling for a fight. Its sleek body, clad in fine silver-blue scales, was attached to a head with staring eyes and a mouth full of long teeth. Two canine-like sabers projected from its lower jaw, and everything about it suggested a life of swift, merciless attack. Rambo posed with it for a moment, holding its tail in one hand and opening its jaws with the other, and I realized that this was what fishing used to be like: easy. In fifteen minutes we'd caught enough to feed us for the next two days. Brian paddled us back to shore, where Rambo presented the fish to Jose, and after we ate, he mounted the vampire's head on a stake at the river's edge, where the reflective coating of its eyes glowed in the light of our headlamps.

"For the caracara," Jose said.

The following day, we finally entered the forest. The morning was overcast and cool, the air so heavy with vapor that my breath hung above me in a cloud when I woke. I went down to the kitchen, and found Sean examining an inch-long black ant on his wrist.

"Dinoponera," he said, setting it down gently in the sand. "Female. Probably has a very painful sting." Jose had been awake since well before dawn, cooking strips of fried dough we dipped in killer bees' honey. I put a drop on my finger and watched three stubby, stingless bees alight and drink it away while Sean looked on with interest.

"Those are the ones that eat meat," he said.

Before we left camp, Rambo caught another vampire fish and left it in the boat to use for bait, and I studied its leering face while we motored upriver to a place where a fallen tree formed a ramp into the forest.

"This is the way to the caracara factory," said Brian, pushing a screen of vines aside with his cutlass, and we followed him into a dark thicket where *Green Mansions'* airy paradise was nowhere to be seen. Every surface was slick with last night's rain, and an ankle-deep carpet of rotting leaves gave off an autumnal smell. Jose lagged behind us while Rambo and Brian forged ahead, following a "line" — a faint series of cut branches and missing swatches of bark that meant someone had come this way before. The line wound through the forest, veering and twisting so often that Brian lost it twice, and I started to feel uneasy; we didn't have a compass or a map, and I'd grown up with stories of people who'd stepped off the Appalachian Trail and wandered to their deaths.

"This line cutter was a real bush Indian," Brian said, as we retraced our steps a third time. "He cut it with GPS." He tapped his temple with his index finger. "But his GPS is in here."

Line or no line, Brian seemed perfectly at ease, and watching him stride through the forest eased my fears about deadly snakes and giant spiders. He slashed at the undergrowth with casual precision, lopping off the crowns of saplings, and pointing out useful plants: a vine whose sap could stun fish, a tree whose thin bark made perfect cigarette papers. He identified larger trees by paring off a slice of bark with his cutlass and sniffing it, and at one point he handed me a crescent of pale green wood whose scent reminded me strongly and pleasantly of an ex-girlfriend. When I said so, I made Brian laugh for the first and only time.

Other scents pooled in the still air, exhaled by plants or left behind by animals, and I wished Hudson could have come here to indulge his "smelling hunger." Some were unaccountably familiar — guano, magnolia, even maple syrup — but I wondered what I was missing, since our sense of smell is feeble compared to most mammals. Many forest animals rely more on their noses than their eyes, and for good reason: the chemical world never sleeps, but the visible world is fickle. Even at midday the separate trunks of saplings and low palms collapsed into an ornate and inscrutable plane, like Henri Rousseau's paintings of twisted palms and hidden leopards, and we walked in silence behind the rhythmic smack of Brian's cutlass. The line took us past a perfectly round socket in the ground where a palm tree had rotted away, and we sloshed through a hollow where a herd of collared peccaries had bedded down — furry, porcine creatures who spend their days rooting for fungus, tubers, worms, and frogs. The oval depressions left by their bodies were dusted with the curled green petals of bat-pollinated flowers. I couldn't see a caracara anywhere, and was about to suggest we turn back when a loud, rough cackle sounded above us, followed by a set of pinched yodels, like a rusty gate swinging in the wind. I looked up through fogged glasses at the silhouette of a large, black bird on a high branch, and as it turned its head I saw a splash of red at its throat.

"Spix's guan!" called Rambo.

I was disappointed, but he was right. Guans are odd South American fowl with absurdly decorated heads — one rare species even sports a single red horn, like a cross between a goose and a unicorn. This one wanted us to know we weren't welcome in its home, and repeated its raucous alarm until we were well out of sight.

Sean was quiet at first, but the forest

seemed to energize him, and after an hour we were deep in a pleasantly one-sided conversation about taking a pair of orphaned crows to sea (they loved it), the chemistry and properties of honeybee venom (150 stings can kill most people), and the pink figs scattered on the forest floor that lace themselves with a powerful hallucinogen. But he was most excited when the line crossed a raiding party of army ants — a dense, trembling rivulet of orange-red bodies. They looked overcaffeinated and intent, following scented trails laid down by their sisters at the head of the column.

"Eciton hamatum," Sean said, bending down for a closer look. "If you're a wasp, these guys are the bane of your existence." The ants' orderly procession was mesmerizing, and we watched them overwhelm a tribe of smaller ground-nesting ants and carry off their young in triumph. As the main column pressed forward, a parallel stream of workers carried the spoils back to their bivouac, a fortress built from their own living bodies, where a queen and thousands of hungry larvae waited to be fed. Soldier ants patrolling the column were twice the size of their sisters, with grotesquely swollen heads and long mandibles, but Sean said that the smaller workers do nearly all the scouting, foraging, and defense — as I learned when a few found their way into my shoes. Their bites were more surprising than

painful, but they had the intended effect, and I backed away.

Few animals bother to resist army ants. Almost none eat them. Like wasps, each army ant species has its own culture and preferred diet, and they've been terrorizing the residents of tropical forests since the Jurassic. They're as feared in real life as Hudson's imaginary "hunting-leopards," and creatures of all sizes drop everything and run when they see (or smell) them coming. The stream of panicked spiders, scorpions, cockroaches, centipedes, and lizards fleeing the ants, in turn, provides a feast for predatory songbirds who specialize in consuming refugees — not unlike the chimango caracaras Hudson saw chasing half-scorched rodents from wildfires in the Pampas.

After another hour we paused to rest and wait for Jose, though I couldn't see a surface I'd feel comfortable leaning against, and lying on my back like Abel to gaze at the heavens was out of the question. Rambo idly trimmed the trees around us with his cutlass while Sean examined a leathery mushroom nearly three feet across, and my ears filled with the whine of mosquitoes and the metallic lowing of distant calfbirds. Calfbirds are among the world's strangest birds, with featherless blue heads encircled by a ruff of orange feathers, and hearing their voices was like hearing a whale at sea: it was thrilling just to know they were there.

We were about to start off again when Jose appeared, moving at a thoughtful pace; he'd stopped to fashion a new strap for his backpack from a strip of bark. Another guan called above our heads, and a thin chorus of descending cries answered it from somewhere ahead of us. It took me a moment to recognize it as the same sound I'd heard from Sean's speaker the day before.

"*There* we go," he said, unzipping his bag.

This time it was Brian who ran, vanishing into the undergrowth like an anhinga diving into the river, and I hung back with Jose and Rambo while Sean played his recording at top volume. The caracaras called again, but from even farther away, and Sean looked slightly defeated. "If they did two sets of calls and then nothing," he said, "they're probably just sitting and preening." He scanned the canopy while we waited for Brian to return, and after several long minutes we abandoned the line, with Rambo leading the way. The tangle of vines and saplings grew even thicker, and we passed beneath a group of birds called screaming pihas, whose small bodies are dwarfed by the power of their mighty, swooping cries. When we left them behind we heard the caracaras again, much closer this time — and then a set of three sharp booms.

"The *hell*?" whispered Sean.

I had the same thought: shotguns. We

hadn't seen any other people along the river, but anyone we met here probably wouldn't be pleased to see us. The Rewa would be a tough but plausible route for smuggling contraband from northern Brazil to the Caribbean, and a glance at Jose and Rambo wasn't reassuring; they were frozen, staring toward the sound with narrowed eyes. But after three more booms they relaxed: it was Brian, drumming on the roots of a tree. We found him a few minutes later at the base of an enormous fig, looking philosophical. The caracaras were here, he said, but when they saw him they screamed and flew off.

"Bush auntie-man get away," he declared.

An hour later, we emerged into the warm light of the riverbank, beside a *Hevea* tree crosshatched with century-old scars from the days of the rubber trade. The open sky was a welcome change, but I couldn't shake a sense that we were being followed, and Rambo's paiara had vanished from the boat. The likely thief was waiting for us back at Kwitaro Backbone, where Jose's prediction had come true: a black caracara was perched on the impaled head of the vampire fish, tearing away beakfuls of flesh. It lifted its head and stared as we approached, wearing the suspicious-but-interested expression of every caracara on Earth, then returned to its dinner, pausing now and again to look up and scream.

"Sometimes people scream like this when

they happy," Jose observed. "Sometimes when they crying."

I couldn't help liking this plucky little scavenger, with its widow's peak of black feathers. It seemed like the kind of bird the Addams family would keep as a pet. I almost felt sorry for it when a pair of swallows swooped at its head, forcing it to duck and wobble; under other circumstances, the caracara might have been after their eggs or chicks. But today it was preoccupied with the long-toothed monster at its feet, and it teetered on its grisly perch, glared at its tormentors, and flew off calling peevishly.

Rambo beached the boat, and we ascended the bank to find that Jose's kitchen had been ransacked by vultures. They'd gotten into the leftover porridge, scattered packets of tea across the ground, and kicked over the chairs. I wasn't surprised; unlike the threatened vultures of Africa, black vultures have tied their fortunes to ours. They're increasingly common at roadsides, farms, and garbage dumps throughout the Americas, and though we were a long way from a landfill, the principle here was the same: where there are people, there will be food.

The black caracara seemed less certain about us. It didn't have the vultures' size or strength on its side, but it did have charm, and the next morning as we broke camp it came to visit us again, announcing its arrival

317

in its small, strident voice.

"I think he wants more fish," said Sean, and Jose humored him by setting out a buffet of fish heads and tinned corn on the shore. The caracara landed, took a few nibbles, flew away, and returned with its partners in tow. The three birds were pacing around the feast as our boats pulled away, taking furtive bites and screaming with the same excitement as Evita with her string, while the vampire's skull dangled above them like a trophy.

Above Kwitaro Backbone the Rewa grew narrower and darker, and its animals more abundant; there were more macaws, more caimans, and more tracks in the sand — even the deep, rounded prints of a jaguar. A long-tailed hummingbird with a shining red breast buzzed us near a brake of wild guava, and Rambo eased back on the throttle to let a capybara climb out of the river. She stood on the bank and fixed us with her large, liquid eyes as we passed, her placid expression betrayed by a tremor in her hind legs.

As we approached the waterfalls that marked the end of the lower Rewa, we paused to admire the most incredible feat of animal architecture I'd ever seen: a tree draped with the woven nests of birds called red-rumped caciques. We'd seen caciques' hanging villages before, but these nests were clustered around a peculiar cylinder, about five feet long, like thatched huts around a granary. The cylinder was a deep, ruddy brown, and so perfectly round that it looked man-made.

Sean warned Rambo not to get too close. "That's *Polybia liliacea*," he said. "Really aggressive social wasps." He took pictures while I admired the paper walls of the wasps' citadel, striped in alternating ribbons of cinnamon, rufous, and chestnut brown, and studded with thousands of small black wasps — an army of defenders poised to take all comers. It was hard to believe that creatures so tiny could build a structure of such size and perfection, or that it could support its own weight without collapsing into the river.

"Now look to the left," said Sean, "on the trunk of the tree. You see that thing that looks like a stalactite?" Below the nests of the wasps and caciques was a tumor-like lump the same shade of gray as the tree's bark, about two feet long. "That's an *Azteca* nest," he continued. "There are millions of ants in it. The wasps are probably associating with them on purpose."

We drifted close enough to the hanging metropolis to attract the wasps' attention, but they held fast to their nest, as if sensing that we weren't a threat. We certainly weren't their most dreaded enemies; army ants also feed on wasp larvae, and wasps live in such fear of them that the scent of a single army ant worker can make some wasps abandon their nests. Building their fortress in a tree was a safer bet than building underground, where it's easier for ants to sniff them out — but army ants can climb, too, and the species we'd seen in the forest, *Eciton hamatum,* often pillages wasps' nests in the canopy.

This, Sean explained, is where the *Azteca* ants come in. They're only a tenth the size of army ants, but in battle they can overwhelm them with waves of suicidal defenders, who pin down the army ants and smear them with caustic chemicals from vents in their abdomens. Army ants can defeat *Azteca* colonies in a protracted struggle, but they rarely bother with prey that takes too much work to subdue — there are plenty of easier victims — and usually leave *Azteca* nests alone. For the wasps, the benefit of living above these fierce little ants was obvious: the ants protected them from a ground invasion. The wasps, in turn, reciprocated with air cover, driving away predators like anteaters and woodpeckers that might consider an *Azteca* nest a tasty snack. They also worked on behalf of the caciques, warding off snakes and parasitic flies that deposit flesh-eating larvae on the birds' nestlings.

Whether the wasps draw any benefit from the birds, however, is something of a mystery, though Sean had a theory: the caciques might deter bush auntie-men. Most tropical wasps artfully conceal their nests from prying eyes, and they certainly aren't doing that to evade army ants, which are virtually blind. Sean had calculated that the troop of red-throats he followed at Nouragues devoured at least seventy-five wasp nests every day — more than even an army ant swarm could consume in the same period — and it didn't seem unlikely that wasps might be hiding their nests to outwit the wasp-murdering superheroes of the rain forest.

But this colony of *Polybia liliacea,* in their conspicuous hanging silo, seemed to have opted instead for a mutual defense pact. If you wanted a bird to protect you from cara-caras, caciques are a good choice: they band together to chase away other birds, and their presence might protect the wasps from air attack. It was tempting to draw inferences from this hanging city of ants, wasps, and birds about the value of tolerance, the need for co-operation, even the origins of civilization, but the imperative behind it was simple enough: for these unlikely allies, living together in peace beat the alternative. Sean leaned in to my ear.

"The caracaras probably know this nest is here," he said. "I don't think they miss much." And around the next bend of the river, as if on cue, one launched itself from a perch and soared above our heads.

"Bush auntie-man!" bellowed Sean.

Rambo cut the motor while Jose drew us

toward the riverbank with his paddle, and I saw a broad-winged, long-tailed shape, perfectly black against the blue sky. It landed in a snag and turned to face us, staring wildly through its red eyes, and four more red-throats jumped up from the forest to join it. The quintet began to call, a chorus of dry *KEK*s and screamed *KAAA-OOO*s, and then to *dance* — raising one wing and then the other, lifting their heads to show off their crimson throats and white bellies, thrusting their necks forward. It was an intimidating, martial display, like the Polynesian war dances that show pride, strength, and withering disdain for an enemy.

Sean pulled out his speaker and cued up his recording. "Let's see how they like this," he said. At the sound of the Nouragues birds, the caracaras stopped their performance in mid-stride and fell silent, glaring at us with unmistakable malice — *Say that again. I dare you.* But they seemed uncertain about how to respond. I wondered if I should get ready to duck.

"Are there any anacondas here?" asked Sean.

"I don't think so," Jose said.

"Okay," said Sean, and hopped out of the boat, holding his camera above his head. This seemed to shock the red-throats out of their indecision, and they launched into a chorus of the cascading, jay-like screams we'd heard from a distance in the forest. *"That's the territorial call!"* shouted Sean, waist-deep in the river. A trio of scarlet macaws added their hoarser cries to the red-throats' chorus, a pandemonium unlike anything I might ever have called birdsong, and Sean joined them by yelping in pain: stinging ants were leaping onto his back from the branches of an overhanging tree.

"Fucking *Pseudomyrmex*!" he hissed, slapping the back of his neck as he struggled with his telephoto lens. "Stop stinging me, I order you!" He whooped again as an unseen fish nipped him, and Jose glanced back at me with a look of delight, biting his index finger.

"Sean," he called, "be careful, or the piranhas will bite off your whistle!"

After a third chorus, the caracaras seemed to settle on a course of action. Four of them flew off together while one stayed behind, as if to keep an eye on us, and Sean handed me his camera while he climbed back into the boat, checking his arms and legs for stray ants. He was pink with sun, endorphins, and happiness.

"Are they all you hoped for?" he asked.

I told him I'd never felt so thoroughly taunted by an animal. The red-throats projected the same intensity as the Johnny rooks, but they didn't have the open-faced curiosity of Tina or Evita. Instead, it seemed, they'd seasoned their minds with suspicion, belligerence, and unit cohesion, and they clearly wanted us to know that this was *their* turf. Another chorus of territorial cries sounded from farther upriver — probably the same birds we'd just seen, but possibly a rival group warning them against crossing into their neighborhood.

Jose favored this theory. "Before sundown," he declared, "we will have war!" He shoved us out of the shallows, and Rambo turned the bow upstream toward the waterfalls, the upper Rewa, and the deeper mysteries of the caracaras' world.

"You're listening to Radio Bush Auntie-man," Sean intoned. "All screaming, all the time."

Gentoo penguins come ashore on Steeple Jason in the Falkland Islands, while a young striated caracara surveys the scene. (The author's shadow is in the foreground.) *Photo courtesy of the author*

An adult striated caracara (or "Johnny rook") showing off its yellow legs, pale bill, and distinctive chestnut "trousers." *Photo © Andrew Stanworth*

A mixed-age group of striated caracaras assembles on kelp wrack near the carcass of a sea lion. The green streaks are caracara droppings stained by dye-marked mouse bait. *Photo courtesy of the author*

Falkland Islander Lorraine McGill greets Johnny rooks behind her house on Carcass Island. She enjoys their company, and feeds them kitchen scraps. *Photo courtesy of the author*

William Henry Hudson in 1908, at the age of sixty-seven. By this time, Hudson had lived in England for thirty-five years, published the books that made his name, and co-founded the Royal Society for the Protection of Birds. He grew up in Argentina, and delighted readers (including Darwin) with vivid accounts of the wildlife and people of his home. *Photo by J. G. Short*

An adult southern crested caracara scans the plains of Patagonia. Darwin called these caracaras "false eagles" and shivered at their "necrophagous habits." Hudson saw them as "lords of the feathered race." *Photo © Miguel Saggese*

Three nearly fledged southern crested caracaras—*carranchas* to Darwin and *caranchos* to Hudson—peer over the edge of their nest. *Photo © Miguel Saggese*

A chimango caracara, the diminutive and omnipresent scavenger of Hudson's childhood, forages at a landfill in Tierra del Fuego. "Throughout an extensive portion of South America, it is the commonest bird that we know," Hudson wrote. "I do not know where the naturalist will find a more interesting one." *Photo © Jorge López Moreno*

Tina, the captive striated caracara dubbed "the most intelligent bird in the world" by her trainer, Geoff Pearson, performs at the Woodlands Falconry Centre in Devonshire, England.
Photo © Geoff Pearson

Len Hill, the self-proclaimed "Penguin Millionaire," poses with his avian subjects at Birdland, the private zoo he founded in the Cotswolds. In the 1970s, Hill purchased both Grand and Steeple Jason, from which he imported penguins, geese, and striated caracaras.
Photo © Eric Hosking, courtesy of the Eric Hosking Charitable Trust, www.erichoskingtrust.com

Evita, Tina's successor at Woodlands, carries a favorite toy while exercising on a tether. Dozens of striated caracaras now live in the UK, where they perform astonishing feats for bemused audiences. Several have escaped. *Photo courtesy of the author*

At the southern edge of South America's continental plate, the Diego Ramírez Islands lie only five hundred miles from Antarctica. The striated caracaras who live here are the world's southernmost birds of prey. *Photo © Norberto Seebach*

Brian Duncan, the leader of our trip into the world of tropical caracaras, steers a boat up the Rewa River in southern Guyana. As a Wapishana Amerindian, Brian's ancestors include the Arawak people who had the misfortune to meet Columbus in Hispaniola. *Photo © Sean McCann*

Ramnall "Rambo" Roberts, a skilled fisherman and boat captain, examines a young black caiman during a night drift along the Rewa. Rambo's Macushi ancestors are among the people Europeans called Caribs. *Photo © Sean McCann*

Jose George, expert cook, raconteur, polyglot, and friend to all snakes, wades in the Rewa River. Two days later, we found a nest of red-throated caracaras near this site. *Photo © Sean McCann*

The world's largest spider, *Theraphosa blondi*, poses with Sean McCann, red-throated caracara expert and avid entomologist. Sean's quest to shed light on the rumor that red-throated caracaras produce a wasp repellent revealed previously unknown aspects of their lives.
Photo courtesy of the author

Two red-throated caracaras engage in a territorial display. Troops of as many as eleven birds take part in these striking performances, shaking their wings and tails and screaming at a volume that made Sean's ears ring. *Photo © Sean McCann*

Slabs of rock at the base of the Rewa's waterfalls bear chisel marks where prehistoric Amerindian people sharpened stone tools. The age of these carvings is unknown; they could be thousands of years old.
Photo courtesy of the author

A young red-throated caracara, hidden in a bromeliad in the forest canopy, sees a human being for the first time. Sean McCann watched six adult birds raise it on a diet of wasps' nests, whose remains litter its home. Note the dead millipede in the center of the image; Sean suspects the birds may use its defensive secretions to deter parasites.
Photo © Philippe Gaucher

An adult red-throated caracara stares back at its captors in French Guiana. Its scarlet eyes and bare throat are unique among all falcons.
Photo © Sean McCann

A juvenile black caracara examines our camp in Guyana. Black caracaras scavenge along riverbanks in the South American tropics, avoiding deep forests and human settlements.
Photo © Sean McCann

A five-foot-long nest of the social wasp *Polybia liliacea*, bristling with defenders, hangs above the Rewa. Red-throated caracaras attack nests like this to feed on the wasps' larvae; an unprotected human who jostled it would risk death. *Photo © Sean McCann*

Huáscar, one of the last Inca emperors, wears the feathers of a mountain caracara in his *mascapaicha*. "Such was the majesty of this bird," wrote Garcilaso de la Vega, the son of a Spanish soldier and an Inca princess, "and such was the reverence and respect which the Incas gave it."
Photo © Stadtmuseum Berlin

A mountain caracara, also known as *alkamari*, *chinalinda*, and *avemaria*, regards a human visitor to the ruins of Machu Picchu in Peru. Mountain caracaras are honored as symbols of good fortune in songs, dances, and stories throughout the high Andes.
Photo by Julia Manzerova

Paleontologist Julia Clarke (above) works with students and colleagues at a dig site in southern Chile (below). Julia's research has illuminated the lives of feathered dinosaurs before and after the Cretaceous extinctions, and emphasized the importance of the land bridge that once connected South America to a warm Antarctica. *Photos courtesy of the author*

A black vulture (left) preens a northern crested caracara near the Mexican border in South Texas. Though they're only distantly related, these social, intelligent species often roost together, and they share an affinity for roadkill.
Photo © Patty Murray

Carla Dove, an associate curator at the Smithsonian National Museum of Natural History in Washington, DC, holds the type specimen of the extinct Guadalupe caracara.
Photo courtesy of the author

A black caracara in Guyana, displaced from its meal by a vulture, snatches a morsel in one foot and hops away on the other. *Photos © Sean McCann*

A carunculated caracara or *curiquingue* soars above the Andean moorland at Rucu Pichincha, Ecuador. These inquisitive birds often approach human visitors to their high, cold habitats, and figure in stories and traditions older than the Inca Empire.
Photo © Angus Pritchard

A group of costumed *curiquingue* dancers perform in a traditional parade in Riobamba, Ecuador, in 2020.
Photo © Dominik Alexander Freire Pérez

Vicuñas graze on desert grass in the Chilean *altiplano* beneath the sacred volcano of Pili, whose snows water narrow, lush wetlands called *bofedales* and alkaline lakes teeming with flamingos. The hills in the middle distance bear the tracks of mountain caracaras. *Photo © Luke Padgett*

A white-throated caracara, the shy "walking falcon" first described by Darwin, shares a rainy perch with a black vulture in southern Argentina. *Photo © Martjan Lammertink*

Caracaras often seek out human partners in their search for food, even in cities. This mountain caracara is one of a trio who pay daily visits to a high-rise apartment in La Paz, Bolivia, for gifts of corn, fruit, and ground beef. *Photo © David Mercado / Reuters Pictures*

A northern crested caracara perches in a tree in Skykomish, Washington, forty-five miles east of Seattle, where it caused a stir among birders in 2014. Caracara sightings across the United States and Canada are increasing. *Photo © Doug Schurman*

15
ABOVE THE FALLS

A young black caracara, wearing the dull plumage and pale yellow face of its first year, peered from behind a screen of branches at Jose, who was hanging slabs of flayed catfish in the smoke of a tidy fire. The caracara leaned forward on its perch, bobbing its head and shifting from one foot to the other, and I wondered what it made of our brightly colored hammocks, our blue cylinder of cooking gas, and our tailless, earthbound bodies. It seemed caught in the grip of the same questions as the Johnny rooks who saw Charles Barnard and his fellow castaways wading ashore in the Falklands two hundred years ago: *What are these creatures? And what can they offer me?*

It was midday, the sky was clear, and the morning chorus of macaws and toucans had given way to the whispers of insects and the sigh of the upper Rewa. We were camped on a narrow peninsula inside a hairpin bend of the river — a place Brian called Thorn, after a palm spine he pried from a friend's foot here — and I'd been talking to Sean about his work with the red-throats, with occasional asides from Jose. Sean was always happy to drift on the currents of his own mind, from the finer points of evolutionary theory to the state of the academic job market (grim) to whether or not Earth has a tiny second moon (maybe). Once, deep in an account of an ant infestation at Nouragues, he suddenly asked if I liked the Oak Ridge Boys and launched into a full-throated rendition of "Baby When Your Heart Breaks Down." Now he was poised on the shore in shorts and a T-shirt, steeling himself for a bath in a river that teemed with unnerving life.

"These caracaras, they are warriors to attack the wasps like this," Jose mused, stirring his fire with a stick. "It is not an easy thing. There must be some rank or something in the skin."

"The evidence is against you," replied Sean, easing in up to his chest.

"Yes," Jose agreed. "But I still cannot believe this."

"In that case," Sean said, "it's on *you* to prove it." He dunked his head and scrubbed his scalp with dish soap, then peeled off his shirt and wrung it out. "Stay away, piranhas," he muttered. "Stay away, stingrays."

Jose looked thoughtful. "I think you have to kill a caracara," he said. "Then rub the skin on you, and then try to get the wasps. But I will not volunteer for this."

Sean climbed out of the river unscathed, and Brian stepped forward with a hand line and a spoon lure. In less than a minute, he landed a large black piranha and severed its head with two strokes of his cutlass. "Sometimes the head still bites," he cautioned. No sooner had he said this than a caiman surfaced in the exact spot where Sean had been bathing.

"*Jesus,*" whispered Sean.

"We had one downstream from here we used to feed," said Jose. "We called him Micky. Maybe this is him."

Jose liked to tease Sean about his love of insects, but his own interest in the forest's creatures was just as keen. Where Brian and Rambo seemed more excited by the largest, tastiest, or most useful animals, Jose seemed drawn to them all, large or small, for the simple fact of their being. He relished the story of a half-dozen caiman hatchlings who'd followed him home like ducklings, and he was as delighted by an emerald boa curled on a branch as he was by a nest of terns in reeds at a bend of the river, whose downy chicks gaped their outsized bills at him.

Before his afternoon bath, Jose liked to lie in his hammock and write in a journal or thumb through my copy of *The Naturalist in La Plata,* wearing thick-rimmed glasses that made him look like the professor he might have been in another life. He often peered under rocks and logs in hopes of finding a snake, but he knew the risks of poking around in the forest after dark; one evening, while Sean assembled his camera rig to look for night-roaming spiders, Jose shot me a significant look. "He better be careful the grandpa spider don't come down and web he up," he said. I asked him who the spider grandfather was.

"*Big* spider," he said.

Three weeks had passed since we left the Rupununi for the Rewa, and our shyness toward one another had mostly fallen away. Jose still slept in his makeshift kitchen, and Brian and Rambo still slung their hammocks at a discreet distance from me and Sean, but I no longer felt like an intruder in the conversations that unspooled around the ghost light. We sat and talked in a sort of slow motion, punctuated with long, tranquil silences; Brian, Jose, and Rambo seemed reluctant to pepper me with questions, and I felt the same. But we were curious about each other's lives. News from the distant lands where I'd spent most of my life had only reached them in dribs and drabs, through action films and hearsay — or, more lately, through email, courtesy of their village library. Brian wanted to know if Sylvester Stallone and Ronald Reagan were still alive and if the euro still existed as a currency, and he dimly remembered the Falklands War from his days in the Guyanese army, though he couldn't recall its outcome. ("We were all going to the map," he said, "saying, where *is* this place?")

Jose's questions were usually more cosmic or geographical — whether there were other planets that people can live on, or if there was water under the earth, or how cold it might be in Boston, Massachusetts, if he visited his granddaughter there. I sometimes wondered if he was pulling my leg, but they were reasonable questions, often surprisingly hard to answer, and he betrayed no amusement or exasperation when Sean took them at face value. Sean had been teaching introductory biology before our trip and occasionally seemed to forget we weren't an afternoon lab section as he explained the properties of ultraviolet light, the chemistry of bee venom, and the active ingredients of Russian bioweapons. Jose seemed to enjoy prompting him further, seeing what new information might spill forth from this inexhaustible man.

Rambo sat quietly in his folding chair, following the conversation without comment, but he leaned forward when it turned to large animals, and looked at me in mild disbelief while I enthused about the vanished titans of the Pleistocene. His eyes shone as Sean described still-living behemoths like manatees and Komodo dragons, as did Brian's when

Sean mentioned the giant armadillo he'd met one night at Nouragues. Giant armadillos are one of South America's most secretive animals, rarely seen even by people who live there, and Sean had been lost in thought when an armored creature the size of a German shepherd, with skin like a bed of pinkish-gray pebbles, appeared in the beam of his headlamp. He'd watched in amazement as it swiveled its long, scaly head, sniffed at the air, and galumphed into the forest, looking resolute and unhurried.

"I have also seen him," said Brian. Nearby, in fact, in the dry channel of a seasonal creek. At the sight of Brian the armadillo had resorted to its best and only trick, tunneling into the bank with its huge claws, and Brian caught hold of its tail and pulled. But the armadillo plunged into its excavation, kicking out a torrent of mud and sand, and Brian had to let go. "He was so *strong*," he marveled, shaking his head. "He would have pulled me in with him." If we liked, he said, he could show us the place, and if we went at night, we might see the armadillo again.

"He is not an easy walker," added Jose. "You will hear him." I couldn't resist telling them that a young William Henry Hudson had once tried to catch a hairy armadillo in the same way, pulling at its tail while it dug its way to freedom. It had hurt his "small-boy pride," he wrote, to think that "an animal no bigger than a cat was going to beat me in a trial of strength." But beat him it did, disappearing underground and showering him with clods of ejected dirt.

"Yes," Brian nodded. "Exactly like this."

It had been a week since we ascended the waterfalls into the upper Rewa, a long, exhausting day of hauling our gear and one of the boats up three steep, rutted inclines and two river crossings. I helped Brian, Jose, and Rambo lift the boat by its gunwales while Sean hitched himself to the bow and pulled like an ox. Though I strained and pushed, my contribution wasn't far above moral support, and after the second portage I collapsed on a pile of tarps, feeling embarrassed and overheated. After an hour's rest, Brian gave me an appraising look and handed me a cup of water, and I strapped on my pack to stumble up the third and final portage to the upper falls, where sheets of white water tumbled over immense blocks of gleaming basalt. It really did look like a gateway to another world, complete with gatekeepers: perched atop the tallest boulder were two pale, slender, primitive-looking birds I never knew existed.

"Capped heron!" shouted Rambo.

Seen through a haze of mist rising from the falls, the blue-faced herons looked like prototypes assembled from parts of other tall birds — the cream-white bodies of cattle egrets, the long-plumed caps of night herons. They escorted us upriver for nearly an hour, gliding low along the curves of the shore. At dusk we made camp on a broad white beach, where Jose and I hung our shirts to dry beneath a Good Friday moon blurred by thin clouds, as if we were looking up at it through turbid water. The moon broke free for a moment, throwing our shadows against the sand and revealing the stiff-winged crescent of a nighthawk catching insects above the river.

" 'Remember, man, that ye are dust, and to dust ye shall return,' " Jose quoted. "You know this?"

I did, but I was too tired to talk, and went to my hammock without supper. Sean was already settled in, reading *Birds of Venezuela,* and I heard Jose stowing pots and pans while Brian and Rambo sat to pass the time on the moonlit beach. I drifted off to the sound of their voices, talking quietly and laughing gently, high-pitched and free.

The next morning was clear and still, with a fine layer of mist on the river. My legs and back ached, but I felt a surge of adrenaline when I remembered where I was, and who I was with. This was the part of the river I'd most wanted to see, and after breakfast we began the routine we would keep for the next two weeks: motoring upriver for a few hours, then cutting the engine to drift back in a silence broken only by the swish of Brian's paddle and the cries of animals. In the late afternoons we drifted downstream through twilight and motored back in the dark, and every other day we shifted camp, advancing slowly toward the headwaters of the Rewa.

Above the falls, a sense that we'd entered a different version of the river and its forest was immediate and striking. The trees were shorter, smaller, and closer, the water nearly level with the shore, the wildlife even more bold and abundant. Flotillas of giant otters poked their wild-eyed faces out of the river while legions of macaws cackled and rasped, and every few hours we heard the screams of red-throated caracaras warning their rivals and laying siege to cities of wasps. Howler monkeys peered down from the crowns of the tallest trees while bands of squirrel monkeys raced along lower branches and vines, carrying babies on their backs. Rambo pointed out a sloth dangling from a high snag, its ever-smiling face turned to the sun.

"The land turtle is a fast man for him!" said Brian, approvingly.

It was hard to believe that such a modest-looking river could support so many animals, but I had to remind myself that I was thinking about it backward; the real question was why the lower river didn't seem as thickly inhabited. Hunting had something to do with it, but so did the fearlessness of innocence:

the animals of the upper Rewa, like the elephant seals and penguins of Steeple Jason, had no reason to hide from us. We were simply another thing happening in a place where there was already a great deal going on.

Not sitting comfortably at the top of the food chain added to the feeling of wildness. We hadn't seen an anaconda yet, but they were almost certainly here, and I thought we'd met our first when we saw a dark, bubbling shape in the middle of the river. But it was a tapir who reared her head above the water, as if surfacing out of prehistory itself. Her brush-like mane and purple-black skin were as elegant as her short trunk was bizarre, and only when she lumbered up the bank, favoring one of her legs, could we see the long white gashes on her flank — wounds so fresh I could almost feel the jaguar's claws digging in. Jose said it was probably waiting nearby to attack her again after dark, and it was disorienting to think that both animals were immigrants from the continent where I was born, where their ancestors died out long ago.

In the long hours between drifts, I began to understand why Brian and Jose always seemed to have a task at hand: without one, the forest could feel oppressive. We were alone in a remote wilderness but confined to the slim border between the forest and the river, and a kind of cabin fever crept in. Waking before dawn with nothing to do but scratch mosquito bites and wait for daylight made me impatient, then annoyed with my impatience; I was dismayed that my mind expected the world to be a place where I could speak to distant friends at will, and graze all day on a diet of shrieking headlines and urgent messages.

That world was steadily receding with each mile of the river, and I tried to accept the hours of enforced stillness for what they were: a chance to bathe in a symphony of animals announcing to friends and enemies that they'd survived the night. As pure darkness gave way to blues and grays, the tremulous whistles of owls and nightjars elided into songs of thrushes and wrens, screams of parrots, and the metallic whistles and bonks of South American specialties like bellbirds and fruitcrows. No two performances were the same. One morning I spent a half hour listening to a pair of calling sunbitterns — squat but delicate birds, like a cross between a heron and a hen, who paced along the shore with hypnotic smoothness, swiveling their striped bodies and unfurling golden wing feathers when they flew. Their song was equally beautiful and odd: a set of hollow notes that ascended by quarter tones, so airy and diffuse that they seemed to come from everywhere. As the sun broke through the canopy, they were joined by a bird I couldn't place, singing a descending countermelody in the same octave — then another, whose sparkling seven-note song was like a peal of tiny bells. It was a musician wren, whose song Hudson compared to Rima's voice, and the birds' entwined voices made human music seem primitive.

They reminded me of my favorite scene in all of Hudson's writing, a memory from an early visit to Buenos Aires that had nothing to do with birds. The city was overwhelming for a boy who'd grown up in the Pampas, but moments of beauty also etched themselves in his mind — and none was more entrancing than the chorus of the city's night watchmen. "When night came," he wrote, "it appeared that the fierce policemen, with their swords and brass buttons, were no longer needed to safeguard the people, and their place in the streets was taken by a quaint, frowsy-looking body of men, mostly old, some almost decrepit, wearing big cloaks and carrying staffs and heavy iron lanterns with a tallow candle alight inside." Hudson lay awake through the small hours listening to the cries of these medieval-looking sentinels, and described them in a passage that would have pleased John Cage.

The calls began at the hour of eleven, and then on from beneath the window would come the wonderful long drawling call of *Las on — ce han da — do y se — re — no,* which means eleven of the clock and all serene, but if clouded the concluding word would be *nu — bla — do,* and so on, according to the weather. From all the streets, from all over the town, the long-drawn calls would float to my listening ears, with infinite variety in the voices — the high and shrill, the falsetto, the harsh, raucous note like the caw of the carrion crow, the solemn, booming bass, and then some fine, rich, pure voice that soared heavenwards above all the others and was like the pealing notes of an organ.

Two decades later, Hudson's only journey into a South American wilderness would also force him to lie still by a river for a long time, under very different circumstances from mine. Though he never saw the tropical forests of *Green Mansions,* he made one ambitious trip before he left Argentina forever: a year-long sojourn in the Patagonian desert, where he intended to make his name as a bird collector. Patagonia's cold scrublands and sandstone canyons extend about a thousand miles down the east coast of South America, from the Pampas to Tierra del Fuego, and Europeans considered them a barren, forbidding, and mostly useless place. But for Hudson, a young man with a head of curly black hair and a thirst for adventure, they held the promise of long, solitary rides through a wild landscape. "There is nothing in life," he wrote, "so delightful as that feeling of relief, of escape, and absolute freedom which one experiences in a vast solitude, where man has perhaps never been, and has, at any rate, left no trace of his existence."

He'd also begun to think that sending bird skins to museums might lead him to a living. As he entered adulthood, he focused on birds above all other interests, and sold skins from La Plata to the British Museum and the new Smithsonian Institution in the United States. These museums held few specimens from southern South America, which wasn't as enticing to collectors as the bird-rich forests of the tropics — and here, Hudson reasoned, was his chance. Patagonia might be inhospitable, but it might also contain birds unknown to science, and he dreamed of being the first naturalist to encounter "some bird as beautiful, let us say, as the wryneck or wheatear, and as old on the earth, which had never been named."

Beyond this tempting possibility, he'd also set his sights on a questing beast — a species of rhea first described by Darwin, smaller and darker than the "ostriches" the gauchos chased across the Pampas. Darwin's rheas were difficult to find, and if Hudson could procure one his reputation as a bird collector

338

might rise enough for him to make it his profession.

Little of his Patagonian odyssey, however, went according to plan. The ancient steamer he boarded in Buenos Aires to take him south gave him doubts from the moment he stepped aboard, then confirmed them by running aground on its second night at sea. After several terrifying hours in which even the eighty-year-old captain believed that all was lost, the sun rose to find them beached on the Patagonian coast. Rather than waiting for a rescue that might be days or weeks away, Hudson and three other men decided to wade ashore and walk to the nearest settlement, which the captain assured them was close at hand. For two days, they followed a faint trail across a plain of dry grass and thorn scrub, with no food but a pair of roasted armadillos and a handful of songbirds' eggs.

Hudson had begun to think they were lost when a dust devil on the horizon turned out to be a man driving a troop of horses, who greeted Hudson and his companions with amiable surprise and offered to lead them to the nearby town of La Merced. They rode the last mile with him, bareback, through a stand of feathery-leaved acacias, and pulled up on a bluff overlooking a sudden and surprising vista: the desert river called the Río Negro.

"Never river seemed fairer to look upon," Hudson recalled, "broader than the Thames at Westminster, and extending away on either hand until it melted and was lost in the blue horizon, its low shores clothed in all the glory of groves and fruit orchards and vineyards and fields of ripening maize.

Far out in the middle of the swift blue current floated flocks of black-necked swans, their white plumage shining like foam in the sunlight; while just beneath us . . . stood the thatched farmhouse of our conductor, the smoke curling up peacefully from the kitchen chimney.

A cherry orchard surrounding the farmhouse was heavy with fruit, which "glowed like burning coals in the deep green foliage," and that night Hudson ate his fill, glad that his grand adventure had finally begun. Two weeks later he set out for the wilderness, riding northwest with a young Englishman who wanted to visit friends upriver. For several days they rode beside the sparkling Río Negro, which carried water that had fallen as snow in the distant Andes, and Hudson was surprised by the inaccuracy of its name: it wasn't black but a rich blue-green — a startling contrast to the desert's dull browns, yellows, and grays.

They paused at a small cabin at the halfway

point, built by the Englishman as a homestead on an unpromising patch of ground. It was more garden shed than dwelling: a single, low-ceilinged room stuffed with enough farming implements "to have enabled a small colony of men to fight the wilderness and found a city of the future." Hudson noticed that his companion seemed more devoted to this hoard of tools than to the land he hoped to farm, and grew slightly alarmed at his new friend's fondness. "The way to make him happy," he noted, "was to tell him that you had injured something made of iron or brass — a gunlock, watch, or anything complicated.

His eyes would shine, he would rub his hands and be all eagerness to get at the new patient to try his surgical skill on him. Now he had to give two or three days to all these wood and metal friends of his, to give a fresh edge to his chisels, and play the dentist to his saws; to spread them all out and count and stroke them lovingly, as a breeder pats his beasties, and feed and anoint them with oil to make them shine and look glad.

While the Englishman nursed his chisels and saws, Hudson went outside to look for birds but found only a scene of parched desolation. The cool green water of the river almost seemed to mock the barren valley around it, where the reeds that fringed its banks were yellow and dead. "Dead also," Hudson recalled, "were the tussocks of coarse tow-coloured grass, while the soil beneath was as white as ashes and cracked everywhere." He was relieved when his companion finally started packing to go, and as they sat on the floor of the cabin, talking about the meal they might enjoy at their journey's end, Hudson picked up the Englishman's revolver to examine it.

He had just begun to tell me that it was a revolver with a peculiar character of its own, and with idiosyncrasies, one of which was that the slightest touch, or even vibration of the air, would cause it to go off when on the cock — he was just telling me this, when off it went with a terrible bang and sent a conical bullet into my left knee, an inch or so beneath the knee-cap.

The pain wasn't much at first, like "a smart blow on the knee," but blood began to stream from the wound, and Hudson soon found he couldn't stand or walk. The question now was whether he would survive the night. He lay on the floor beneath his poncho, his leg bound in blood-soaked handkerchiefs, while the Englishman went for help. In the silent, windowless cabin, Hudson felt he'd been buried deep in the earth, unable to think or

342

sleep. At first he heard only the faint hiss of blood rushing in his head, but near midnight another sound made him suspect he wasn't alone. "It was in the cabin and close to me," he wrote. "I thought at first it was like the sound made by a rope drawn slowly over the clay floor. I lighted a wax match, but the sound had ceased, and I saw nothing."

The silence resumed, the hours passed, and at last Hudson heard a voice he knew: the thin, dry twittering of a flycatcher perched in a willow tree. This was followed by the "dreamy, softly rising and falling, throaty warblings" of swallows, then the chatter and fuss of red-billed finches and sparrows in the reeds, and at last the "long, leisurely-uttered, chanting cry" of a chimango caracara on its daily patrol for the weak and wounded — a sound, he knew, that meant "morning was beautiful in the east." Little by little, a suggestion of light returned to the room, as did the Englishman, who'd found a farmer with an oxcart to carry him back to La Merced.

The Englishman was pleased to find Hudson alive and lucid, and boiled water for tea, but when he bent to help Hudson to his feet, the night's mysterious sound revealed itself as a large, venomous snake — a *Bothrops* — that slithered from beneath Hudson's poncho and into a hole in the wall, having slept beside him all night. Hudson was surprised but not frightened, and later admitted he was

343

secretly glad that his friend's arms were occupied in helping him stand, denying him the chance to attack the snake with a saw or a hammer.

The next two days passed in pain and delirium as the cart lurched along a hot, dusty road while Hudson lay in back, facing the sky, and ruminated on his dashed hopes. In the coming months there would be no rheas, no solo rides through the desert, no unknown birds — only hours of heat and silence on a bed in the headquarters of the South American Missionary Society, and weekly meetings with a doctor who probed his wound without finding a bullet. But as they neared La Merced in the early morning, he felt unexpectedly peaceful. Swallows were "rising in wide circles into the still, dusky air" as the stars faded, and their liquid trills and whistles reassured him.

This feeling of peace came and went through the long days and nights at the mission. With nothing to do but lie still, and no company but a cloud of houseflies "perpetually engaged in their intricate airy dance," Hudson had to explore a new wilderness: the one inside his own mind. He'd meant to give some thought to the mysteries of bird migration — how they did it, what compelled them, and where they went — but that couldn't absorb every ounce of the day. In mounting desperation, he began to sift through other "small unpainful riddles of the earth" that had preoccupied him since he was a child, but nothing could hold his attention, and after a while he began to see his thoughts at a remove, like the flies that hovered above him. They were "flitting, sylph-like things," he later wrote, "that began life as abstractions, and developed, like imago from maggot, into entities:

I always flitted among them as they performed their mazy dance, whirling in circles, falling and rising, poised motionless, then suddenly cannoning against me for an instant, mocking my power to grasp them, and darting off again at a tangent. Baffled, I would drop out of the game, like a tired fly that goes back to his perch, but like the resting, restive fly I would soon turn towards them again; perhaps to see them all wheeling in a closer order, describing new fantastic figures, with swifter motions, their forms turned to thin black lines, crossing and recrossing in every direction, as if they had all combined to write a series of strange characters in the air.

This was a new and frustrating experience for Hudson, but he had no choice. He had to let his thoughts simply flow, noting them without effort or judgment, and the result was curious: though his muscles grew weak in the mission bed, he left it feeling obscurely fortified. There had been no grand revelations or discoveries ("I caught nothing," he admitted, "and found out nothing"), but something in him had been broken and remade; and many days of nothing made him reconsider his single-minded pursuit of birds. "Seeing one class of objects too well," he reflected, "had made all others look distant, obscure, and of little interest."

When he finally emerged, gaunt and hobbling, into the streets of La Merced, the world looked subtly different, richer in detail and flavor. "Our waking life is sometimes like a dream," he wrote, "which proceeds logically enough until the stimulus of some new sensation, from without or within, throws it into temporary confusion, or suspends its action; after which it goes on again, but with fresh characters, passions, and motives, and a changed argument."

In his first days as a free man, Hudson found that an old craving had left him: a compulsive hunger for news of the larger world. When he first saw a newspaper again, he snatched it up "mechanically, just as a cat, even when not hungry, pounces on a mouse it sees scuttling across its path." But as he scanned its columns, he felt little interest; his taste for "the ambitious schemes of Russia, the attitude of the Sublime Porte, and the meeting or breaking up of parliaments" had gone, never to return. He compared himself to an alcoholic giving up the bottle, suspecting that "the passion for politics, the perpetual craving of the mind for some new thing, is after all only a feverish artificial feeling . . . from which one rapidly recovers when it can no longer be pandered to."

Without it, a fresh space had opened in his mind, and the world he could see, touch, and smell in the valley of the Río Negro grew to fill it. He still loved birds, and mourned the loss of the town's purple martins when they flew north to winter in the tropics. But the lives of the men and women who lived by the river interested him as they had not before, when he'd been eager to leave them behind for the wilderness. "How fresh and how human it seemed," he recalled, "to feel a keen interest in the village annals, the domestic life, the simple pleasures, cares, and struggles of the people I lived with."

The colonists led a timeless life in their valley, cut off from the rest of the world, and the thought of being out of sight of the Río Negro for more than a few hours filled them with dread. Hudson "was disposed to laugh a little," he admitted, "at the very large place THE RIVER occupied in all men's minds." But a few months on its banks made him regret his disdain, feeling he'd "made a jest of something sacred." For the settlers, the river was life itself. One afternoon in La Merced, as he sat sipping *mate* and talking with the members of a large family, a young boy asked him where he lived:

My home, I said, was in the Buenos Ayrean Pampas, far north of Patagonia.
"Is it near the river," he asked, "right on the bank, like this house?"

Hudson explained that it was not, that there was no river in the Pampas, and that he could ride across its plains in any direction he liked — and the boy laughed at him. "It was as if I had told him that I lived up in a tree that grew to the clouds," Hudson wrote, "or under the sea, or some such impossible thing." The settlers were bound to the river not only by water but by fear: travelers in the desert risked meeting a hungry puma, or even a jaguar. But the colonists were most afraid of meeting the Amerindians they'd recently evicted from the valley. This was "the one cloud always on [their] otherwise sunlit horizon," Hudson wrote, and the sudden boom of a cannon from one of their defensive forts, signaling the approach of a raiding party, could come at any time.

The Amerindians had ample reason to be upset. Since the days of General Rosas, Argentina's military leaders had pursued a cruel and relentless campaign against its native people, and the livestock brought by

European colonists like Hudson's family steadily displaced the wild animals Amerindians relied on for food and clothing. They retaliated by raiding settlements and military outposts, and the Argentine government dug a trench more than two hundred miles long across the open range to deter them, while the rival government of Chile, seeing an opportunity, encouraged the Mapuche people of northern Patagonia to steal Argentine cattle. When the trench failed to deter the Mapuche, Argentina sent its army to slaughter them, claiming that its soldiers were fighting for civilization itself. Argentina's minister of war (and later president) Julio Argentina Roca chillingly declared that "our self-respect as a virile people obliges us to put down . . . this handful of savages who destroy our wealth and prevent us from definitely occupying, in the name of law, progress and our own security, the richest and most fertile lands of the Republic." Thousands of men, women, and children were slaughtered or enslaved in the offensives that became enshrined in Argentine mythology as the Conquest of the Desert — a southern echo of the campaigns the U.S. Army was waging against Native Americans in the western United States.

The bloodiest days of the conquest were several years away when Hudson arrived at the Río Negro, but the colonists had already made it a beachhead of the Argentine state.

Evidence of this grand theft was everywhere, and Hudson noted that the settlers' livestock had made it all the more obvious: beyond the irrigated fields of La Merced, herds of cattle and sheep had stripped away the valley's fragile carpet of rushes and native sedge, leaving gloomy landscapes like the barren land at the Englishman's cabin. Without its protective shroud of vegetation, the ruins of Amerindian villages emerged from the valley floor, and though the settlers showed little interest in these sites, they drew Hudson like a magnet.

Where the village had been a populous one, or inhabited for a long period, the ground was a perfect bed of chipped stones, and among these fragments were found arrowheads, flint knives and scrapers, mortars and pestles, large round stones with a groove in the middle, pieces of hard polished stone used as anvils, perforated shells, fragments of pottery, and bones of animals. My host remarked one day that the valley that year had produced nothing but a plentiful crop of arrow-heads.

Hudson collected a small hoard of these items, but what began as idle prospecting for artifacts became a search for their makers. Amerindians had always hovered on the periphery of Hudson's life, and though he was raised to regard them as savages, the finely worked arrowheads in the lost villages of the Río Negro troubled his conscience. "Not only were they minute," he wrote, "but most exquisitely finished, with a fine serration, and without an exception, made of some beautiful stone — crystal, agate, and green, yellow, and horn-colored flint.

It was impossible to take half-a-dozen of these gems of colour and workmanship in the hand and not be impressed at once with the idea that beauty had been as much an aim to the worker as utility.

Some villages seemed to have specialized in certain kinds of tools, suggesting a broad division of labor, and the bones in their rubbish piles reflected their residents' intimate knowledge of the desert's wary animals. Hudson found the remains of armadillos, guanacos, rheas, peccaries, nutrias, guinea pigs, upland geese, and other smaller birds and mammals among them, but not glyptodonts or ground sloths; the villages were far too recently occupied. But in places where the river had cut down through older sediments, he unearthed longer, rougher blades, fashioned by people hunting much larger game. They reminded him of the Paleolithic spear points of Europe, the fluted weapons of people who'd hunted woolly rhinos, aurochs, and cave bears.

Sifting through the ruins of these villages became a preoccupation for Hudson as he recovered his strength, and his discoveries came with a piercing sense of loss. He tried to keep this feeling at bay with two lies that comforted many Europeans in the New World: that the Amerindians' demise was somehow inevitable, and that the people who had survived disease, war, and exile had been so debased by the ordeal that they no longer resembled their ancestors, who might have deserved respect. "The red men of today may be of the same race and blood," he assured himself, "but they are without doubt so changed, and have lost so much, that their progenitors would not know them, nor acknowledge them as relations."

On the Río Negro, he couldn't sustain this pretense. The more he peered into the lives of the "savages" who'd made the valley their home, the more he saw people like himself looking back: clever, resourceful, keenly observant. They had been "alone with nature," he wrote, "makers of their own weapons and self-sustaining, untouched by any outside influence" — qualities he surely envied — and he must have seen that emptiness and innocence were not the same. Like the carefully managed forests of the Amazon, Patagonia's deserts had been touched for many centuries by the skilled hands of people with a deep knowledge of the natural world, a knowledge that lay forever beyond his reach. "Merely to think on the subject," he admitted, "sometimes had the effect of bringing a shadow, a something of melancholy, over my mind, [a] temper which is fatal to investigation."

But not, in the end, to reverence. Burial grounds adjoined the ruined villages, and at a site "strewn thick with crumbling skeletons," Hudson began to feel he'd crossed a line between archaeology and grave robbing. "I would sit and walk about on the hot yellow sand," he wrote, "careful in walking not to touch an exposed skull with my foot, although the hoof of the next wild thing that passed would shatter it to pieces like a vessel of fragile glass." The skulls, especially, called to him: he would lift them, examine them, and replace them where they lay. Sometimes, cradling one in his hand, he would pour out the sand that filled it, pondering another facet of the great Patagonian absence that troubled Darwin. Each skull had contained a world of sense, thought, and belief Hudson would never know, and their polished craniums, smooth as a rhea's egg, "reflected the noonday light so powerfully that it almost pained the eyes to look at them." Above him in the blue were chattering flocks of chimango caracaras, on their way to glean pests from the settlers' livestock or tuck into their garbage, and on still days he could hear the rattling calls of caranchos, who were no strangers to picking through scattered bones.

"Jonathan," said Jose, "what do you think is dreams?"

It was well after dark at Thorn camp. Jose had set the ghost light next to his kitchen, which allowed him to lie invisibly in his hammock, cocooned in a mosquito net, and still join in the conversation. It was easy to forget he was there until the cocoon spoke and moved, and Rambo playfully rocked it with his foot.

As far as I knew, I said, dreams were your mind thinking about itself.

"Sometimes I wake up and I'm crying," said Brian. "I don't know why."

We'd returned an hour earlier from a night drift, a subdued and spooky experience: bats thrummed around our heads, twisted branches loomed from the water like skeletal hands, and the eyes of fawn-sized rodents called pacas glowed in Jose's spotlight. Two disoriented piranhas jumped into the boat, and Rambo giggled and chucked them back, and the sky was so dark and clear that calm stretches of water mirrored stars I'd rarely seen — the fine curve of Orion's bow, the horns of Taurus. Just before we arrived back at Thorn, we passed a row of swallows huddled on a branch inches above the surface of the river. All of them faced the same direction except one, as if he'd had enough company for the day.

Around the ghost light, the conversation turned from dreams to village politics, and then to the voices you sometimes hear in the river, especially at night. Just below the falls, Jose said, a young man had been killed by a falling tree, and you could hear him crying all night if you slept in that place. "Today," added Brian, "when I walked down to bathe, I hear a body call me — like one of you call me. But there is no one."

The moon erupted from trees across the river, so huge and bright it almost seemed to make a sound. Jose admitted he was thinking about the annual rodeo he was missing back home in the savanna. It was held in Lethem, a hamlet on the border with Brazil where Jose had some history: he'd spent a couple of years there in a Bible school, where the students had to cook for themselves and buy their own Bibles. ("Only the teaching was free," he said.) He'd finally lost his patience when the instructor, a British priest who wore a military beret, flew into a rage at two young boys who'd tried to steal mangoes from his tree.

"All the time teaching us about love, you know — *love* your parents, *love* your teachers," Jose said, "and he chasing after them with a stick. A lot of them old army guys, old English guys, want to pretend to be good

355

guys now."

I asked if he was still a churchgoing man.

"Believe ye in the Lord and have eternal life!" boomed the hammock, sending Rambo into a laughing fit.

"Sometimes I start going to church," he continued, "but then I stop again. Religious people always say, 'The world going to end, and the righteous will be saved.' And sometimes I just have a shot of rum, forget about everything."

Rambo's big shoulders heaved.

"But when I drink," Jose added, "I am probably more evil than you see me now."

"We can't see you," said Sean.

"True," Jose allowed. "But Uncle Brian, now, he's civilized. He believe in Christianity, read his Bible every day, everything."

Brian admitted that he liked to listen to gospel music in the mornings, but he seemed to hold his piety lightly. He mentioned a footprint-shaped hole in a rock near his home village of Aishalton, said to mark the place where Jesus took his last step before vaulting into heaven, then veered into a description of the open-pit gold mine that had brought strangers, money, alcohol, and motor vehicles to a place that had rarely known them. He was even more suspicious of Chinese logging operations in the Essequibo basin, fifty miles east of the Rewa, and the "exploratory" permits recently granted them by the government.

"What are they exploring?" he asked, rising from his chair. "What is their purpose here?"

Brian headed off to bed, and I thought of the sodden Guyanese bank notes I'd found in my pocket earlier in the day and spread on a flat stone to dry. Each bill had a small map of the country on its reverse, inset with emblems of its natural resources, as if to assuage any doubts about its worth. The northern coast bristled with tiny bundles of sugarcane, while pyramids of gold bars and diamonds encrusted its central highlands, and in the deep south, hovering ominously above our camp on the Rewa, lay a pile of logs and the word "timber."

After a long silence, Jose spoke again. "My friends tell me the Milky Way is a river," he said, "and if you are a bad man, when you die you cannot cross over it. You have to stay here, till the end of the world. But Rastaman says heaven is here."

"What do *you* think?" asked Sean.

Jose's arm rose from the hammock and pulled the netting away, and he lifted his head over the side. "I think man is like a tree," he said. "Strong on the outside." He grinned. "Inside, all rotten."

"SEAN!" called Brian, his voice sharp. "There is a *Theraphosa* here!"

Sean ran to his hammock and returned

wearing a T-shirt that read A SPIDER DID NOT BITE YOU — a private joke he shared with his girlfriend, an arachnologist. He handed me his camera, and we walked toward the light of Brian's headlamp, which was shining on the largest spider in the world. Brian had set the Goliath birdeater on a palm leaf to show it off to maximum effect, but it didn't need help: it was really and truly as big as a dinner plate, its long legs covered with hairs the same reddish brown as Sean's beard. Despite my fear of spiders, I didn't feel especially rattled by it; maybe it was so large that my mind refused to accept it as real. I was more than happy to admire it from a distance, but Sean wanted to get closer, and Brian offered the birdeater the rake we used to clear our campsite. The spider clambered onto its tines, and then Brian held the rake against the leg of Sean's trousers.

"Do not shake," Brian whispered.

The spider froze for a moment, then scurried up to Sean's abdomen — at which Sean flinched, and Brian chuckled. Then it assumed a patient, thoughtful pace, as if exploring an interesting new landscape. It climbed to Sean's left shoulder, then to the top of his head, and came to rest above his right ear, like a piece of costume jewelry.

"Ow," whispered Sean. "Its claws are sharp." He was beaming. The birdeater's back legs were clinging to his beard, its inch-long fangs beside his eyes. I clutched his camera in one hand and a flashlight in the other, wondering how he intended to remove it, but he seemed unconcerned and walked into the forest with the spider still clinging to his head. "They can live a really long time," he said, his voice dimming as he disappeared. "Five or six years for a male. Maybe twenty for a female."

Brian, watching him go, looked bemused. I told him I'd never met anyone quite like Sean.

"I don't think scientists are ordinary people," he said.

The next morning we woke to the sounds of a caracara turf war. Two rival troops of redthroats had assembled on opposite sides of the river to taunt each other like Sharks and Jets, shaking their tails and flashing their wings as if daring the other to make the first move. "This could go on for a while," said Sean — and it did, all through our breakfast of coffee and cornmeal porridge, winding down inconclusively as Brian revved up the boat's motor. He had something special to show us, but wouldn't say what it was. An hour later we arrived at a deep eddy where curtains of bubbles rising through the water made it look carbonated, and a kingfisher whipped the head of a catfish against a snag.

"Now we will have a contest," said Brian, handing out spools of fishing line while

Rambo tried and failed to suppress a smile. Sean dropped his hook into the water, and something hit it with such force that he nearly lurched out of the boat.

"Fuck!" he yelled, pulling hard on the line, and a huge fish with bulging, dog-like eyes, fearsome jaws, and a coat of pewter-gray scales rolled at the surface: an *aimara,* or wolffish. It was nearly three feet long and fat as a tuna. Sean's hands reddened as it rolled again, smacking the surface with its tail and soaking us with spray. Then it went limp, as if playing dead, and Sean lifted it warily from the water. Rambo pulled the hook from the aimara's mouth and held it for us to admire, gripping its head behind its armor-plated gills. It reminded me of a coelacanth, with stubby pectoral fins and a squared-off tail as wide as its body. Sean, catching his breath, said he'd seen them in a river in French Guiana, and that they liked to lie concealed in underwater dens and ambush their prey with a single, hard strike. They had little stamina, it seemed, because they didn't need it.

"But they have really big teeth," he added. "And it's your turn." I wasn't eager to catch a wolffish, but I couldn't see a dignified way out, so I dropped my line with the same result — *bang* — and Brian and Rambo laughed at my yelps of amazement and fright while I struggled with another prodigious aimara.

Ten minutes later, five glistening fish lay at Rambo's feet; roasted and smoked, they would last us for a week.

We drifted back to camp in silence, passing the rusted, hand-lettered sign of a mining claim from a half century ago, when prospectors had ascended the falls to look for gold in the upper Rewa. At noon we paused at a wide platform of shield rock, where we stretched our legs and rested while Rambo cleaned the aimaras with his cutlass. Scales peeled off their bodies in handfuls, each one a perfect hexagon, and floated on the river like petals of a geometric flower until unseen fish pulled them under. In the late morning sun, the forest seemed benevolent, almost familiar; I might have been on a fishing trip with my uncle on one of the ancient rivers of north Georgia. Sean pointed out a chorus of redthroats at the edge of my hearing, and Brian pulled his cap over his eyes and lay back on the rock with his arms folded, wearing a look of deep contentment.

"I think we could live here for a long time," Sean said.

He wasn't the first to have this thought. Sitting on a billion-year-old rock, watching Rambo scale the wolffish, I felt we'd arrived at a version of the Guiana Shield as it first appeared to human eyes — or to the caracaras' eyes, for that matter: a place whose animals had no reason to fear us, whose rivers were bursting with edible monsters. Since the Cretaceous extinctions, the largest animals in the forest have always been aquatic, including some true dragons: a fossil crocodile from the western Amazon called *Purussaurus* was nearly identical to the Rewa's black caimans except that it was forty feet long, and a giant snake called *Titanoboa* was three times the size of a modern anaconda. No land animal, however, has ever surpassed humans in pulling meat from the water, and caracaras like the young bird at Thorn must have sensed an opportunity in the first people to travel up the rivers of the shield. Brian said that the Wapishana word for black caracaras means "tapir bird" — more evidence for Helmut Sick's account — but the young bird watching Jose prepare our dinner seemed to be evaluating his potential as an ally.

Half an hour later, Brian and Rambo hung the two smallest aimaras from a tree near our camp, hoping to attract scavenging birds, and we found Jose in his hammock perusing my copy of Hudson's *Birds and Man.* The warmth and deep quiet of early afternoon descended, and Brian fed scraps of fish to Micky the caiman while Rambo tied perfect knots on an arsenal of fishhooks. Across the river a forest falcon called, a nearly human-sounding *Oh . . . oh . . . ohhh!,* and Sean and I watched a black caracara take a bath on the shore. It dipped its body three times in the river, shook a curtain of spray from its feathers like a dog, and settled down to feed on a pile of fish guts Jose had left at the waterline.

It wasn't alone for long. A black vulture twice its size landed and strode up to it, looking intent and menacing, and the caracara retreated to a spot a few paces away, where it scratched in the warm sand to reveal a cooler layer beneath and settled into it like a bean-bag. The caracara was the picture of contentment, basking in the sun with fluffed feathers, but it glanced at the feeding vulture now and again, as if thinking through a problem. A few minutes later it stood up, stretched, and charged headlong at the larger bird. The vulture stepped back in surprise, and the caracara snatched a sandy morsel in one foot and hopped away on the other, holding out its wings for balance. It was a textbook caracara move — clownish, ingenious, and effective — and the vulture looked annoyed, but didn't give chase.

"I could watch these guys forever," Sean sighed. "Too bad I'd never get funding to study them."

It was the last day before we'd need to turn back, and for our final trip Brian wanted to take us as far upriver as possible, with a stop at the creek where he'd wrestled the giant armadillo. He threaded the boat through a labyrinth of submerged and exposed boulders for hours, until the ever-narrowing Rewa began to resemble the upper Chattahoochee: a shallow, rock-studded stream where the air smelled of raw clay and leaf mold. Trees undermined by the river formed natural arches above us, and green ibis and sunbitterns rested in their shade while barn swallows skimmed the river — visitors from North America, like me. Dead limbs lay so thick in the stream that Rambo had to clear them away with his cutlass, but Brian pressed on until a clear, swift creek called Anka entered the Rewa from the east.

Beyond it the river was too low for our boat to proceed, and I hopped out to savor a few minutes in the deepest part of the Guiana Shield I would ever see. South and east of us lay a hundred thousand square miles of unbroken forest, a wilderness like no other on Earth, and the late afternoon at its edge was so hushed and still that it seemed nothing might ever happen again. Sean lifted a stick from the ground that was still coated with dried mud from last year's rainy season, and I watched a pair of jacamars — needlebilled relatives of woodpeckers — sally into a sunbeam to snatch insects from the air, and land among the huge, silver-frosted leaves of a cecropia tree. At the stream's edge, the only animal tracks were the fine prints of a sandpiper, and I dipped my hands in the water and drank. It tasted as cold and pure as snowmelt.

Brian unbuttoned his shirt and leaned back against the outboard, gazing upstream. He seemed faintly disappointed; he'd hoped to take us to a place where the river was barely as wide as the boat, a place he'd seen only once in his life. "There you will find tapir," he murmured, "so tame, you can touch them."

On the return drift, the sky filled with shoals of white-collared swifts, and kingfishers called sharply in the failing light. After sundown Rambo's spotlight played over the shore and the trees, seeking the eyeshine of mammals and reptiles, and I wondered what the creatures of the upper Rewa made of our lantern-eyed, five-headed monster, surely the scariest animal in the forest. A slim red snake wriggled past us in the water, and a puzzled family of capybaras stood on a sandbar in midstream, two calves peeking out from behind their parents' legs. I'd nearly forgotten the giant armadillo until Brian drew up at an indentation in the riverbank, where the mouth of a seasonal creek was clogged with vines.

"Our walk begins here," he said. We hauled the boat ashore while Brian attacked the vines with his cutlass, revealing a V-shaped tunnel into the forest. At midday it might have been inviting and mysterious, but at night it looked like a portal to the underworld. I asked Brian what to do if we met a jaguar.

"Kneel down, and pray to almighty God to help you," he replied, at which Rambo and Jose laughed, and I did too, but not without a lump in my throat. Brian had once fought off a jaguar with a cutlass and his bare hands, and seemed to feel he could do it again, but there wouldn't be much room to maneuver in a narrow creek bed, and I couldn't help thinking how screwed we'd be if one of us startled a *Bothrops.*

"Do not get the panic!" advised Jose, stepping into the void, and I followed him.

We might as well have crawled into a cave. Our breath condensed in the cool, wet air seeping down the channel, and the trees above us blotted out the star-filled sky. The steep walls of the creek glittered with iridescent droplets, which I thought at first were dew. Then I saw they were the eyes of tropical wolf spiders, and the blood drained from my face. Some were nearly the size of my hand. Brian brushed past them without concern, pointing out another *Theraphosa* crouched beneath a rotting log. It was as large as the one we'd seen at Thorn camp, but somehow less unnerving than its cousins that lurked in every crevice of the bank. Though most scurried away in our lights, a few stood their ground, as if daring us to approach.

I tried to remind myself that they were (mostly) harmless, that they were there in the day, too, and that we'd lived among them for weeks without incident, but I felt light-headed with fear. Every turn of the creek revealed hundreds more, many of them running down their favorite prey — cockroaches — at an alarming speed. After twenty minutes I'd seen enough for a lifetime, but Brian pressed on for nearly an hour, stepping blithely over two columns of army ants and a quivering mass of termites while I focused on breathing, and on placing the capitals of the fifty states in alphabetical order.

I'd have asked to turn around, except that the signs of a giant armadillo were everywhere. Its huge front claws had scored the soft wood of fallen limbs, and a set of three-toed tracks the width of my palm were divided by the sinuous imprint of a long, dragging tail. Patches of wet, upturned leaves had collected where it probed with its long snout for worms, and Brian finally came to a halt at a rounded, fresh-looking excavation in the bank, almost large enough for me to crawl inside, where the closest living relative of the glyptodonts had carved a temporary shelter.

"Here I found him," he said.

I worried that Brian might sit down to wait or continue up the creek, but to my great relief he promptly turned back. A small eternity later we emerged at the river, where my heartbeat slowly returned to normal and I checked and rechecked my trousers for eight-legged hitchhikers.

"So many spiders," Brian sighed, wiping his brow with his forearm. I was relieved that it wasn't just me. Rambo pushed us off from shore, and a boat-billed heron appeared in his spotlight, perched on a rock in the river. Its huge, dark eyes, black headdress, and pale body made it look like the lord of the dead in animal guise, bidding us a solemn farewell.

We broke camp in the morning under an unsettled sky, with thunderheads mounting in the distance and a light wind in the trees. The black caracaras were nowhere to be seen, and a pair of black-cowled nunbirds repeated a short, lilting phrase that seemed to ask and answer its own question.

"That's the rain song," said Jose, kneading dough for our breakfast of fried bread. *"'The rain — will kill you!'"* As he worked, I confessed to feeling that if we'd gone farther upriver, we'd have found a secret patch of savanna or a hidden village, concealed somehow from the satellites that see this part of the world as an unbroken sea of green. It was easy to see why so many people, including Hudson, had filled this place with dreams.

Jose poured oil into a skillet and offered a story from his childhood. Like Brian, he said, he'd grown up in a small village in the savanna, where the mountains loomed enticingly above the plain — mountains his parents forbade him to visit. But he couldn't resist, and snuck out at night with friends to climb to a ledge where they could see the lights of Boa Vista, thirty miles away in Brazil. "Growing up, it was all we talked about," he said. "Boa Vista, going to Boa Vista. I wanted to learn Portuguese, dance *forró* —"

He was cut off by a burst of laughter from Rambo and Brian, who were taking down their tarps and hammocks. "You can't do that!" called Brian. "You can't dance!"

"Well, that is my dream!" Jose called back.

He'd lived it to the letter. After he left Bible school in Lethem, he stayed with an aunt in Boa Vista and learned Portuguese from her children. Once he'd found his feet, he worked odd jobs all over northeastern Brazil, moving on when he liked. "A Wapishana is a river man," Jose said, "like the black caracara. And when he finds a place he likes, maybe fall in love with a local girl, he stay." As he spoke, a toucan across the river began yelping its head off — high, ascending whoops that meant *I'm here, and I see you,* while a curve of the riverbank duplicated its cries with a single, perfect echo. I wondered if it was excited at finding such a worthy opponent or if it was just having fun, and Jose mimicked its call to himself as he laid strips of fried dough in a bowl and drizzled them with honey.

Sean joined us with his rolled-up hammock tucked under his arm, saying that he'd just seen the shadows of several large vultures.

369

He thought we should check on yesterday's aimaras, and after breakfast we took the boat around the bend with Rambo and Brian, where the half-eaten fish dangled from an overhanging limb like medieval convicts at a gibbet. Several black vultures were assembled nearby on a sandbar, but they were waiting their turn: in the tree above the fish sat a king vulture in its snowy robes, its distended crop bulging through its breast feathers like a ripe peach.

Kings are the most enigmatic of the New World's vultures. They live only in tropical forests, and like red-throated caracaras, little is known and even less has been written about their lives. Their elegant plumage — pure white, with black flight and tail feathers — seems to violate the somber dress code of most vultures, and their bare heads are wrapped in a Pharaonic mask of colorful wattles that highlights their red-and-yellow necks, orange beaks, and blue-white eyes. They have the same regal bearing as their nearest relatives, the condors, but they're legendarily shy and usually seen alone when they're seen at all.

This one, however, had a companion: a newly fledged chick, whose all-black plumage was surprisingly drab for a royal heir. Its soft-featured face was dull gray, as were its eyes, but it wore a curious, contemplative expression, and it craned its neck to peer at us as we drifted closer, first with one eye, then the other.

The two kings clambered heavily into the higher limbs of the tree, giving us the widest possible berth, while a pair of yellow-headed vultures joined the black vultures on the sandbar. They too were oddly handsome, like turkey vultures in bold face paint, and a third came circling in only to be intercepted by a red-throated caracara, which zoomed out of the forest with its talons held out to strike.

"Auntie-man!" cried Rambo.

The vulture teetered in the air and veered off while the caracara landed on a snag, throwing back its head to summon a quartet of fellow red-throats, who warmed up with a round of agitated *ka-o*s and performed their territorial call and dance. It seemed they were challenging the vultures to a scream-off, which wasn't at all fair; vultures can only croak and hiss, while the caracaras were armed with one of the loudest voices in the forest, and their wild chorus rang across the river.

"There's *got* to be a nest in there," muttered Sean, nearly beside himself with excitement. An emergent tree set back from the bank struck him as a likely candidate, so we beached the boat and climbed into the forest to find it. The red-throats didn't like this one bit, and they harangued us mercilessly while Brian thrashed through the undergrowth with

Sean at his side. I did my best to keep up, but the understory was a thick and confounding mass of spiny palms and fallen trees, and I blundered into a rotten stump that housed an army ant bivouac. Thousands of ants boiled out of the ground, bent on defending their queen and her brood, and I bounded away as fast as I could, spiders and snakes be damned.

Scarlet macaws joined the caracaras in screaming up a storm, adding to the feeling that we'd tripped an alarm, and a pair of oropendolas stirred up by the excitement mated on a branch above me while Brian struggled with a thicket of palms. The male made a few deft leaps over the female's back before mounting her for a hard-flapping instant, then collapsed into the understory, and Rambo stifled a laugh while Sean pointed at the crown of the tree he'd seen from the river. In its heart was a dark mass of vegetation: a giant bromeliad.

"Betcha twenty bucks that's it," he said.

The red-throats did little to persuade us otherwise. Their cries reached a fever pitch as they dashed from one branch to another, as if trying to appear more numerous than they were, and one feinted at me, talons out, while another gave a weird, keening cry Sean hadn't heard before. If this wasn't their nest, it was hard to imagine what else they could be protecting. "If I could climb up and get a picture," said Sean, "that'd be the sixth recorded nest. Ever."

It was an extraordinary moment: here was another group of red-throats nesting in a bromeliad, hundreds of miles from Nouragues, confirming that their taste for breeding in giant epiphytes wasn't just a local quirk — and I wished, for the first time in my life, for a crossbow and a climbing harness. But there was nothing to be done, and we had to turn back. A strong wind stirred the forest while we retraced our steps, blurring the canopy into a jumble of swaying limbs, but a gap above us showed a shred of clear blue. In it was a king vulture, its bright wings stark and bold against the sky.

"Pretty soon it darkened up, and begun to thunder and lighten; so the birds was right about it," wrote Mark Twain.

Directly it begun to rain, and it rained like all fury, too, and I never seen the wind blow so. It was one of those regular summer storms. It would get so dark that it looked all blue-black outside, and lovely; and the rain would thrash along by so thick that the trees off a little ways looked dim and spiderwebby; and here would come a blast of wind that would bend the trees down and turn up the pale underside of the leaves; and then a perfect ripper of a gust would follow along and set the branches to toss-ing their arms as if they was just wild; and next, when it was just about the bluest and blackest — FST! it was as bright as glory, and you'd have a little glimpse of treetops a-plunging about away off yonder in the storm, hundreds of yards further than you could see before; dark as sin again in a second, and now you'd hear the thunder let go with an awful crash, and then go rum-bling, grumbling, tumbling down the sky towards the under side of the world, like rolling empty barrels down stairs.

Twain, a contemporary of Hudson, could easily have been describing a storm on the Rewa. Over the next two days we weathered a series of afternoon cloudbursts, awesome in their intensity — a taste of the coming rainy season, when the skies would open for days on end. Brian worried that the river might rise enough to make the waterfalls impass-able, but the parched forest soaked up the rain like a sponge, and we arrived at the top of Corona Falls to find their size and volume unchanged. On the way up I'd been so tired that I hadn't paid much attention to the falls themselves, but now we paused to admire their wide, broken shelves of volcanic rock, where the river cascaded over green curtains of water-weed. In a month the falls would be foaming, wild, and fatal to anything swept over the edge, but for now the cracks and hollows beside the main channel of the river held delicate masses of frogs' eggs, and our shadows sent little brown crabs scuttling for cover beneath boulders tumbled smooth by thousands of wet seasons. Carrying our boat down was easier than the ascent, and Brian opted for a route that led to a broad, shallow pool at the base of the falls where orange, vegetarian piranhas called pacus stirred in the water like koi. We set down our gear and bathed, and Brian showed me a place where the pool emptied into a long, dark channel, hemmed in by smooth walls of basalt: the start of the lower Rewa.

"Tomorrow we will come here," he declared, "and catch monsters."

The channel was deep enough to appear still, and nothing moved beneath its surface; if it held monsters, they were invisible. I looked up at the opposite bank and was startled by a face looking back at me, chiseled into the rock.

"Many of them here," said Brian.

I'd heard rumors of petroglyphs along the Rewa but never expected to see them; stone carvings in the tropics are quickly obscured by the relentless growth of forest. But once I tuned my eyes to find them, a gallery of rough but artful images emerged from the boulders at the base of the falls, where the river's seasonal pulses swept them clean.

Rambo said that one reminded him of a spectacled owl, and the figure of a man with a heart-shaped face became a monkey when Brian pointed out the faint curve of its tail. But most were inscrutable spirals and curlicues or patterns of crosshatched lines, nothing like the fastidious carvings of Mayan or Inca ruins. These seemed older, wilder, and deeply alive, like the spare images of antelope and bighorn sheep in the cliffs of the western United States.

When they were made was impossible to say. The charcoal in cave paintings can be carbon-dated, but there's no way to date petroglyphs; these could even have been the work of the first people to enter South America, who traveled across the Guiana Shield before they ever saw the Amazon or the Andes. Farther down the channel, a wide shelf of rock was scored with oblong divots where hunters had sharpened their stone tools. Each held a few tablespoons of rain, and they looked so freshly carved that it seemed their makers might return at any moment.

And in a way, of course, they'd never left at all. Though the figures inscribed on the rocks didn't seem to hold a particular significance for Brian and Rambo, they regarded them with the curiosity and pride anyone might feel for the work of their ancestors, especially in a place where it wasn't impossible to

376

imagine their lives — or even, for a moment, to live them. After a short rest, we carried our gear down to the beach where we'd stashed the second boat weeks ago, and made camp to the approaching thunder of a storm that raged all night.

The next morning was thick, wet, and slow, and we were all tired. Brian and Rambo led me back to the channel while Jose stayed in camp with Sean, who was busy photographing a basilisk lizard and a small green tarantula he'd found in a rotten log. Rambo wanted a tiger catfish for dinner, but Brian still had monsters on his mind, and I watched him tie his hook to a line as thick as the strings of a bass guitar. The first bite was mine — a black piranha, of course — and Rambo and Brian followed with a pair of exceptionally large vampire fish, whose curved teeth and shining blue scales dazzled me again with their beauty and ugliness. We kept the largest to eat, and on his second throw Rambo caught another piranha, which he stunned with his cutlass and laid on the rocks to use for bait. I was about to cast my line again when Brian's went taut as a bowstring.

"First monster!" he called.

I sat down to watch. Brian's jaw set and the muscles bulged in his arms, and after a brief struggle he wrested a great, black, torpedo-shaped catfish from the river that must have weighed fifty pounds. Its barbels were two feet long, and a galaxy of tiny white spots decorated its body.

"This is a *jau*," said Rambo, looking on while Brian freed his hook from the fish's enormous mouth. He held it up for me to admire while it grunted in protest — a deep, bone-shaking note — and then, to my relief, released it, and it vanished in the dark water with two flips of its tail. I assumed this was the grand finale, but Brian rebaited his hook, and five minutes later his line tightened again.

"Second monster," he said, and hauled up a catfish even larger than the first. Rambo called it a "banana fish," perhaps because of its shape: it was sleeker and more shark-like, with orange fins and a white belly, and its staccato grunt was a few steps higher than the jau's booming bass. I gazed at it, unsure how to feel, or what to say, in the presence of yet another mind-boggling animal I never knew existed. The Rewa's supply of fantastic creatures seemed unlimited, and I half expected a saurian relic of the Cretaceous to rise from the depths of the channel. I had to remind myself again that there was nothing magical about this river — that the whole world was once like this, not so long ago.

Brian cradled the fish in his arms, looking every inch a proud and accomplished hunter, then let it go; it would be vampire fish for dinner tonight. He seemed pleased to have lived up to his promise, but as we gathered our tackle he saw that the piranha Rambo left for dead was still alive, gasping for air on the warm black stones. Brian looked pained. "Still breathing," he murmured, and carried it to the river where he tenderly stroked its flanks, coaxing water through its gills. But it was too far gone, and tumbled lifelessly in the channel.

Back at camp, we found Jose sitting on a folding chair in his kitchen, carving a bow from a fallen limb. "Taking blows, eh?" he teased, chiding Brian for bringing him only one huge fish, and I followed him to the river's edge to clean it. The vampire's scales and viscera drew a crowd of hungry minnows, which grew even more agitated when Jose opened its swollen belly and released two long, plump egg sacs. My heart sank. She'd probably traveled up the Rewa to spawn, and we'd cut her life short at a critical moment, before she could give her offspring the best possible start in life.

"We can fry them up if you want," said Jose, rinsing his knife in the water. "You can eat a million fish for breakfast." Then he lurched forward, as if struck on the back of the head — and I could have sworn the dead paiara did, too. After a moment of confusion, Jose pointed to a long shadow lurking behind the minnows: a young electric eel. It rose to sip air from the surface, exposing the tiny eyes

379

its own electrical field would one day render useless. The minnows shivered in its probing beams, caught in the grip of a sensory world I couldn't imagine.

"When he release the power," said Jose, "you see the fine fish move." He brandished his knife. "But I have the power to shock he back!"

After dinner we repacked our gear for an early start on the long ride back to Kwitaro Backbone, and I went with Sean to pay a last visit to the monsters' pool. We sat in the dark on sun-warmed boulders, talking about the slim chance that he'd ever study the red-throats again, even though he'd have liked nothing more. His girlfriend had just secured a grant to study black widow spiders in a lab in Toronto, which would take him away from the western forests he loved, and though he looked forward to assisting her, it wasn't his favorite kind of science. But "in the end," he said, "you have to go where the money is."

He meant this as a statement of fact, but there was a note of defeat in his voice that made me think of Hudson in London, far from the animals of his childhood, trying and mostly failing to wring a living from his pen. It had taken decades for him to be seen for who he really was, but I didn't know whether Sean would find that reassuring or depressing, so I kept it to myself. On the path back to camp we paused at a pile of bones that were once a black vulture, cleaned to shining perfection by ants. The hook-billed skull was nearly weightless in my hand, and its empty sockets stared back at me. Where had it slept at night? What had it seen of the world? Who were its friends?

"Look at this cane toad," said Sean, shining his lamp on an amphibian the size of a football. "Doesn't it have beautiful eyes?"

Rambo had gone to bed when we returned, but Brian was sitting in a chair by the ghost light, making sure we came back before he turned in. Sean went straight to his hammock, and Jose called to me from the kitchen, where he handed me a mug of tea and invited me to sit.

"As you know," he began, "my great-grandmother used to tell me stories, about the days when the animals were people."

I loved these stories. He'd been rationing them out in the afternoons, and through them I'd been able to glimpse his great-grandmother Madeleine, who lived long enough to see a picture of Jose's eleventh grandchild, born in Boston — her great-great-great-granddaughter. Madeleine had been a widow for many years when Jose was born, and had little use for men. But she was fond of him, and from the time he was old enough to walk she took him on long rambles through the forest, where she spent her days fishing and collecting useful plants. Her tales of the feats and follies of the animal-people were full of sleep-inducing asides and embellishments, and rarely had a discernible moral or a definite ending; one concerned a cacique who enlisted a carpenter bee to build a chair in the shape of the king vulture's head, hoping to win the king's favor; another explained, in a roundabout way, why opossums have a strong fishy smell. But the look in Jose's eye suggested he'd been holding this one in reserve.

"A long time ago," he began, "the caracaras used to be human beings, as I told you. And the crested caracara was like a security man, patrolling up and down the savanna, letting all the other animals know if there's danger. And the black caracara was the same for the rivers — patrolling the river banks, whistling, so other animals know. And the bush auntie-man is the forest guard. And it is still like that now, today.

"Well, one day an old retired horse on the savanna is eating grass, and he come up under a tree and lie down on his side. And the vulture, the black vulture, is the great hunter; he comes to see the horse, and he is talking to the caracara, and he says, 'I think he is dead.' And the horse lets out a great fart, and the hunter say, 'I think he is dead, he smells so, like he all rotten.'

"And the caracara say, 'No, I think he is alive.' And the vulture say, 'I think he is dead,

382

and to prove it I will stick my head inside him.' So the horse let another wind pass, and the vulture stick his head inside the horse's anus — because that is vulture's favorite part to eat, the anus — and then the horse clamp down on his head!

"And the caracara *laugh,* man, with his head back so far, like he does. And that is why the caracara is always laughing, and the vultures have no feathers on the head. And even today it's still true, crested caracara is the savanna man, black caracara is the river man, bush auntie-man is the forest patrol, security guy. And that is the story I have to tell you."

Jose held my eyes through the entire tale, as if daring me to laugh — then he looked down, suddenly shy, while I gulped down my tea. I wanted to tell him that spending time with him in the bush auntie-man's ancient home had been one of the greatest privileges of my life. But I couldn't think how to say it in a way that wouldn't sound insincere — or, worse, make him wonder if I was mocking him. So I am saying it now.

I walked down to the river to brush my teeth, turning off my headlamp to gaze at the Milky Way. Then I remembered where I was and turned it back on — and the shining green eyes of a black caiman lit up in the water, fixing me with its implacable smile: *I've been waiting for you for 70 million years.* A month earlier I'd have been scared, but now I only felt chastened; the Rewa was still the caiman's domain, not mine, and I respectfully backed away. I joined Brian by the ghost light, and after a few moments I asked if he'd also heard the story of the caracara, the vulture, and the horse. But he shook his head.

"Jose is the world creation," he said, with deep affection. "Created together when God created the heavens and the earth."

■ ■ ■ ■

Part IV
Between the Sky
and the Sea

■ ■ ■ ■

Everything on this southern continent has
been effected on a grand scale.
— CHARLES DARWIN

Cunas ch'iyar awayunim c'iyar bayetani,
jank'o phajilani, wila cayuni, jachac
jacht'asqui pampanacanija? Ucajj allkama-
riwa.

(What is it that wears a black shawl, black
head scarf, white skirt, and has red legs,
while it cries all the time in the fields? An
alkamari.)
— AYMARA RIDDLE

16
LAST DAYS OF THE GUADALUPE CARACARA

On the morning of December 1, 1900, a compact, sinewy Californian named Rollo Beck stepped ashore on a dormant volcano off the Pacific coast of Mexico and entered the annals of extinction. Isla Guadalupe's desolate crags and cliff-bound coast had little to attract a casual visitor, but Beck was no tourist: he was a professional bird collector, and museum curators revered his ability to collect, prepare, and deliver complete sets of study skins from legendarily remote places.

Beck was especially admired for his skill in collecting seabirds, which range unpredictably over vast areas of ocean. Most ornithologists in the late nineteenth century doubted that birds had an olfactory sense, but Beck knew from experience that seabirds can smell food from miles away, and on calm days he would row out into Monterey Bay in a dory and drift with the current, trailing an oily mixture of fish guts and blood behind him. Then he would row back along the shimmering slick, picking off the petrels, terns, and gulls that gathered on it to feed. Once he recovered their floating bodies, he cleaned and prepared them on the spot — removing their organs and muscles, stuffing them with cotton, and stitching them up with an offhand elegance you can spot at a glance in museum collections. Then he roasted and ate the birds' carcasses over a small fire he built in a sandbox. If night fell before he was through, he lay down beside it and went to sleep.

Like William Henry Hudson, Beck was an autodidact. He never finished the eighth grade, but he was hardy, brilliant, and brave (a colleague once described him as "a tough little bastard"), and together with his wife, Ida, he became one of the most accomplished bird collectors of all time. The Becks were an ornithological power couple — childless, adventuresome, and equally handy with a scalpel or a rifle — and they spent the early decades of the twentieth century gathering tens of thousands of specimens from South America and the South Pacific for museums and collectors in the United States and England, including birds new to science or presumed lost.

But all these adventures lay ahead of Rollo when he landed on Guadalupe, which lies about two hundred miles west of Baja California. He was barely thirty, nearly a decade away from his marriage to Ida, and he'd just made his first paid collecting trips to California's Channel Islands, where he suggested — correctly — that the islands' scrub jays might be a distinct species. Guadalupe was a brief stop on the way to his biggest job yet, a months-long collecting trip in the Galápagos for the California Academy of Sciences, and though the island wasn't widely known as a haven for unusual species, Beck was hoping to find a unique bird there that lived nowhere else in the world.

Guadalupe is about four times the size of Manhattan, and its brittle slopes of volcanic scree are every shade of brown, yellow, and orange. Since it was never connected to another landmass, all its plants and animals arrived by chance — blown in by the wind, or washed ashore in rafts of driftwood and seafoam — and over many thousands of years, these colonists built their own ecosystem on the island. A forest of pines, junipers, and oaks ran along the crests of its dormant calderas, and some of its birds had evolved into separate species from their mainland ancestors, including a woodpecker, a nuthatch, and a burrowing petrel. Cut off from the rest of the world, these birds lived in an isolated paradise, free from the predators that plagued their ancestors in mainland North and South America. There were no snakes, no rats, no cats, no pigs, and no foxes.

There was, however, a Guadalupe caracara,

whose ancestors also blew in on the wind. They were impressive birds, about the size of a barnyard rooster, with the same yellow faces and black crests as the caranchos Hudson admired thousands of miles away in the Pampas. Like most caracaras they were unfussy eaters, and probably consumed their share of insects and shellfish, but their bread and butter was likely Guadalupe's most notable animal residents — seals. Like the Falklands, Guadalupe is an oasis of land in the open sea, and thousands of sea lions, fur seals, and elephant seals crowded its slender beaches to bask in the sun, nurse their pups, and escape the orcas and white sharks cruising offshore. Guadalupe caracaras probably didn't attack healthy seals, but dead pups, afterbirths, and adults wounded in fights or raked by sharks' teeth might have enticed a scavenging opportunist, and the seals' feces contained enough partly digested fish, squid, and sea urchins for the caracaras to give them a second pressing. If you ever end up downwind of a seal colony, you won't soon forget its fierce, acrid scent or its threnody of strangled cries; these were the sounds and smells of the Guadalupe caracaras' world for thousands of years.

Their lives might have gone on like this for centuries more if it hadn't been for humans, who came for the seals in the late eighteenth century and introduced goats to the island to supply themselves with meat. The seals were soon wiped out, but the goats grew fat and numerous on the vegetation of an island that had never known grazing animals, and new settlers from Mexico and California attempted to catch and farm them. The goat farmers regarded the caracaras as pests, and killed as many as they could, but their settlement failed in less than a decade, and by the time of Beck's visit, Guadalupe was once again uninhabited by humans.

The settlers' parting gift to the caracaras, however, was a deadly measure of fame. Stories of Guadalupe's strange "eagles" eventually reached the mainland, and fortune seekers traveled to the island in hopes of catching and selling the few birds that remained. One was a former goat hunter named Harry Drent, who turned up at the pier in San Diego in 1897 with four living Guadalupe caracaras, demanding $150 apiece for them (about $15,000 today). Drent told a local newspaper that he'd written to the Smithsonian Institution and was "confident I shall secure a high figure." He also seems to have had a real — if slight — attachment to the birds. "I have them all named," he boasted, "and each one will come to me when called."

A month later, the birds were dead. Daniel Cleveland, a member of the San Diego Society of Natural History, regretted the loss bitterly, telling the naturalist Clinton Abbott in 1933 that he'd been "very anxious" to purchase a pair but couldn't afford them; Drent had refused to budge on the price. "The man's greed resulted in our failure to rear some of these birds in captivity," Cleveland lamented, "and in his own loss from his failure to sell the birds." Another member of the society, A. M. Ingersoll, recalled that two of Drent's birds were displayed as a curiosity in a saloon.

At first [they] were in their cage in the back room, but then chicken-wire was put across the show window and the two birds were placed there. They attracted lots of attention and had a peculiar characteristic of lowering the head, something like a Barn Owl, and swinging it from side to side. Thereafter they were taken away from the saloon, on account of their dirty habits, and later on one of the birds escaped and was caught and killed in a chicken coop near the waterfront. The bird was taken to Frank Holster, who mounted it and had it on exhibition in his taxidermy shop. . . . This shop later burned, and the specimen was consumed.

Unlike Harry Drent, Rollo Beck's interest in the birds wasn't purely mercenary. But his job was to collect study skins, and the Guadalupe caracaras made it easy. A group of curious birds came winging in to check him out when he landed, perhaps mistaking him for one of the sea's mysterious gifts, and "of 11 birds that flew toward me," he wrote, "9 were secured. The other two were shot at but got away . . . [and] judging by their tameness and the short time that I was on the island I assumed at the time that they must be abundant."

Beck's account is tinged with an odd mixture of regret and pride — why mention shooting at the escapees? — and it's hard to believe his claim that he thought the birds were abundant, since their rarity probably drew him to the island in the first place. One thing, however, is certain: Guadalupe caracaras were never seen alive again. The thousands of specimens the Becks collected in their long career are still an invaluable resource for scientists, but Rollo is the only person to have single-handedly pushed a bird of prey from rarity into extinction — an indelible blemish on the career of a field naturalist, and one at which Hudson would have shuddered.

Today Isla Guadalupe is a barren and desolate place, home to a fishing village and a lonely military outpost. The goats have finally been removed, and seals and sea lions once again breed on its beaches, but much of the island remains denuded and silent: the goats scraped away most of its vegetation, and cats that came ashore with the goat farmers doomed its native birds. A survey of Guadalupe's terrestrial life found it teeming with earwigs and black widow spiders, as if to underline the damage that a small group of people can do to a fragile landscape, and a crestfallen visitor from the San Diego Natural History Museum called it a "moonscape" and a "ghost island." If there are ghosts, the Guadalupe caracaras are among them.

"This is the one you don't want to be in," said Carla Dove, unlocking a tall metal cabinet with a heavy ring of keys. We were standing in the ornithology collection of the Smithsonian National Museum of Natural History in Washington, DC, where Dove, an associate curator, runs the museum's feather identification lab. A good portion of her work involves sifting through the pulverized remains of birds that collide with aircraft.

This cabinet was one she rarely opened, however, since it contained species that would never see an airplane. Dove carefully pulled out a long metal shelf that held the skins of a Labrador duck (a handsome black-and-white sea duck, extinct since the 1850s) and an artfully mounted Guadalupe caracara — one of thirty-four that still exist. Study skins rarely convey a bird's personality (and aren't meant to), but this one had once been displayed to the public, and a taxidermist had fitted it with dusty glass eyes that gave it an expression of faint surprise.

It wasn't one of Beck's nine birds. It was the "type" specimen — the one from which it was first described as a species in 1875. Dove lifted it gently from the tray. A few of its breast feathers had fallen out, but it stood proudly and naturally on a wooden perch, its head turned slightly to the left, its chin lifted in a way that suggested confidence, interest, and the bold spirit all caracaras seem to share. It wore the same black cap as the crested caracaras I'd seen in Guyana and Tierra del Fuego, but the feathers of its body and wings were ringed with fine black and white bars, like a herringbone suit. To its left and right, other members of the same unfortunate club lay sealed in identical cabinets — ivory-billed and imperial woodpeckers from Louisiana and Mexico, Carolina parakeets from Florida, even the pelvic girdle of a dodo.

But one object in the caracara's mausoleum caught me off guard: a human skull, brown with age, that had been part of a children's exhibit in the nineteenth century. Dove opened a hinged panel on the back of its cranium to reveal the nest a wren had built in its brain case, using its eye sockets for a front door. I was impressed by the bird's taste in living quarters, but a human skull seemed out of place — to say the least — in a cabinet of extinct birds, and I asked the obvious question: Who was this?

"We don't know," Dove replied quietly, closing the panel and fastening its tiny brass latch.

I stared at the skull's convoluted seams, absorbing its contradictions: it was an object too powerful to discard, too uncomfortable to display. I thought of Hudson contemplating the bones along the Río Negro, sensing a world of knowledge and experience that would always be closed to him; of Darwin, who ransacked ancient graves in Patagonia during his voyage on the *Beagle;* of Jose, under the moon, saying, "Remember, man, that ye are dust." The thought that a bird could one day build its home in my head was reassuring, a reminder that the natural world will always be heedless of human time, human history, human interest.

It also reminded me that even without Beck's coup de grâce, the Guadalupe caracaras were probably doomed. Islands are sometimes called laboratories of evolution, since their unique opportunities and constraints can produce strange and wonderful creatures — dwarf elephants, giant tortoises, flightless birds. But they can also be an evolutionary trap. Their ecosystems are fragile and unsophisticated compared to those of the mainland, and they're vulnerable to disruption by natural disasters like earthquakes, diseases, or the sudden appearance of a new predator. Like the giant mammals of the Americas, many animals endemic to islands have died out shortly after we arrived — including the warrahs of the Falklands, the mammoths of Wrangel Island, the ground sloths of the Caribbean, and most of the native birds of Polynesia.

You might imagine that birds would be better equipped to escape from us than mammals, though the record suggests otherwise. Plenty of continental birds have colonized islands, but no bird species that evolved on an island has ever found a foothold on a larger landmass, and the caracaras are no exception: the Guadalupe caracaras were the latest of several island caracaras to vanish in the fairly recent past, including two extinct species identified from tar pits in Cuba, and a third found in an underwater sepulcher called a "blue hole" in the Bahamas, beside the bones of a giant sloth.

The fate of these birds hangs ominously over the Johnny rooks. Striated caracaras' small population and range are red flags of impending extinction, and humans have done them few favors in the Falklands, where introduced predators and decades of persecution have taken a toll on their numbers, their prey, and their habitats. But even without human intervention their prospects would be uncertain, as a final extinct caracara suggests:

in the ancient peat bog where Robin Woods and Mark Adams unearthed the bones of five-thousand-year-old striated caracaras, they also found the bones of an eagle-sized bird, a sort of mega–Johnny rook, that no one has ever seen.

Why this large caracara disappeared will likely remain a mystery, since the answer probably lies under the sea. When the world was last at its coldest — about seventeen thousand years ago — huge glaciers captured and held enough of our planet's water to lower global sea level by about four hundred feet, inflating the Falklands from a constellation of islands to a range of low mountains, connected to the mainland by a strip of grassy tundra that's now the submerged Patagonian Shelf. In this colder, drier world, animals from continental South America could travel over land to the Falklands — but they were marooned there when the world warmed and the seas rose.

Darwin intuited this past in the fjords of Tierra del Fuego, where the *Beagle* sailed through deep channels left by retreating glaciers. "Tierra del Fuego may be described as a mountainous land, partly submerged in the sea," he wrote, "so that deep inlets and bays occupy the place where valleys should exist." By five thousand years ago, the Falklands were much like they are today — an isolated haven hemmed in by rising seas, and poised to shrink still further. In the next century, sea level is projected to rise enough to drown the meadows of Steeple Jason where Johnny rooks scratch for worms and grubs today, and it seems unlikely that they'll still be with us five thousand years from now.

But a nagging feature of their lives may be troubling you, just as it's troubled me since the day I met them: they don't *act* like rare birds. Endangered species are often threatened for obvious reasons — because they're highly specialized, or delicious, or too dependent on resources humans covet. Striated caracaras combine the small range of a threatened species with the confidence and adaptability of a common one, and their confinement, as Darwin put it, seems "a singular precaution in so tame and fearless a bird." If they're really so clever and flexible, why didn't they conquer the world?

17
THE MYSTERIOUS FALCON
OF MANCO CÁPAC

In the ruddy, volcanic dust of northern Chile, on the shoulder of a road across the high desert between San Pedro de Atacama and the Bolivian border, I stooped to touch the desiccated hide of a vicuña. Vicuñas are the rarest and smallest of South America's camels, about the size of a white-tailed deer, and they spend their lives in the stony, arid uplands called *puna,* chewing at wiry desert grasses and drinking meltwater from snow-capped volcanoes. This one lay in the shadow of a mountain named Curiquinca, where it had dried to a husk in the thin air of the high Andes. It was tufted with the fine golden fur people have prized for thousands of years, and surrounded by the footprints of mountain caracaras, the shy, sacred birds I'd come to see.

Mountain caracaras might be the most beautiful of their tribe. They're one of three species of caracara that live only in the chilly deserts and moorlands of South America's highest mountains — all of whom resemble brightly painted ravens, with red faces, yellow legs, and white bellies and underwings. Their silhouettes are as much a signature of the Andes as the mighty arc of a condor, but they're often seen pacing solemnly across the desert, pausing to scratch like chickens for insects and lizards. Unlike the tropical forests' bellicose red-throats or the Pampas' companionable chimangos, mountain caracaras are cautious and uncommon, which gives them an aura of mystery, as does the fact that their favorite habitats seem perversely unwelcoming to life.

In 1968, the ornithologists Leslie Brown and Dean Amadon — the same ones who called the caracaras "a rather unimpressive lot" — described mountain caracaras with a confession: "It is difficult to imagine a raptorial bird," they wrote, "with less falcon-like characteristics." Scientists place the three Andean caracaras in the genus *Phalcoboenus,* Latin for "walking falcon," and like all caracaras they show flashes of ingenuity: Brown and Amadon noted that they visit "the dwellings of Indians in search of refuse of animal origin, and . . . even learned to follow cars, toiling over the slopes like gulls following a ship, to catch in the air bits of food thrown from the vehicles." A BBC crew once filmed a group of carunculated caracaras, the northernmost of the walking falcons, tearing strips of meat from a dead cow and stashing them behind a tuft of grass — a tactic whose purpose became clear when a condor arrived to claim the carcass for itself. And in 1995, a Canadian graduate student named Jason Jones watched three mountain caracaras in Peru perform a feat that made them unique among all birds.

Jones was driving along a highway through a remote desert valley when he saw them — two black-and-white adults and a mottled youngster, standing near a large flat rock — and slowed to a stop to watch as one of the adults circled the rock on foot, lifted its head, and gave "a high-pitched *kieer.*" Its two companions ambled over to join it, and all three "proceeded to work together to flip the rock from its resting place, with each bird using one of its talons." After several minutes of effort, the first bird caught and ate a small creature that dashed from beneath the rock — a skink, perhaps, or one of the mouse-like Andean rodents called tuco-tucos.

Though Jones wasn't an ornithologist, he felt sure he'd seen something special, and he was right: no other birds have been seen cooperating to lift heavy objects. He returned to the valley every day for the following week and watched the caracaras flip four more rocks, and on one occasion an adult passed a captured morsel to the younger bird. It was tempting to think they were parents sharing a lesson with their chick, perhaps even a technique they'd invented. Jones hefted the stones they'd pried loose, and was impressed by their weight. "I do not believe," he concluded, "that one individual could have turned over any of the rocks by itself."

"This handsome bird," Darwin wrote, "from what little I saw of its habits, appears to resemble the Carrancha . . . it is however much shyer, and generally seen in pairs." This passage, from his private journal, seems more congenial than his public mutterings about "false eagles," perhaps because mountain caracaras presented him with another geographical mystery. He was very surprised to see them in northern Chile, since they looked nearly identical to a bird he'd seen (and shot) three thousand miles away, in the foothills of southern Patagonia. These caracaras "were in no part numerous," he noted, and this rarity intrigued him. How could they be so scarce but so far-flung?

The answer lay in the titanic sweep of the Andes themselves, whose power over their continent defies all superlatives. Rising along the seam where South America's continental plate meets the slabs of oceanic crust called the Pacific and Nazca plates, the Andes are the longest chain of mountains on earth — over twice as long as the Himalayas, with more than eight hundred peaks that exceed the highest of the Rockies. They define the west coast of South America for forty-five hundred miles, from Venezuela to Tierra del Fuego, and dominate the landscape even where they can't be seen: they dictate the flow and course of rivers, the fertility of soils, and the character of the weather, and their rain shadow looms over the coastal deserts of Peru and Chile, where decades can elapse between cloudbursts.

None of these facts can prepare you for their presence. Looking east from the central plaza of San Pedro de Atacama, with its cordon of pepper trees and tourist shops, you face an unnervingly imminent wall of giant volcanoes, some rising above eighteen thousand feet, whose profiles alternate between the jagged spires of magmatic rock and wind-sculpted cones of compacted ash. At night, the lights of trucks ascending their pediment from the desert floor seem to defy gravity, and by day it's easy to see why the Incas regarded them as living beings, as ill-tempered and magnanimous as the Old Testament God. The Incas forged their supremely organized civilization in this unlikely place, and to appease the mountains they carried gifts to their frozen summits: gold, textiles, even children, whom they killed and ritually buried in mountaintop tombs.

It's less well-known that the Incas also held caracara feathers among their most prized objects. Headgear signified rank and identity at all levels of Inca society, and Garcilaso de la Vega, the son of an Inca princess and a Spanish military commander, wrote that only the emperor — the Sapa Inca — was permitted to wear the black-and-white plumes of a bird called *corequenque*. Each new emperor received a fresh set of its wing feathers to set in the band he wore on his temples, and was buried with them when he died. Corequenques were so rare that they lived only by a sacred lake at the foot of a mountain fifty miles from Cuzco; "Never more than two of them, a Male and Female, are seen together," Garcilaso wrote. "But whence they come, or where they are bred, is not known."

The true identity of the corequenques has been debated. Some authors have suggested that they might have been quetzals, or one of the Andes' many dazzling hummingbirds. But Garcilaso's description matches the behavior, plumage, and habitat of mountain caracaras, and he noted that the Incas venerated them not only because they were rare, but because the birds symbolized "their two original parents, man and woman, which descended from heaven." Inca rulers and mythmakers loved symbols of duality — heaven and earth, sun and moon, dark and light, male and female — and the caracaras' black-and-white wardrobe might have appealed to their sense of cosmic order.

So, too, did the birds' fondness for the high mountains, nearer to the sacred summits and the realm of the sun god, Inti. The first ruler to style himself Sapa Inca was a man named Manco Cápac, who claimed descent from Inti himself; but he also derived his authority from a corequenque who gave him oracles and advice. When Manco Cápac's great-grandson Mayta Cápac ascended the throne, he consulted this bird before launching campaigns that would enlarge the Inca empire to nearly half the size of imperial Rome, and in time the corequenque ranked among the Incas' most powerful symbols, depicted on the tall banners they carried into battle. "Such was the majesty of this bird," Garcilaso wrote, "and such was the reverence and respect which the Incas gave it."

They probably weren't the first Andean people to ascribe a special significance to the walking falcons. The Incas' flair for pageantry and grand architecture makes it easy to forget that their empire was short-lived, spanning about three hundred years from the rule of Manco Cápac to the sack of Cuzco by Spanish marauders. But Amerindians had arrived in the high Andes at least ten thousand years earlier, and persist there today with a unique cultural strength and coherence. The Wapishana language spoken by Jose and Brian in Guyana might have no more than ten thousand native speakers today, but the Quechua and Aymara languages spoken by subjects of the Inca Empire are still spoken by as many as *ten million* people in the highlands of Peru, Ecuador, Bolivia, and Chile — a number nearly equal to the population of the Empire at its zenith, when it stretched from present-day Ecuador to Chile.

Within this highland realm, a special regard for Andean caracaras has also persisted, along with a broader sense of the birds as emblems of cosmic benevolence. Many highland people are intensely religious, blending Catholic rituals with the veneration of the goddess Pachamama and her male counterpart, Viracocha; the festival of Inti Raymi, honoring the winter solstice, is still celebrated with parades in towns and villages throughout the former extent of the Inca Empire. In Ecuador, these parades often feature troupes of dancers in stylized bird costumes with conical headpieces and comma-shaped wings who bow, peck, scrape, and kick as they wind through the streets, bestowing good fortune on everyone for the coming year. Their dances mimic the foraging movements of Andean caracaras, and they're called *curiquingues* — a near twin of Garcilaso's corequenque.

This name, curiously, has fallen out of use in the Inca heartland of central Peru, where mountain caracaras bear the Spanish nickname *chinalinda,* "beautiful Amerindian woman," or the Aymara name *alkamari,* which describes their piebald plumage. (In Bolivia, they're also called *avemarías,* which enigmatically links them to the Virgin Mary.) But in Ecuador and Colombia, "curiquingue" refers to not only the costumed dancers of Inti Raymi but also the living birds called carunculated caracaras, who forage and scavenge in fog-bound islands of alpine moorland called *páramos.* Páramos' misty, gray-green slopes are wetter than the deserts above Cuzco, and carunculated caracaras are slightly gaudier than mountain caracaras; they sport a bold pattern of white spots on their dark breasts, a curly black crest atop their heads, and a down-curved beak that makes them look perpetually indignant. Their English name emphasizes the small red wattles on the faces of adult birds, as if this were their most important attribute, but in Ecuador curiquingues are totems of fertility and good luck, with a gift for predicting the future.

In 1983, the biologist Tjitte de Vries and his students at Quito's Catholic University published a unique book about the curiquingues' natural and cultural history, combining a study of their lives with a survey of legends attached to them. One tradition held that mating a curiquingue with a chicken would produce a fearsome fighting cock. Another practice involved tying a dead curiquingue to the grille of a bus or truck as a charm against misfortune on treacherous mountain roads. A third maintained that a pair of circling curiquingues augurs a future wedding — recalling the Incas' connection of the birds with their divine parents. But the most haunting custom was recounted by elders in a Quechua-speaking village near the mighty peak of Chimborazo. If a woman in the community bore a child out of wedlock, they said, the child's father was a curiquingue, and if she died without marrying, she was buried with one tied to her coffin.

Not all tales of Andean caracaras involve magical powers. In an exploration of Andean narratives called *Foxboy,* the anthropologist Catherine Allen relates an earthier story, told by a man from Bolivia named Don Ángel, that hews closer to the birds' actual lives. In Don Ángel's story, Taytacha (God) leaves Fox, his spoiled brat of a son, to his own devices for one day, a privilege Fox abuses by overcooking his breakfast of quinoa. As punishment, God casts Fox and his brethren, Condor, Puma, and Alkamari, out of Hanaq Pacha — the upper world — to live in exile on Earth. The four chastened brothers slide down a rope to our world, where they present themselves to four human sisters for marriage. The first sister wisely chooses Puma, the most capable of the bunch, but the second chooses Alkamari, because he's so smartly dressed in his dark suit and white trousers. She soon regrets her choice. The other three husbands provide good meat for their wives, but Alkamari brings only lizards, animal guts, and worms. "Alkamari was always a lazy good-for-nothing," Don Ángel confides, "even in heaven."

He clamored to be served first at the table, and when God replied, "No, son, one must always serve from elder to younger," Alkamari smashed his plate in a tantrum. Then God threw him from the table, saying, "Eat what you like. There will be days when you have to eat human excrement!"

Excrement of many kinds — even human — isn't off the menu for the walking falcons. Even so, their appearance is generally seen as a blessing. Farmers throughout the highlands regard them as heralds of a good harvest, and honor them in songs and dances; they're especially welcomed in the late summer, when they descend from the peaks to glean harvested fields of quinoa, amaranth, potatoes, and maize. In Ecuador, the traditional song "El curiquingue," which combines descriptions of caracaras' calls and movements with lines of joyous nonsense, is a sort of unofficial national anthem: an online search turns up not only costumed dancers in highland parades but mashups, dance mixes, and parodies, including one featuring a Korean pop star.

In another video, simply titled "Curiquingue," an unseen man addresses a carunculated caracara standing before him on the heights of the volcano Rucu Pichincha, above the thickly populated valley of Quito. "You're a beautiful bird," the man says. "But I don't have anything for you." He seems entranced, and the bird does, too; it blinks, takes a step toward the camera, steps back again. It might be used to receiving gifts from hikers who've paused to admire the view, but it's easy to imagine it as a guardian spirit of the mountain. It seems fitting that many peaks in Ecuador, Peru, Chile, and Bolivia bear versions of its name, including Alqamari, Allqamarinayuc, Alqamarine, Chinalinda, Corequenque — and Curiquinca, whose long profile rose above the dead vicuña on the highland road.

William Henry Hudson never saw the Andes, and never knew that a group of caracaras had mastered them as thoroughly as chimangos and caranchos mastered the farms and grasslands of the Pampas. But the mountains loomed in his mind, and in one of *Green Mansions'* most endearing scenes, Abel builds a scale model of South America and holds forth on its wonders to a curious but impatient Rima. Rima hopes Abel will reveal the homeland of the people who speak her unique language, but Abel insists that there are no such people, and to prove it he subjects her to an hours-long catalog of her continent's landscapes. "In a sudden burst of inspiration," Abel says, "I described the Cordilleras to her — that world-long, stupendous chain; its sea of Titicaca, and wintry, desolate Paramo, where lie the ruins of Tihuanaco, older than Thebes."

Many words — how inadequate! — of the summits, white with everlasting snows, above it — above this navel of the world, above the earth, the ocean, the darkening tempest, the condor's flight. Flame-breathing Cotopaxi, whose wrathful mutterings are audible two hundred leagues away, and Chimborazo, Antisana, Sarata, Illimani, Aconcagua — names of mountains that affect us like the names of gods, implacable Pachamama and Viracocha, whose everlasting granite thrones they are.

It's easy to feel, as Hudson did, that the Andes must be unfathomably old. But in geological terms they're relatively new, especially compared to the Guiana Shield or North America's Appalachians, which rose nearly half a billion years ago. The Andes' most intense period of growth, by contrast, is the last thirty million years, while the caracaras were enjoying their continent's splendid isolation along with the glyptodonts and saber-toothed marsupials. The rising Andes forced the west-flowing Amazon River to reverse course and flow east, and their most recent growth spurt commenced around the time the two Americas finally met.

Genetic evidence shows that the Andean caracaras' lineage departed from their forest-dwelling brethren at about this time; they might even have followed a wave of northern immigrants into the mountains, including the vicuñas' camelid ancestors and now-extinct species of mastodons and horses. The Andes are long but narrow, averaging only thirty miles wide for most of their length, and for millions of years these animals made a home in the long, cool ribbon of desert, grassland, and moor that towers above the sweltering forests of the tropics and descends to the sea in Tierra del Fuego. Like a snake that's swallowed an egg, this ribbon broadens at a massive central swelling, a soaring plateau called the Altiplano, whose brick-red deserts, shimmering salt pans, and hissing calderas sit at the intersection of Chile, Peru, Bolivia, and Argentina. It's the highest and largest plateau on Earth after Tibet, and like the Guiana Shield, it's one of the wildest and least inhabited places on the continent.

It's also the heartland of mountain caracaras. Like Darwin, I only glimpsed them there, but I saw their footprints everywhere, often in places where the only other animal tracks belonged to vicuñas, pumas, the shy blond foxes called culpeos, and me. All of us were immigrants from North America except the caracaras, who'd learned to survive in South America's harshest environment despite the biological challenges of the great interchange, the megafaunal extinctions, and a landscape that's still bubbling up from under the earth. The Altiplano rose from sea level to an average height of twelve thousand feet in less than three million years, and the peaks that rise above it, draped in curtains of fresh-baked lava, look as if they belong to a lifeless planet; scientists have used its sun-blasted expanses of volcanic glass to stand in for the surface of Mars. A few miles from San Pedro de Atacama, the world's most powerful array of telescopes points skyward, underlining the fact that outer space is nearer to the high Andes than to most other places on Earth.

But the Altiplano's desolation is as deceptive, in its way, as the lushness of the tropical forests. Though its mountains cough up rivers of superheated mud and rock that kill everything in their path, the snows gathered on their slumbering peaks send clear, cold water rushing through hidden canyons. Some of these desert streams combine to reach the Pacific Ocean, 150 miles away, but most end within sight of their headwaters, pooling and evaporating in basins where mounds of precipitated salt project like icebergs from pink and blue-tinted lakes.

One of these alkaline oases is the Salar de Pujsa, in the heart of the Chilean Altiplano, where I spent one of the coldest nights of my life. Pujsa's lake bed, caked with dried mud and rimmed with powdered salt, lies nearly fifteen thousand feet above sea level — higher than any mountain in the lower United States — and to call it "otherworldly" misses the mark: it's simply a version of our world I had never imagined. In the late afternoon its hummocks of salt seem lit from within, and its gleaming surface reflects a ring of enormous foothills, carved and smoothed by winds that descend from the mountains at night. Its vastness and silence suggest a place where animal life has yet to evolve, or has already come to an end. But on its shore, a single row of caracara tracks suggested a casual visit, and a pinkish haze on the far side, seen through my binoculars, resolved into one of the most extraordinary sights in all of South America, if not the world: the shimmering forms of thousands of flamingos.

The high Andes are home to three species of flamingo — a fact that surprises those of us who associate them with the Caribbean or East Africa. Some travel long distances to summer in the Altiplano and winter in the grassy lowlands of Chile and Argentina; one of the highlights of Hudson's childhood was a glimpse of three Chilean flamingos — birds nearly twice a young boy's height — wading solemnly through a flooded meadow after a rain. But the birds at the Salar de Pujsa were James's flamingos, the shortest on Earth at only three feet tall. They never leave the Altiplano, and during the day they feed constantly, dipping their bright yellow bills in the lakes' caustic water to filter out red algae that gives them their famous color. At night they huddle together at the outlets of thermal springs, standing for hours with their heads tucked under their wings while the temperature drops below zero.

That these fragile-looking birds could spend a lifetime in this freezing, toxic place seemed impossible. Yet here they were, standing resolutely in the lagoon while the sun sank behind the mountains, taking the day's heat with it. I shivered through the night in a sleeping bag, listening to the deep roar of the wind across the basin, and in the small hours of the morning a wild, undulating chorus of stuttering whistles took its place. It was the flamingos, reassuring each other of their existence: *I'm here. I'm here. I'm here.* When I rose just before dawn, the stars had faded and the birds had gone quiet. In the dim light they were more grove than flock, their bodies pulled into tight pink orbs, their feathers fluffed against the cold.

The Altiplano's salt lagoons are so compelling that they draw both the eye and the mind, but it's easy to be seduced by them and miss broader patterns of life in the high desert. Salt pans are havens for flamingos and their microscopic food, but little else lives in them, and the true cradles of life in the high Andes are narrow green deltas above the basins called *bofedales,* where clear streams fan out into marshes of cushion plants and short grasses. These oases are rarely obvious, since they're usually tucked inside creases of the landscape, and their sudden green is shocking. Bofedales look as delicate as they are improbable, but they're insulated by deep layers of underlying peat, and their braided rills teem with birds. Ducks, geese, gulls, and sandpipers crowd these isolated wetlands throughout the year, and though some birds are only passing through, others live nowhere else, including oddities like horned coots and puna tinamous.

An especially fine bofedal lies a few miles north of the place I found the dead vicuña, where a wetland called the Vado de Putana gathers water from the peaks of four volcanoes: the humped ridges of Apagado and Curiquinca, the cone-shaped Cerro Colorado, and Putana itself, whose summit is wreathed in a thin yellow cloud of sulfur. Their profiles rise and fall on the horizon as the highway climbs their foothills, and the wetland gives no sign of its presence until the crest of a hill reveals a wide, shining lens of water and vegetation. On the morning I saw it, a family of vicuñas was descending toward the water in wary single file, on alert for pumas lying in the grass, and shallow pools swarmed with giant coots — plump, black, hen-sized waterbirds with bony yellow shields on their foreheads. Through my binoculars I could make out a small flock of Andean geese resting among lush cushion plants, and beside them stood a pair of mountain caracaras.

I couldn't have imagined a more dramatic or appropriate place to see them. The Vado de Putana was a small lake below a mountain, just as Garcilaso de la Vega described, and the two birds stood so near to each other they were almost touching, suggesting a close partnership. They looked relaxed, even contemplative, with the morning sun on their black wings and white bellies. There was nothing for them to fear here — only an oasis where they could drink and bathe before venturing back into the desert to look for a puma's kill, or a truck's, and they probably carried a map of the Altiplano's hidden wetlands in their minds. Later in the day I would see them again, soaring purposefully above a featureless plain of orange gravel, and wonder what else was obvious to them that was invisible to me. It seemed an enviable life.

Two loose ends remain in the story of the Andean caracaras, and both connect to Darwin. One is the enigmatic bird he shot in Patagonia, three thousand miles south of the Altiplano. It wasn't a mountain caracara, though he wasn't too far off in thinking so; it was a new and different walking falcon. The ornithologist John Gould named it the white-throated caracara, *Phalcoboenus albogularis,* and Darwin's specimen still resides in the collection of the British Museum, neatly tucked inside a paper sleeve. It doesn't have the spots or wattles of a carunculated caracara, but it's almost a dead ringer for an *alkamari,* except that the white feathers of its underbelly extend all the way up to its chin.

White-throated caracaras are so infrequently seen that they're rarely mentioned, and they've never been formally studied; descriptions of them usually contain a phrase like "presumed similar to mountain caracaras." Their habitats aren't as heroically scaled as those of curiquingues, since the southern Andes are much lower than the younger peaks to the north. But like their northern cousins, white-throated caracaras usually keep well away from people, preferring remote uplands and meadows where pumas and foxes supply them with carrion.

In the valley where Julia Clarke found the dinosaur, I glimpsed four white-throats scraping the last bits of skin and hair from the carcass of a guanaco, and they fled when I was still hundreds of yards away. One of their regurgitated pellets, tumbling in the wind, was a tawny packet of fur and beetle shells.

A few white-throats, however, may be changing their minds about us — perhaps under the influence of more worldly caracaras. One of the surest places to see them today is the sprawling port of Ushuaia, Argentina, which spills down the slopes of a forested mountain in Tierra del Fuego. Ushuaia is the main port of departure for Antarctic cruise ships, and most visitors have points farther south on their mind; but a unique moment in the history of the walking falcons is unfolding on the outskirts of town.

To see it, you have to walk uphill from the port, past the crowds of red-jacketed tourists and kiosks crammed with glass penguins, and turn east at the spooky old prison (now a spooky old museum) from Ushuaia's former life as a gulag. Beyond this point, the only roads out of town are a highway which can take you to Alaska or a dirt track that leads to the municipal landfill. The dump sits beneath the jagged face of a small but imposing peak called Monte Olivia, and when I arrived at its gated entrance a few years ago, the guard shyly accepted a package of *mate,* noted my binoculars, and asked if I was looking for the little black-and-white ones. I was, I said — and he smiled knowingly and raised the gate.

I took a vantage point on the berm above the dump's open pit, where a bulldozer sorted piles of Ushuaia's refuse. A cloud of gray dust trailed in its wake, along with a parade of about thirty ragged-looking birds that followed it like mourners in a funeral procession. All of them were caracaras. Most were chimangos, the ingenious little scavengers of Hudson's childhood, though a pair of larger caranchos strutted among them, and bringing up the rear were three white-throated caracaras. Their breasts were dulled with dirt and grime, and their movements seemed tentative, as if they were unsure what to make of this place: they worried scraps of plastic with their beaks, raked in the dust with their feet, and glanced up every few seconds at their companions, making sure they weren't missing anything. They reminded me of the rock-flipping birds Jason Jones saw in Peru, and like him, I felt I was witnessing something extraordinary: the chimangos and caranchos were used to dealing with humans, but these white-throats were probably among the first of their species to see a city and choose to approach it. Like most animals who've decided to move in with us, they were learning about us through our garbage.

And as dumps go, this one was especially scenic. Looking south from its berm, beyond the cascading tiers of Ushuaia's roofs, your eyes land on a narrow seaway called the Beagle Channel, and then the long, snowy ridge of Isla Navarino, the Chilean island that marks the southern limit of human settlement in South America. Beyond Navarino, a labyrinth of uninhabited islands and fjords extends ninety miles to the edge of the continent, where beech forests give way to stands of the same tussac grass that lines the wildest coasts of the Falklands.

Humans rarely see these exposed margins of the continent, but they bear a surprising resemblance to the páramos of the curiquingues, four thousand miles away — and they, too, have their own unique species of caracara. These birds, long exiled from the heights of the Andes, bear the scientific name *Phalcoboenus australis:* the southern walking falcon. Darwin knew them by the misleading name *Polyborus Novae Zelandiae* ("New Zealand eater of everything") due to an earlier taxonomist's mistake, but they have nothing to do with New Zealand.

In the Falklands, they're called Johnny rooks.

18
A NEW CAREER
IN A NEW TOWN

Ten miles from the Gothic turrets and emerald courtyards of Oxford University, a striated caracara named Boo lives in a falconry park behind Millets Farm Centre, a produce market and tourist attraction that advertises fresh-made quiche, afternoon tea, giant trampolines, a petting zoo, and the UK's first corn maze. It's an unlikely place to meet a Johnny rook, and I found it only because of internet videos of Boo and her keeper James Channon, a boyish, dark-haired man in his early thirties. In the videos James seems charmed and bemused by Boo, and their rapport reminded me of Geoff Pearson's early days with Tina.

By the time I met them, Boo had grown from a scrappy youth into a sleek young adult, but James still regarded her with a fondness that seemed beyond his ability to explain. Boo's airy enclosure was littered with stuffed animals, like the bedroom of a hyperactive toddler, and James said that she'd become a favorite among his patrons, despite (or perhaps because of) her appetite for imaginative chaos. She surprised him one afternoon by devouring a plate of biscuits he set out for human visitors, and during one memorable flying demonstration, she'd jumped a tall hedge into the garden center next door, where James found her a few minutes later, eating strawberries.

Like Geoff, James told me that Boo had trained *him,* and like Tina, she'd come into his life by chance. He'd gone to the London Zoo to purchase a scavenging hawk called a black kite, only to find that it was no longer available. But Boo was, so he'd brought her home instead. Once he'd installed her in an aviary behind his house, James tried to train her as he would a kestrel or a peregrine, using jesses and a hood. But she wasn't having it — she especially hated the hood — and became so loud, aggressive, and intractable that he gave up and let her do as she pleased.

After that, to James's amazement, Boo became companionable and cooperative. She was the first raptor he'd ever met that didn't have to be broken to accept him, and she seemed to enjoy performing. On a typical day at Millets, Boo runs and hops around the flying arena, darts between patrons' legs, knocks over a bin labeled FALKLANDS WASTE, and solves multi-step puzzles involving flowerpots. Each task comes with a food reward, but

James says Boo will perform them even on a full stomach — a fact that still astonishes him, since it breaks a cardinal rule of falconry.

Another curious thing about Boo is her relationship with her neighbor, a raven named Loki. James keeps about ninety birds at Millets, from an imposing steppe eagle to a trio of burrowing owls his daughter christened Jo, Jo, and Jo, but Loki is the only feathered resident of the center who isn't a bird of prey. Ravens are the biggest and brainiest of the world's crows, known for their love of play, mischief, and abstract reasoning, and James placed Loki and Boo side by side not only because of their none-of-the-above-ness, but because he feels they're his most intelligent birds.

"These two are the only ones," he said, standing beside their enclosures, "that will poke their heads through the mesh to see what's going on outside." Loki and Boo can't see each other — there's an inch of plywood between them — but Boo throws a screaming fit if James doesn't feed her first, and Loki strikes a silver bell with his beak if he feels he's not getting enough attention. They can make quite a racket if they're both feeling slighted at the same time, and they aren't friends. "Which is funny," James added, "because they're so much alike."

They are indeed. Though they're not close relatives, Loki and Boo look almost like two versions of the same creature; they're about the same size and shape, with a similar air of alert curiosity. Their long wings, perfectly shaped for catching and holding strong winds, are so nearly interchangeable that they'd be easy to mistake for each other in flight, and Loki's apartment, like Boo's, is strewn with plush toys. In the wild, however, the difference between their species is stark: striated caracaras live only on a handful of islands, but ravens are among the most widespread birds on Earth.

Their similarity, oddly enough, may reflect the fact that they've never met. Two species rarely occupy the same ecological niche for long, since competition tends to push their lives apart, but ravens and striated caracaras have never had the chance to compete. The walking falcons have never left South America, and large crows have never reached it; they might as well have evolved on different planets. And while Boo's ancestors were climbing into the young peaks of the high Andes, ravens were occupying a newly available swath of the northern world.

Genetic evidence suggests that the first crows evolved in central Eurasia, and ravens appear to have found their identity as a species by advancing into regions that had been wiped clean by the massive glaciers of the last ice age, more properly called the Pleistocene epoch — the time between two million

426

and ten thousand years ago, when the two New Worlds were teeming with giant animals, and global temperatures averaged about eleven degrees Fahrenheit lower than today. This was enough to bury huge swaths of our planet under ice. As the glaciers melted, they left behind a freshly scrubbed landscape where pioneering plants and animals raced to build new lives for themselves, just as the holocaust of the Cretaceous extinctions cleared the way for the age of mammals.

In the Northern Hemisphere, this post-glacial landscape of desert, steppe, and tundra dwarfed the alpine zones of the Andes; ice sheets had pulverized much of northern Asia, along with almost every square inch of what's now Canada and the northern United States. The mega-glacier that covered the northern New World is all but gone today, but you can still sense its presence on snow-bound islands of the high Arctic, where a monthlong summer briefly reveals a land-scape of bare rock, as if the earth had been stripped to its mineral bones.

But it isn't lifeless. The Arctic is home to plants and animals that do most of their living in a single month of unending sunlight, and ravens learned long ago that the country along the glaciers' retreating front was a place of opportunity. Their curiosity and social intelligence served them well in a world as bountiful as it was unpredictable, where they could scavenge on carcasses of moose, elk, and buffalo, and fill gaps in their diet with small mammals, seeds, insects, and other birds' eggs. Today ravens live throughout the Northern Hemisphere, though they seem especially fond of stark environments like high mountains and fierce deserts; the biologist George Schaller, walking in the Himalayas, was amazed by their persistence even in the severest landscapes he'd ever seen. "Wherever you go, the crow shows up, sooner or later," he remarked. "At forty below, no sign of life — and there's the raven!"

Schaller may not have given himself enough credit as an object of interest. Like the caranchos who trailed gauchos across the Pampas, ravens learned to follow more powerful hunters whose kills could be shared or stolen: saber-toothed cats, bears, wolves, humans. Some ravens may even guide predators to prey so they can take a share, and following people is a rewarding strategy for a savvy scavenger, since we leave a trail of edible refuse in our wake.

Even so, the first ravens to take an interest in us might have done it out of pure curiosity. Like us, they seem to have a deep need to fill their lives with more than the search for food and mates, and they sometimes act as if their most dreaded enemy isn't starvation but boredom. Among their pastimes are sledding down snowbanks on their backs, playing tricks on other animals, flying upside down, and dropping pebbles and bones from great heights, only to dive and catch them in the air.

Prehistoric humans spent many hours watching ravens — and vice versa — and the birds' mastery of the world seemed so effortless that some people suspected them of creating it. Ravens figure in many northern mythologies, playing roles from the reincarnated forms of damned souls to benevolent spirits who brought light to the world. But they also have a reputation as tricksters and thieves — as the biologist Bernd Heinrich noted in his book *Mind of the Raven* (in which Schaller also appears):

> George Schaller told me of watching raven pairs in Mongolia *cooperate* in snatching rats from feeding raptors. Similarly, in Yellowstone Park, Ray Paunovitch reported seeing a red-tailed hawk with a ground squirrel. Two ravens approached. One distracted the hawk from the front while the other handily snatched the squirrel from behind. Carsten Hinnerichs saw the same maneuver repeated three times in a row in a field near Brücke, Germany, where a fox was catching field mice.

You could easily exchange striated caracaras for ravens in these stories. In the Falklands, pairs of Johnny rooks sometimes cooperate to chase rockhopper penguins off their nests, for example; one bird diverts the penguin's attention while the other makes off with a chick or an egg. But they also share the ravens' knack for finding new and unlikely sources of food. Katie Harrington, a biologist who studies striated caracaras in the Falklands, recently spent an austral summer on an island where caracaras gathered on the shore at low tide to pick through fronds of kelp and peer under rocks for limpets. This was unusual behavior for a bird of prey, but she was used to seeing Johnny rooks do funny things; she'd spent afternoons watching them play with balls of dried kelp, rolling them around and snatching them from one another like Tina with Geoff's keys. But even Katie was astonished when an enterprising bird dragged a large red octopus out of a tidal pool. "The Johnny rook immediately pulled the octopus up onto a rock," she wrote, "where it laid overturned, struggling to right itself.

> Within six minutes, more than thirty birds encircled the octopus, which had been reduced to portions of its head. . . . With full crops, the group dispersed; some birds sheltered under nearby ledges to digest, while others retreated to a freshwater seep on the adjacent cliff to wash down the meal.

This is the only record of a falcon hunting and killing an octopus; Katie noted that the only other predators of southern red octopuses are sea lions, gentoo penguins, and people. But at this point, I imagine, you're probably not too surprised to hear about another unlikely item in a caracara's diet, since versatility seems to be written into their DNA. The Johnny rooks at the ocean's edge in the Falklands complete the walking falcons' conquest of the entire Andean world, from equatorial volcanoes to sea level — and Katie marveled at the minds that had allowed them to do it. "Octopus may be clever," she wrote, "but they have met their match in the Johnny Rook."

That may be. But for all the Johnny rooks' resourcefulness, a troubling fact remains: even if ravens and striated caracaras are mental equals — even if Boo were definitively *smarter* than Loki, by any measure you wanted to use — it might not be enough to save her species from extinction. Loki's ancestors inherited a vast kingdom when the glaciers ebbed in the northern world, and Boo's ancestors did the same when they left the forests for the rising Andes; but there's a glaring difference between the Northern and Southern Hemispheres. The ravens' domain includes the former extent of the northern ice sheets and then some — many thousands of square miles, encircling the globe in the high latitudes. But in the far south, the Johnny rooks are hemmed in by the circum-polar vortex, a frozen Antarctica, and the polar oceans: a geographical dead end. The same climatic forces that allowed ravens to become themselves, it seems, may have also created the Johnny rooks — and then put them behind bars.

Unlike North America, the southern New World wasn't paved over with ice; it was too warm for that in the tropics, where most of South America's land is concentrated. But glaciers did spread throughout the Andes, slicing their ribbon of alpine habitat into islands and dividing the walking falcons from one another. Their slightly different plumage is a signature of this isolation, and genetic analysis shows that they parted ways exactly when you might expect them to: during the last half-million years, when ice sheets advanced and retreated several times. You could even say that the Johnny rooks are about the same age as us; their lineage diverged from other walking falcons at about the same time the lineage of hominins that produced modern humans diverged in Africa. It's likely that rivers of ice isolated the ancestors of striated caracaras from their nearest relatives, then pushed them south and west toward Tierra del Fuego.

These forerunners of the Johnny rooks, trapped between the pincers of ice and ocean, could easily have been driven off the continent and into the sea, but a stroke of good fortune seems to have rescued them: at the last possible moment, the Patagonian Ice Sheet ground to a halt on the doorstep of a mountainous island whose surviving peaks include Cape Horn itself. The shores of this island probably looked much like its half-drowned remnants do today — covered in seabirds, seals, and tussac, whipped by the southwesterly winds of the polar vortex. In this cold but ice-free refuge, ancestral Johnny rooks adapted to a new life as coastal scavengers, and the winds could easily have carried them north and east to the Falklands.

Seen in this light, striated caracaras' puzzling range suddenly makes sense: it's the remnant of an ice age refuge that's now mostly sunk beneath the waves. They survive there today by a combination of ingenuity and luck, but Darwin's conjecture was wrong: the Johnny rooks never chose the Falklands for their metropolis. Glaciers drove them down from the high Andes to the uttermost end of the earth, and the wind marooned them there.

The tiny cluster of islands called Diego Ramírez is perched on the very lip of South America's continental shelf, south even of Cape Horn. Its only human inhabitants are a few Chilean sailors who maintain its lighthouse and weather station, and its grassy peaks look much the same as they did in 1834, when Darwin glimpsed them from the deck of the *Beagle.* The ship had nearly capsized in one of the Cape's legendary storms, and its waterlogged crew didn't stop to poke around on a set of exposed rocks at the bottom of the world. But sealers had told Darwin that striated caracaras lived there, and he could hardly believe that a bird of prey could survive in such an isolated place. "Their whole sustenance," he marveled, "must depend on the sea."

And so it does. Diego Ramírez, like Steeple Jason, is a breeding ground for the prey striated caracaras learned to favor during the ice age — penguins, albatrosses, and burrowing petrels — and its Johnny rooks are the southernmost falcons on earth. Between them and Antarctica, there's only the Drake Passage: five hundred miles of howling winds and thirty-foot waves that made Darwin shudder with fear and awe. "The sea looked ominous, like a dreary waving plain with patches of drifted snow," he wrote, but "whilst the ship labored heavily, the albatross glided with its expanded wings right up the wind."

For Diego Ramírez's seabirds, the Drake Passage isn't ominous at all: it's home. Its roaming mountains of water mean food, drink, even a bed; they can curl up on its surface and fall asleep. But for Diego Ramírez's striated caracaras, the sea might as well be Death Valley. They can't swim in it or drink its salt water, and they have no way of knowing that they're as close as any living falcons have come to their ancestral home, a continent that long ago helped save the animal world, then lifted its drawbridges and froze to death.

A more tragically minded writer might be tempted to leave them there. Barring a profound shift in our species' approach to life on planet Earth, there's good reason to eulogize the Johnny rooks as a slender branch of a lineage whose members have explored South America to its farthest edges, only to arrive back where they started and slowly fade away. Striated caracaras depend on the health of oceans that we're over-fishing, acidifying, warming, and choking with plastic, and if the food web of the southern oceans collapses, larger predators like seabirds will lie in extinction's crosshairs. They would almost surely take the Johnny rooks with them.

There's also the matter of rising seas. The Falklands will shrink considerably over the next century, and many of their smallest and lowest islands will simply disappear. Albatrosses and penguins may be able to find new breeding grounds in a warmer Antarctica, but striated caracaras are unlikely to follow them, for the same reason they haven't colonized the seabird-rich island of South Georgia, eight hundred miles southeast of the Falklands: it is simply too far. The polar vortex would blow any wandering caracaras north, into the open waters of the South Atlantic.

The "flying monkeys" that troubled and amused Darwin, it seems, are entering the most precarious moment of their lives. Unlike the Guadalupe caracaras, they've survived long enough for us to care about them — but their island homes are poised to shrink even further, and their most important prey could soon move beyond their reach. This may be the way of things on a warming planet, as we're forced to accept the extinction of species we've run off the road; but every time I think about the prison of their tiny range, I can't help dreaming up ways to break them out. If it's still possible to save the Johnny rooks, it feels heartless — and unimaginative — not to try.

Every species has its own cradle, a place and time when it first left its ancestors' path. Ours was the heart of Africa in a cool and well-watered age, a place of low mountains, rivers, and rolling grasslands filled with animals. Its imprint remains in our genes, if not our conscious minds — even though much of it is now the Sahara. Perhaps its image still appears to us in our instinctive sense of beauty, the way we're unaccountably drawn to certain landscapes, the shape of the worlds we build around ourselves.

But if a longing for our first home is embedded in our minds, we're probably not alone. Most animals now live far from their origins, and every species' ideal would be different. The few remaining Siberian tigers might wander through a genetic memory of the searing light and broad marshes of India, while a ruby-throated hummingbird in the North Carolina piedmont might dream of the lower slopes of the Andes. A camel in Egypt might pine for the great, golden center of North America; a deep-sea shrimp, a hydrothermal vent pumping heat and minerals into the abyssal plain. But a few species have never really known exile: marine iguanas, snub-nosed algae eaters that lie in blissful dog piles in the equatorial sun, still live in their Eden in the Galápagos, and probably always will.

The Johnny rooks, in their ancient refuge at the bottom of the world, have also never left the place where they finally became themselves. But they may need to — and their escape route, like ours, may lie along the coast. It took a long time for humans to leave Africa, but we did it by hugging the shores — a route that eventually led us into Europe, India, Asia, Australia, and the Americas. To make this great trek, we relied on the same traits and strategies that sustained the crows and caracaras we met along the way: we were social, curious, innovative, and ate almost anything.

In this sense, striated caracaras are as much a mirror image of us as they are of ravens — and if they're going to survive, their journey will have to begin in the place ours ended. Two large fragments of the Patagonian Ice Sheet remain in the southern Andes, but they no longer bar the way north, and some striated caracaras seem to have realized this: single birds have been seen hundreds of miles north of Cape Horn, among inlets and islands of the Chilean coast that once lay beneath two thousand feet of blue ice. If they keep island-hopping, they'll eventually reach a very different world from the one they've known for the last quarter-million years. People living on the island of Chiloé, halfway between Cape Horn and Santiago, may yet wake up one morning to find a group of curious, crow-like raptors sitting in their gardens.

That journey, however, could take more time than they have left. Even if some of the Chilean Johnny rooks can escape the confines of the far south, the Falkland birds may not be so lucky. Like the lost chimango on Steeple Jason, the Falklands' Johnny rooks are held in place by the invisible wall of the polar winds, and as their islands dwindle,

G7's family members on Steeple Jason may face only one possible future that doesn't lead to their extinction — one in which we come to their aid, in a large-scale version of Len Hill's Operation Birdlift.

There's at least one precedent for this. In the 1920s, chimango caracaras were released on Easter Island (also called Rapa Nui), a supremely isolated island two thousand miles west of Chile. Chimangos were introduced in the hope that they might tamp down an infestation of rats, but they quickly settled into the same lives Hudson saw them pursuing in the Pampas: scavenging at farms and refuse piles, grooming livestock, and stealing the eggs of unwary chickens. (Easter Islanders, with a mixture of affection and annoyance, call them *manu toke-toke* — "thief birds.") Polynesian colonists took down Rapa Nui's forests centuries ago, along with most of its wildlife, but chimangos seem at home in the open grasslands that replaced the trees, and often perch on the giant heads of the island's famous statues. They face no competition, and like ravens chasing the retreating ice sheets, they're in the vanguard of a wave of colonists, building a new world from the wreck of an old one.

Maybe Johnny rooks, given the chance, could do the same. When we talk about "threatened" animals, it's implied that we're the ones doing the threatening, and we usually think of saving them from us in two ways. The first assumes that animals who've been hunted or driven out of a place they once lived could be returned to it; the ongoing effort to reintroduce California condors, the largest birds in North America, to their historic range is the poster child for this approach. The acrobatic hawks called red kites are another example: they were persecuted to near extinction in Britain in the early twentieth century, but the relocation of wild birds from Spain to sites across the UK has made their fork-tailed silhouettes a common sight again in much of England, Scotland, and Wales.

The second strategy follows the first: giving animals a safe haven from us. Sometimes this means creating reserves to keep humans out, but simple changes in the behavior of people who live near them can have a similar effect, as when the Falkland Islands government stopped paying bounties on caracara beaks; as one scientist noted, "it's not habitat if you get shot in it." In the United States, it became a federal crime to kill birds of prey in 1972, and since then the populations of most North American raptors have grown even as their available habitat has, by some measures, shrunk.

But we're entering an era in which entire ecosystems face extinction, and protecting every habitat won't be possible — especially on islands. As the oceans rise, a growing host of nonhuman refugees around the world will soon have no homes to return to, and we'll need to use our imaginations more forcefully if we want them to survive. We might laugh at Len Hill's wonderland of penguins, macaws, and flamingos in the Cotswolds, but we might also have to contemplate something like it, on a much grander scale, for newly homeless species whose fate lies in our hands. We might even have to ask them to live a new kind of wild life — not "out there" in a vanishing wilderness, but *in here,* in the world as we've remade it.

Some aren't waiting for an invitation. Coyotes, for instance, were almost unheard of in eastern North America only a few decades ago, but they've become common residents in many cities and suburbs along the Atlantic coast, following the example set by squirrels, raccoons, opossums, foxes, and ravens. Like the caracaras, these animals are skilled at seeking out and exploiting new opportunities, and the evolutionary pressures of urban environments are shaping them further; one recent study found that city-dwelling small mammals have larger brains than their rural counterparts.

And in the botanical world, there's the wonderful example of the ginkgoes. Ginkgoes are beautiful but peculiar trees that grow in most cities of the temperate world, where many people would recognize their fan-shaped leaves and the sour smell of their abundant fruit in the spring. Few, however, know that they're virtually extinct in the wild. What destroyed them wasn't weakness, competition, or logging — just a long run of bad luck. After surviving a quarter-billion years of continental ruptures and climatic swings, ginkgoes were confined to a part of central Asia whose fortunes were upended when the giant fragment of Gondwana we call India crashed into it, shoving up the crinkled ranges of the Himalayas. During the ice ages, the glaciers that feed the Indus and the Ganges today swelled to gigantic proportions and mowed down forests throughout the mountains — and ginkgoes, like Johnny rooks, survived only in isolated refuges.

Today there are no wild ginkgoes, with the possible exception of a few trees that might remain in the vertiginous Dalou Mountains of the eastern Tibetan plateau. Beyond that, they live only where humans have planted them — but they've proved to be very good neighbors. So long as there's enough water and sunlight, city life seems to suit ginkgoes just fine, and they're so legendarily hardy that six trees even survived the atomic blast in the center of Hiroshima. But they've made it to the present only because we took them under our wing, moved them in with us, and refused to let them die.

■ ■ ■

I can't help wondering if Johnny rooks might also thrive in cities. They evolved on one of our planet's wildest margins, but street smarts owe more to curiosity, flexibility, and opportunism than anything else, and striated caracaras would seem to tick all those boxes: they're quick students, unfussy eaters, don't mind a crowd, and don't need large territories. In a city, it's not as if they'd risk disrupting a fragile ecosystem — and cities would provide them a nearly unlimited supply of the novelty they crave. On Steeple Jason in 2012, Kalinka and the rest of the mouse team saw a striking example of striated caracaras' adaptability when the team's dye-marked mouse bait began to disappear faster than they'd expected — a mystery that solved itself when Johnny rooks began painting their roosts with green droppings and coughing up pellets of mealy yellow goo. Luckily for the birds, the bait wasn't poisonous, but no one had expected them to develop a taste for fluorescent rabbit food, and Kalinka wrote her field report with some resignation. The bait seemed likely to work on Steeple's mice, but the Royal Society for the Protection of Birds would need to find a way to kill them that didn't suit the palate of a nosy, omnivorous falcon.

Almost eight thousand miles away, the adventures of escaped Johnny rooks in the UK hint at a more explicit aptitude for urban life. A nine-year-old striated caracara named Wendy recently made a lunge at freedom during a flying demonstration at the Dartmoor Zoo, and though her keeper claimed she'd been "disoriented by high winds," she might simply have wondered about the world beyond the one she knew. Over the next two weeks, she was seen looking fit and well in the Devonshire villages of Sparkwell, Venton, and Ugborough, where she was finally lured into a truck and driven back to the zoo. In 2009, a Johnny rook at a falconry center in Worcestershire jumped a wire fence into a tennis court and retrieved errant balls for astonished players; the *Daily Mail* declared him the "Tennis-Mad Falcon Who Thinks He Is a Ball Boy." And in January 2018, a young striated caracara named Louie escaped from the London Zoo in Regent's Park and took up residence in nearby Kilburn, where he was spotted walking down a high street and, per the *Camden New Journal,* "ripping into a whole cooked chicken." After ten days on the lam, Louie was recaptured, examined, and declared none the worse for wear; a zoo spokesman noted that he seemed "well equipped for surviving in the urban environment," and that "as a meat-eating forager, he clearly found plenty of scraps to dine on."

Hyde Park, the site of the Rima memorial, might be as good a place as any to introduce Johnny rooks to the big city, an island of green space amid the bustle of central London. The precariously small gene pool of the UK's captive striated caracaras could be replenished with birds imported from the Falklands' most crowded islands, and the experiment might enrich our lives as much as theirs. People would surely enjoy watching them learn to navigate the city, and might even post photos of their progress on the internet — like the viral images of pigeons who've learned to use the London Underground. It's not hard to imagine Johnny rooks following suit, running under turnstiles of the Circle Line at Paddington Station and riding out to Hampstead Heath (or Wimbledon), then returning home to roost at night. In time, they might go from odd curiosities to celebrated mascots, like the ravens at the Tower of London.

I'm only half-serious, of course. This scheme would face incredulous and reasonable opposition, and there are good arguments against introducing a threatened raptor from another continent into a new and dangerous habitat. But our world is changing in ways we've never seen it change before, and we may need to stretch our ideas of wildlife conservation in ways that seem risky, even reckless, if we want to save animals like the Johnny rooks. Since we're the ones destroying their homes, it seems only fair to see if we could learn to live together, and when you consider all their lineage has accomplished, from the wasp-eating tropical red-throats to the rock-turning alkamaris of the high desert, it seems unlikely that the challenges of our cities would be beyond them.

There's also their curious knack for bonding with people, as if they recognize a kindred spirit when they see one. Like them we're a contradictory species, obstinate but flexible, and even though we chafe at change, we can bend our lives to fit almost any shape. A friend at the American Museum of Natural History had the same feeling about ravens when he saw one stashing half a bagel in a gutter in Queens, and I've never felt more struck by humans' adaptability than on a recent evening in Brooklyn, in a neighborhood where many of its residents were born outside the United States. I'd just stepped out of a laundromat on a residential block when I heard a brass band coming up the street, playing a dignified, antique-sounding music I couldn't quite place. It was confident and cheerful, if not entirely in tune; and for a moment I wondered if it was part of the recent wave of punk marching bands.

The procession that swung around the corner was nothing like what I'd pictured. A red pickup truck, advancing at a stately pace, was clearing the way for a group of about thirty Amerindian people dressed in the traditional costumes of the Andean highlands: black bowler hats and fedoras, white shirts, red skirts and capes. They were celebrating the annual feast of the Virgin of Urkupiña, a Bolivian apparition of the Virgin Mary, whose statue rode in the bed of the truck framed by a nimbus of flowers — though the feast also, more informally, honors the Inca goddess Pachamama. Some of the marchers carried trumpets and mellophones. Others carried a rainbow-hued flag associated with the Inca nation, a country whose boundaries can't be found on any map, but nonetheless exists. A few, wearing ornate masks, twirled and bowed like the curiquingue dancers from Ecuador and Peru. They hailed from a world four thousand miles away, but here they were, a stone's throw from the East River, celebrating a new avatar of an ancient god. I couldn't have imagined a clearer reminder that transplants and migrants of all kinds can be surprisingly resilient, and that though their lives might take new forms in new places, they always carry their first homes within them.

19

LAND'S END

The hamlet of Zennor lies on the west coast of Cornwall, twelve miles above the southwest cape of Britain called Land's End. The Cornish peninsula's basalt cliffs and stone-walled pastures are England's most striking and primeval landscape, and Zennor's Norman church and stone cottages huddle in a crease of land below a looming hill surmounted by a pile of granite boulders called a tor. One of the boulders bears an inscription that reads "W.H. Hudson often sat here," and I climbed the hill to look for it on a bright fall afternoon, with a cool wind blowing from the west.

Hudson was drawn to Cornwall's rough-hewn scenery and people in the last fifteen years of his life, and though he kept a room in the sheltered port of Penzance, the moors and sea cliffs of its southwest coast were the places he liked best. Unlike London, or even Savernake Forest, the Cornish coast had a palpable wildness that stretched beyond the confines of human history, a feeling Hudson treasured above all others. He liked to sit on the tor "and gaze by the hour, thinking of nothing, on the blue expanse of the ocean and the more ethereal blue of the sky beyond," he wrote, "with perhaps a few floating white clouds and soaring white gulls in the void to add to the sense of height and vastness." If he looked inland, he could make out the ruin of an Iron Age tomb called a quoit, a chamber built of giant stones where prehistoric people interred their dead after leaving their bodies in the open to be cleaned by ravens. Hudson loved being able to touch this vanished world with all his senses, as he did in the valley of the Río Negro, and think about his place in the grand and imperfectly known history of human and animal life. "We ourselves," he wrote, "are the living sepulchres of a dead past."

Hudson didn't believe in reincarnation, but he did think that our unwritten history was woven into our bodies, and that civilization was only a "crust of custom around the still-burning core" of a deeper and older human nature. A passage from *Idle Days in Patagonia* prefigures the discipline of evolutionary psychology, which sees the human mind as a product of the time and place in which we first evolved. "What has truly entered our soul and become psychical is our environment," he wrote, "that wild nature in which and to which we were born at an inconceivably remote period, and which made us what we are." For Hudson, this wasn't a scientific conclusion so much as a revelation in the desert.

> It is true that we are eminently adaptive, that we have created, and exist in some sort of harmony with new conditions . . . but the old harmony was infinitely more perfect than the new, and if there be such a thing as a historical memory in us, it is not strange that the sweetest moment in any life, pleasant or dreary, should be when Nature draws near to it, and, taking up her neglected instrument, plays a fragment of some ancient melody, long unheard on the earth.

These melodies reached his ears more often in Cornwall than in London, and he spent as much time there as he could — especially in the long, quiet winters, when the peninsula's rocky skeleton showed through its threadbare pastures. On clear days, adders emerged from dens beneath the stones to warm themselves, as they had since long before people arrived, and to Hudson their cold-blooded happiness was a vision of the bliss that lies beyond thought. "The entire visible world," he wrote, "sea and land, is a glittering serpent, its discontent now forgotten, slumbering peacefully, albeit with wide-open eyes, in the face of the sun." Cornwall is as close to South America as you can be without leaving Britain, and as Hudson gazed westward it must have crossed his mind that only water lay between him and his native home. Like his life, his writing was always divided between these two worlds, and no matter how British he became in speech, manner, and citizenship, the Pampas never left him.

Far Away and Long Ago, his most admired book, was an impressionistic memoir that literally came to him in a fevered rush. He'd fallen ill after a long, cold walk along the coast of Dorset in 1916, and as he shivered under a blanket in London, he was astonished to find his childhood rushing back to him. "It was as if the cloud shadows and haze had parted," he wrote, "and the entire wide prospect beneath me made visible." Afraid this vision would vanish as quickly as it came, Hudson did his best to set it down on paper, and when his fever relented he was left with a draft of a book that defies easy description. *Far Away and Long Ago* conveys not only the events but the innermost feelings of Hudson's early life, and it reads like what it is: an old man's ramble through the country of his young mind. It was the book in which he described his botched raid on the caranchos' nest, the conferences of snakes beneath the floorboards of his bedroom, and the cries of night watchmen in the streets of Buenos Aires.

These were happy memories, by and large, but he chose to open the book with a portrait of a figure whose loneliness had haunted him all his life. The first visitor Hudson could recall at his family's home was a mentally ill man who roved around the Pampas, appearing every few months to demand food in an unintelligible language and stare down his hosts with eyes "clear grey and keen as a falcon's." Adding to his strangeness was his outfit, which seemed drawn from another age, if not another planet. "He wore a pair of gigantic shoes," Hudson recalled, "about a foot broad, at the toes, made of thick cowhide with the hair on; and on his head was a tall rimless cow-hide hat shaped like an inverted flower-pot.

The outer garment, if garment it can be called, resembled a very large mattress in size and shape, with the ticking made of innumerable pieces of raw hide sewn together. It was about a foot in thickness and stuffed with sticks, stones, hard lumps of clay, rams' horns, bleached bones, and other hard heavy objects; it was fastened round him with straps of hide, and reached nearly to the ground . . . and if this awful burden with which he had saddled himself was not sufficient, he had weighted the heavy stick used to support his steps with a great ball at the end, also with a circular bell-shaped object surrounding the middle. On arriving at the house, the dogs would become frantic with terror and rage at the sight of him.

William and his siblings called the man "Con-stair Lo-vair," a phrase he often repeated in a high, singsong voice, and his story ended when his body was found on the plain, crushed beneath the weight of his costume. Hudson called him "the strangest of all strange beings I have met with in my journey through life," but the figure of a solitary wanderer, understood by no one, must have touched a nerve. Just before William boarded the steamer that took him away from South America forever, his younger brother Albert looked at him for a long time and said, "Of all the people I have ever known, you are the only one I don't know."

Fifty years later, Albert's words still stung. Hudson hadn't left La Plata because it was inhospitable, but because of a passion that would not let him rest. "In all the years of my life in the Pampas," he wrote, "never did I have the happiness to meet with anyone to share my interest in the wild bird life of the country I was born in." Reading Darwin and collecting birds for the British Museum had led him to believe that England was a place where he would find people like himself and be accepted among them, and his early disappointment when he didn't was bitter and lasting. A streak of martyrdom surfaces occasionally in his work; at the end of *Green Mansions,* Abel fails to save Rima from immolation and carries her ashes back to Georgetown, a hallucinatory journey that leaves him broken in mind and body, and the owner of a story no one else can understand.

One way to read this is as tragedy. But it's also a parable of doggedness, a stubborn refusal to renounce something precious. Like Abel, Hudson never gave up — and his combination of erudition, imagination, and plainspokenness finally connected with public tastes after three decades of effort. Intellectual and social companions were available in his last years if he wanted them, but he often did not want them, and an expression of what one admirer called "soul-loneliness" rarely left his face. To once again hear the cries of upland geese wintering in the Pampas, he wrote, "I would willingly give up, in exchange, all the invitations to dine which I shall receive, all the novels I shall read, all the plays I shall witness, in the next three years; and some other miserable pleasures might be thrown in."

Birds of La Plata, published in 1920, was a wistful farewell — a revision of descriptions he'd written thirty years earlier, when the memory of South America was fresh. Like *Far Away and Long Ago,* it immersed him again in the landscapes of his childhood, and revising it made him rue his choice to leave. "When I think of that land so rich in bird life," he wrote, "those fresher woods and newer pastures where I might have done so much . . . the reflection is forced on me that, after all, I probably made choice of the wrong road of the two then open to me."

But the home he remembered no longer existed. The days of the open range in the Pampas were over, just as they were over in the United States, and the places Hudson loved as a child had changed beyond recognition — their broad marshes drained, their pastures fenced and plowed under. This was a loss he knew he could not bear, and he settled on a writer's compromise: if he couldn't return to the people and animals of his youth, he could at least bring them to life for his new countrymen and give them back some of the wildness he felt they had lost.

And in this, he was a success. His books about the English countryside and its wildlife helped urban readers see their own country with new eyes, while readers who fell under the spell of *Far Away and Long Ago* included Ernest Hemingway and Virginia Woolf, who wrote that "one does not want to recommend it as a book so much as greet it as a person." But the price Hudson paid, like Abel, was to live in a state of perpetual longing — and, like Rima, to feel he was alone in the world. When he grew too frail to walk on the moors of west Cornwall, Hudson stayed as close to them as he could, dividing his time between his second-floor flat in Penzance and a local public library. In the last months of his life he was seen striding down the beach in all weathers as he gradually retreated from a civilization whose endless wars and political intrigues saddened and perplexed him. "The world is a shambles," he wrote to a friend, "but I wasn't born to set it right."

Hudson was largely dismissive of his late fame, feeling it had waited too long; but he couldn't conceal his pride at seeing his books displayed in shops, and felt a deep satisfaction that he'd finally reached an audience that shared his belief in the value of the natural world. The club he'd helped found to protest the use of feathers in women's fashion had grown into the Royal Society for the Protection of Birds, and he could sense a growing popular appreciation for free-living animals, not just their stuffed remains or their caged bodies in a zoo. On the night before he died, Hudson was still revising *A Hind in Richmond Park* — a unique blend of memoir, natural history, and philosophy, bathed in the light that naturalists like Darwin and Wallace had shed on the mysteries that consumed him as a child.

The power, beauty, and grace of the wild creature, its perfect harmony in nature, the exquisite correspondence between organism, form and faculties, and the environment, with the plasticity and intelligence for the readjustment of the vital machinery; and thus, amidst perpetual mutations and conflict with hostile and destructive forces, to perpetuate a form, a type, a species for thousands and millions of years! — all this was always present to my mind.

"Yet even so," he added, "it was but a lesser element in the complete feeling." To the last, Hudson remained wary of the closed spheres of expertise, feeling that only imagination and curiosity could reach beyond their borders. "One must shake off . . . the curse of books," he wrote, "the delusion that they contain all knowledge, so that to observe and reflect for ourselves is no longer necessary." This reverence for the unknown often drew him back to the mysticism of his early life, and in the end he felt that a sense of nature as a vast and secretive intelligence was something to be cherished, not outgrown. No matter how much he learned about its inner workings, the world beyond the knowledge and concern of human beings called to him in the same clear voice, like Rima calling to Abel in the forest. "The main thing," he concluded, "was the wonderfulness and eternal mystery of life itself; this formative, informing energy — this flame that burns in and shines through the case . . . which in lighting another dies, and yet dying endures for ever.

And the sense, too, that this flame of life was one, and of my kinship with it in all its appearances, in all organic shapes, however different from the human. Nay, the very fact that the forms were inhuman but served to heighten the interest; — the roe deer, the leopard and wild horse, the swallow cleaving the air, the butterfly toying with a flower, and the dragon-fly dreaming on the river; the monster whale, the silver flying-fish, and the nautilus with rose and purple tinted sails spread to the wind.

This was his greatest theme: that only by looking to the nonhuman world, with all the tools of science and art, can we see what we really are — and that we aren't as alone as we feel.

On the day I visited, the tor above Zennor was bathed in a warm, kind light. Wild blackberries tore at my coat and stained my fingers, and I pushed through a thicket of gorse and bracken to reach its overgrown boulders. But I couldn't find Hudson's stone. Maybe it had fallen over when the earth shifted; maybe I looked too closely at one side of it and missed the chiseled letters on the other. After a while I started to feel I was missing the point, and picked my own spot to sit and look at the sea, thinking of the grave in Worthing with its inscription about wild places and the wind on the heath. Below me, a buzzard circled slowly over the village, holding a thermal under its wings, riding it up until it was a black speck in the sky.

The light and the landscape reminded me of my last day with Julia Clarke and her students in southern Chile, where guanacos and white-throated caracaras replaced the ravens and sheep of Cornwall. The morning had dawned crisp and clear, but the gaggle of field-weary paleontologists were unusually slow to get moving: celebratory bottles of wine had come out the night before, and gusts of laughter were still booming from the kitchen tent when I crawled into my own at three a.m. The shadows of the mountains ebbed while we broke camp, and six of us carried the sauropod femur down to a pickup truck that had crawled bravely up the valley of the Río de las Chinas to receive it. Then we shouldered our packs and descended the steep, rugged track, warmed by the slanted rays of the sun.

Like the deserts of the Altiplano, the tree-less peaks and deep ravines of the surrounding mountains looked utterly barren, but animals revealed themselves whenever we stopped to rest. A pair of long-winged harriers careened above the valley's carpet of dry grass, ready to drop on anything that moved; a spry Patagonian fox pounced on insects in a meadow where a stream dropped into the river; and on the sandstone heights, families of wild guanacos turned red and gold in the sun, snorting and whinnying to let us know we were seen. Like the caimans and red-throated caracaras of the Rewa, the valley's animals seemed to have decided that we deserved caution but not fear, and I had the same feeling of slipping back thousands of years in time.

For Julia the trip had been a success, worth a journey halfway around the world. She'd found enough tantalizing fossils to justify another visit, and Sarah was trying to figure out how to modify her PhD research so she could return, too; there was enough here to occupy an army of graduate students for years. Hector, who envisioned a future in oil and gas, seemed knocked out that he was here at all: this was far beyond any life he'd imagined growing up in South Texas, and when our eyes met he broke into a broad, steady grin. We'd been scratching in the dust on our knees for days, and hiking down the valley let us take in the full sweep of a place few people had seen, and that he and I were probably leaving for the last time.

As we walked, Julia noted how good it felt

to escape the clutches of the internet, and how hard it is to avoid the trap of thinking that everything worth knowing is a Google search away. For the moment, no one but us knew about the fossils we carried in our packs, any one of which might have the power to change our understanding of the past, and there was an undeniable sweetness in standing at the very edge of a small part of human knowledge.

But more mundane concerns couldn't be kept at bay, even here. At a lunch break beneath cliffs whitewashed with condors' droppings, Julia confessed that her mind had already wandered back to her office in Austin — to unfinished manuscripts and grant applications, the endless search for funding, and the eternal challenge of explaining what her research meant to people outside the scientific world. The researchers who study our planet today live in an age as full of insights and discoveries as the nineteenth century, and it must be maddening to be confronted again and again with the fact that many people simply don't care. Every scientist I'd met seemed to wonder how often they'd have to repeat that there's far more to learn about the world than we already know, that much of it lurks in the guise of the unimportant, and that all it takes to break new ground in the pursuit of knowledge is a desire to do the hard work of seeing.

Knowing where to look, however, might be the hardest skill to master, and some of it seems innate. I thought of Julia sleeping under a truck in Mongolia, Sean hauling a guitar amp through the jungle at Nouragues, and Hudson's "idle days" in Patagonia, and couldn't help feeling that a very special restlessness plagues the people who devote their lives to understanding the natural world. Despite their occasional griping, their fondest wish seems to be that the rest of us will one day come to meet them there, gaze with wonder and curiosity at the hidden story of life on our planet, and marvel at how little of it has been revealed.

We walked on, leaving the alpine world behind, and soon dwarf stands of southern beeches and *calafate* bushes, heavy with purple berries, appeared on the banks of the river. The tin roof of a nineteenth-century farmhouse heaved into view at the valley's mouth, and in the high blue of the sky, a southern crested caracara soared with five Andean condors — a scene as old as the joining of the Americas. A few minutes later we came upon a second carancho, feasting on a cow that lay dead in the grass. A dark stream of blood trailed from the cow's empty eye socket, and the martial-looking bird glared at us from beneath its dark crest, unwilling to abandon its prize: *Yes, I eat dead things; and I look good doing it.*

"That's *so* cool," muttered Sarah, pulling out her phone to take a picture. Below us the thin, clear river sighed in its gorge, and an outraged chorus of distant lapwings screamed at one of their enemies — a fox, maybe, or a chimango. The carancho lifted its chin and called, *karruk-karruk,* then bent to tear into the cow's head, just as its ancestors had done at the carcasses of ground sloths and glyptodonts. Meat is meat.

"HEY, DINOSAURS!" called Julia.

I turned to see a pair of Darwin's rheas break from the bushes to our left and barrel down the valley — the same birds Hudson tried and failed to find on the other side of the mountains. They held their long necks upright as they ran, their shaggy gray plumes shivering with every step, and at a bend of the river they jumped a wire fence and disappeared. It was easy to imagine that they'd sailed through the Cretaceous extinctions unscathed. Julia was glowing, staring after them, and she lifted her arm and waved: *I'm here. I see you.*

She might as well have been waving to the great feathered beasts of the past who had lived and died where we stood, back when we could have walked south across dry land into the forests of Antarctica. The frozen continent still holds its history close, and for now Julia and her colleagues can only probe its edges for clues. But our impending return to a greenhouse world, despite its dangers, holds the promise of Antarctica's rebirth as a place where life is once again possible — and the unveiling of its buried secrets. Julia's scientific heirs might even find that the big, flightless dinosaurs survived there long after the Cretaceous extinctions and succumbed to ice, not fire, after their flying relatives dispersed into the fragments of Gondwana.

"The more I think about it," said Julia, "the more I think this idea — that the world is *known* — is what keeps people from committing to a life of discovery." Then she took a swig from her water bottle, picked up her hiking poles, and marched down the valley, where the rheas had gone.

On the one-lane road from Zennor to Penzance, the evening sun lit the paddocks of Cornwall in chiaroscuro, gilding the ocean and shading out most traces of modern life. William Henry Hudson might have approved; it turned his favorite corner of England into a severe, Paleolithic world, as forlorn as the Patagonian desert. Cornwall attracted few tourists in his day, but it's long since become a holiday destination, and I sat in a long line of cars crawling between hedges and stone walls, playing timid games of chicken at blind curves.

As I rounded one of them, I had to step hard on the brakes — not for another motorist but for a magpie, a fancy little crow of the northern world, which was dragging a flattened rabbit into the bushes. Like all magpies, this one looked overdressed for its work, with a vest of white feathers over its black gown; its slender tail, as long as its body, gleamed with a metallic blue sheen. Magpies aren't quite as arresting as ravens, but they're extraordinary in their own right; they can recognize their own reflections, mimic the human voice, and ritually mourn the deaths of their friends.

This one, however, seemed preoccupied only with thoughts of dinner, and raised its head to cock a shining black eye at me: *Just a moment, please.* It gazed right at the windshield — as if it knew, somehow, that I was in charge of the car — and I wanted to tell it to take its time. But it had to gauge my intentions for itself. It stared at me, and I stared back, and for a long moment, each of us waited for the other to move.

EPILOGUE:
RETURN OF THE
MEXICAN EAGLE

In January of 2015, an unexpected visitor turned up at Bear Mountain State Park, fifty miles north of New York City. Bear Mountain sprawls across a forested peak overlooking the Hudson River, and it's hardly a remote wilderness; you can see the Manhattan skyline from its summit. But it's popular with visitors all the same, and the Appalachian Trail runs directly through its headquarters, where a small zoo houses injured animals, including black bears, bald eagles, and a family of river otters. In summer Bear Mountain teems with backpackers, but winters are quiet, and on the chilly morning of January 5 the park's affable director of science, Ed McGowan, arrived at sunrise to conduct a survey of winter wildlife. This was an annual tradition at the park dating back to the 1940s, and McGowan was joined by a trio of veteran bird-watchers who liked getting up early. For the first hour, the morning brought the usual suspects: chickadees, blue jays, crows, cardinals, a raccoon. But as they approached the suspension bridge that spans the Hudson near the park's entrance, they saw a large, colorful bird flying toward them that none of them recognized.

That's not local, McGowan thought, reaching for his binoculars as his colleagues called out the bird's distinctive marks: a white tail, yellow legs, an orange face, a black crest. It circled for two minutes in the clear sky, lit by the morning sun, then sailed away to the east, and the men looked at each other in disbelief. Gerhard Patsch, the most experienced birder among them, was the first to suggest that it might have been a caracara, but if so it was a once-in-a-lifetime sighting — about as unlikely as a macaw alighting on the Christmas tree at Rockefeller Center. McGowan was chagrined: he'd been so intent on identifying the bird that he hadn't photographed it, and he rushed back to his office to consult a field guide, where he saw that Patsch was right — they'd just seen the first crested caracara ever recorded in New York State. "Wherever it came from," he later wrote, "it was a sight to behold — a tropical apparition on a brisk winter's day."

Bird-watchers cherish sightings of "vagrants" — birds who appear hundreds or even thousands of miles from their usual homes — but they don't usually signify much. In 2016, for example, an amethystthroated hummingbird, a bird almost never seen north of Mexico, appeared at a feeder in Quebec; a Siberian sandpiper called a great knot paid a visit to West Virginia; and a homeowner in an Arizona suburb snapped a picture of a Juan Fernández petrel flying over his house — a seabird that breeds on a single island off the coast of Chile, five thousand miles away. It's probably safe to say that a rare Chilean seabird in Arizona was blown off course by a storm, or suffering from a defect in its navigation system.

But as McGowan searched for other sightings of caracaras in the United States, the Bear Mountain bird seemed less like a vagrant and more like the leading edge of a wave. Crested caracaras were rarely seen north of Florida or Texas until the late 1990s, but in the past twenty years they've been recorded as far north as Maine, Montana, and Washington State. A few have even reached Canada, where a caracara at Cape Breton Island attracted a small army of birders bristling with spotting scopes and zoom lenses, hoping to see it before it moved on. The caracara surprised them by staying put for years. "It's just been stuck here," said David Currie, the president of the Nova Scotia Bird Society. "Or maybe it's enjoying our province."

Both might be true. Crested caracaras thrive in the tropics, but they aren't allergic to cold weather — they live in Tierra del Fuego, after all — and though they've been away for a while, they aren't strangers to North America. They first came up from the south with the ground sloths and glyptodonts when the two New Worlds met, and by the end of the ice ages they'd made themselves at home across the Great Plains, whose broad grasslands and open forests were something like the wildest parts of East Africa today: filled with grazing animals and the predators that ate them. Instead of elephants, zebras, giraffes, and wildebeests, North America had mastodons, horses, camels, and elk; instead of lions, leopards, and hyenas, it had sabertoothed cats, jaguars, and dire wolves.

Where there's murder, there's meat, and crested caracaras joined a well-established club of feathered scavengers in North America that included condors, ravens, and leggy raptors called walking eagles. Caracara bones lie among the remains of jaguars, camels, and dwarf antelopes in the La Brea Tar Pits in downtown Los Angeles, where a mural depicts the area as it might have appeared twenty thousand years ago. In the painting, Los Angeles looks as busy and crowded as it is today, with the same folded ranges of the San Gabriel Mountains in the distance; but instead of tangled highways and soaring glass towers, it shows an open savanna, thick with mammoths, bison, and giant bears.

The caracara lurks in the lower right corner, eyeing the half-eaten carcass of a wolf beside a larger scavenging bird called a teratorn. The teratorn's six-inch beak and menacing expression suggest that it probably ate first, but its days were numbered. The wave of extinctions that followed humans into North America largely disbanded the scavengers' club, sending the teratorns and walking eagles into oblivion with the mastodons and saber-tooths. Of the largest birds, only the condors hung on in a sliver of their former range, living off the bodies of whales and seals on the California coast. The caracaras retreated south of the Rio Grande — except for an isolated population that hung on in the savannas of central Florida, where John James Audubon saw and painted them in 1831.

A few hundred crested caracaras live there still, in a shrinking island of grassland surrounded by suburban housing estates. Like the Johnny rooks of the Falklands, they don't migrate; they've been stuck between closed forest to the north and the Everglades to the south for at least ten thousand years. But they've made the most of their isolation. The biologist Joan Morrison, who studied them for three decades, was amazed by their scrappy versatility: she watched them feeding on fish, frogs, lizards, snakes, eggs, nestlings, insects, and carrion, and memorably described their diet as "any animal matter, living or dead, that [they] can catch or find." Morrison noted that the Floridian caracaras were especially fond of armadillos — a culinary relic of their South American past — but equally willing to embrace foods made by (and for) humans: one young bird scarfed down a pile of discarded macaroni, and a family group squabbled over a half-empty tub of cream cheese. Like the caranchos that impressed William Henry Hudson on the plains of La Plata, the Florida birds' broadmindedness probably helped them hang on through the Pleistocene extinctions; and their small size, compared to teratorns and condors, meant they weren't entirely dependent on huge bonanzas of dead meat.

Meanwhile, across the Gulf of Mexico, their Central American counterparts regrouped. Saber-tooths and giant bears might have disappeared, but the Mesoamerican crested caracaras switched their allegiance to the two-legged hunters that replaced the ice age predators. For the next ten thousand years, they stood by as Amerindian civilizations rose and fell, and they probably regarded the first Americans as caracaras always regard potential allies: with interest.

Their interest was returned. Brian, Jose, and Rambo's ancestors could hardly have missed the long-legged, regal-looking birds with resourceful habits, and the Amerindians who settled in the dry Gran Chaco forests south of the Amazon basin elevated them nearly to the status that ravens had attained in the Pacific Northwest. In legends recounted to the anthropologist Alfred Métreaux by Qom people of northern Argentina, the supernatural figure of Carancho is a wise and powerful warrior who vanquishes monsters and evil men, outsmarts the vain and selfish Fox, and offers advice to humans he considers his friends. One story relates how the first women descended from the sky, but the men waiting below couldn't have sex with them until Carancho removed a set of teeth from their vaginas; another credits him with the invention of medicine. But his most precious and significant gift is the same one the ancient Greeks attributed to Prometheus.

"Now," said Carancho, "bring me branches of the pi'taladik and of the kuwak'á." The people came back with the wood. Carancho was busy; he bored a small hole in the middle of a stick, and inserted another one into the shaft of an arrow. He twirled this stick rapidly, and after a while the wood smoked and glowed. He took some caraguatá tinder and built a big fire.

Carancho's gift echoes a curious and persistent legend about crested caracaras: that they understand fire, and spread it by dropping

472

flaming sticks in dry grass. Helmut Sick mentioned it in his book on the birds of Brazil (qualifying it with "local peasants allege"); Joan Morrison heard it from colleagues in Mexico; other ornithologists have reported it from Nicaragua. No one has confirmed these rumors, but a pair of Australian researchers recently concluded that some birds probably *do* spread fire on purpose — and, moreover, that Aboriginal Australians have known about and commemorated this behavior in ceremonies and legends for centuries, if not millennia.

A fire-wielding caracara is strangely plausible. Humans suffer from a touch of magical thinking where fire is concerned, as if its use had been declared off-limits to other species, but it's hard to imagine birds more likely to discover it than crested caracaras. Wildfires have swept their grassland homes for millions of years, and they often carry long sticks, bones, and other objects in their talons and beaks as they build and maintain unwieldy nests like the one Hudson tried to raid as a child. It's a fairly short step to the discovery that fire is portable, and a caracara armed with this knowledge might pass it on to its more observant friends. No one has photographed a caracara carrying a smoldering branch, but that doesn't mean it hasn't happened, and a grueling PhD project awaits a daring graduate student with an interest in raptors and a touch of pyromania.

Whether or not they can wield it, crested caracaras are certainly attracted to fire — a trait that might have endeared them to the Aztecs, who venerated the sun as the ultimate source of all life. Like the Incas, the Aztecs were technologically adept and elaborately religious, and devoted vast amounts of treasure and blood to rituals meant to placate cosmic forces, in which totemic animals like jaguars, rabbits, snakes, and vultures played important roles. Caracaras seem to be missing from the Aztec pantheon at first glance, but a closer look suggests that they're hiding in plain sight: the bird that the Spanish placed on the Mexican flag is an *águila real* — a golden eagle — a symbol derived from the Aztec myth of a bird of prey who showed their Nahuatl ancestors where to build their capital of Tenochtitlán (now Mexico City).

The Aztecs called this bird *cuauhtli,* which Spanish colonists translated as "eagle," but the Mexican ornithologist Rafael Martín del Campo argued in 1960 that it was most likely a crested caracara. As evidence, he pointed to images of cuauhtlis in surviving Aztec manuscripts, which depict birds with gray and white plumage, unfeathered yellow legs, and upturned crests — all hallmarks of caracaras, not eagles — and some even have their heads thrown back in the posture that surprised Darwin. Golden eagles aren't unknown in

Mexico, but they live only in its northern mountains, far from the Aztecs' southern heartland. It's possible that the Spanish didn't bother to distinguish between birds of prey in the New World, but del Campo suspected that they transformed the cuauhtli into an eagle for reasons of political convenience: a golden eagle was already a symbol of royal authority in Spain, a mascot its Hapsburg monarchs inherited from the Romans.

The national bird of Mexico, in other words, may be a caracara in disguise. A vague sense that caracaras are the true cuauhtlis, no matter what the flag says, persists on both sides of the border; in Mexico, most people know crested caracaras informally as *águilas,* which turns the Spanish substitution on its head, while in South Texas, where they've been common residents for centuries, some people still call them Mexican eagles or Mexican buzzards.

One of my favorite caracara videos on the internet is called "San Jacinto Festival Mexican Eagle (National Bird of Mexico Crested Cara Cara)." It features a Texas-accented falconer named Mike, who introduces a northern crested caracara to a listless audience of toddlers and their parents at a regional fair near San Antonio. Mike calls her "a bird who didn't quite know what she wanted to be when she grew up," compliments her intelligence, notes that her species is becoming more common in the United States, and persuades a member of the audience to offer her a rolled-up dollar bill. Like Tina in England, Mike's caracara seems to know exactly what to do. She gently takes the dollar in her beak, leaps from her keeper's gloved hand, and glides about thirty feet to alight on a donation box the size and shape of a fence post, where she nudges the money into a slot and flies back for a food reward. The audience applauds weakly, unaware that most raptors couldn't be taught to use a vending machine if their lives depended on it.

"All right!" says Mike. "Has anybody got a twenty?"

Whether or not crested caracaras have mastered fire, their tendency to follow other hunters and scavengers may be urging them north in the company of an old friend. Black vultures — the canny opportunists who raided our camp at Kwitaro Backbone in Guyana — once fed beside crested caracaras at the carcasses of ground sloths and mastodons in North America, and they too retreated south after the Pleistocene extinctions. But they've come roaring back in the past few decades, and caracaras might be riding their coattails. The two scavengers' relationship is surprisingly cordial: they often feed together and sleep in the same evening roosts, and vultures have been photographed preening caracaras' neck feathers. Though they come from disparate lineages, they're natural partners; both species are smart, social, and observant, and they'd rather eat the dead than the living.

Why black vultures and caracaras have chosen this moment to return to their old stomping grounds isn't entirely clear. A warming world might have something to do with it, but it's hard to see the connection, since Pleistocene North America was often much colder than it is today. It seems more likely that they're learning to exploit the habits of a new predator that rivals even the saber-tooths and dire wolves: cars. In 2017–18, at least 1.3 million deer were struck by automobiles along the highways of the United States — a number equal to the wildebeest population of the Serengeti — and if you throw in millions of raccoons, coyotes, squirrels, rabbits, opossums, and armadillos, you've assembled a scavengers' buffet of Pleistocene proportions, conveniently laid out along predictable routes. Crested caracaras might be grassland birds, but the shoulders and medians of highways form corridors of treeless habitat everywhere, and the light poles along their peripheries are increasingly festooned with the dark, hooked silhouettes of their old companions. Like the black caracaras patrolling the banks of the Rewa, the northbound cuauhtlis of Mesoamerica may be deciding that long, thin strips of open country, lined with food and friends, will do just fine.

This explanation appeals to Ed McGowan, who's been coping with a recent invasion of black vultures at the Bear Mountain zoo. Black vultures were a rare sight in the Hudson Valley as recently as the 1990s, but hundreds now roost every night above their captive kin in the zoo's aviary, as if visiting them in jail. Cleaning up after the birds is a smelly and time-consuming chore, and McGowan sometimes wishes they'd take their business elsewhere, but admits that the zoo probably draws them in. "They like being around other animals," he says, "and these animals aren't going anywhere."

The vultures might also like Bear Mountain because the New York State Department of Transportation feeds them there. NYSDOT personnel deposit the carcasses of road-killed deer every day at a dump less than a mile from the zoo, a scavengers' paradise that attracts eagles, ravens, and vultures like a backyard feeder draws chickadees. It wouldn't surprise McGowan if the caracaras are starting to join them, and the thought gives him some satisfaction; in a cave forty miles from Bear Mountain, the remains of prehistoric black vultures have been found among the bones of giant sloths, caribou, musk oxen, tapirs, and California condors. Even if their living descendants are a nuisance, watching their return carries the rare thrill of witnessing a reversal of the Pleistocene extinctions.

If this is indeed the trend, it's possible that crested caracaras could become as common in New York City as the ravens and peregrines that have reoccupied it in my lifetime. If caracaras can make it to New Jersey and Nova Scotia, there's nothing to stop them from building one of their ungainly nests in a transmission tower on the shores of Jamaica Bay in Queens, or the fire escape of an apartment building facing Manhattan's Central Park. Like the army of opossums that scour the garbage cans of Brooklyn every night, they'd be a reminder that the terms of the Great American Biotic Interchange are still being negotiated, and that it doesn't belong only to the past.

But for Florida's crested caracaras, trapped in their ancient refuge, the most momentous event in many generations will almost certainly happen soon, if it hasn't happened already. It might be a summer's day, with thunderheads on the horizon and the thin pulse of cicadas in the air, along a dirt road lined with cabbage palms and loblolly pines in the savannas east of Fort Myers. In the early morning a few turkey vultures might collect there, drawn in by the scent of a road-killed deer, alighting heavily in the trees before descending to feed on its eyes and tongue. A gang of black vultures might turn up a few hours later, tearing open the carcass's swollen abdomen. By late afternoon there'd be little but skin clinging to its exposed ribs, and a Floridian crested caracara might be tearing it away in long strips when the first pair of newcomers arrive.

They'd probably strike their Florida cousin as odd. Like us, birds are quick to spot subtle differences among members of their own species, and the Floridian bird would surely notice a variation in the strangers' plumage, a peculiar intonation in their calls, as they greet each other for the first time in thirteen thousand years.

Pleased to meet you, the Florida bird might say.

Igualmente, one of the strangers might reply.

A brief, awkward pause might follow while a pickup truck roars by, trailing a cloud of dust.

Forgive me for staring, the Florida bird might continue, *but I always thought we were the only ones.*

At which its cousins might throw back their heads and *karruk-karruk* for a long time.

Señora, one might say at last, *there are more of us than you could imagine. We have an entire continent.*

480

THE EVOLUTIONARY JOURNEY
OF THE CARACARAS

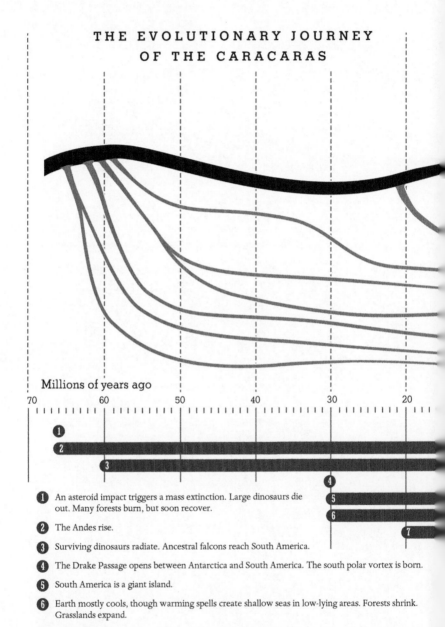

Millions of years ago

70   60   50   40   30   20

① An asteroid impact triggers a mass extinction. Large dinosaurs die out. Many forests burn, but soon recover.

② The Andes rise.

③ Surviving dinosaurs radiate. Ancestral falcons reach South America.

④ The Drake Passage opens between Antarctica and South America. The south polar vortex is born.

⑤ South America is a giant island.

⑥ Earth mostly cools, though warming spells create shallow seas in low-lying areas. Forests shrink. Grasslands expand.

⑦ "True" falcons occupy the northern world, while forest falcons and most caracaras remain in South America.

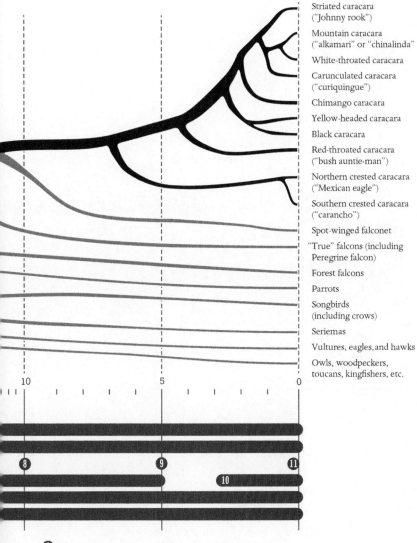

Striated caracara
("Johnny rook")

Mountain caracara
("alkamari" or "chinalinda"

White-throated caracara

Carunculated caracara
("curiquingue")

Chimango caracara

Yellow-headed caracara

Black caracara

Red-throated caracara
("bush auntie-man")

Northern crested caracara
("Mexican eagle")

Southern crested caracara
("carancho")

Spot-winged falconet

"True" falcons (including
Peregrine falcon)

Forest falcons

Parrots

Songbirds
(including crows)

Seriemas

Vultures, eagles, and hawks

Owls, woodpeckers,
toucans, kingfishers, etc.

10   5   0

⑧ The rising Andes reverse the flow of the Amazon.

⑨ The two Americas connect. The Great American Biotic Interchange begins.

⑩ Glaciers grow, shrink, and grow again. Andean caracaras diversify.

⑪ The Last Glacial Maximum. Amerindian people reach South America.

Data sources: Prum *et al* 2015, Fuchs *et al* 2015

ACKNOWLEDGMENTS

This book took a long time, and would not have been possible without the support of many people and several institutions. First among the latter is the Thomas J. Watson Foundation, which funded a young man's proposal to spend a year in remote communities around the world — a project that was transformed by my accidental meeting with striated caracaras. Since then, the incomparable Kay McCallum is one of many Falkland Islanders who've welcomed me to the Johnny rooks' wild and beautiful home, including (but not limited to) Michael and Jeanette Clarke, Steve Massam, Mike and Sue Morrison, Rob and Lorraine McGill, Roddy and Lily Napier, Matthew McMullen, Jeremy Smith, Micky Reeves, Sarah Crofts, Andy Stanworth, Alec and Gisele Hazell, and the Pole-Evans family. Special thanks are due to the directors and staff of Falklands Conservation, who graciously allowed me to take part in fieldwork in the Jason Islands; to Michael

Steinhardt, whose gift of Grand and Steeple Jason to the Wildlife Conservation Society ensured their protection; and to Adrian Schiavini and Andrea Raya Rey at the Centro Austral de Investigaciones Científicas in Ushuaia, who back in 2001 allowed me to piggyback on their penguin research at Isla de los Estados — the island where Georg Forster, traveling with Captain Cook in 1775, saw and painted the bird on this book's cover.

In Brazil, the peerlessly observant Bret Whitney took me up the Aripuanã River with his colleagues Micah Riegner, Albert Burgas, Moraes Eberson and Caitetú, a journey which does not appear in the book only for reasons of length; I will always cherish meeting a jaguar in the forest, holding the claw of a giant armadillo, and hearing the call of a nocturnal curassow. Bret also accompanied me, the filmmaker Luke Padgett, and the mountaineer and guide Jorge Jerez in northern Chile, where he introduced us to salt lagoons and *bofedales,* the pioneering work of the ornithologist A. W. Johnson, and the unlikely wonders of the Andes' giant coots.

Across the ocean, in the United Kingdom, Mary and Simon Lowth provided me an ideal space to write and think in London at a critical moment, which also allowed me to meet my gracious UK editor Stuart Williams (at The Bodley Head) and agent Caspian Dennis (at Abner Stein) in person. Outside London,

Geoff Pearson at Woodlands Falconry Centre, James Channon at Millets Farm Centre, Campbell Murn at the Hawk Conservancy Trust, Simon Blackwell at Birdland, and Davide Giorgi and Jade Stott at Cotswold Wildlife Park and Gardens all made time for a Johnny rook–curious visitor. And Robin and Anne Woods fed me from their minds, library, and kitchen in Newton Abbot for almost twenty years, always reminding me that not everything known is written, and not everything written is known.

I would never have visited Guyana without the help and advice of the intrepid ichthyologist Lesley DeSouza, who connected me with Ashley Holland and let me accompany her and her assistant Piper Kimpel on arapaima fieldwork when my trip with Brian, Jose, Rambo, and Sean came to an end. Debra Sutherland of Travel Experts and Syeada Manbodh at Rainforest Lodge in Georgetown made the trip logistically possible, and I owe a special debt of gratitude to the people of Rewa village and the caretakers of Rewa Eco-Lodge, particularly Dicky Alvin, Rudolph and Irmalinda Edwards, Darlene Alvin, and Winston Edwards.

In the United States, Jynne Martin, Becky Saletan, and Laura Perciasepe were the first to urge me to write a book, and let me feel it was possible. A few years later, the Logan Nonfiction Program at the Carey Center for

Global Good gave me space to write in the book's middle stages; I especially thank Tom Jennings, Carol and Josh Friedman, Emma Beals, MT Conolly, Cathy Otten, Laura Murray, Hazel Thompson, Josh Kron, Catherine Buni, Taran Khan, Megan Buskey, Jonathan Katz, Julia Siler, Mariya Karimjee, and Finbarr O'Reilly (among others) for their friendship and feedback in snowy Rensselaerville. At the American Museum of Natural History, Paul Sweet, Peter Capainolo, and Mary LeCroy helped me locate archival material related to Rollo Beck; Chris Meyer, Carla Dove, and Storrs Olson at the Smithsonian National Museum of Natural History granted me generous access to their time, expertise, and collections on very short notice; and Julia Clarke at the University of Texas honored me with her invitation to search for fossil birds in southern Chile, where Marcelo Leppe and his colleagues at the Instituto Antártico Chileno housed and fed us in the field and shared their findings and work space in Punta Arenas. Back in Texas, Carson and Branson Fustes offered a place for me to bring the book to an end, and the clear-eyed Katie Harrington helped immeasurably in sustaining the book through its final stages and reshaped a crucial chapter. I would also like to thank Maria Matthiessen for her unexpected friendship, good counsel, and green ink — and for pointing out that *gloam-*

ing means dusk, not dawn.

Many of my musical comrades have been swept up in this project in one way or another — especially Emily Lee, who spent many hours helping me transcribe notes, revise chapters, and think aloud; Dan Duszynski and Anastasia Wright, who plied me with tea, sympathy, and vegan tacos; and Will Sheff, who bravely waded through an early version of the manuscript. Other readers whose attention vastly improved this book include Justin Morimoto, Polly Harrington, Jenna Moore, Sarah Tweedt, and Alex Harrington. For more reasons than I could possibly list here, I bow deeply to Jamie Dobie, Chris Kasabach, Steve Rinella, John Schaefer, Jonathan Kade, Diane Hall, Branan Edgens, Sharon Her, Jonathan Poneman, Michael Azerrad, Louie Saletan, Bob Barth, Noreen Damude, Claudia and Carlos Jofre, Monika Schillat, and my extended human and animal families.

Lastly, I owe deep thanks to my thoughtful, passionate, and unfailingly generous agent, Farley Chase, at Chase Literary, as well as Erin Sellers, Nora Reichard, Gabrielle Brooks, Abigail Endler, Sara Eagle, Morgan Fenton, and everyone at Knopf Doubleday — most of all my editor, Jonathan Segal, whose faith, patience, and sound advice kept this book afloat and steered it home.

489

Robin Woods (1936–2020) holds an adult striated caracara on Steeple Jason.

NOTES

Abbreviations

People
BC: Bernabé Cobo
CD: Charles Darwin
WHH: William Henry Hudson
LH: Leonard Hill
RWW: Robin W. Woods

Selected Books by William Henry Hudson and Date of First Publication
BAM: *Birds and Man* (1901)
BIL: *Birds in London* (1898)
BLP: *Birds of La Plata* (1920)
BON: *The Book of a Naturalist* (1919)
FALA: *Far Away and Long Ago: A History of My Early Life* (1918)
GM: *Green Mansions: A Romance of the Tropical Forest* (1904)
IDIP: *Idle Days in Patagonia* (1893)
NLP: *The Naturalist in La Plata* (1892)

TLE: *The Land's End: A Naturalist's Impressions in West Cornwall* (1908)

Other

BBC: British Broadcasting Corporation
BLI: BirdLife International
CCD: Correspondence of Charles Darwin (available at darwin-online.org.uk)
IUCN: International Union for Conservation of Nature
RSPB: Royal Society for the Protection of Birds
WCS: Wildlife Conservation Society

1. An Unanswered Question

Charles Darwin saw: The tropical forests overwhelmed Darwin's powers of description. "In these fertile climates, teeming with life," he wrote, "the attractions are so numerous, that [I am] scarcely able to walk at all" (CD 1845:26). In another moment of wonder, contemplating the "exceedingly great" diversity of small beetles he met in the tropical forest, Darwin wrote that "it is sufficient to disturb the composure of an entomologist's mind, to look forward to the future dimensions of a complete catalogue" (CD 1845:34).

"in these still solitudes": CD 1845:210.

Without ants or termites: Magellanic woodpeckers (*Campephilus magellanicus*) are close relatives of North America's famously extinct ivory-billed woodpeckers (*Campephilus principalis*) and imperial woodpeckers (*Campephilus imperialis*). Magellanic woodpeckers depend on large stands of mature trees, just as their northern cousins once did; and old-growth *Nothofagus* forests are critical to their survival (IUCN 2020: *Campephilus magellanicus*).

The *Beagle* and its companion: CD 1845:26, 188.

"I can very plainly see": CD 1945:83.

He'd been invited aboard: The *Beagle*'s captain, Robert FitzRoy, had asked a friend to

493

share his quarters on its five-year voyage, in part because the ship's previous captain had killed himself under the pressures of a lonely command. When his friend declined, FitzRoy decided that a "gentleman naturalist" might do — opening the way for Darwin, who was put forward when other candidates turned down the opportunity. FitzRoy later served a tempestuous term as governor of New Zealand and pioneered the technique (and the term) of weather "forecasting" by using a network of barometers at fixed stations. Nearly thirty years after returning from the *Beagle*'s voyage with Darwin, FitzRoy died by suicide.

Darwin's only real qualification: Henslow letter in CCD.

he was simply an amiable and wealthy young man: Wedgwood letter in CCD.

Riding and shooting: "Rather more than half" of the penal colony's residents, Darwin noted, "were runaway rebels and murderers" (CD 1845:188).

Among the former prisoners were a contingent of gauchos: The Falklands' wild cattle were descended from a herd set loose on the islands in 1764 by a French expedition, which also put horses ashore and set fire to several of the smaller islands in the hopes of "improving" them for agriculture at some future date. The islands' deep seams of peat smoldered for years, but the French never returned (Wilson 2016).

For five days, they rode: The feral bulls that roamed the Falklands in Darwin's time "wander about single, or two and three together," he wrote, "and are very savage. I never saw such magnificent beasts; they equalled in the size of their huge heads and necks the Grecian marble sculptures" (CD 1845:190).

Grazing flocks of native geese: "In the Falklands," Darwin noted, "the sportsman may sometimes kill more of the upland goose in one day than he can carry home" (CD 1845:400).

These gullible carnivores: CD 1845:194. DNA studies have revealed that warrahs' nearest living relatives are the maned wolves of northern Argentina and Uruguay, lanky creatures sometimes described as foxes on stilts. The warrahs' ancestors appear to have crossed over to the Falklands from the South American mainland, possibly via an ice bridge, during the last glacial period — sometime between thirteen thousand and seventeen thousand years ago — and remained there until large-scale sheep farming began in the late nineteenth century. The last warrah is said to have been killed by a sheep farmer in 1876 (Slater et al. 2009).

Unlike the wary hawks: CD 1845:57–58.

"The sailors who visit these islands": Barnard 1979:75.

The most common: Darwin also noted that southern crested caracaras (*Caracara plancus*) were "said to be very crafty, and to steal great numbers of eggs" (CD 1845:56).

Both birds "possess one family air": CD 1963:239.

The sound of crested caracaras' weird, rattling call: CD 1845:57.

"they are very evident": CD 1845:56.

Scientists have combed through: Darwin's comment that "rarity, as geology tells us, is the precursor to extinction" (CD 1876:85) seems obvious only because our concept of endangered species is built on it.

"from their point of view": James Hamilton letter to Falkland Islands Government, personal archive of RWW.

scientists and falconers: Figueroa et al. 2015.

"false eagles": CD 1845:56.

"shiftless wanderers of rubbish pits": Neruda 1985:64. This English translation by the author and Katie Harrington.

"a rather unimpressive lot": Brown and Amadon 1968:738.

"They're dirty birds": Joan Morrison, personal communication, 2001.

"Bad falcons": A recently published satire called *The Field Guide to Dumb Birds of North America* continues in this vein, calling the only species of caracara to regularly visit

North America "an embarrassment to real raptors." "This big, lazy son-of-a-bitch should have its bird-of-prey-license revoked," it complains. "You'd think a member of the [falcon] family could make more of an effort" (Kracht 2019:128).

"all manner of subsistence": Azara 1809, trans. and quoted in WHH, BLP 1920 Vol 2:62.

a "sub-family of which even grave naturalists": WHH, BLP 1920 Vol 2:63.

2. Johnny Rooks

It was a visit: FIGAS flights leave every day from Stanley to points around the islands. To find out when your flight departs, you tune in to the Falkland Islands Radio Service the night before to hear when each flight is leaving, where it is going — and the names of all the passengers. Each plane holds about eight people.

he cursed them elaborately: Barnard 1979:82.

"I have known these birds": Barnard 1979:75.

"quite white, and very good eating": CD 1845:58.

"the most mischievous of all the feathered creation": Barnard 1979:75.

Penguins seem purpose built: The nineteenth-century American sailor, author, and crackpot John Cleves Symmes Jr. believed that the remarkable wildlife of polar regions, including penguins and whales, was evidence of a separate world inside the earth, to which they passed back and forth through giant portals. "I declare the earth is hollow," he wrote in 1817, "and habitable within; containing a number of solid concentrick spheres, one within the other, and that it is open at the poles 12 or 16 degrees; I pledge my life in support of this truth, and am ready to explore the hollow, if the world will support and aid me in the undertaking." Edgar Allan Poe later drew on this idea as the basis for his novel *The Narrative of Arthur Gordon Pym of Nantucket,* which starts off as a high-seas adventure but soon becomes an otherworldly nightmare. It also includes a scene at a penguin rookery on Grand Jason Island.

a bounty on Johnny rook beaks: Cawkell, Maling, and Cawkell, 1960:75.

"There is an irresistible, shambolic clownishness": James Hamilton, "Memorandum on the Johnny rook," undated, in personal collection of RWW.

"had not learnt that man is dangerous": Hamilton, "Memorandum on the Johnny rook."

"there is an indefinite expectation": CD 1845:282.

"The beasts that roam over the plain": Cowper 1782:305–308.

The Johnny rooks are among the last outliers: You can feel a sense of first contact with most animals in the Falklands. Albatrosses will ignore you unless you make a sudden move; sit in the path of a column of penguins marching to or from the sea, and they'll walk around or over you. Elephant seals, which fear only orcas and white sharks, sprawl belly up on the beach to snooze, and snipe will let you come close enough to see the fine details of the stripes and patterns that make them nearly invisible in reeds and tall grass. None of these animals are dim; they've just reserved their caution for the threats they know.

But there's one poignant exception. Even in the remotest of the Falklands, sea lions and fur seals flee at the first sign of a human being, hurling themselves from rocks and cliffs in a frenzy of mortal fear that makes you want to call out that the danger has passed. But only wary animals survived the sealers' onslaught. If you stumble across a sleeping sea lion in the tall grass, they bolt awake with a deep, hair-raising snarl, and if you're unlucky enough to be standing between them and their escape route, they might attack. From their point of view, you're a figure from an ancestral nightmare — the boogeyman, come to life.

In their previous job: Cuthbert et al. 2013.

Mice had also brought: "The thing is, I really

like mice," Kalinka said one evening as we washed up from supper. "It's one of the contradictions of the job."

3. A Half-Tamed Hawk

A few discreet signs: Mary Hughes died, aged ninety-one, in 1931.

"The air, the sunlight, the night": Jefferies 1901:49.

"I found him arrayed": WHH 1925:125.

"the monkey people": WHH, AHRP 1923:238.

"Take this horror out of the park": Epstein 1940:106.

"the obscenities that did not exist": Epstein 1940:25.

"To most of our wild birds": WHH, AHRP 1923:38.

"It lives on the ground": CD 1845:270.

"A man with the strength of an ant": WHH, AHRP 1923:242. A road engine is a type of locomotive. The heading at the top of this page in AHRP is "Man the Weakling."

"As neither the enjoyment nor the capacity": CD 1874:569.

"They are just as useless": WHH, AHRP 1923:263.

"You may try him with a variety of sounds": WHH, AHRP 1923:303.

"All that is in our minds": WHH, AHRP 1923:272. Hudson wasn't afraid to pursue this thought even further. "The more the psychologists dig down to get at the roots of [our mental] faculties," he continued, "the deeper they find them . . . What we call spirituality is not ours by miracle; it was inherent in us from the beginning: the seed germinated and the roots and early leaves were formed before man, as man, existed, and are ours by inheritance." Animal spirituality is a wide-open field (to put it mildly), but behavioral science that proceeds from our essential similarity — rather than difference — with animals is slowly coming into fashion. Behavioral science has wandered for a long time in a wilderness where animals are treated as emotionless "black boxes" who can only be understood by measuring their responses to various stimuli; de Waal 2016 beautifully probes the assumptions and problems of this approach.

"She was not concerned about me": WHH, AHRP 1923:3.

"a great quarrel": WHH, AHRP 1923:138.

"interested armed detachment": Roberts 1924:23.

"a half-tamed hawk": Roberts 1924:22.

"However poor our creature": WHH, BLP 1920 Vol 2:63.

"By turns he is a Falcon": WHH, BLP 1920 Vol 2:62.

"the merest apology": WHH, BLP 1920 Vol 2:64.

"It is generally the last": CD 1845:57.

"A species so cosmopolitan": WHH, BLP 1920 Vol 2:63. See also Solaro and Sarasola (2015) on chimangos' nesting success in urban areas.

"I should not be surprised": WHH, BIL 1898:42.

"The gauchos have a saying": WHH, BLP 1920 Vol 2:71. "While feeding on a carcase [sic]," Hudson added, "it incessantly utters a soliloquy of the most lamentable notes, as if protesting against the hard necessity of having to put up with such carrion fare — long querulous cries resembling the piteous whines of a shivering puppy chained up in a bleak backyard and all its wants neglected, but infinitely more doleful in character."

"As a rule": WHH, BLP 1920 Vol 2:67.

"a chafed saddle-horse": WHH, BLP 1920 Vol 2:69–70.

"The mind in beast": WHH, AHRP 1923:6.

"a sort of poor relation": WHH, BLP 1920 Vol 2:63.

4. The Birth of a Naturalist

"a man of shining defects": WHH, FALA 1918:119.

"Murder": WHH, FALA 1918:20.

"brightly colored garments": CD 1845:42.

"where the people are accustomed": WHH, FALA 1918:65.

Darwin crossed paths with Rosas: CD 1845:73. Rosas was courteous to Darwin and gave him a formal document granting him safe passage within the land controlled by the Argentine state, but his laughter was a sound men feared, and Darwin described the atmosphere surrounding the general's army in a scene worthy of Cormac McCarthy. "During my stay at Bahia Blanca," he wrote, "while waiting for the *Beagle,* the place was in a constant state of excitement, from rumours of wars and victories, between the troops of Rosas and the wild Indians. One day an account came that a small party forming one of the postas on the line to Buenos Ayres, had been found all murdered. The next day three hundred men arrived from the Colorado, under the command of Commandant Miranda. A large portion of these men were Indians (mansos, or tame), belonging to the tribe of the Cacique Bernantio. They passed the night here; and it was impossible to conceive anything more wild and savage than the scene of their bivouac. Some drank till they were intoxicated; others swallowed the steaming blood of the cattle slaughtered for their suppers, and then, being sick from drunkenness, they cast it up again, and were besmeared with filth and gore."

Darwin nonetheless expressed hope that Rosas would be a good leader for his country — a hope he amended in a footnote to the 1845 edition of his *Beagle* narrative. "This prophecy," he wrote, "has turned out entirely and miserably wrong" (CD 1845:73).

By the time Hudson was born: Hudson never saw General Rosas, but he did see one of his fools during a boyhood visit to the capital. "I had been sent with my sisters and little brother to spend the day at the house of an Anglo-Argentine family in another part of the town," he recalled, "and was in the large courtyard playing with the children of the house when some one opened a window above us and called 'Don Eusebio!' That conveyed nothing to me, but the little boys of the house all knew what it meant; it meant that if we went quickly out to the street we might catch a glimpse of the great man in all his glory. At all events, they jumped up, flinging their toys away, and rushed to the street door, and we went after them. Coming out we found quite a crowd of lookers-on, and then down the street, in his general's dress — for it was one of the Dictator's little jokes to make his fool a general — all scarlet, with a big scarlet three-cornered hat surmounted by an immense aigrette of scarlet plumes, came Don Eusebio. He marched along in tremendous dignity, his sword at his side, and twelve soldiers, also in scarlet, his bodyguard, walking six on each side of him with drawn swords in their hands. (WHH, FALA 1918:106)

One of Hudson's playmates whispered to him that if anyone in the crowd laughed at Don Eusebio, they would be cut to pieces. This was thrilling to a little boy, but it induced a different shiver in him later, when he saw how precarious his family's lives really were.

Nothing seemed to make his parents happier: WHH, FALA 1918:318.

"little wild animal running about": WHH, FALA 1918:17.

"So powerful it was": WHH, FALA 1918:323.

"standing motionless among the tall weeds": WHH, FALA 1918:93.

"the pleasure of living": CD 1845:505.

the bolas of the gauchos: Darwin described this weapon and his own attempt to wield it.

The bolas, or balls, are of two kinds: the simplest, which is chiefly used for catching ostriches, consists of two round stones, covered with leather, and united by a thin plaited thong, about eight feet long. The other kind differs only in having three balls united by the thongs to a common centre. The Gaucho holds the smallest of the three in his hand, and whirls the other two round and round his head; then, taking aim, sends them like chain shot revolving through the air. The balls no sooner strike any object, than, winding round it, they cross each other, and become firmly hitched. . . . One day, as I was amusing myself by galloping and whirling the balls round my head, by accident the free one struck a bush, and its revolving motion being thus destroyed, it immediately fell to the ground, and, like magic, caught one hind leg of my horse; the other ball was then jerked out of my hand, and the horse fairly secured. Luckily he was an old practised animal, and knew what it meant; otherwise he would probably have kicked till he had thrown himself down. The Gauchos roared with laughter; they cried out that they had seen every sort of animal caught, but had never before seen a man caught by himself. (CD 1845:45)

"When riding late": WHH, AHRP 1923:240.
"one with animals": WHH, FALA 1918:327.
"altogether unique among books": Wallace 1892.
"In winter they hibernated": WHH, FALA 1918:208.
"the feathered people": WHH, NLP 1892:208.

"whenever I was in the wild arboreal mood": WHH, FALA 1918:190.

"Here was a bird as big or bigger": WHH, FALA 1918:191. It was the screamer's freedom that Hudson coveted most, not just its power of flight. "This desire has continued with me through my life," he added, "yet I have never wished to fly in a balloon or airship, since I should then be tied to a machine and have no will or soul of my own. The desire has only been gratified a very few times in that kind of dream called levitation, when one rises and floats above the earth without effort and is like a ball of thistledown carried by the wind."

"lord[s] of the feathered race"; "wonderfully bold and savage spirit": WHH, BLP 1920 Vol 2:76.

"On one of my early rides on my pony": WHH, FALA 1918:84.

"In the convenient hollow": WHH, FALA 1918:83.

"They roosted in it by night": In Argentina, people sometimes compare their windblown hair to a carancho's nest.

"unspeakably savage and fearsome"; "I managed to swarm"; "Just then I heard the harsh grating cry": WHH, FALA 1918:84.

"Where anything is wrong"; "intelligently keeping at a safe distance": WHH, BLP 1920 Vol 2:82–83.

had a gift for finding partners: One of Hudson's friends proved this point when he was out riding during a "thistle season," when the ten-foot stalks of wild artichokes turned the Pampas into a maze of twisting paths. He noticed several caranchos hovering ahead of him, and assumed that a large animal had wandered into a patch of thistles and died; but when he arrived in a small open patch, he found himself in a far more ancient scene. "The attraction," Hudson wrote, "was a large male Rhea squatting on the ground and sheltering with its extended wing a brood of not fewer than twenty-five or thirty young birds, small tender things, only a day or so out of the shell." The appearance of a horse and rider was a boon for the caranchos. "As soon as he rode into the open space of ground," Hudson continued, "the old Ostrich sprang up, and with lowered head, clattering beak, and broad wings spread out like sails, rushed at him; his horse was greatly terrified, and tried to plunge into the dense mass of thistles, so that he had the greatest difficulty in keeping his seat. Presently the Ostrich left him, and casting his eyes around he was astonished to see that all the young Ostriches were running about, scattered over the ground, while the Caranchos were pursuing, knocking down, and killing them. Meanwhile the old Ostrich was frantically rushing about trying to save them; but the

Caranchos, when driven from one bird they were attacking, would merely rise and drop on the next one a dozen yards off; and as there were about fifteen Caranchos all engaged in the same way, the slaughter was proceeding at a great rate."

At this point, Hudson's friend became preoccupied with staying on his horse, and rode away without seeing the final outcome of his intrusion — but not before he saw that "at least half the young birds were dead, and that these were all torn and bleeding on the small of the neck just behind the head, while in some cases the head had been completely wrenched off" (WHH, BLP 1920 Vol 2:81).

"The snarer has a long slender cane": WHH, BLP 1920 Vol 2:87.

They were playful, intelligent birds: WHH, BLP 1920 Vol 2:71.

"undisturbed by any sense of incongruity": WHH, BLP 1920 Vol 2:70.

"The moment the smoke of a distant fire is seen": WHH, BLP 1920 Vol 2:65.

"sometimes attack birds": WHH, BLP 1920 Vol 2:68.

"In all times and in all places": WHH, BLP 1920 Vol 2:65.

"The Peregrine": WHH, BLP 1920 Vol 2:54.

"In the beginner's mind": Suzuki 2010:1.

5. The Most Intelligent Bird in the World

An off-the-cuff lecture: The island where Geoff saw human bones is Sir Abu Nu'ayr, which belongs to the Emirate of Sharjah. A wooden cottage apparently still stands on the island, which male members of the Bin Hada family visited each autumn during much of the twentieth century to catch wild falcons and hawks that were passing through on migration; these birds were then sold into falconry. Geoff describes the island as a depot for smugglers ferrying human slaves across the Persian Gulf.

"Don't ask how many": Geoff's wife Rita is a patient, quick-witted English teacher from Hungary a few decades Geoff's junior. She fended off his marriage proposals for years, but finally yielded when he ambushed her at a family wedding with an elaborate speech in Hungarian that he'd memorized phonetically. She appears to regard him with a mixture of affection, exasperation, and bewilderment; when he talks for too long, she tugs at his sleeve and reminds him to listen. Geoff sometimes delights Rita's students by bringing an eagle to her classroom.

Calipers, pliers, and other tools: Every Christmas, Geoff presents each bird with a dead mouse or a rat, tied up with a ribbon.

Later he tended falcons: In Malaysia, "I'd

show them how they do it in the West,"
Geoff says, "and they'd show me their
methods. And after we'd finished all that,
they'd give me a tour of the place, and I'd
see more and enjoy myself a lot better than
getting put into jail for the night, you know,
waking up with a hangover, and not knowing if you're going to catch gonorrhea."

Geoff assumed that Tina: Parent-raised birds,
as Geoff puts it, "know that they're birds"
and have a self-assurance that makes them
easier to deal with than hand-reared birds,
who often suffer from crippling identity
problems if they think their parents — and,
by extension, they — are human. These
"imprint" birds live frustrated lives, stuck
between two worlds, at home in neither.

6. The Court of the Penguin King

a "lovable rogue": Simon Blackwell, Man-
ager, in conversation with author, 2015.
A pair of hyacinth macaws: Hill wrote that
his flamingos were useful for predicting the
local weather; if a cold front was due to arrive overnight, they always marched, in solemn single file, to a heated shed he'd left
open for them hours earlier.
"Often, on a dark winter's morning": LH
1976:13.
"The rods would be wiggled": LH 1976:40.
"walking into a great children's tea party":

Johnny Morris, quoted in LH 1976:10.

His best animal friend: When Joey the pigeon arrived in the church, "all the choristers were tittering in amusement," Hill wrote, "and I must confess that a little light relief did us all no harm, although the congregation were not so pleased and the canon administered a sharp reprimand when he caught me alone. Strange how times change, isn't it? I always think that today someone would be only too pleased to deliver a sermon on such a story" (LH 1976:15).

"taught me vital lessons": LH 1976:13.

He began to travel: LH 1976:44–49. Len's hummingbird-smuggling caper, discovered by the airline, was a hit with the company brass, and Hill restaged it for a "BOAC takes good care of you" ad campaign.

In a final letter: Scott 1993:475.

"As we flew over Patagonia": LH 1976:71.

"The gentoo nest": LH 1976:92.

Most delicious of all: This would not be so easy today. The Convention on International Trade in Endangered Species of Wild Flora and Fauna, or CITES, came into force in 1975, after Hill's first visits to the Jasons. If Hill owned the islands today, he might still be able to capture and export penguins and caracaras, but it would be a far more complicated and expensive undertaking — and it would leave a paper trail.

The islands' current owner, the Wildlife Conservation Society (formerly the New York Zoological Society) prohibits any trade in the islands' birds.

One of Len's legacies: The story of Hill transporting striated caracara eggs back to the UK comes from Rob McGill, a Falkland Islander who is the Wildlife Conservation Society's official agent for Grand and Steeple Jason.

He returned to the Falklands: A film taken in 1973 at Birdland shows imperial shags and steamer ducks, probably taken from the Jasons, swimming in its artificial ponds.

Such a small gene pool: Severe inbreeding among the captive Johnny rooks is more or less inevitable; as one keeper noted, "they're all brothers and sisters now." This is likely to lead to genetic disorders, neurological problems, and hatching failure in succeeding generations; the arthritis that crippled Tina in her later years might be a warning sign. Campbell Murn remembers a rare Eurasian owl that was common in captivity in the 1980s, when he was a teenager; a decade later they were gone, having ceased to lay viable eggs.

Peebles has her own Instagram feed: www .instagram.com/icbp_peebles/.

"This bird": theshellmeister, "Fallowfields Falconry — Meet Boo the Intelligent Cara-

cara," December 28, 2011, https://www
.youtube.com.

7. In the Wake of the Dinosaurs

"I saw a dark object": WHH, AHRP
   1923:225.
But the scale of his dream: Later in life, Hudson came to believe in telepathy; he felt certain that he'd seen the face of a young girl he knew in a cloud at a moment when she was in distress. In *A Hind in Richmond Park*, he wonders at length about what secrets and abilities remain to be discovered in "the unexplored wilderness of the mind" (WHH, AHRP 1923:228).
When the asteroid: The Australian biologist Tim Flannery gives an excellent account of the asteroid's impact and its effects on North America in his 2002 book *The Eternal Frontier: An Ecological History of North America and Its Peoples.*
the largest volcanic eruption to occur in human history: There have been some corkers. An eruption in western North America once buried Wyoming under sixty feet of ash, and the largest eruption we know about was the Lake Toba supervolcano in Indonesia, which exploded about seventy thousand years ago and dropped significant quantities of ash as far away as East Africa. It cooled the earth by a staggering five to fif-

teen degrees centigrade, and may have killed most people; our species bears the genetic signature of population bottlenecks in India and East Asia that can be traced to about the time of Toba's eruption.

But evidence for it: In 1980, a team of scientists led by the physicist Luis Alvarez first suggested that a meteor strike had caused the Cretaceous extinctions. They based their hypothesis on the presence of a thin layer of widely distributed metallic ash, rich in iridium, which has been found all over the world and dated to the time of the Yucatán impact and the end-Cretaceous extinctions. Iridium is a very rare element on Earth but common in asteroids (Alvarez et al. 1980).

A conference of experts: Schulte et al. 2010.

Plants were better equipped: Plants handled the end-Cretaceous impact better than animals for several reasons. They didn't need to eat in sudden bursts, for one thing, or chase after their food, and they'd had hundreds of millions of years to refine their approaches to living. Many long-lived plants could vary their growth rate in times of scarce resources, letting them take temporary vacations from life; they could also absorb physical damage that would kill most animals, and stored up reserves of nutrients and water in their tissues to draw from in lean times. Their ingenious strategies even

515

extended to their offspring: many plants produce seeds that can lie dormant, encased in a hard shell, until conditions are right — sometimes for many years, if that's what it takes. As long as they weren't incinerated, they stood a good chance of living through a dark and difficult time.

Even farther south: Donovan et al. 2016.

The oldest known primate skeleton: Ni et al. 2013.

as the animal world rebuilt itself: Not all mammals of the dinosaurs' world were tiny; a few raccoon-sized mammals have been found that appear to have been predators, and might very well have eaten small dinosaurs. Another Mesozoic fish-eating mammal of about the same size had a flattened tail like a beaver.

many of them could fly: I've tried to run down striated caracaras in the Falklands a few times by walking slowly toward them and gradually picking up speed. When they realize you're coming after them, they turn and slowly walk away: *Surely you're not interested in me.* But if you pick up speed, they'll break into a trot, then a run. If you run faster, they'll open their wings, giving them an extra burst of speed as the lift reduces their weight. Run faster still and they'll finally take to the air with a few strong flaps, curling up and away from you in a graceful arc while peering down at the weird, long-legged creature with the temerity to chase them. It's like watching flight evolve in front of you.

The fossils we've found so far: The feathered dinosaurs even include several species of tyrannosaurs, though probably not *T. rex* itself, which seems to have been clad only in tough scales, at least as an adult.

But a mixed-age group of one species: Funston et al. 2016.

Late-Cretaceous fossils: Longrich et al. 2011.

At least a dozen separate lineages: Ksepka et al. 2017. The only reason we still think of birds as anything *other* than dinosaurs is that most scientists were resolutely wrong about them for decades. Darwin's friend Thomas Henry Huxley suspected the link, but the prevailing opinion through most of the twentieth century was that *all* the dinosaurs had died in the Cretaceous extinctions, and that birds were survivors of a separate group of reptiles. When the debate reopened in earnest in the 1990s, some researchers wore buttons reading BIRDS AREN'T DINOSAURS at academic conferences. But in recent years the evidence has become overwhelming: birds are to dinosaurs what Italian is to Latin. If you're a fan of scrambled eggs or fried chicken, you've been eating dinosaurs all your life.

They'd already evolved into the forty major groups: Prum et al. 2015.

Only about seven hundred dinosaur species: Starrfelt and Liow 2015.

The variety of their sizes: Amphibians also have a surprisingly strong claim to the Cenozoic title. There are more than 6,700 species of living frogs, and their lineage predates the dinosaurs. Like birds, they radiated explosively in the time that followed the Cretaceous extinctions, and most living frogs can trace their ancestry to frogs that lived in southern Africa, South America, and (probably) Antarctica — still more evidence that the southern world was the best place to live if you wanted to survive the asteroid.

A few even feed on leaves: Hoatzins hatch with saurian claws on their wing digits, and for a while, there was some speculation that they might be more closely related to early birds like *Archaeopteryx,* which lived about 120 million years ago, than to other living birds. But this doesn't seem to be the case; the most recent molecular research suggests that hoatzins' nearest relatives may be cuckoos. But even this is in some doubt, and they're often referred to as "enigmatic." Hoatzins seem to have been far more widespread in the distant past, when tropical forests covered more of Earth's surface.

they're probably the most widespread: IUCN 2020.

finding a new bird of prey: The Cryptic Forest Falcon, a secretive hunter that lives in South American tropical forests (Whittaker 2002).

Birds of prey: There are slightly more species of birds of prey than there are primates; on Team Primate, we can boast only about 450 species.

the unique secretary birds: Secretary birds, named for the long black feathers on their heads that resemble the quill pens secretaries tucked behind their ears in the eighteenth century, have one of the best scientific names on record, *Sagittarius serpentarius.* In 2003, French paleontologist Cécile Mourer-Chauviré described a fossil genus of secretary birds with the tongue-in-cheek name *Amanuensis.*

Hollywood's version: Turner et al. 2007.

full coats of feathers: There's been a long-running debate among evolutionary biologists about why feathers evolved from scales in the first place. They clearly preceded flight; like hair, the earliest feathers probably evolved for thermal insulation, and might later have become useful in displays meant to communicate or impress mates, which could have led to the long, rigid plumes that eventually became useful in flight. In any case, feathers remain more essential to birds' physiology than the ability to fly; there are flightless birds, but none are featherless.

T. rex and its contemporaries: I paid a visit to the *T. rex* skeleton in the American Museum of Natural History just after her species had made the news — again — for a new estimate of the crushing force of their jaws: eight thousand pounds of pressure per square inch, enough to shatter the bones of sauropods and suck out the marrow. She was as imposing as ever, leaning forward with her tail held off the ground, her skull tilted at an angle that suggested focus and interest. I stared for a while into her sobering maw, but then looked down and noticed that her feet looked almost exactly like Evita's. I shouldn't have been surprised, since the tyrannosaur's theropod lineage includes living birds. But it was startling to see their connection written so plainly in stone.

none are large enough to put us on their menu: With the possible exception of a giant eagle the Polynesian ancestors of today's Maori met when they arrived in New Zealand about a thousand years ago. Haast's eagle, *Harpagornis moorei,* weighed around thirty pounds and was about 40 percent larger than the largest living bird of prey. It struck its victims with what Richard Holdaway described in 1989 (https://www.nzgeo.com) as the force of a cinder block dropped from an eight-story building and pierced them with claws as long as the claws of a polar bear. These giant raptors had to be huge to prey on even larger grazing birds called moas, which were like massive, wingless ostriches or emus — the avian equivalent of cows or antelopes.

Until the Maori appeared, New Zealand had no indigenous mammals except three species of bat, and birds were free to occupy niches in New Zealand that were taken by large mammals elsewhere. Haast's eagles were like flying tigers; but like tigers, they met their match in human beings. The ancestors of today's Maori had hunted the moas to extinction by about 1400, and the giant eagles disappeared around the same time. They live on in Maori lore as Pouakai, a giant bird that killed and ate people.

We're hunters, too: One way to see Geoff's art of falconry, with its arcane vocabulary and customs, is as a symbolic ritual of absorbing a raptor's powers by subordinating its will. For many years in Europe and Asia, falconry was a pastime reserved for royalty, and it remains a sport of kings in the Middle East, where a thriving trade supplies royal falconers with birds that are as valued as symbols of prestige as a yacht or a Lamborghini.

8. A Family Secret

among her discoveries: Clarke et al. 2010, Clarke et al. 2016, Riede et al. 2016, Li et al. 2012, Peteya et al. 2017, Hu et al. 2018, Legendre et al. 2020.

We'd already passed up: These large Cretaceous clams from the genus *Panopea* have virtually identical living descendants today, which brings up the confusing problem of species that appear to have "stopped" evolving. Why do modern sharks and crocodilians, for example, look so similar to their ancestors? Did evolution somehow declare them finished and stop working on them? The answer is no; they're just as subject to it as anything else; but they've found a comfortable, well-bounded niche in the world from which nothing's yet been able to dislodge them. Natural selection hasn't abandoned species like this; it's *maintaining* them, and without a selective pressure to change, they don't.

One result of this process is that the living world resembles a complex mosaic of earlier versions of itself, a bit like a billboard that's been papered over and then peeled away in places to reveal hints of its previous iterations. This is part of the fun of hunting for fossils: finding them feels like the moment when you're stripping paint from a wall and suddenly expose a swatch of color from a room's former life.

This didn't just isolate: Livermore et al. 2007, Van Den Ende et al. 2017.

among this season's discoveries: Manríquez et al. 2019, Goin et al. 2020.

A need to organize the world:
>
> Oh! Blessed rage for order, pale Ramon,
> The maker's rage to order words of the
>   sea,
> Words of the fragrant portals, dimly-starred,
> And of ourselves and of our origins,
> In ghostlier demarcations, keener sounds.
>
> — WALLACE STEVENS,
> "The Idea of Order at Key West," 1934

Its true age was most recently revised: Dalrymple 2001.

Cobo spent most of his adult life: Cobo published his magnum opus, *Historia del Nuevo Mundo,* only four years before his death; of that only a portion has survived. He is also said to be the author of a work on botany, which has never been found.

"the richest jewel": BC 2010:21.

"Acknowledging jointly what we know": BC 2010:58.

"If this solution does not meet": BC 2010:59.

"I should infer from analogy": CD 1860:484. The common ancestor of all life had to remain an inference for Darwin and Wallace, since it left no physical traces they could discern, nor did they know how the ancestor itself came into being — a question for which there is still no definitive answer. Nevertheless, the ancestor's existence has since been supported by many lines of evidence, especially in the molecular realms of life that scientists have now been peering into for more than a century. Chief among them is the arbitrary but universal chemical language called the genetic code, present in all living things, which points to the same conclusion Darwin reached: that if you could travel back to the right moment and place, you could find an organism from which all life on Earth today descends. This doesn't mean, however, that the last universal common ancestor, affectionately known as LUCA, was alone, or even the first organism; it's just the earliest living thing whose genetic material survived to be passed down to its progeny, including us.

Years ago, in the lonely corner of southwest Texas called the Big Bend, I sat outside one night looking at the stars with an ornithologist friend, training my binoculars on glowing objects that were many light-years away: the faint powder puff of Andromeda, the bright smudge of the nebula in Orion's sword. After a half hour or so, my friend cleared his throat. "You know," he said, "evolution is a great theory. But it doesn't explain why all this shit is *here*."

"There is grandeur in this view": CD 1876:429.

Most of the tree's forking limbs: If you examine a scientific illustration of the tree of life, sometimes called a cladogram, it's easy to mistakenly conclude that there are more species now than there have ever been. But the actual tree itself, as scientists currently understand it, is so dense and convoluted that it's almost impossible to take in all at once — even if you're only talking about animals, to say nothing of the other kingdoms of life. Fungi, for instance, are pitifully neglected; you can probably expect major discoveries in the fungal world in the coming decades. And the fossil record is so spotty (and biased toward larger organisms) that there are many smaller branches we may never know about.

But some have arrived: All ancestries, of course, eventually meet somewhere on their way to the base of the tree, since all life stems back to the same last universal common ancestor (LUCA), which probably lived somewhere around four billion years ago. When scientists say something like *X isn't related to Y,* they don't mean it in an absolute sense.

But they're an undeniably handy group: It's fairly easy to tell most bird species apart at a glance, because that's how they do it, too: like us, birds lean heavily on their eyes to tell them about the world, though some can see well into the UV spectrum — the optical equivalent of a dog's ultra-high-frequency hearing — and communicate with visual signals that are invisible to us.

It's impossible to overstate DNA's importance: It's still a bit jarring to think that Darwin died seventy-one years before DNA was described, though it was first isolated by a Swiss chemist named Johannes Friedrich Miescher in 1869, thirteen years before Darwin's death (and only four years after the end of the American Civil War). Miescher suspected that DNA might have something to do with heredity, but its molecular composition wasn't described until 1953, by the American chemists James Watson and Francis Crick.

it offers physical evidence: In the past few years, paleontologists have even begun to recover fragments of DNA from fossils, a feat once thought impossible. But where most extinct animals are concerned, they're still forced to rely on traditional methods, using details of fossil skeletons to infer relationships among creatures of the deep past. This technique led scientists to improbably but correctly link a group of pre-dinosaurian animals called synapsids (which include those weird creatures with bony sails on their backs you might remember from *Fantasia*) to mammals through a skeletal feature that all their descendants share, including you and me. But it also led them to the mistaken conclusion that birds aren't dinosaurs.

The last ancestor common to both birds and mammals belonged to a pre-synapsid group of organisms called amniotes. (Next time you hear someone express skepticism that humans could share a lineage with apes, you might ask them if they'd be more comfortable with a salamander-like creature from the Carboniferous period.) Here's another way to think about this: it means that though the evolutionary distance between Geoff and his distant cousin Tina is enough to make you want to lie down, *three hundred million years* of our planet's history couldn't keep them from befriending one another.

And it still bears the chemical fingerprints: Darwin suggested a "warm little pond" for life's place of origin; hardly a garden of Eden, but an idea that lost and recently regained favor in light of new evidence of early life preserved in the rocks of ancient Australian hot springs.

This is a nice, clean, intuitive division: There's an iconoclastic owl that hunts by day (North America's northern hawk owl) and a hawk that hunts by night (Australia's letter-winged kite).

The falcons' genomes: Prum et al. 2015. This discovery didn't entirely surprise Carla Dove, a curator of birds at the Smithsonian

National Museum of Natural History (see chapter 16). One of her projects involves identifying the pulverized remains of birds that have struck airplanes, using DNA and isotopic analysis of feathers (which can tell you something about what the birds were eating). Another technique Dove and her colleagues use for identifying birds is examining the microscopic structure of their feathers, which yields a kind of low-resolution fingerprint, not quite fine enough to pinpoint them by species, but enough to resolve them a few clicks back to the "family" level. Dove had noticed that the structure of falcon feathers was easy to tell apart from that of hawks or eagles. She'd even noticed that falcon feathers looked similar to parrot feathers. Like many significant discoveries, this fact didn't seem especially important at the time.

In the wild, most parrots: Monk parakeets, a species native to southern Argentina, provide an interesting twist on sociality, because they build a parrot version of residential high-rises. They've been introduced several times in the United States, where they thrive in cities as far north as New York and Chicago; unlike most parrots, which live in hollows or burrows, monk parakeets build large, communal nests of sticks in which several pairs keep their own chambers. They often place these nests near a source of heat, like an electrical transformer on a power line, providing their apartments with central heating all winter long.

their innate sociality makes them good companions: It can also make them sullen and miserable if they're left alone for too long. Neglected parrots often rip out their feathers in an agony of boredom or become addicted to repetitive behaviors. Life without friends, for them, hardly seems worth living.

captive parrots will readily eat meat: Historically, some keas even took this practice a step further and attacked live sheep, digging into their hindquarters to feed on calorie-rich mutton fat. This practice didn't endear them to New Zealand's sheep farmers, who persecuted keas nearly to extinction. They're now considered threatened, with an estimated population of about 3,300 birds (IUCN 2020: *Nestor notabilis*).

Keas belong to the oldest: Bond and Diamond 2019.

This seems unlikely: Nearly all living parrots are social, even members of the oldest surviving lineages like New Zealand's keas, kakas, and kakapos. Another old and very social group are the Australasian parrots called cockatoos, which have been separate from their cousins in the New World for more than fifty million years. If I were going to test an evolutionary hypothesis within these groups, I'd probably start with the presumption that the parrot-falcon ancestor was a social bird, and that this trait was lost in the true falcons and forest falcons but maintained in the caracaras.

The more divergent: The molecular clock assumes that genes in organisms' DNA that aren't under intense selective pressure to remain the same from generation to generation naturally "drift" away from each other at a predictable baseline rate as random DNA copying errors accumulate over time, in a sort of genetic game of telephone.

By comparing the same parts of these genes among different organisms and seeing how much they've diverged from one another, the thinking goes, we ought to be able to calculate roughly how much time has passed since they were the same. Known-age fossils, when they're available, are used to "calibrate" these estimates by pegging their estimated ages to species we know to have existed. Another way fossils can be used to support these conclusions involves a "morphological clock" hypothesis that posits a gradual and predictable rate of change for physical characteristics that can drift more or less without penalty.

This method is simple in theory but complex in execution, and its results yield ranges of probable divergence times, rather than exact dates. There are many disagreements about how to calibrate the rate of the molecular clock for different organisms and different genes in different situations; it's still very much a work in progress.

This is an enormous target area: "Australasia" refers to the combined landmasses of Australia (including Tasmania), New Guinea, New Zealand, New Caledonia, the Solomon and Cook Islands, and a few nearby scraps of land that share geographical and biological affinities. They were once all part of the same portion of Gondwana.

The oldest surviving lineages: One of the most significant scientific results of Robert Falcon Scott's doomed Antarctic expedition was his discovery of the fossil remains of two kinds of trees within two hundred miles of the South Pole. One was an extinct cycad that's also been unearthed in India, but the other was a southern beech, closely related to trees that flourish in southern Chile, Argentina, and New Zealand today. They're the main component of the forests Darwin found so gloomy and magnificent in Tierra del Fuego.

it's possible — if not likely: If you're wondering what parrots are doing in South America today, genetic analysis indicates that they evolved first in Australasia, and that some parrots then crossed into South America via the coast of Antarctica, giving rise to macaws, Amazons, and other distinctively South American parrots (Tavares et al. 2006).

Connecting the biological journeys: I once found a spider on the garden gate of a house in Windhoek, Namibia, that was very clearly a *Latrodectus* — a widow spider, like the black widows I used to find under logs in North Carolina. Namibia lies on the southwest coast of Africa — very far from North America — and widow spiders certainly didn't swim or fly there. Realizing that these spiders had been around, more or less in the form we find them now, since the days of Pangaea, gave me a kind of temporal vertigo.

They span enormous swaths of time: Human cultural history beyond 150,000 years ago, for example, is almost entirely speculative, but DNA evidence can drill down a thousand times as far in our genetic record.

the stories embedded in the caracaras' DNA: Fuchs et al. 2012.

Within this family: The odds of someone finding a falcon that no one's ever identified before are low, though there could yet be another tiny falconet lurking in Borneo or Cambodia. More likely to add to the total species count would be the recognition of separate species within a widespread population of falcons that have previously been considered to be only one species. (The aplomado falcon, which ranges from the southern United States to Tierra del Fuego, might be a candidate.) DNA analysis has contributed to multiple cases of "splitting" by illustrating genetic diversity that's not especially visible to the naked eye; it's also contributed to the opposite phenomenon, "lumping," in which populations of similar animals previously regarded as separate species have been shown to be genetically alike.

the so-called true falcons: Less well-known than the powerful hunters like peregrines and sakers, but no less "true," are a handful of tiny falconets that live in the forests of southeast Asia; these handsome little creatures, barely the size of lovebirds, are every bit as deadly for their size as the larger peregrines.

like most true falcons: A species called Eleonora's falcon (*Falco eleonorae*) nests in large colonies on islands in the Mediterranean sea, where they prey on migrating songbirds passing overhead; these falcons then fly south and east to spend their winters in Madagascar.

Many peregrines commute seasonally: The Falkland peregrines, oddly enough, don't appear to migrate at all; like the Johnny rooks, they seem unaware that the rest of the world exists.

There's an interesting example of this phenomenon in the human world. A small group of Maori, the Polynesians who were the first humans to settle in New Zealand, sailed away from mainland New Zealand several centuries ago and ended up in the Chatham Islands, a tiny archipelago about 450 nautical miles east of Christchurch. Over time, these people lost all memory of the mainland; they also lost the seafaring and agricultural skills and traditions that larger Polynesian groups maintained, and reverted to hunting and gathering. This was easy enough in the islands, where fish and seabirds were plentiful, and they didn't want for food. When a British frigate "discovered" the islands in 1790, the people living there, who called themselves the Moriori, were astonished; they'd come to believe they were the only people on Earth.

One bird banded in Nome, Alaska: Pyle and Pyle 2017.

Along with these prodigious feats: According to one example, peregrines would see a 24-frame-per-second film, which appears fluid to you and me, as a series of distinct, stuttering images. For a peregrine, the images would only begin to smooth out at 192 frames per second.

a human with eyes in the same proportion: Baker 2005:35.

But DNA tells us: Fuchs et al. 2015.

Fossil evidence is scarce: Becker 1987.

In the meantime: DNA evidence suggests

that the odd South American falcons called spot-winged falconets might be a living example of what the common ancestor of both "true" and "false" falcons was like. They do seem intermediate between the two groups, if you squint; even their voices seem somewhere between a forest falcon's repetitive cries, a caracara's hoarse screams, and a true falcon's chattering calls. Today they live in the dry, scrubby forests of the Gran Chaco, a region of Paraguay, Bolivia, and Argentina that's home to an endemic suite of flora and fauna; it seems to be a refuge for species that thrived in an earlier, cooler period in South America's history.

Some are barely known: Forest falcons, like caracaras, are beautiful and unusual-looking birds, with orange-yellow or red faces and finely barred blue-gray and brown plumage. They sometimes run down their prey on foot along the high branches of trees. Their voices are mellow and oddly musical, and the call of one species sounds almost exactly like a woman repeatedly exclaiming "ohhhh!" in mild, pleasant surprise.

Their DNA suggests: Fuchs et al. 2015.

There are risks: A DNA-based analysis of the relationships among African parrots, for example, suggested that several lineages were "seeded" by birds that crossed the Indian Ocean from Australia, including the peculiar, long-necked vasa parrots of Madagascar (Kundu et al. 2012).

It's possible that the falcons' origins lie somewhere else: A twenty-million-year-old fossil bone from a falcon-like bird unearthed in Idaho could represent an early colonist from the south, perhaps even one of the immigrants whose lineage gave rise to the "true" falcons (Becker 1987).

But the genetic evidence points toward Antarctica: Claramunt and Cracraft 2015, Benton 2010.

It's a tarsometatarsus: Cenizo et al. 2016.

9. The Curious Case of the Missing Crows

"The whole retina": Baker 2005:35.

Johnny rooks' skills are harder to define: Striated caracaras do seem to have at least one special visual ability: they see surprisingly well at night. This makes sense, since the small seabirds that form an important part of some Johnny rooks' diets return to their burrows after sundown, presumably to avoid predators. (On Beauchene Island, the southernmost of the Falklands, researchers trying to catch returning seabirds at night with mist nets had to give up when they kept catching striated caracaras instead [Smith and Prince 1985]). On Steeple Jason, the striated caracaras I saw at the seal carcass continued to feed until well after sundown; when I returned after dark to check on them, I saw my headlamp reflected back in a dozen sets of gleaming, violet-tinged eyes. They looked like a huddle of goblins.

No scientist has ever: Potier et al. 2016.

The first scientists to examine birds' brains: Marzluff and Angell 2013:23.

Some birds have even reached levels of fame: Pepperberg 2009.

Birds, he believed: I've often thought that striated caracaras build their nests in locations that seem not just practically functional but aesthetically "right" — snug, tidy, and attractive, with a good view of a food source and other prominent features of the landscape. This probably says more about me than it does about them, but it's harder to explain away the fact that the nests, which are mostly composed of dead grass, are sometimes decorated with bits of colorful garbage washed up by the sea. Scraps of bright green fishing net from trawlers seem especially popular.

"When Santayana": WHH, AHRP 1923:285.

"It is in us all": WHH, AHRP 1923:321.

"It is a depressing experience": WHH, BAM 1923:213.

There was one parrot: Polly was a yellow-headed Amazon, a species now officially endangered in the wild. They're known as excellent talkers and singers — according to one parrot enthusiasts' website, yellow-headed Amazons have "a naturally power-ful, operatic voice." Their popularity in the pet trade saw their wild population crash from seventy thousand to about seven thousand in the 1970s, and their numbers have halved again since then. The Lamb, where Polly lived, still stands in the town of Hindon in Wiltshire and is still an inn.

"had two favorite songs": WHH, BAM 1923:221.

"half a century of fried eggs": WHH, BAM 1923:223.

researchers have even subjected crows: Marzluff and Angell 2013:183.

The biologist Laura Biondi: Biondi et al. 2010.

"The gregarious habits": Biondi et al. 2010.

If the ability to train your own intuition: Several years ago, I was standing in the shadow of the Brandenburg Gate in Berlin when I noticed a hooded crow — a large crow of central and eastern Europe with a gray breast and back that make it look as if it's wearing a cowl — sticking its head inside a trash bin attached to a lamppost. After a moment, the crow pulled out a crushed Dunkin' donuts box, opened the lid with its bill, and started feasting on a half-eaten chocolate-frosted donut that was still inside. I wondered how the crow had learned about donuts, and if it was shown this trick by a friend.

But though the structures: Marzluff and Angell 2013:23–26.

Geoff and Tina: There are, of course, several significant differences between our brains and birds' brains, but not all of them are in our favor. Crows' brains are especially good at self-maintenance, for instance; though their bodies grow more frail in old age, their brains continue to produce new neurons and slough off old ones throughout their lives, storing new memories and reinforcing successful pathways, thoughts, and behaviors while allowing useless knowledge to wither (as Polly the parrot's mind did, perhaps, as she gradually switched from Spanish to English) (Marzluff and Angell 2013:35).

Another side effect of a large brain: Lendvai et al. 2013.

This isn't to say: I can't help thinking, here, of the fearlessness of captive striated caracaras. Fearlessness might be both a cause and effect of what we call intelligence.

their lives consist: I sat very still for an hour one afternoon at the pinched waist of Steeple Jason, where gentoo penguins who've escaped prowling sea lions emerge from the sea and gather to snooze and preen among their friends. A few penguins stopped short of my feet and craned their necks at me, but most of them galumphed over and around me like I was part of the scenery. They'd just run a gauntlet of sea lions, and as far as they were concerned, they were safe. Their parents, I thought, must have forgotten to warn them about Len Hill, who'd abducted penguins for Birdland at this very spot.

If we didn't need our giant brains: An iconic Australian mammal may be trading in its brain as you read these lines. Koalas' brains only occupy about two-thirds of their cranial cavities (the balance is spinal fluid), and their slow metabolisms make them reluctant to move unless they have to — not unlike the woozy South American sloths, to which naturalists once thought koalas might be related. Koalas' larger-brained ancestors lived in a wetter, lusher version of Australia with more varied and available food; but as the continent dried out, their descendants adapted to a monotonous, mildly toxic, nutrient-poor diet of eucalyptus leaves. The demands of this lifestyle forced koalas to become as energy-efficient as possible — even, perhaps, at the expense of their minds. (Maybe there's a kindness in this; a koala's life, from a human perspective, seems painfully dull.)

just as we long ago lost: Some mammals seem to have regretted this loss, and thought better of it. None have re-evolved gills, but the cetaceans — dolphins, porpoises, and whales — are descended from animals that

540

once lived on land. Their ancestors began reentering the sea around fifty million years ago and had become fully aquatic thirty million years later. (Hippos, which spend as much time in the water as they do on land, are whales' closest terrestrial relatives.)

Less well-known flightless birds: A recent genetic study suggests that steamer ducks may be in the process of losing flight *right now,* or perhaps separating into two new species: some steamer ducks can fly, but others can't (Fulton et al. 2012).

Once there was even a giant: Olson 2008.

flightless caracara: There may well have been other flightless caracaras in other places, too; this is the only one whose remains have been discovered so far.

Most birds would have ignored: When Robin threw the caracaras an actual dead mouse, their reaction was comparatively muted; one of them carried it off and stashed it under a rock, as if saving it for later, then went back to digging for worms.

Robin and his colleague Mark Adams: Adams and Woods 2016.

Charleses Darwin and Barnard: I once called Jemima Parry-Jones, the owner and head keeper at the International Centre for Birds of Prey in Newent, Gloucestershire, and asked her if she had any odd or interesting stories to share about her striated caracaras. There was a pause on the other end of the line. "Too many to mention," she said.

It's as if they *enjoy* testing our limits: Heinrich 1999, Ch. 19.

"well supply the place of our carrion-crows": CD 1845:55. Strictly speaking, Darwin and Cobo were both wrong. There are crow relatives living in South America they didn't know about, or didn't recognize as crows: a few striking, brightly colored jays — one is even aptly named "beautiful jay" — live in the Amazon basin, which they appear to have colonized after South America docked with North America a few million years ago. Little is known about these tropical jays beyond what they look like; one species was described as recently as 2013. But Darwin's larger point still holds: the birds you probably think of when you hear the word "crow" — big, black birds like ravens and rooks, which are common on every other continent except Antarctica — have never become established in South America.

Two centuries earlier: Geographically speaking, Mexico is as much a part of the North American continent as Canada, a fact that surprises many residents of the United States. Cobo knew it as New Spain.

"Who distributed and picked out": BC 2010:62.

Cobo, like most of his contemporaries: In a four-thousand-year-old world, which is where Bernabé Cobo believed he lived, this idea of unchanging species seems far more comprehensible (and forgivable). If you traveled back four thousand years from today, you'd hardly notice any difference in the plants or animals you know (except that there'd be a lot more of them).

"I do not want to mention": BC 2010:61. Vicuñas and guanacos are wild relatives of the domesticated animals we call llamas and alpacas; but unlike the extinct wild ancestors of cows, goats, and horses, they still roam free in remote stretches of southern South America. Vicuñas are the smaller and more delicate of the two, and live among the highest elevations of the Andes.

Cobo might have been astonished to learn that vicuñas and guanacos aren't native to South America: they're actually fairly recent arrivals from the far north. Unlike the sloths, armadillos, and anteaters, whose lineage evolved during South America's long isolation, vicuñas, guanacos, llamas, and alpacas all descend from a migratory North American lineage that died out in its native range but survived elsewhere: they're camels.

Darwin shipped these bones: It can be difficult to remember that the theory of evolution by natural selection was published late in Darwin's life, after he'd spent decades ruminating on the natural world and his discoveries aboard the *Beagle;* we tend to jam the older and younger versions of him together in our minds. Several decades lay between them, however, and his haul of giant bones added as much to his fame in life as *The Origin of Species.*

"Professor Owen": CD 1845:84.

Neither Owen nor Darwin: It's very tempting to call this the "Cotton-Eyed Joe" conundrum.

"It is impossible": CD 1845:173.

But here he could go no further: I wish I could slip a note back in time to Darwin, and let him in on this secret of the world. In photographs he looks glum, almost haunted, and though the solution to the problem of the bicameral "American continent" created another set of questions, it might have removed at least one of the deep furrows from his brow. If I could grant him the same ability, I'd like to imagine that he'd also have sent messages to other worried thinkers before him. *Father Cobo,* one might read, *I write you with good news, as one admirer of Reason to another. We have both seen through a glass darkly. The surface of the earth is in constant motion — and there have been many arks.*

10. The Island of Giants

Their fondness for tipping over trash cans: White-faced or Virginia opossums are often struck by motor vehicles as they try to cross roads at night, and most North Americans know them only as mangled corpses on the side of the road, which isn't the best look for anyone.

The supercontinent of Pangaea: McIntyre et al. 2017.

Beneath the earth's crust: Laurasia's modern remnants are North America and Eurasia (except for India); the surviving fragments of Gondwana are Africa, Antarctica, India, Australia, New Guinea, New Zealand, New Caledonia, and South America.

This pair of titans: As a child, you were probably shown how South America fits neatly into the coast of Africa, which is exactly where it used to be; the skeleton coast of Namibia was once a stone's throw from Hudson's childhood home in La Plata, and the Guiana Shield once lay cheek by jowl with the rocks beneath present-day Ivory Coast and Ghana.

a sliver of geologic time: This date for the connection of the Americas has been contested recently, with some geologists suggesting an earlier, short-lived connection between twenty-three million and twenty-five million years ago. The distribution of some South American salamanders does seem to suggest an earlier land-based connection than the generally accepted date of three million to five million years ago, but the jury is still out.

"one of the most extraordinary events": Simpson 1980.

Many creatures who took part: There were also some giant beasts in the north with no modern equivalents — like the chalicotheres, which were like giant horses with hands (Simpson 1980).

thirty years after Darwin's death: Hudson had folded at least a partial version of plate tectonics into his worldview by the time he published *Birds of La Plata* in 1920. In its introduction, he noted that the birds of South America include groups whose lineages occur nowhere else, and suggested them as evidence of planetary-scale changes. "They are survivals of an incalculably remote period in the earth's history," he wrote, "when the greater part of the Southern Hemisphere was land; when South America, South Africa, and Australasia were parts of one continent. Among these forms . . . are the Rheas, the Crypturi (the Partridges of South America), and the Crested Screamer, which Huxley supposed to be related by descent to the *Archaeopteryx*." Screamers belong to a very old lineage, though Huxley was wrong in the strictest sense; there's no direct line of descent between them and *Archaeopteryx* itself. But it probably pleased Hudson to think that the odd, ungainly birds he loved as a child might be a living connection to the dinosaurs; and in this, Huxley was entirely correct.

Even so, it was regarded as a fringe theory: Conniff 2012. The notion of an ancient, Pangaea-like landmass dates from at least the late sixteenth century; but it wasn't until 1912 that a German meteorologist and Arctic adventurer named Alfred Wegener argued persuasively that the continents could and did move, and had slowly come apart. Wegener's ideas were rejected in academic circles for decades, partly for political reasons; one American paleontologist, tellingly, dismissed them as "Germanic pseudo-science." But by 1960, a newly minted generation of geologists, some of them barely out of graduate school, had proved that Wegener was right: the continents rest on giant "plates" that float on a denser layer of semi-liquid rock. They are still moving, forming, and disintegrating — oozing out of the earth's liquid mantle along spreading oceanic ridges and grinding together in rumpled "suture zones."

This theory wasn't accepted without furious arguments, which often rested on pride as much as fact; one of David Attenborough's college professors assured him that continental drift was "moonshine," and Harold Jeffreys, ironically the first scientist to suggest that the earth had a liquid core, remained unshakably convinced that continents could not move when he died in 1989. But Jeffreys was one of the last holdouts: by then, the study of the earth's plates had revolutionized geology and helped lay some of the biological mysteries that bedeviled Darwin and Cobo to rest. Some living things that were inexplicably present in some places and missing in others had simply gone along for a ride; others had wandered into new realms when their worlds collided.

The opossum on my back porch: Some North American animals also migrated west into Asia over the Bering land bridge, in a reversal of the human migration into the Americas — which is how horses ended up in Asia and Europe, tapirs in Malaysia, and camels in Africa and Mongolia. Camels first evolved in North America, and the first humans to enter that continent met (and ate) them there — but there haven't been camels in North America for more than ten thousand years, though they've survived in South America (see chapter 17). Horses died out in both Americas during the Pleistocene extinctions and didn't reappear until Europeans reintroduced them in the sixteenth century. The Incas in Peru and the Aztecs in Mexico were astounded by the horses of the Spaniards, and wondered if they might be giant deer.

From the raw materials: Like a human mom, a marsupial mother gives milk, but her young emerge from her body as tiny, wriggling creatures that crawl into her belly pouch, where they find a nipple and attach themselves to it until they've grown enough to be born a second time — a decidedly less risky (and, to all appearances, more comfortable) approach to live birth than ours (but not quite as low-maintenance as that of the monotremes, the third group of living mammals, which, like our amniote ancestors, still lay hard-shelled eggs).

Marsupials, it turns out, don't come from Australia: See Nilsson et al. 2010. If you're wondering how marsupials ended up on the opposite side of the world, the answer seems to be that they walked. Genetic and skeletal evidence indicates that a few surviving marsupials headed south to the shores of Antarctica (which didn't freeze over, if you recall, until after its connection to South America collapsed). Some of them probably set up shop in its coastal plains and evergreen forests, but other marsupials kept moving, traversing another set of land bridges into Australia, where they flourished both obscurely and famously. You may not have heard of a bilby, a quokka, a wambenger, a numbat, or a marsupial mole, but almost everyone can picture a kangaroo or a koala.

But some never left South America: Male yapoks, uniquely among marsupials, also have a belly pouch — in which they tuck their genitals while they swim in rivers filled with hungry fish.

If you could take a safari: "It is a remarkable circumstance that so many different species should be found together," Darwin wrote; "and it proves how numerous in kind the ancient inhabitants of this country must have been" (CD 1845:82). You might have seen the bones of some of these animals in a museum and not known quite what you were looking at or when it had lived; at the American Museum of Natural History in New York, for example, the hall of early mammals adjoins the dinosaur halls, and since both dinosaurs and ground sloths are presented as articulated skeletons, it's easy to subconsciously lump them together as contemporaries. But they're very far apart in time: ground sloths were still around when humans first entered the Americas, while the big dinosaurs had been gone for sixty-five million years.

The glyptodonts were well protected: Sloths, anteaters, armadillos, and the extinct glyptodonts belong to a uniquely South American lineage of mammals called xenarthrans, who share several distinctive traits, including excellent noses, huge front claws, and terrible eyesight. These traits

550

suggest that their common ancestor probably lived a mole-like existence underground — a life that might have helped it survive the fires, cold spells, and darkness that followed the end-Cretaceous asteroid.

Most surviving members of this group are fairly small, but there are still two giant xenarthrans left. The most familiar is the giant anteater, a dog-sized, brush-tailed creature with shaggy fur and a long, curved snout that slurps up ants and termites with an absurdly long, rubbery tongue. The other is less famous but no less remarkable: a giant armadillo that can weigh as much as 120 pounds. It's the closest surviving relative of the glyptodonts, and so rarely seen that few have ever been photographed, but giant armadillos are presumed to live throughout the tropical forests of the Amazon basin and the Guiana Shield (see chapter 15). They excavate burrows nearly sixteen feet deep and spend most of their days underground; at night, they emerge to scour creek beds and flood plains for worms, termites, and other invertebrate prey.

One other lasting relic of the giant xenarthrans' existence has recently come to light: their architecture. Modern tree sloths use their long, curved claws like grappling hooks to hang from branches, and don't spend much time on the ground; but ground sloths appear to have excavated giant burrows for shelter. More than fifteen hundred of these "paleoburrows," with the deep gouges of the sloths' claws still visible in the walls, have recently been found in southern Brazil; and though some have filled with sediment, others have been mistaken for geologically formed cave systems. One particularly impressive complex of burrows in the state of Rondônia contains a branching network of tunnels more than six feet in diameter, stretching for thousands of feet; it seems to have been the work of multiple generations of sloths who moved more than four thousand cubic meters of dirt and rock to construct it. Archaeological evidence suggests that prehistoric Amerindians later used these burrows for dwellings and burial sites (Frank et al. 2012).

One look at a terror bird: At least one species of terror bird, *Titanis walleri,* even made it across the isthmus into North America; its fossil remains have been found in Texas and Florida. But it disappeared about two million years ago, and so far as we know, no human ever met one. A recently described species from Uruguay, however, may have lived long enough to meet *Homo sapiens* (Alvarenga et al. 2010).

But if you've never thought to imagine: See Fariña et al. 2013 for a comprehensive description of South America's pre-interchange megafauna, including ecological and physiological studies. Naish 2012 also provides a thoughtful discussion of smaller South American mammals that didn't make it through the interchange.

Fossil evidence shows: Jones et al. 2013, Jones et al. 2015.

bears twice the size of modern grizzlies: Soibelzon et al. 2011. The closest living relatives of these massive bears are the elusive (and rather small) spectacled bears (*Tremarctos ornatus*) of Andean cloud forests.

a fossil bird unearthed in the Pampas: Jones et al. 2013, Jones et al. 2015. To me, the loss of *Caracara major* is a crying shame; I'd love to see what an eagle-sized bird could do with a caracara's mind.

One of these, *Argentavis magnificens:* Chatterjee et al. 2007. So far, *Argentavis magnificens* has been surpassed in wingspan only by the extinct giant fishing birds of the genus *Pelagornis,* which presumably snatched live prey in the tooth-like grooves of their long bills, and probably spent most of their lives soaring like albatrosses over the open sea.

"can be described": CD 1845:503. Years later, this absence still troubled Darwin. "In calling up images of the past," he wrote, "I find that the plains of Patagonia frequently cross before my eyes; yet these plains are pronounced by all as wretched and useless . . . why then, and the case is not peculiar to myself, have these arid wastes taken so firm a hold on my memory?"

In less than a thousand years: Prado et al. 2015.

Small asteroid strikes: Like the thirty-one-kilometer-wide crater recently discovered beneath the Hiawatha Glacier of Greenland, which appears to have been formed by an object at least one kilometer wide sometime in the past twenty thousand years (Kjær et al. 2018).

Though monkeys had arrived: The arrival of primates in South America is one of the great mysteries of animal biogeography: there are 125 species of South American monkeys, but their nearest relatives live in West Africa. Genetic evidence suggests that they arrived in South America about thirty million years ago, give or take — an incredible feat, given that the continent was completely surrounded by ocean at the time. The most favored hypothesis today is that they accidentally sailed across the Atlantic Ocean on mats of floating vegetation, with possible assistance from oceanic islands that may have emerged during a period of lower sea level. But even if these islands existed, the New World monkeys faced a long journey by sea; and they beat Columbus by a wide margin.

Humans' precise role: Borrero 2009, Steadman et al. 2005, Lyons et al. 2004. See also
Metcalf et al. 2016 for a discussion of the
synergistic effects of climate change and
human presence on Patagonia's large animals.

Archaeological evidence: In 2017, divers exploring an underwater cave in Mexico
found the oldest known human remains in
the Americas: the skull of a woman who
lived fifteen thousand years ago. The submerged cavern was also littered with the
bones of giant bears (from the north), giant
sloths (from the south), and the saber-
toothed marsupials that died out long before humans arrived (Society of Vertebrate
Paleontology 2017).

This disruption: The first Americans probably couldn't have imagined that they could
exhaust the world's supply of animals; and
it can be hard to believe that hunters armed
only with spears, arrows, and fire could
wipe out two continents' worth of giant
mammals. But they wouldn't have had to
mount a deliberate campaign of extermination to do it, or slaughter everything they
saw willy-nilly. They'd only have needed to
put a finger on the scales of predation so
that the biggest herbivores died out slightly
faster than they could reproduce; and the
largest animals tended to grow and breed
slowly. Even if this didn't cause the animals

to go extinct, it might have made them especially vulnerable to the effects of climate
change.

"horrible and revolting": CD 1845:122.

"To this spot were driven": WHH, FALA
1918:286.

"Some of the old, very long walls": WHH,
FALA 1918:286.

In the logic of this story: The idea of a sweeping victory for North America in the interchange has begun to ebb. Plants and animals from tropical South America, for
instance, have so completely occupied the
land between Panama and southern Mexico
that it's easy to forget they're geologically
part of the North American continent.

South America might have imported: Weir et
al. 2009.

a host of South America's birds: Seriemas are
the closest living relatives of the terror
birds. They're about four feet tall, with an
odd little poof of silver-gray feathers at the
base of their beaks, and a strange, whooping call that can be heard half a mile away.
Like African secretary birds (which they
slightly resemble), they've developed a special technique for snapping the necks of
snakes.

South America's birds have an even more
tangled history: See Navarro-Sigüenza et
al. 2017, who unraveled the wildly complex
biogeographical history of woodpeckers in

the Americas using DNA analysis.

It's tempting to imagine: Despite what the song says, lions don't sleep in the jungle. They sleep in the grasslands, where their food lives.

tropical forests are such: Rumors persist that ground sloths may yet survive somewhere in the western Amazon, and there have been earnest attempts to find them; but so far, there's been no proof.

The last ancestor: Fuchs et al. 2012.

The full extent of these inland seas: Jaramillo et al. 2017, Claudia et al. 2013, Nores 2004.

These two seaways: In North America, a shallow inland sea also split the continent essentially in two during the Cretaceous period, dividing it into a western landmass scientists call Laramidia and an eastern one known as Appalachia. This shallow sea is responsible for the huge deposits of limestone and sandstone that lie beneath the southwestern United States.

11. Bush Auntie-Man

Brian, Jose, and Rambo: For a genetic analysis of Amerindian immigration into Central and South America, see Posth et al. 2018.

I'd first seen Sean online: Sean named his blog (and his Twitter handle) *Ibycter,* after the scientific name of red-throated caracaras, *Ibycter americanus.*

"Red-Throated Caracaras Are Way Cool": McCann 2014.

earnest captions and Latin names: For example: "Turns out this is *Naphrys pulex,* indeed a *Habronattus* relative, and such a handsome fellow!" (https://www.ibycter .com).

Many related pairs: One theory held that the entire Amazon basin dried up and became grassland during cooler glacial periods before humans arrived, leaving the shield and other peripheral areas around the edge of the basin as "islands" of forest in an ocean of savanna. This idea was popular among scientists in the 1970s and '80s, but studies of ancient pollen from the basin are ambiguous. More recently, some researchers have suggested that a shallow sea might have covered much of the basin during times of higher sea level, much like the inland sea that left the remains of marine reptiles in the hills of central Texas (Bush and Oliveira 2006).

Signs of Amerindian civilizations: Barlow et al. 2012, Mann 2005.

Veteran creatures of the forest: Kricher 2017 is an excellent and accessible primer on the basic ecology of South America's tropical forests.

Black caracaras prefer wilder stretches: Typical range maps for black caracaras show a contiguous blob the size of the Amazon basin and the Guiana Shield — but this includes stretches of closed forest where you probably wouldn't see one no matter how hard you tried. An ornithologist friend told me that a more accurate map of black caracaras' range would look like you'd thrown a brick at a windshield.

where they were surprised: Krakauer and Krakauer 1999.

Red-throated caracaras: The ancestors of today's tropical caracaras split off from the line of crested caracaras about twelve million to fourteen million years ago, and the ancestors of red-throated caracaras left this second line about six million years later — a divergence that might reflect their mastery of a new food source.

No one keeps: The ornithologist Emil Goeldi, traveling in the Brazilian Amazon in 1898, captured a red-throated caracara and kept it alive for a time by feeding it small birds. "It was an old, savage, and sturdy individual," he wrote, "darting deadly hate from its blood-colored eyes, and gave us much trouble" (Goeldi 1903).

"necrophagous habits": CD 1845:56.

"The angry hectoring cries": WHH, BLP 1920:81.

This was a peculiar nickname: I asked a young man at Rewa village about the reason for red-throated caracaras' nickname "bush auntie-man," and he smiled and said,

"It's because they give away your secrets."

At the current pace of deforestation: Red-throated caracaras have also disappeared almost entirely from Central America and southern Mexico, where they were common even a few decades ago; and an increase in logging, hunting, and human populations probably has something to do with it. Unlike other large forest birds, red-throated caracaras aren't sought after for their meat — they're rumored to taste terrible — and they don't threaten or molest livestock; but they might be easy targets for trigger-happy people, as birds of prey in the United States were only a few decades ago. Sean McCann spent a harrowing summer trying to reach an isolated group of red-throats in the rugged, mountainous pine forests of central Honduras, and though he found them, he wasn't able to do much else. His photographs are the only evidence that they still live there — or did, at least, in 2013.

Guyana's old-growth woodlands: The recent discovery of offshore oil has suggested the slim but real possibility that Guyana will be able to avoid raiding its forests for money, at least in the short term (Krauss 2018).

12. Hymenopteran Dreams

Others tell us about food: I was sitting in a restaurant once with a friend when the smell of frying bacon reached us from the kitchen. My friend had given up pork when he converted to Islam, but he closed his eyes and inhaled deeply, wearing a look of unabashed pleasure. "It's not *haram* to smell," he said.

"When I first came to England": WHH, AHRP 1923:58.

"Intellectually," he wrote: Proust and Hudson both died in 1922. They never met.

"The heavy greasy smell": WHH, AHRP 1923:55.

"So far as a smell": WHH, AHRP 1923:53.

"I can stand knee-deep": WHH, AHRP 1923:59. "Also bracken," he added, "when it first unrolls its broad fronds, and I crush it to get the unique smell, which suggests castor-oil and the fish-and-cucumber odour of smelts — a strange and fascinating combination."

"It is useless": WHH, AHRP 1923:78.

"cows and sky": WHH, AHRP 1923:112.

"With a horse maddened by terror": WHH, AHRP 1923:114–15. Hudson recalled smelling an encampment of Amerindians at a distance of a mile or so, and compared it to "the familiar homely smell of a rag-and-bone shop in a city slum."

This was an ingenious use: Like many writers in North America of European descent, Hudson had a conflicted relationship with the Amerindian people of the country where he was born. He feared them but also respected their birthright, and acknowledged the brutality of General Rosas's campaigns against them. By the time he was a young man, he had begun to view them with some admiration, and by the time of *A Hind in Richmond Park* he was nostalgic for them, as he was for all aspects of life in his home country. "This was the state of things on all the Argentine frontiers in my time," he wrote, "and it had been so from the time the country was first colonized, and it continued so down to the eighties of the last century, when at long last the war was carried into the desert and the tribes beaten and their raiding spirit broken for ever" (WHH, AHRP 1923:113).

"as long as you are satisfied": WHH, AHRP 1923:53.

"infinitely more subtle . . . insect realm": WHH, AHRP 1923:79.

The term "pheromones": Karlson and Lüscher 1959.

Sean was especially drawn: The order Hymenoptera also includes the wasp-like insects called sawflies, which don't concern us here (and aren't social). There are about 115,000 known species of hymenopterans on earth — more than ten times the number of bird species — and many remain undescribed.

ants are social creatures: It's possible that there might be a solitary ant species somewhere, but no one's found it yet. Even species in the most ancient surviving lineages of ants gather in small groups of thirty or forty individuals, though they're all capable of laying eggs and don't depend on queens, as other ants do.

Peering into the world of ant societies: Holldöbler and Wilson 1990 provide a beautifully illustrated and readable overview of the fascinating world of ants.

Though ant societies have absorbed evolutionary biologists: Unlike ants, not all wasps are social; in fact, most of them aren't. Thousands of species of wasps live solitary lives, and the inventive ways they provide for their young have made them objects of fascination for researchers with a taste for the macabre. Most adult wasps feed on nectar and pollen; but for certain insects and spiders, solitary wasps are a living nightmare. Many solitary wasp mothers paralyze a larger arthropod — like a cicada or even a tarantula — with a well-placed sting, then drag the helpless giant back to a burrow and lay an egg on its abdomen. When the egg hatches, its defenseless host is slowly eaten alive by a hungry wasp nymph.

Other wasps take this even further, injecting a complex toxin into the brains of cockroaches that renders them as docile as a horse on a halter; they allow themselves to be led by an antenna to their doom. Another group of solitary wasps deposit their eggs on the living bodies of caterpillars, which are hollowed out from within as the larvae burrow into them and grow. Wasps' many disquieting variations on these strategies can make them seem almost sadistic, and even Darwin admitted to a friend that the elaborate cruelties of solitary wasps led him to doubt the existence of God.

coordinate the behavior: Ross and Matthews 2018.

the members of at least one species: Sheehan and Tibbetts 2011.

Social wasps also share a skill: Under the right conditions, wasp nests can reach awesome sizes even by human standards. In China, where giant hornets killed thirteen people in a single province in 2012, soldiers have turned flamethrowers on massive nests that plague rural villages (Park et al. 2013); and in the United States, an exterminator in Florida was summoned to deal with a freestanding metropolis of yellow jackets the size of a telephone booth. It was the product of years of effort by its residents, and he guessed it contained a million workers and hundreds of queens (Golgowski 2013).

Some weave delicate envelopes: O'Donnell and Jeanne 2002.

and a few, taking no chances: In the United States, anyone who's ever mowed a lawn knows the fear of running over an underground nest of the social wasps called yellow jackets. Huddie "Lead Belly" Ledbetter spoke for most of eastern North America in his song "Yellow Jacket," in which he threatens a nest of wasps with incineration if they won't stop stinging him.

Yellow jackets are among the wasps who've learned to live closely with humans. Like crows, raccoons, and rats, these species tend to be especially good at sniffing out and exploiting resources they haven't seen before, and we obligingly provide them with exciting food options. Faced with the challenge of understanding our ever-changing habits and products, social wasps can't rely simply on instinct; they use curiosity and social learning to help them make sense of our world, like the innovative chimango caracaras in Laura Biondi's experiments.

it might also save lives: In Australia and the United States, for example, bees and wasps send more people to the hospital each year than any other nonhuman animals (Gunderman 2015).

The quest for a wasp-repellent bird: The pitohui's chemical was identified as homobatrachotoxin — an alkaloid poison that's 250 times more toxic, by weight, than strychnine. This was an accidental discovery; a scientist preparing a pitohui's skin

565

for a museum touched his tongue with his fingers, and his tongue went numb (Dumbacher et al. 1992).

The most vivid description: Skutch's many works include books with titles like *The Minds of Birds* and *A Bird Watcher's Adventures in Tropical America*.

"When the big bird bent": Skutch 1959.

The red-throat in Skutch's backyard: The American ornithologists Leslie Brown and Dean Amadon fastened on this line of Skutch's account in their survey of the world's birds of prey, speculating that "one can only imagine that some sort of chemical repugnance has evolved" — but they didn't pursue this thought any further (Brown and Amadon 1968 Vol 2:729–730).

"When, proceeding in this fashion": Skutch 1959.

"an accelerating sequence of *ghehs*": Sick 1993.

"which the birds scraped laboriously": Thiollay 1991.

"As soon as one bird reached a nest": Thiollay 1991.

All social wasps: Bruschini et al. 2010, Sonnentag and Jeanne 2009. The tribe of swarm founders is called the Polybiini.

A handful of scouts: Sonnentag and Jeanne 2009. A similar impulse appears to underlie honeybees' response to smoke, which is why beekeepers can pacify their hives with it. Smoke doesn't stupefy bees; they seem to reasonably interpret it as a chemical signal of an approaching wildfire, and switch from defending their highly flammable hive — which, after all, is made of wax — to gorging themselves on honey as they prepare to abandon ship. When the smoke subsides, they go back to their regular duties.

13. The Lost World

"That is a mysterious voice": WHH, BAM 1923:70.

"The suggestion is ever of a vast concourse": WHH, BAM 1923:70.

Being proved right was bittersweet: McCann et al. 2013.

Sean wondered if the birds: Millipedes are some of the first animals to live on land, with recognizable ancestors from long before the days of Pangaea. They seem unlikely to have survived for so long: they're docile and slow-moving creatures, without heavy armor or powerful jaws (unlike their cousins, the centipedes), and though they're good at hiding under fallen leaves and rotting logs, they don't seem stealthy enough to have escaped extinction for half a billion years.

The secret of their success seems to lie in the fact that they taste really, really bad. A few species squirt poison at predators from several feet away, but most merely ooze a noxious goo when disturbed, and the few animals that have learned to eat them, like meerkats in Africa and coatis in South America, prepare them by rolling them on the ground first to rub off their distasteful secretions.

the millipedes' strong-smelling secretions: Weldon et al. 2003, Valderrama et al. 2000. Monkeys and lemurs might also be using the millipedes as recreational drugs: in Madagascar, some lemurs chew on millipedes to induce them to release their toxins, then enter a buzzy, trancelike state in which they salivate heavily and rub toxin-laced saliva all over their bodies.

One of the first: Raleigh 1848.

Raleigh, a poet and naval commander: Raleigh's expedition was a dream he'd nursed for a decade. During one of his maritime adventures, he'd captured and questioned a Spanish navigator, mapmaker, and "cosmographer" named Pedro Sarmiento de Gamboa, who'd lived in Spanish-occupied Peru and written a deeply sourced history of the Inca empire; Sarmiento was returning to Spain after an ill-fated attempt to establish a colony in Tierra del Fuego. Raleigh brought him to Elizabeth herself as a prize, and Elizabeth and Sarmiento, to everyone's surprise, hit it off. They shared a common language — Latin — and she gave him an official letter of friendship; Sarmiento, in return, shared his maps of South America with Elizabeth's royal cartographers and offered her a strange and tantalizing story. Some of the defeated Incas had fled to the east, he said, and built a new city in the remote highlands between the watersheds of the Amazon and the Orinoco — a short but mighty river, filled with crocodiles. As evidence, Sarmiento offered the account of another Spaniard named Juan Martínez de Albújar, who saw the Orinoco in 1570 and claimed to have been captured by Caribs who held him in a mysterious golden city on a giant lake called Parima. Spain had already sent several expeditions to find Parima, but none had yet succeeded; and it was still there, waiting.

Raleigh was nothing if not an opportunist, and Sarmiento's story stayed with him; several years later, in a moment of necessity, he decided to chase it down himself. Raleigh had fallen from Elizabeth's good graces when he impregnated and secretly married one of her ladies-in-waiting, and the jealous queen sent him through the Traitors' Gate to cool his heels for a while in the Tower of London. He secured his release with a plan daring enough to restore his fortunes: he would go to the Orinoco, find the city of the unconquered Incas, and bring back their unclaimed treasures. It did not go well.

Raleigh was sure: El Dorado is Spanish for "the Golden Man."

They would almost certainly have died: The Spanish may have inadvertently assisted Raleigh by giving him a fearsome reputation at odds with his ragged appearance; they'd assured Caribs and Arawaks alike that the English were cannibals.

Raleigh finally halted: "There appeared some ten or twelve overfalls in sight, every one as high over the other as a church tower, which fell with that fury, that the rebound of water made it seem as if it had been all covered over with a great shower of rain; and in some places we took it at the first for a smoke that had risen over some great town" (Raleigh 1848:81).

He was sure: Raleigh, ever the self-promoter, set down his descriptions of his failed expedition in a book with the humble title *The Discoverie of the Large, Rich, and Bewtiful Empyre of Guiana, with a relation of the Great and Golden Citie of Manoa (which the Spanyards call El Dorado) and of the Provinces of Emeria, Arromaia, Amapaia, and other Countries, with their rivers, adioyning.*

As he faced them: "The common soldier shal here fight for gold," Raleigh insisted, "and pay himself, instead of pence, with plates of half-a-foot broad" (Raleigh 1848:111).

"The face of the earth": Raleigh 1848:115. Despite this portrait of Guiana as a ripe fruit waiting to be plucked, Elizabeth never granted Raleigh his landing force, and he fell again from royal favor when he was convicted of plotting against her successor, James I. This offense landed Raleigh back in the Tower, where he passed a lonely decade writing an impassioned and wildly inaccurate history of the world; but Guiana never left his thoughts, and he financed other attempts to find Manoa from prison. Even after years in a cell, Raleigh's silver tongue was untarnished, and he finally persuaded his captors to release him to direct one more expedition himself — a disastrous adventure that led to the death of his son Wat during a botched raid on a Spanish garrison in Venezuela. The raid was a violation of peace treaties between England and Spain, and Spain demanded Raleigh's head, which King James was happy to give them. Raleigh was executed at the Tower of London in 1618, and his last words, as he lay with his head on the block, were "Strike, man, strike!"

"There is no countrey": Raleigh 1848:111.

"some carnation": Raleigh 1848:54. "Watched," or "watchet," is a very pale blue, similar to sky blue, named for a town on the English coast whose cliffs are rich in alabaster.

"like a phantom": Humboldt and Bonpland 1895:48. Humboldt continued: "It is in the nature of man, wandering on the earth, to figure to himself happiness beyond the region which he knows, [and] El Dorado, similar to Atlas and the islands of the Hesperides, disappeared by degrees from the domain of geography, and entered that of mythological fictions."

They were a perfect setting: Arthur Conan Doyle's 1912 natural science fiction fantasy *The Lost World* takes place in the mountains west of the Rupununi, where the granite rocks of the shield terminate in the flat-topped mountains called *tepuis* that Raleigh glimpsed at the end of his journey. In Conan Doyle's story, a brave (but foolish) expedition under the leadership of a man named Professor Challenger finds that the tepuis' mist-covered plateaus are home to a host of prehistoric monsters, including dinosaurs, giant deer, and pterodactyls — creatures of Earth's past whose existence had only been revealed to his readers a few decades earlier.

Waugh's dark satire: Waugh 1934. "Let us read *Little Dorrit* again," Mr. Todd says, in the story's chilling last line. "There are passages in that book I can never hear without the temptation to weep."

No book is quite like *Green Mansions*: Rima,

sadly, ticks many of the boxes for "The Manic Pixie Dream Girl," a term coined in 2007 by the film critic Nathan Rabin to describe a type of female love interest familiar to movie audiences that "exists solely in the fevered imagination of sensitive writer-directors to teach broodingly soulful young men to embrace life and its infinite mysteries and adventures" (https://film.avclub .com). The 1959 film version of *Green Mansions*, starring Audrey Hepburn, underscores Rima's shortcomings: and the London *Times* skewered her as "a fey child of nature communicating with her dead mother, imitating the songs of birds and running about the forest in a kind of nightdress" (Tomalin 1982:199–200).

The book's late success: Alfred A. Knopf published *Green Mansions* in the United States. It was the fledgling publisher's first major success.

"seeing a dead thing": Letter to Alfred A. Knopf, quoted in Tomalin 1982:222.

"a vulgar farrago": *Saturday Review,* quoted in Tomalin 1982:126.

Like Hudson, Abel lives in self-imposed exile: "With the object of replacing it by more worthy men — ourselves, to wit" (WHH, GM 1916:20).

"In answer to": WHH, GM 1916:13.

"The sterile ground": WHH, GM 1916:31.

14. Sweet Fishes to Eat

"Now, that is a sweet fish to eat": As of this writing, a single three-hundred-pound arapaima can fetch more than a thousand dollars on the black market — a king's ransom in southern Guyana. The fine for catching them illegally is one million Guyanese dollars, about five thousand U.S. dollars. The huge fish attract foreign anglers to the Rewa, who pay handsomely to catch and release them on fly rigs in closely supervised trips — and the tourists' dollars, in turn, support the village. But the arapaimas' pale, succulent flesh was a staple of the local diet for many years, and it's sorely missed.

Jaguars can weigh: In a pinch, some jaguars will even attack caimans, leaping onto their backs and snapping their necks with jaws as strong as a lion's.

They're usually seen: There is only one published description of a black caracara's nest: a shallow platform of sticks, ten stories up in a tree (Whittaker 1996).

a German ornithologist named Helmut Sick: Sick 1993.

Tapirs, Sick wrote: "The tapir begins to squeal on hearing the call of the caracara, which then goes to the tapir, for it likes eating its ticks. The tapir lies down, belly up,

574

so the bird can get at the parasites" (Sick 1993).

I told Sean I was surprised: This behavior still hasn't been documented for black caracaras — but it has been for yellow-headed caracaras (Coulson et al. 2018).

"What a roof was that": WHH, GM 1916:33. Overcome by the forest's beauty, Abel can't resist an aside about the inadequacy of human architecture: "The human artist," he says, "is only able to get his horizontal distance by a monotonous reduplication of pillar and arch, placed at regular intervals, and the least departure from this order would destroy the effect. But Nature produces her effects at random, and seems only to increase the beautiful illusion by the infinite variety of decoration in which she revels, binding tree to tree in a tangle of anaconda-like lianas, and dwindling down from these huge cables to airy webs and hair-like fibres that vibrate to the wind of the passing insect's wing." These are lofty thoughts for Abel, whose concerns are usually more earthbound; but the passage rings with his author's frustration at the limits of human art and imagination — and from an architectural point of view, it could almost have been written by Hudson's contemporary Antoni Gaudí, whose unfinished masterpiece is a basilica that looks like a jungle of stone. "Gothic art is imperfect, only half

575

resolved," Gaudí wrote; "it is a style created by the compasses, a formulaic industrial repetition. Its stability depends on constant propping up by the buttresses: it is a defective body held up on crutches. . . . The proof that Gothic works are of deficient plasticity is that they produce their greatest emotional effect when they are mutilated, covered in ivy and lit by the moon" (Gaudí, quoted in Flores 2002:119).

But the forest's crowning glory: Hudson's fancy gets the better of him in the passage that follows. "I often listened to this tinkling music," Abel says, "and it had suggested the idea that the place was frequented by a tribe of fairy-like troubadour monkeys, and that if I could only be quick-sighted enough I might one day be able to detect the minstrel sitting, in a green tunic perhaps, cross-legged on some high bough, carelessly touching his mandolin, suspended from his neck by a yellow ribbon" (WHH, GM 1916:43).

Most of Hudson's readers: Pitta-thrushes, now called ant thrushes, belong to a uniquely South American family of birds; their close resemblance to another group of Indian and Australasian birds (still called pittas today) confused scientists until genetic analysis revealed their separate ancestries.

"a pack of those swift-footed": WHH, GM 1916:49. This is pure fiction: there are no such animals.

"would outroar the mightiest lion": Hudson's imagination was running away with him again. A concert of hundreds of howler monkeys has probably never happened, since howler troops usually range in size from six to fifteen members, and they call in part to warn other howlers away. But he was right about their incredible volume: Howlers have been recorded at 140 decibels, making them not only louder than roaring lions but also jet engines. A single male can be heard calling from two miles away.

their scientific name: This name was given to them by a Dutch naturalist in 1783, describing specimens collected in French Guiana; a French naturalist had already given them another non-Latin name, which didn't stick (alas): American eagle.

The line took us: Peccaries are amazingly piglike, but they're not closely related; peccaries and "true" pigs belong to different families of mammals that evolved in different parts of the world. Another convergence.

after an hour we were deep: N,N-Dimethyltryptamine, an organic chemical secreted by many plants and animals including some poisonous frogs, is known for

577

its short-lived but intense mind-altering effects, including "profound time-dilation, visual and auditory illusions, and other experiences that, by most firsthand accounts, defy verbal or visual description" (www .floridacenterforrecovery.com). I had a brief vision of the peccaries writhing on their muddy beds in hallucinatory bliss, squealing and waving their stubby legs in the air.

Soldier ants patrolling the column: Of the hundreds of thousands of ants in an army ant colony, all are the offspring of a single queen, and nearly all are female — though the queen sometimes lays a small batch of unfertilized eggs which develop into males. Male army ants are winged and look wasp-like, with long, curved abdomens and tiny mouth parts; most die shortly after they hatch out of their pupal cocoons, but a few manage to locate other army ant queens and mate with them. Other than that, males play almost no role in the elaborate social life of the colonies, and don't participate in the massive raiding parties that define them.

Like wasps: Army ants aren't only invincible, they're basically immortal. Once a colony reaches a certain size — somewhere around a half a million workers — it divides into separate swarms, like a cell undergoing mitosis, and a daughter of the original swarm's queen takes charge of the new colony; so, in a sense, the swarm never dies. The queens themselves are rarely seen, since they're nearly always hidden behind a mass of their workers' bodies. They can survive in the safety of their living fortresses for as long as five years, and bear more than four million children.

Calfbirds are among the world's strangest birds: They look something like a combination of Beast Man and Skeletor.

As we approached the waterfalls: See Somavilla et al. (2013) for a description of mutual defense among ants, wasps, and birds.

army ants also: Note to anyone seeking a wasp-repellent compound: look here.

The quintet began to call: This call is the source of another of the red-throats' many nicknames, *chupacacao,* which attaches to them in Venezuela and Ecuador.

I wondered if I should: At the American Museum of Natural History, I once cut my finger on the talons of a red-throated caracara that died in the nineteenth century.

15. Above the Falls

He relished the story: Jose returned the crocodiles to the river, but he was tempted to take one of the young terns home and raise it. He'd once done this with a white-winged trumpeter he named Brethren, who would come when called. Jose said he used to play hide-and-seek with this bird, and it always found him.

Jose's questions were usually more cosmic: One afternoon, Brian asked if it was cold in New York in the winter, but he furrowed his brow when I asked him if he used Fahrenheit or Celsius. "I don't know," he said. "I never studied temperature."

I couldn't resist telling them: WHH, FALA 1918:51. "This made me hold on more tenaciously than ever," Hudson continued, "and tug and strain more violently, until not to lose him I had to go flat down on the ground. But it was all for nothing; first my hands, then my aching arms were carried down into the earth, and I was forced to release my hold and get up to rid myself of the mould he had been throwing up into my face and all over my head, neck, and shoulders."

We were simply another thing: It struck me that this was what people usually mean when they describe a place as "Edenic": a palpable sense of being only one species among many, and not the most important one, either.

Her brush-like mane: Tapirs can bite, but they're no match for two hundred pounds of hunting cat, and the scratches were indicative of her best defense: to run, preferably into dense, thorny bushes where the cat might be dislodged. Once a jaguar reaches your neck, it's all over.

No two performances: On clear mornings, the parrots were so loud that I reached for my earplugs; but on close, cloudy days the dawn chorus was spare and subdued, sometimes little more than a deep, listening hush, broken every few minutes by the low double hoot of a motmot.

One morning I spent: Though sunbitterns slightly resemble herons, they're taxonomically puzzling; scientists regard them as the sole members of their own family. Their nearest relative seems to be a leggy, flightless bird from New Caledonia, on the other side of the Pacific Ocean, called a kagu — suggesting that their last common ancestor probably lived in Gondwana before it fragmented into today's southern continents. Sunbitterns' placid, otherworldly demeanor suits this ancient origin, and they look so fragile and fancy that it's hard to understand how they survive in the merciless world of the forest. Captive sunbitterns will call back to even a vague imitation of their song; after a few minutes' conversation, it's hard not to want one for a pet.

"When night came": WHH, FALA 1918:99.

Hudson lay awake: John Cage (1912–92) was an American composer who considered every sound to be a kind of music. "There is no such thing as an empty space or an empty time," he wrote. "There is always something to see, something to hear. In

581

fact, try as we may to make a silence, we cannot" (Cage 1961:8).

"The calls began": WHH, FALA 1918:100. The *serenos,* sadly, were frequently harassed by Buenos Aires' equivalent of marauding frat boys. "I loved the poor night-watchmen and their cries," Hudson wrote, "and it grieved my little soft heart to hear that it was considered fine sport by rich young gentlemen to sally forth at night and do battle with them, and to deprive them of their staffs and lanterns, which they took home and kept as trophies."

"There is nothing in life": WHH, IDIP 1893:5–7. "It was not, however, the fascination of old legends that drew me," Hudson wrote, "nor the desire of the desert, for not until I had seen it, and had tasted its flavor . . . did I know how much its solitude and desolation would be to me, what strange knowledge it would teach, and how enduring its effect would be on my spirit. Not these things, but the passion of the ornithologist took me. Many of the winged wanderers with which I had been familiar from childhood in La Plata were visitors, occasional or regular, from this grey wilderness of thorns."

Patagonia might be inhospitable: "I do not know how it is with other ornithologists at the time when their enthusiasm is greatest," wrote Hudson, "but of myself I can say that my dreams by night were often of some new bird, vividly seen; and such dreams were always beautiful to me, and a grief to wake from" (WHH, IDIP 1893:6).

The ancient steamer: The ship was "a very curious boat . . . long and narrow, like a Viking's ship, with the passengers' cabins ranged like a row of small wooden cottages on the deck" (WHH, IDIP 1893:1).

They rode the last mile: Argentina's Río Negro is different from the one in Brazil, which is one of the two main tributaries of the Amazon.

"Never river seemed fairer": WHH, IDIP 1893:17.

"to have enabled a small colony": WHH, IDIP 1893:21.

"The way to make him happy": WHH, IDIP 1893:21.

"Dead also": WHH, IDIP 1893:22.

"He had just begun": WHH, IDIP 1893:23.

In the silent, windowless cabin: "From my experience during those black anxious hours," Hudson added, "I can imagine how much the sense of hearing must be to the blind and to animals that exist in dark caves" (WHH, IDIP 1893:24).

"dreamy, softly rising and falling": WHH, IDIP 1893:25. Here is Hudson on the morning songs of swallows: "A loved and beautiful bird is this, that utters his early song circling round and round in the dusky air, when the stars begin to pale; and his song, perhaps, seems sweeter than all others, because it corresponds in time to that rise in the temperature and swifter flow of the blood — the inward resurrection experienced on each morning of our individual life."

Hudson was surprised: "I rejoice to think," he wrote, "that the secret deadly creature, after lying all night with me, warming its chilly blood with my warmth, went back unbruised to its den" (WHH, IDIP 1893:26).

"flitting, sylph-like things": WHH, IDIP 1893:19.

"the ambitious schemes of Russia": WHH, IDIP 1893:77. "The Sublime Porte" is an old synecdoche for the Ottoman Empire (now Turkey); it's like using "the White House" to refer to the United States or "Downing Street" for the UK.

"the passion for politics": WHH, IDIP 1893:76. "I was delighted," Hudson noted, "to discover that the stimulus derived from many daily telegrams and much discussion of remote probabilities were not necessary to keep my mind from lethargy."

"How fresh and how human": WHH, IDIP 1893:77.

"My home, I said": WHH, IDIP 1893:47.

Since the days of General Rosas: Darwin saw evidence of the Argentine army's campaign against the Indians firsthand, and the brutality of one skirmish shook him. "Some Indians," Darwin wrote, "who had been taken prisoners, gave information of a tribe living north of the Colorado. Two hundred soldiers were sent; and they first discovered the Indians by a cloud of dust from their horses' feet, as they chanced to be travelling. The country was mountainous and wild, and it must have been far in the interior, for the [Andes] were in sight. The Indians, men, women, and children, were about one hundred and ten in number, and they were nearly all taken or killed, for the soldiers saber every man. The Indians are now so terrified that they offer no resistance in a body . . . but when overtaken, like wild animals, they fight against any number to the last moment. One dying Indian seized with his teeth the thumb of his adversary, and allowed his own eye to be forced out sooner than relinquish his hold . . . This is a dark picture; but how much more shocking is the unquestionable fact, that all the women who appear above twenty years old are massacred in cold blood! When I exclaimed that this appeared rather inhuman, he answered, 'Why, what can be done? they breed so!' Everyone here is convinced that this is the most just war" (CD 1845:102).

They retaliated by raiding settlements: Known as the Zanja de Alsina, from the general who directed its creation, remnants of this giant network of trenches and wooden watchtowers are still visible today. Where it crosses a modern highway, a blue sign still proclaims that you are crossing the Zanja de Alsina, "the frontier of civilization" in 1876.

"our self-respect as a virile people": Julio Argentina Roca is quoted in Roth 2002:45.

Thousands of men, women, and children: See the Latin Americanist Jens Andermann's online essay "Argentine Literature and the 'Conquest of the Desert', 1872–1896" (http://www.bbk.ac.uk) for a bracing exploration and analysis of contemporary accounts of this period in Argentina's history.

"Where the village": WHH, IDIP 1893:37. "The anthropologist could not have wished for a more favourable year or for a better crop," Hudson continued. "I collected a large number of these objects; and some three or four hundred arrow-heads which I picked up are at present, I believe, in the famous Pitt-Rivers collection [in Oxford]. But I was over-careful. The finest of my treasures, the most curious and beautiful objects I could select, packed apart for greater safety, were unfortunately lost in transit — a severe blow, which hurt me more than the wound I had received on the knee."

"Not only were they minute": WHH, IDIP

1893:39.

He mentioned a footprint-shaped hole: The irony of this was piercing; Brian's hometown of Aishalton lies almost exactly in the place where Manoa, the golden city of El Dorado, was supposed to be. The company that operates the mine, a Chinese-Canadian venture, has recently renamed itself Guyana Goldstrike, and its website extols its kindness to its workers in Aishalton, with particular emphasis on the variety of local food it offers them at mealtimes. See Hammond et al. 2008 for more on the effects of gold mining in the Guiana Shield region.

"What are they exploring?": See Bulkan 2016 for a history of Amerindians' struggle for territorial rights in the Guiana Shield.

"My friends tell me the Milky Way": This belief is common to Amerindian cultures across the Americas. López and Benítez 2008 record it from the Mocoví of the Gran Chaco of Argentina, Paraguay, and Bolivia — a region of dry forests one thousand six hundred miles south of the Rewa.

Since the Cretaceous extinctions: Moreno-Bernal 2007.

Then I saw: The hunting spiders in the armadillo's creek weren't closely related to the "true" wolf spiders of the genus *Lycosa* that I grew up with in the southeastern United States; they belonged to a uniquely South American family of hunting spiders called the Ctenidae. Like South America's many tarantulas, most ctenid spiders are harmless to humans, with one notable exception: the large "wandering spiders" in the genus *Phoneutria,* known for their aggressive behavior and venomous bites, which can cause paralysis and death (sometimes preceded, in men, by a painful attack of priapism). They're occasionally called banana spiders for their tendency to hide in bunches of bananas, which occasionally make their way to other continents — hence the "deadly black tarantula" in Harry Belafonte's "Day-O," even though strictly speaking, *Phoneutria* spiders aren't tarantulas.

Some were nearly the size: Sean later identified these giants as *Ancylometes rufus,* among the largest spiders on Earth that aren't tarantulas. Their specialty is catching fish and frogs. They can run across the surface of water and spin webs beneath it.

A strong wind stirred the forest: When we returned to camp, Jose said he'd heard the red-throats calling, and assumed we had something to do with it; Sean said the caracaras had chased the vultures away. "Like the Bob Marley song," Jose replied. "He gonna chase them crazy bald-heads out of town."

"Pretty soon it darkened up": Twain 1884:74.

"Second monster": Redtail catfish, *Phracto-*

cephalus hemioliopterus, can grow to almost six feet in length and weigh up to two hundred pounds.

It rose to sip air: Electrical senses alone appear to be enough for electric eels, which can live for at least thirty years and grow to seven feet long. At that size they can stun prey with heart-stopping blasts of up to eight hundred volts.

Madeleine had been a widow: The compression of generations in Jose's family compared to mine was staggering; one of my great-great-grandfathers had fought in the American Civil War.

16. Last Days of the Guadalupe Caracara

Cunas ch'iyar awayunim: Scott 1963.

On the morning: Abbott 1933.

Beck was especially admired: Dumbacher and West 2010, Mearns and Mearns 1998:337.

Most ornithologists in the late nineteenth century: Beck, like Hudson, was decades ahead of his time in making this leap. Serious study of the sense of smell in birds didn't begin until the 1960s, and has been very slow in progressing — partly because of an irrational but persistent belief among ornithologists (including John James Audubon) that birds don't have one.

Despite these headwinds, Gabrielle Nevitt, a professor at the University of California–Davis, has pushed the frontiers of research on bird olfaction for the last few decades — even though the program officer of a grant once told her, "Your idea that birds can smell is ridiculous." Her work has been especially focused on seabirds, and she discovered that they're sensitive to a gas called dimethyl sulfide, or DMS, which is released by dying organisms, most notably when tiny shrimp called krill — a major food source for seabirds — feed on phytoplankton. As Nevitt compared a satellite map of DMS plumes to underwater topography, she realized that seabirds can, in effect, "see" the topography of the ocean floor by smell. "They have their own map," she said. "An odor landscape, in the air above the water" — a discovery that would have pleased (and validated) Hudson (Averett 2014). The only study to examine smell in a caracara found suggestive evidence that southern crested caracaras use smell to locate food (Potier et al. 2019); it also seems possible that red-throated caracaras, for example, might use their olfactory senses as well as their sharp eyes to help them find wasp nests in the tropical forest.

Once he recovered their floating bodies: A word about study skins. Birds are unusual among animals in that their feathers, more than their bones and muscles, give them their distinctive shapes; unfeathered, most birds resemble a plucked chicken. Turning a bird into a "skin" (which, unless there's a freezer handy, has to be done within a few hours of its death) is a sort of shorthand taxidermy that preserves its feathers and overall form for study. The process involves opening its abdomen with a vertical incision, removing its muscles and viscera (including the brain, which is drawn from the skull after turning the neck inside out), stuffing the body cavity with a filler like straw or cotton, and stitching it back up, leaving the beak, feet, wings, and tail intact.

In the hand, these skins have a talismanic power, since they evoke not just the animal they once were but the moment in which they were collected: ID tags attached to the feet of specimens usually list the species, the collector's name, and where and when the bird was killed. Once in a while they reveal something more: a skin at Harvard's Museum of Comparative Zoology, for example, includes the note "See me for locality" in the hand of a long-dead curator. On the back of a tag attached to a snowy-white kelp goose at the American Museum of Natural History, another collector wrote "Shot flying by moonlight."

I've placed two striated caracaras from Steeple Jason in museums. Though both were dead when I found them, I still feel vaguely guilty when I think about taking their remains so far from home. One was an adult female, curled up on the ground in a territory her mate was still defending; her skeleton, scraped clean of flesh and packed in salt, was sent to the American Museum of Natural History, where it now resides in a cardboard box. The other is G7, whose body I left at the Falklands museum in Stanley with the artful taxidermist Steve Massam — a former butcher from England who visited the islands, fell in love, and stayed.

"a tough little bastard": Matt James, quoted in Wolfe 2006.

Guadalupe was a brief stop: See James 2019 for a complete account of the California Academy's collecting expedition to the Galápagos, the last of its kind, which helped provide evidence to confirm Darwin and Wallace's theory of evolution by natural selection.

One was a former goat hunter: Abbott 1933. Drent said that he'd captured the birds "by a trick I learned while in South Africa," and was pleased to explain his methods in detail. "The first bird I winged with a shotgun," he said. "I then made him a prisoner, and staked him near a large boulder. I then took a string, fastened it to a stick, and made a loop similar to a cowboy's lariat. I then hid myself behind the rock, knowing the other birds would come to the captive.

I threw the rope and captured a second bird. I then made him a prisoner with the other. By this method I secured four out of the seven birds on the island." This last assertion is almost certainly a lie, since there's no way Drent could have known how many caracaras remained on an island of Guadalupe's size; but drumming up demand for the birds was clearly on his mind.

"I have them all named": Try that with a group of red-tailed hawks or peregrines; you'll be waiting a long time.

"At first [they] were in their cage": Abbott 1933.

"of 11 birds that flew toward me": Abbott 1933.

One thing, however, is certain: With the possible exception of a single, unconfirmed sighting in 1903 (Abbott 1933).

cats that came ashore: Keitt et al. 2005.

a crestfallen visitor: San Diego Natural History Museum 2000.

A good portion of her work: The height record for a flying bird is thirty-seven thousand feet — almost twice the height of Kilimanjaro — set when a Rüppell's vulture struck an airplane above Ivory Coast (Laybourne 1974).

To its left and right: In a separate row of cabinets, we found several more Guadalupe caracaras, including three fledglings that had been exhibited along with the type specimen, one of which might even have been its offspring. They had comically large feet and plaintive expressions, and were covered head to toe in golden down, except for a patch of brown fuzz atop their heads. I was relieved when Dove put them away; it was hard for me to imagine killing a nest of young caracaras, even for science.

But one object: Lewis 2012:42.

Dove opened a hinged panel: The skull, catalog number 18285, was given to the museum by Albert Kenrick Fisher, who found it near Ossining, New York, in 1881. Fisher was an employee of the USDA and a founding member of the American Ornithologists' Union, and part of his job was preventing farmers from needlessly killing birds of prey. In 1893 he published *The Hawks and Owls of the United States in Their Relation to Agriculture,* and a 1951 obituary of Fisher in the AOU's journal, *The Auk,* noted that "as a result of this work the destruction of harmless hawks and owls has been greatly reduced, and they are no longer threatened with extermination." Birds of prey would not be officially protected by law in the United States until 1972.

"We don't know": Except that it probably wasn't an Amerindian person. According to Dove, an anthropologist examined the skull as part of the Smithsonian's repatriation program and determined that it was not of

Native American origin.

I thought of Hudson: Oddly enough, the skull at the Smithsonian is not the only one in history to house a wren's nest; there are references to at least two others, both from England. In 1872, a young "J.H. Gurney, jr, Esq." in a recurring column of the amateur journal *The Zoologist* called "Ornithological Notes from Norfolk," described a wren's nest built in a hat — then added that "on the 24th of last July Mr. Baker, of Cambridge, showed me a wren's nest in a human skull." William Stewart Ross, a Scottish secularist and freethinker who sometimes used the pen name Saladin, mentioned another (or is it the same?) skull nest in a collection of essays called *Roses and Rue*, published that same year; this one came from the village of Etal in Northumberland.

"A few years ago," he wrote, "it was discovered that somebody, perhaps having found it was of very little use to him, had left his skull in the Etal woods. But the useless thing, which had in all probability rendered its owner subject to headache and blockheadism, had been found and ingeniously utilized by Jenny Wren for incubatory purposes."

Stewart then reprinted a poem about the skull by a writer from the region, William Weaver Tomlinson, now remembered (when he is remembered at all) for a 1915 book about the history of English railways. If I haven't scared you off yet with this digression, you might as well read it, too (Ross 1890:206).

Strange bower, O lively wren! is this
To dwell in when the heart is full
Of love and song and vernal bliss.
Oh! is not living in a skull
A little dull?

One would not think so, tiny bird,
To hear thee trill thy joyous lay;
Sweeter perhaps than any word
That this old skull, when young and
 gay
Could sing or say.

Thou warblest not for our delight
Who linger near these ruins, yet
How much we owe thee, merry sprite!
Ah! that we cannot pay our debt
Is our regret.

What can we give thee — we whose
 voice
Awakens in thee such unrest?
When we are gone thou wilt rejoice,
For sorely art thou troubled lest
We find thy nest.

These Etal woods are all thy world,
And glad must be thy heart to see
The tender bracken fronds unfurled,
And all the long-pent leaves set free
On bush and tree.

Ah! if once more on Flodden fell
A host of heroes, brave and strong,
Still blithely, through this ferny dell
Would ring thy dainty little song
The whole day long.

This skull, I doubt not, in its prime
Has harboured — like a robber's cave

—

Unholy dreams of love and crime,
With thoughts and passions that
deprave
The soul, their slave.

Yet happy he, though dark his past,
Whose skull can be of service when
His brain is dust; yea, be at last
Of service to a little wren
That sings to men.

The thought that a bird: This book, if nothing else, is proof that one has already done it.

Their ecosystems are fragile: See Quammen 1996 for a thorough and entertaining journey through the world of island biogeography — and its implications for threatened species everywhere.

Like the giant mammals: Duncan et al. 2013 found that the expansion of Polynesian peoples into the islands of the South Pacific was responsible for the greatest human-caused mass extinction of birds in history, in which at least thirteen hundred species were lost — more than 10 percent of the species of birds on Earth. Steadman et al. 2003 describe the extinctions of giant sloths on Caribbean islands, where they lingered quite a while longer than their cousins did on the mainland.

Plenty of continental birds: Newton 2003:244.

Guadalupe caracaras were the latest: Suárez and Olson 2003, Olson 1976.

A third found: Steadman et al. 2007.

in the ancient peat bog: Adams and Woods 2016. The authors named this bird *Phalcoboenus napieri* in honor of Roddy Napier, the owner of West Point Island, where the bones were found. At first glance, it's tempting to imagine that this eagle-sized caracara was simply an ancestral form of the modern Johnny rook, and that the species had shrunk over time. But the small fraction of the deposit that Robin and Mark excavated also contained the remains of sixteen birds nearly identical in size to modern Johnny rooks — so the two birds almost certainly knew each other as distinct species.

"Tierra del Fuego": CD 1845:209.

"a singular precaution": CD 1845:58.

17. The Mysterious Falcon of Manco Cápac

Unlike the tropical forests' bellicose red-throats: Mountain caracaras in particular have evaded attempts to know them better (perhaps because of the Incas' fondness for their feathers). One Chilean ornithologist crossly described them as "evasive, unsociable and cowardly" after searching in vain for their nests (Housse 1938).

"It is difficult to imagine a raptorial bird": Brown and Amadon 1968:732.

A BBC crew once filmed: BBC 1998.

And in 1995, a Canadian graduate student: Jones 1999.

It was tempting to think they were parents: "No begging vocalizations were uttered by the younger bird," Jones noted, "nor did it adopt any unusual posture."

"This handsome bird": CD 1963:238.

He was very surprised to see: The white-throated caracara Darwin collected still resides in the collection of the British Museum. On a yellowed paper tag tied to one of its feet, the word "albigularis" is written in faint pencil.

They define the west coast: South America's

599

good fortune is Africa's loss; if Earth turned in the opposite direction, the moisture that blows in from the Atlantic and waters the Amazon basin would caravan into the Sahara instead. The Amazon would be a huge desert, walled off from the Pacific by the Andes; and on their western slopes, the Atacama would be a deep green ribbon framing the continent's scorching, arid center.

Headgear signified rank: Steele and Allen 2004:107.

Each new emperor: "These Feathers were planted over the coloured Wreath which bound their Temples," Garcilaso wrote, "the peak feathers pointing upwards, removed at a little distance one from the other, as they were naturally spread" (Garcilaso 1609:335–336). This wreath or crown, called the *mascapaicha,* was depicted in the illustrations of Garcilaso's chronicle of the history and customs of the Incas, and clearly shows the black-and-white pattern of a mountain caracara's primary feathers.

Corequenques were so rare: This lake, called Villcanota by Garcilaso, is probably one of three small lakes at La Raya pass in Peru, on the boundary between the provinces of Cuzco and Puna. La Raya is named for two parallel rows of large stones that were probably placed there by the Incas; today, it's also home to stone corrals of indeterminate age still in use by shepherds, and an informal market and rest area.

"Never more than two of them": Garcilaso 1609:335.

"their two original parents": Garcilaso 1609:335. By "Man and Woman," Garcilaso meant the Incas' creator gods, Viracocha and Pachamama, the most powerful figures in their cosmology.

"Such was the majesty": Garcilaso 1609:336. As an aside, Garcilaso added that though the corequenques were certainly rare, he didn't think they were magical, or confined to a single lake — and that there were probably more of them in other parts of Peru. He also noted that in the days since the Spanish (and their diseases) overthrew the Inca emperor Atahualpa, the wearing of corequenque feathers had proliferated among people claiming royal blood. "It is certain that the feathers of these birds were highly esteemed in those days," he sniffed, "though they are more common now, being worn by many, who falsely pretend to a descent from the royal blood of the Incas."

But Amerindians had arrived: Lindo et al. 2018. Andean Amerindians today include the descendants of many people who never — or never fully — submitted to Inca rule.

Their dances mimic: Curiquingue dances also take place at the turn of the new year. A ten-minute video clip on YouTube titled "Danza de Curiquingues — Riobamba —

Ecuador" shows a group of costumed dancers enacting important moments in the birds' lives, from courtship to the hatching of their young.

This name: Arnold and Yapitamoya 1992.

gray-green slopes: The alpine moorlands of Colombia and Ecuador bear a striking resemblance to the shores of the Falklands, nearly four thousand miles away.

In 1983, the biologist Tjitte de Vries: de Vries et al. 1983.

One tradition held that mating: The authors of the study saw several young curiquingues kept in corrals with domestic fowl, apparently in the hope that they would mate (de Vries et al. 1983). Curiously, this tradition doesn't necessarily postdate the Inca, and could even be much older than their empire; archaeological evidence suggests that domestic chickens were present in South America more than seven hundred years ago, long before Europeans arrived. Any attempt to crossbreed a falcon and a chicken is wildly unlikely to succeed, however, even if people insist they've seen it happen. Chickens and their nearest relatives belong to a lineage of birds that last shared a common ancestor with falcons about ninety million years ago, long before the Cretaceous extinctions. For these distant relatives to produce viable young together would be like cross-breeding a dog with a horse.

If a woman in the community: The authors noted that this practice was dying out, and that only the oldest members of the community remembered it — though it had occurred, they said, as recently as 1980 (de Vries et al. 1983).

"Alkamari was always a lazy good-for-nothing": Allen 2011:106.

"In a sudden burst of inspiration": WHH, GM 1916:156.

The rising Andes: Perkins 2014, Hoorn et al. 2010.

Genetic evidence shows: Fuchs et al. 2012.

for millions of years: The site where Julia Clarke found the dinosaur in Chile lies only five thousand feet above sea level, but it's nearly identical to habitats at thirteen thousand feet in Ecuador.

The high Andes are home: Johnson et al. 1958. All of Africa, Europe, and Asia, by contrast, can boast only two species of flamingos.

At night they huddle: A resting position in which the fossils of sleeping dinosaurs have been found (Watson 2017).

in the small hours: The midnight choir of Andean flamingos was a sound Hudson never heard, but he grew up with others like it. Vast flocks of geese arrived each year from southern Patagonia to spend the winter in

La Plata, and he remembered listening to them chattering from his bedroom until the early hours of the morning:

> On clear frosty nights they are most loquacious, and their voices may be heard by the hour, rising and falling, now few, and now many taking part in the endless confabulation — a talkee-talkee and concert in one; a chatter as of many magpies; the solemn deep, *honk-honk,* the long, grave note changing to a shuddering sound; and, most wonderful, the fine silvery whistle of the male, steady or tremulous, now long and now short, modulated a hundred ways — wilder and more beautiful than the night-cry of the widgeon, brighter than the voice of any shore bird, or any warbler, thrush or wren, or the sound of any wind instrument.

These oases are rarely obvious: Fonkén 2014. Ducks, geese, gulls, and sandpipers: It's fairly easy to find bofedales today by poring over satellite images, but it wasn't always so. They're rarely marked on maps, and the British-born ornithologist Alfred W. Johnson spent years seeking them out in his pioneering efforts to find and study the unique birds of the high Andes. Johnson's life was, in some ways, the reverse of Hudson's: born in 1894, he grew up in England, then moved to Chile in 1912 as a young man, fell in love with its wildlife, and never went back; and it was Johnson and his friends who "rediscovered" James's flamingos in the Altiplano. They were never really lost, however: once Johnson turned up near the birds' breeding grounds, Amerindian people who occasionally harvested the birds' eggs told him where they lived (Johnson et al. 1958).

shallow pools swarmed: A. W. Johnson's description of the breeding grounds of the hen-like waterbirds called Andean giant coots on the lake of Cotacotani, a highland series of connected ponds and bofedales along the northern border of Chile and Bolivia, read like a glimpse of the life Hudson might have enjoyed if he'd never gone to England:

> Setting out the next morning with the first rays of light, we reached the shores of the lake just as the sun was rising behind the peaks and were witness to a scene of such grandeur as, once seen, lingers for ever in the memory. Cotacotani lay placid at the foot of the twin volcanoes which, lifting their snow-clad caps to over 20,000 feet, reflected their crystal-clear images in the placid waters of the lake to which they had given birth and which owed its very existence to their continually melting snows.
>
> Here, amid this scene . . . of immense and almost terrifying solitude, where the

inclemencies of weather in its moments of anger are such that not a single Indian is bold enough to pitch his camp, the Giant Coot has taken up his abode, a far cry from the world of man, but if we may judge from the size and vigor of the colony, a favourable habitat for the propagation of the species (Johnson 1964).

The ornithologist John Gould: Gould 1837.

But like their northern cousins: I have not been able to find an Amerindian name for white-throated caracaras, but there's probably a grim reason: native people are few and far between in the far south, thanks to the purges and massacres of the Chilean and Argentine armies, the disruptive if sometimes well-meaning efforts of missionaries, and the corrosive effects of disease. These forces decimated the Tehuelche and Mapuche people of the mountains, and wiped out the Yamana and Ona people of the fjords and coasts of Tierra del Fuego, among others. Any traditions related to white-throated caracaras, if they still exist, do not seem to be recorded anywhere.

These birds, long exiled: A. W. Johnson, in his exhaustive and celebrated book *The Birds of Chile* (1965), had to admit, "This is one of very few birds I still do not know personally."

18. A New Career in a New Town

I found it only because: James Channon opened his first falconry center behind a small hotel when he was only sixteen years old. Fifteen years later, he and his wife, Sharon, moved into the present facility at Millets Farm Centre, where they keep a growing collection of other animals along with the birds. Newer enclosures house families of ferrets and meerkats, a pair of skunks named Renée and Pepé, and a miscellaneous assortment of unwanted exotic pets from animal rescue centers, including tarantulas, bearded lizards, and hissing cockroaches. All the animals seem well cared for, but there's an unmistakable sense that James and Sharon are unable to resist an interesting animal that needs a home, even if it exceeds the usual mission of a falconry center.

Ravens are the biggest: The difference between a raven and a crow is slightly confusing. A raven *is* a crow, in the sense that "crow" refers to any of the large black birds in the genus *Corvus* — a group of about forty species whose members are spread across most of the world. Each species is different, but you'd recognize all of them as crows if they were set in front of you. Common ravens are crows in the same way that Johnny rooks are caracaras.

They are indeed: The similarity between striated caracaras and ravens seems to have fooled the birds themselves at least once. A pair of captive striated caracaras who've lived at Cotswold Wildlife Park and Gardens in the UK for more than twenty years once became strangely excited by a pair of wild ravens who nested nearby for a season. Each time the ravens flew overhead, the caracaras performed a territorial display, throwing their heads backward and calling in unison — a behavior they usually reserve, in the wild, for other Johnny rooks.

In the wild: James Channon noted that Loki the raven seems to have a slightly stronger ego than Boo the striated caracara. Loki, he said, isn't very interested in performing routines, and lacks a sense of "boundaries." ("If I let him out here," he said, "he'd climb all over you.") Boo might be demanding, but she's slightly more reserved than Loki, and less worldly-wise. This might reflect a difference in Loki's and Boo's individual personalities, but it might also be an evolutionary effect of their species' experiences with humans. Ravens have had many thousands of years to study our habits and add us to the long list of animals whose ways they understand; but Johnny rooks have known us for less than two hundred, and may still be taking us on a case-by-case basis.

608

Genetic evidence suggests: Ericson et al. 2002, Ekman and Ericson 2006.

about eleven degrees Fahrenheit: i.e., about six degrees Celsius.

In the Northern Hemisphere: Present-day Manhattan, which lies near the Pleistocene glaciers' southern limit, was still buried under ice fifteen thousand years ago. Rocks dragged along the glaciers' underbellies carved the deep, parallel grooves on the giant outcrops of granite in Central Park.

But it isn't lifeless: Life in the Arctic bides its time. Unlike a glacier, a few feet of snow doesn't grind the world beneath it to lifeless dust, but living things that can survive many months of freezing temperatures have to snap into action during the brief Arctic summer. Within days of the snow's departure, the plants and animals of the high Arctic transform the landscape in a fevered spasm of life as beautiful as it is abrupt. Years ago, I spent an Arctic summer on the shore of Hudson Bay in Canada's Nunavut province, and was amazed to see sudden meadows of pale yellow poppies and lush grasses springing from cracks in the stones, while clouds of mosquitoes rose from meltwater puddles to seek out roaming herds of caribou. In the hills surrounding the Inuit village of Kimmirut, teenagers cannonballed into ponds that were barely above freezing, while their grandparents scoured the hills for delicacies like fireweed and sweet-vetch to add to their diets of whale meat, flour, salt and sugar. High above their heads, there were always the dark, long-fingered shapes of ravens.

Their curiosity and social intelligence: On the west coast of Ireland, I found a raven's regurgitated pellet composed entirely of the iridescent shells of blue-green tiger beetles. It looked like a conglomerate gemstone.

Today ravens: Kristan et al. 2004.

"Wherever you go, the crow shows up": Matthiessen 1978:76. Matthiessen added: "GS had a pet raven while attending the University of Alaska, and this bird brought about his first encounter with the girl who became his wife: her attention was drawn to a man shouting at the sky, commanding an unseen raven to come back."

Some ravens may even guide predators: Heinrich 1999, chapter 19, describes interactions between ravens and wolves in Yellowstone National Park. The biologist Joan Morrison told me that ravens in Los Alamos, New Mexico, regularly appeared in residential areas on Thursday mornings — trash collection day — so they could plunder the town's household garbage as homeowners brought it to the curb. Tearing into garbage bags isn't all that remarkable a behavior for the famously clever birds; the surprise, for Morrison, was that the ravens almost seemed to have grasped the idea of Thursday.

"George Schaller told me": Heinrich 1999:133.

"The Johnny rook immediately pulled the octopus": Harrington and Bildstein 2019.

glaciers did spread throughout the Andes: Vuilleumier 1970, Clapperton 1993, Hulton et al. 2002.

their lineage diverged: Fuchs et al. 2012.

It's likely that rivers of ice: Hulton et al. 2002. This scenario fits the most recent algorithmic models of the Patagonian Ice Sheet, a minor complex of glaciers compared to the titanic Laurentide Ice Sheet that covered Canada, but still large enough to contain ten feet of global sea level. It radiated from the southern peaks of the Andes to cover most of the far south, carving the valleys and fjords of Tierra del Fuego and Chilean Patagonia. Fragments of it remain among the wildly sculpted mountains called the Torres del Paine.

These forerunners of the Johnny rooks: The New Zealand sailor Gerry Clark's description of a coastal colony of king shags, at the base of one of the glacial remnants of the Patagonian Ice Sheet in southwestern Chile, illustrates the situation in which animals fleeing from the ice sheets might have found themselves. "In the basin at the glacier face," Clark wrote, "a mighty wall of jagged blue ice, divided into two arms by a massive rock, reached high up into a vast icefield which stretched away out of sight into the clouds . . . making loud cracking and groaning noises on either side of us. Occasionally, with a thunderous roar a great avalanche of ice tumbled down into the basin . . . On the big rock between the two arms of ice was a very large colony of King Cormorants — we could not count how many thousands — to which the flocks we had seen had been coming. Close by, squeezed into a nearly horizontal crack in a cliff of rock, was a colony of seals, with three Striated Caracaras in attendance" (Clark 1988).

"Their whole sustenance": CD 1845:57.

"The sea looked ominous": CD 1845:217.

Unlike the Guadalupe caracaras: see Rignot et al. (2019) for a sobering illustration of ice-sheet losses in Antarctica since 1979.

single birds have been seen: Marín et al. 2006.

tamp down an infestation of rats: Easter Island's chimangos, like the Johnny rooks, have also learned to associate with its few remaining colonial seabirds. Albatrosses and penguins would probably be too large for a chimango to handle, but Easter Island is home to smaller, tern-like seabirds called red-tailed tropicbirds, whose nestlings are just the right size to provide a snack for a hungry chimango.

Easter Islanders, with a mixture of affection and annoyance: Flores 2016.

They face no competition: Easter Island has only five species of land birds today, all of them introduced by humans in the past century. Two are our companions almost everywhere we go: house sparrows and rock doves, also known as city pigeons, who rarely get the credit they deserve for learning to accommodate and take advantage of humans in all our manifestations. Easter Island's other two land birds are South American imports: Chilean tinamous, the same birds the gauchos caught with the aid of crested caracaras in the Pampas, were presumably introduced as game; and little gray finches called diucas were probably brought in as pets. Easter Island's extinct native birds, known only from fossils, include two parrots, two large moorhens (not unlike the giant coots of the Andes or New Zealand), an owl, and a heron.

The first assumes: Conservationists captured all 27 of the last wild California condors in the early 1980s, bred them in zoos, then released them into parts of their historical range; as of 2018, their population stands at 446.

"it's not habitat": Keith Bildstein, personal communication.

In the United States: The 1972 amendment to the Migratory Bird Treaty Act of 1918

613

finally granted protection to birds of prey; before that, it was legal to shoot hawks, owls, and falcons (and people often did). It was a banner year for birds of prey, since 1972 also brought a ban on the agricultural use of DDT, a pesticide that accumulated in the tissues of raptors and thinned their eggshells, leading to widespread nesting failure that nearly drove peregrine falcons, among others, to extinction.

We might even have to ask them: This process isn't new. Over the past few millennia, humans have deliberately and accidentally carried many species to new lives in places that might have taken them millions of years and a mountain of luck to reach in the past. Even if every person on Earth vanished tomorrow, an alien biogeographer would scratch its head(s) at the mysterious forces that somehow placed Norwegian rats in the Falklands, goats in the Galápagos, tigers in Texas, beavers in Tierra del Fuego, raccoons and rheas in Germany, macaques in Gibraltar, eucalyptus trees in California, rabbits and camels in Australia, and hedgehogs in New Zealand.

Coyotes, for instance: Levy 2012. In 2016, I saw a coyote standing calmly at a railroad crossing in the suburbs of Atlanta, waiting for a train to pass.

After surviving a quarter-billion years: Fossil ginkgoes date from as far back as 270 million years ago, making them older than any dinosaur. Ginkgoes have been cultivated in China for at least fifteen hundred years, and Europeans first saw them as ornamental trees in the imperial court of Japan in 1629 (where a ginkgo leaf is still the emblem of Japan's Tokyo prefecture). Whether any "wild" ginkgo trees survive at all is a matter of some debate; if any old-growth ginkgoes remain, they may live in the remote Dalou Mountains of the eastern Tibetan plateau, atop isolated limestone cliffs. Ginkgoes are only distantly related to other living trees, and their taxonomic affinities are somewhat uncertain; they seem to be closest to a primitive group of vascular plants called seed ferns.

In a city, it's not as if: And what is a seabird colony, with its thousands of shrieking, clucking, and cooing birds nesting mere inches from each other, if not an avian metropolis?

The bait seemed likely to work: Rexer-Huber et al. 2013. The Johnny rooks' regurgitated pellets glowed like nuggets of kryptonite under Kalinka's UV flashlight.

A nine-year-old striated caracara named Wendy: Horton 2017.

"ripping into a whole cooked chicken": McLennan 2018. The article includes several memorable quotes from astonished Londoners, including this one from Tareq

Ashry, who photographed Louie near Kilburn Grange Park: "There were several eyewitnesses stood around, wondering what it was. . . . It was walking along the road and then a car came by and it flew up to the top of the church on the High Road."

After ten days on the lam: A few other striated caracaras have notably gone walkabout from UK collections, including an unnamed adult bird that escaped from a falconry exhibit at a garden center and was last seen at the gravel pit at Little Marlow, on the banks of the Thames, where a bird enthusiast named Jim Rose photographed it on April 13, 2002. "The bird was chased by a Crow [sic] and hid under a bush where it stayed for some time," he wrote. "It was clearly very tame." He added that "it seemed to like wandering around on the ground and spent some time in an open field," and that it "had apparently escaped from the falconry centre at Thames Valley Garden Centre two days earlier when it was being flown . . . the owners were alerted from their after work drink in the Kings Head Pub and were soon on its trail" (www .bucksbirdclub.co.uk).

People would surely enjoy: BBC 2012.

In time, they might go from odd curiosities to celebrated mascots: Back in the New World, I can't help thinking that Johnny rooks might also do well in New York. It's not too difficult to imagine them bathing in the fountain in Washington Square after strutting down Fifth Avenue, or nesting under the Brooklyn Bridge (where they'd probably meet some resistance from our resident peregrines). Signs reading DO NOT FEED THE CARACARAS would need to be made, and they might have to be shooed out of sections of Central Park if they started digging up the flowerbeds. But there's a great deal of food in any city for a curious scavenger, especially one that doesn't mind walking. Striated caracaras wouldn't seem at all out of place soaring with gulls over the Statue of Liberty, gorging on discarded french fries at Coney Island, or picking through the day's deliveries at the Staten Island landfill.

there are good arguments: If you really had to introduce Johnny rooks somewhere else, the island of South Georgia, might be a good candidate–or better, at least, than most other options. It's immense, tall, and covered in seabirds and tussac grass; the only reason Johnny rooks aren't there now seems to be pure chance.

A friend at the American Museum of Natural History: Peter Capainolo, a senior museum specialist in the department of ornithology.

They were celebrating the annual feast: Which religious tradition has more successfully absorbed the other, in this case, is in the eye of the beholder.

They hailed from a world: If I'd been holding a mountain caracara on my arm, they might have cheered.

19. Land's End

Hudson was drawn: *The Land's End: A Naturalist's Impressions in West Cornwall,* originally published in 1908, is one of Hudson's most entertaining books — a long essay about the region and its people, whose antique dignity he saw nowhere else in his adopted country, though they were also prone to surprising outbreaks of whimsy. The tradition of "Guize-dancing" in the town of St. Ives, a midwinter celebration with pre-Christian roots, especially delighted him:

A considerable portion of the inhabitants turn out in masks and any fantastic costume they can manufacture out of old garments and bright coloured rags to parade the streets in groups and processions and to dance on the beach to some simple music till eleven o'clock or later. This goes on for a fortnight. Just think of it, men, women and children in their masks and gaudy get-up, parading the little narrow crooked muddy streets, for long hours in all weathers! And they are Methodists, good, sober people who crowd in to their numerous chapels on Sundays to sing hymns and listen to their preachers! (WHH, TLE 1923:165)

Unlike London: Some of Cornwall's cliffs predate even animal life; the outcrop of serpentine near the promontory of Lizard Head at Land's End is a rare example of exposed oceanic crust from the Precambrian era, the earliest part of Earth's geologic history.

"and gaze by the hour": WHH, TLE 1923:193.

"What has truly entered": WHH, IDIP 1893:225.

"It is true that": WHH, IDIP 1893: 225.

"The entire visible world": WHH, TLE 1923:193.

"It was as if the cloud shadows": WHH, FALA 1918:3. "Over it all my eyes could range at will," he continued, "choosing this or that point to dwell on, to examine it in all its details; and, in the case of some person known to me as a child, to follow his life till it ended or passed from sight; then to return to the same point again to repeat the process with other lives."

"clear grey and keen as a falcon's": WHH, FALA 1918:13.

"The outer garment": WHH, FALA 1918:14.

"the strangest of all strange beings": WHH, FALA 1918:16.

"Of all the people I have ever known": WHH, FALA 1918:313.

"In all the years of my life": WHH, BLP 1920:xi.

"soul-loneliness": Louise Chandler Moulton, a Bostonian poet who spent summers in London between 1876 and 1898, as quoted in Kernahan 1934.

"I would willingly give up": WHH, BAM 1923:170.

Birds of La Plata: Birds of La Plata (1920) was a revised version of the bird descriptions published in a book called Argentine Ornithology, which had been issued in 1889 in a (very) limited edition with taxonomic notes by Philip Sclater, the British Museum's South American bird specialist. Sclater's reputation far exceeded Hudson's at the time, and he took most of the credit (and profit) from the book; but Hudson's lively descriptions, which impressed Darwin, were the only parts of the book that weren't outdated thirty years later. Hudson published Birds of La Plata to make his accounts available to a new audience.

Like Far Away and Long Ago: In the introduction to Birds of La Plata, Hudson quoted a piercing letter from his older brother Edwin that arrived after the commercial failure of Hudson's first novel. "Why are you staying on in England," Edwin demanded, "and what can you do there?

I have looked at your romance and find it not unreadable, but this you must know is not your line — the one thing you are best fitted to do. Come back to your own country and come to me here in Cordova. These woods and sierras and rivers have a more plentiful and interesting bird life than that of the Pampas and Patagonia. Here I could help you and make it possible for you to dedicate your whole time to observation of the native birds and the fauna generally.

"I read the letter with a pang," Hudson wrote, "feeling that his judgement was right; but the message came too late; I had already made my choice" (WHH, BLP 1920:xiii). The pang must have been one of chagrin: it was Edwin who'd kindled the thought in his younger brother's mind that there might be a place for him across the sea when he lent him a new and controversial book called *The Origin of Species*.

Why it was too late for Hudson to return home is hard to say. Pride might have played a role, and marriage, too; Emily couldn't stand crossing the English Channel, much less the Atlantic Ocean, and Hudson probably assumed life in Argentina would be beyond her. But by the time he finished *Birds of La Plata*, Emily had nearly vanished from his life. She was living with family and caretakers in Worthing, suffering from dementia, and no longer knew him. They're buried side by side.

"When I think of that land": WHH, BLP 1920:xiv.

Virginia Woolf: Woolf tried to meet Hudson, but she was too late. On the day after his death, she wrote to a friend that "I was to have been taken to see Mr Hudson this winter by [Dorothy] Brett, who adored him. I think her sister was in love with him? No, I have got it wrong . . . Anyhow, I wish I had seen him" (Woolf 1975:549).

"one does not want to recommend it": Woolf 1918.

In the last months of his life: An acquaintance remembered seeing Hudson on his walks, and described him as "an impressive figure as he battled with the storm and bent to the wind" (Charles A. Hall, quoted in Tomalin 1982:229).

"The world is a shambles": Tomalin 1982:224.

The club he'd helped found: The RSPB has more than a million dues-paying members today. It maintains a network of nature reserves in Britain and supports wildlife conservation projects around the world. Hudson left most of his estate to it, and considered it his most important legacy.

"The power, beauty, and grace": WHH, BON 1920:23.

"One must shake off": WHH, AHRP 1923:78.

"The main thing": WHH, BON 1920:24.

622

Epilogue: Return of the Mexican Eagle

"Wherever it came from": McGowan 2015.

In 2016, for example: Swick 2017.

"It's just been stuck here": McGregor 2015.

They first came up from the south: See Ducey 1992 for a fossil crested caracara from Nebraska.

The caracaras retreated south: John James Audubon saw northern crested caracaras in 1831, two years before Darwin met them in Argentina. Audubon was at the height of his artistic powers, having just published the first series of plates for *Birds of America;* but the book was still a work in progress, and he spent months searching for new birds to illustrate (and sell). Later he would describe watching caracaras wade in shallow water to catch baby alligators, and perch like vultures with their wings outstretched in the sun; but his first instinct on seeing a new bird was to shoot. He was walking with his gun near the town of Saint Augustine, Florida, on November 24 when he saw an unknown bird "flying at a great elevation, and almost over my head.

Convinced that it was unknown to me, and bent on obtaining it, I followed it nearly a mile, when I saw it sail towards the earth, making for a place where a group of Vultures were engaged in devouring a dead horse. Walking up to the horse, I observed

the new bird alighted on it, and helping itself freely to the savoury meat beneath its
feet; but it evinced a degree of shyness
far greater than that of its associates, the
Turkey Buzzards and Carrion Crows. I
moved circuitously, until I came to a deep
ditch, along which I crawled, and went as
near to the bird as I possibly could.

The distance was too great for a clean
shot, so Audubon stood up, and the vultures took off; but the caracara surprised
him by deciding to approach him, circling
above him and looking down, "as if desir-
ous of forming acquaintance of me." He
shot again and missed, and the bird landed
hundreds of yards away in an open field.
Determined not to miss his chance, Audubon tried again.

I laid myself flat on the ground, and
crawled towards it, pushing my gun before me, amid burs and mud-holes, until I
reached the distance of about seventy-
five yards from it, when I stopped to observe its attitudes. The bird did not notice
me; he stood on a lump of flesh, tearing it
to pieces . . . until he had nearly swallowed the whole . . . I shot a second time,
and probably touched him; for he dropped
his burden, and made off in a direct
course across the St Sebastian River, with
alternate sailings and flappings, somewhat in the manner of a Vulture, but more

gracefully. He never uttered a cry, and I followed him wistfully with my eyes until he was quite out of sight.

Audubon pursued this bird for two days without success, until his assistant finally killed it and brought it to him. Audubon marveled at the caracara's strangeness, noting that its skin quickly changed color after death from yellow to a "near-livid purple," and that its stomach contained "the remains of a bull-frog, numerous hard-shelled worms and a quantity of horse and deer hair" — an odd meal for a bird that looked more like an eagle than a vulture. His painting duplicated it as a quarreling pair, so that both sides of it could be seen, and his written description returns several times to its surprising beauty in flight. "It sailed off in large circles," he wrote, "gliding in a very elegant manner, and now and then diving downwards and rising again" (Audubon 1832:350–352).

"any animal matter": Morrison 2006. Even this broad description doesn't give the full picture; northern crested caracaras were recently recorded eating the fruits of peach palms in Costa Rica (Rojas Carranza and Anderson 2019). Morrison has also been studying crested caracaras in Arizona, where they've learned to crack and eat pecans at pecan orchards, making them one of the very few nut-eating birds of prey.

These enterprising birds may offer us a glimpse of what ancient parrots might have been like as they began to shift to a vegetarian diet.

a family group squabbled: One of Morrison's colleagues put a photograph of one of these birds on the cover of *Southeastern Naturalist* after photoshopping out the container of cream cheese at the editors' request (Morrison et al. 2007).

In legends recounted: Métraux 1939, 1946.

" 'Now,' said Carancho": Métraux 1946:55.

No one has confirmed these rumors: Bonta et al. 2017 list black kites, whistling kites, and brown falcons as birds they believe likely to spread fire. Brown falcons are "true" falcons from Australia, more closely related to the peregrine than to G7. The authors speculate that early humans in Africa might have been inspired to use fire by watching birds.

The Aztecs called this bird: Gonzáles Block 2012.

The national bird of Mexico: Regardless of the identity of the bird on the Mexican flag, it's hard not to feel that crested caracaras are a fitting symbol for a resourceful and long-suffering people who have also defied extinction. Amerindians have suffered terribly from disease, war, and open persecution in both of the New Worlds, and many remain confined to reservations in the

United States and Canada. But they survived in greater numbers in the south — and some are beginning to make their way north again. The Amerindians crossing the border today often go unrecognized; many have lost their tribal histories and languages, and most speak Spanish. But their genetic signature is unmistakable, and the anti-immigrant paranoia seizing the United States today is, at least in part, just the newest iteration of the old European prejudice against the first true Americans.

in Mexico, most people know crested caracaras informally as *águilas:* Or occasionally *quebrantahuesos* ("bonebreakers"), a term reserved in Europe for bearded vultures. Only in southern South America is *carancho* a common name for crested caracaras.

Mexican eagles: Pearson 1917.

"San Jacinto Festival": NYCYankinTexas, "San Jacinto Festival Mexican Eagle (National Bird of Mexico Crested Cara Cara)," April 18, 2011, https://www.youtube.com.

Though they come from disparate lineages: Like caracaras, black vultures also don't mind walking. There are stories of injured black vultures who've adapted to a fully terrestrial life; one wild bird near Hawk Mountain Sanctuary in eastern Pennsylvania survived at least two harsh winters on a diet of household garbage and cat food.

In 2017–18, at least 1.3 million deer: State

Farm, "Deer Collision 2017–2018," October 1, 2018, https://www.statefarm.com.

Like the black caracaras: It's possible that the crested caracaras seen in the northern United States and Canada are Florida birds who've broken out of their ice age refuge, but it seems more likely that they're coming up via Texas and Arizona; the birds seen near Seattle and Vancouver probably didn't make their way there from the shores of Lake Okeechobee.

Black vultures were a rare sight: Dendis 2017.

"They like being around other animals": author interview with Ed McGowan, October 29, 2016.

in a cave forty miles from Bear Mountain: Steadman et al. 1987. Before the Pleistocene extinctions, California condors lived throughout North America, and their remains have been found from Nevada to New York State. The disappearance of the megafauna was a continent-wide catastrophe for them, as it was for the extinct teratorns; but they appear to have survived on the California coast by feeding on the carcasses of whales and seals washed up from the sea. Marine mammals were relatively unaffected by the mass extinctions caused by human hunters, and it would be thousands of years before people plundered the oceans with the same deadly efficiency they used on land.

BIBLIOGRAPHY

Abbott, Clinton G. "Closing History of the Guadalupe Caracara." *Condor* 35, no. 1 (1933): 10–14.

Adams, Mark P., and Robin W. Woods. "Mid-Holocene Falkland Islands Bird Bones from a Peat Deposit, Including a New Species of Caracara." *Emu-Austral Ornithology* 116, no. 4 (2016): 370–378.

Allen, Catherine J. *Foxboy: Intimacy and Aesthetics in Andean Stories.* Austin: University of Texas Press, 2011.

Alvarenga, Herculano, Washington Jones, and Andrés Rinderknecht. "The Youngest Record of Phorusrhacid Birds (Aves, Phorusrhacidae) from the Late Pleistocene of Uruguay." *Neues Jahrbuch für Geologie und Paläontologie-Abhandlungen* 256, no. 2 (2010): 229–234.

Alvarez, L. W., W. Alvarez, F. Asaro, H. V. Michel. "Extraterrestrial Cause for the Cretaceous-Tertiary Extinction." *Science* 208 (1980): 1095–1108.

Andermann, Jens. "Argentine Literature and the 'Conquest of the Desert,' 1872–1896." From *Relics and Selves: Iconographies of the National in Argentina, Brazil and Chile, 1880–1890.* Birkbeck College, University of London, 2004. http://www.bbk.ac.uk/ibamuseum.

Arnold, Denise Y., and J. D. D. Yapitamoya. "Fox-Talk: Addressing the Wild Beasts in the Southern Andes." *Latin American Indian Literatures Journal* 8, no. 1 (1992): 9–37.

Audubon, John James. *Ornithological Biography,* vol. 2. United States: n.p., 1832.

Averett, Nancy. "Birds Can Smell, and One Scientist Is Leading the Charge to Prove It." *Audubon,* January–February 2014. https://www.audubon.org.

Azara, Félix de. *Voyages dans l'Amérique méridionale depuis 1781 jusqu'en 1801.* N.p.: GA Walckenaer II, 1809.

Baker, John Alec. *The Peregrine.* Introduction by Robert MacFarlane. New York: New York Review of Books, 2005.

Barlow, Jos, Toby A. Gardner, Alexander C. Lees, Luke Parry, and Carlos A. Peres. "How Pristine Are Tropical Forests? An Ecological Perspective on the Pre-Columbian Human Footprint in Amazonia and Implications for Contemporary Conservation." *Biological Conservation* 151, no. 1 (2012): 45–49.

Barnard, Charles H. *Marooned: Being a Narrative of the Sufferings and Adventures of Captain Charles H. Barnard, Embracing an Account of the Seizure of His Vessel at the Falkland Islands, & C., 1812–1816.* Middletown, CT: Wesleyan University Press, 1979.

Becker, Jonathan J. "Revision of *'Falco' ramenta* Wetmore and the Neogene Evolution of the Falconidae." *Auk* 104, no. 2 (1987): 270–276.

Benton, Michael J. "The Origins of Modern Biodiversity on Land." *Philosophical Transactions of the Royal Society B: Biological Sciences* 365, no. 1558 (2010): 3667–3679.

Biondi, Laura Marina, María Susana Bó, and Aldo Iván Vassallo. "Experimental Assessment of Problem Solving by *Milvago chimango* (Aves: Falconiformes)." *Journal of Ethology* 26, no. 1 (2008): 113–118.

Biondi, Laura Marina, Germán Oscar García, María Susana Bó, and Aldo Iván Vassallo. "Social Learning in the Caracara Chimango, *Milvago chimango* (Aves: Falconiformes): An Age Comparison." *Ethology* 116, no. 8 (2010): 722–735.

Bond, Alan, and Judy Diamond. *Thinking Like a Parrot: Perspectives from the Wild.* Chicago: University of Chicago Press, 2019.

Bonta, Mark, R. Gosford, E. Eussen, N. Ferguson, E. Loveless, and M. Witwer. "Intentional Fire-Spreading by 'Firehawk' Raptors in Northern Australia." *Journal of Ethnobiology* 37, no. 4 (2017): 700–718.

Borrero, Luis Alberto. "The Elusive Evidence: The Archaeological Record of the South American Extinct Megafauna." In *American Megafaunal Extinctions at the End of the Pleistocene,* pp. 145–168. Netherlands: Springer, 2009.

British Broadcasting Corporation. "Meat Eaters." *The Life of Birds,* episode 4, 1998.

British Broadcasting Corporation. "The Unnatural History of London." *Natural World,* June 14, 2012, http://www.bbc.co.uk.

Brown, Leslie, and Dean Amadon. *Eagles, Hawks and Falcons of the World,* vol. 1. New York: Hamlyn Publishing Group, 1968.

Bruschini, Claudia, Rita Cervo, and Stefano Turillazzi. "Pheromones in Social Wasps." *Vitamins and Hormones: Pheromones* 83 (2010): 447–492.

Bulkan, Janette. " 'Original Lords of the Soil'? The Erosion of Amerindian Territorial Rights in Guyana." *Environment and History* 22, no. 3 (2016): 351–391.

Bush, Mark B., and Paulo E. de Oliveira. "The Rise and Fall of the Refugial Hypothesis of Amazonian Speciation: A Paleoecological Perspective." *Biota Neotropica* 6, no. 1 (2006).

Cage, John. *Silence.* Middletown, CT: Wesleyan University Press, 1961.

Cawkell, E. M., D. H. Maling, Mary Cawkell. *The Falkland Islands*. London: Macmillan, 1960.

Cenizo, M., J. I. Noriega, and M. A. Reguero. "A Stem Falconid Bird from the Lower Eocene of Antarctica and the Early Southern Radiation of the Falcons." *Journal of Ornithology* 157 (2016): 885–894.

Chatterjee, Sankar, R. Jack Templin, and Kenneth E. Campbell. "The Aerodynamics of *Argentavis*, the World's Largest Flying Bird from the Miocene of Argentina." *Proceedings of the National Academy of Sciences* 104, no. 30 (2007): 12398–12403.

Clapperton, C. *Quaternary Geology and Geomorphology of South America*. London: Elsevier, 1993.

Claramunt, Santiago, and Joel Cracraft. "A New Time Tree Reveals Earth History's Imprint on the Evolution of Modern Birds." *Science Advances* 1, no. 11 (2015): e1501005.

Clark, Gerry. *The Totorore Voyage: An Antarctic Adventure*. London: Ebury Press, 1988.

Clarke, Julia A., Sankar Chatterjee, Zhiheng Li, Tobias Riede, Federico Agnolin, Franz Goller, Marcelo P. Isasi, Daniel R. Martinioni, Francisco J. Mussel, and Fernando E. Novas. "Fossil Evidence of the Avian Vocal Organ from the Mesozoic." *Nature* 538, no. 7626 (2016): 502–505.

Clarke, Julia A., Daniel T. Ksepka, Rodolfo Salas-Gismondi, Ali J. Altamirano, Matthew D. Shawkey, Liliana D'Alba, Jakob Vinther, Thomas J. DeVries, and Patrice Baby. "Fossil Evidence for Evolution of the Shape and Color of Penguin Feathers." *Science* 330, no. 6006 (2010): 954–957.

Claudia, J., Miguel Griffin, John M. McArthur, Sergio Martínez, and Matthew F. Thirlwall. "Evidence for Early Pliocene and Late Miocene Transgressions in Southern Patagonia (Argentina): 87Sr/86Sr Ages of the Pectinid *'Chlamys' actinodes* (Sowerby)." *Journal of South American Earth Sciences* 47 (2013): 220–229.

Cobo, Bernabé. *History of the Inca Empire: An Account of the Indians' Customs and Their Origin, Together with a Treatise on Inca Legends, History, and Social Institutions.* Austin: University of Texas Press, 2010.

Conniff, Richard, "When Continental Drift Was Considered Pseudoscience," *Smithsonian Magazine,* June 2012, http://www.smithsonian.com.

Coulson, Jennifer O., Emmanuel Rondeau, and Manuel Caravaca. "Yellow-Headed Caracara and Black Vulture Cleaning Baird's Tapir." *Journal of Raptor Research* 52, no. 1 (2018): 104–107.

Cowper, William. "The Solitude of Alexander Selkirk" in *Poems: by William Cowper, of the*

Inner Temple, Esq. London: J. Johnson, 1782.

Cuthbert, R. J., H. Louw, G. Parker, K. Rexer-Huber, and P. Visser. "Observations of Mice Predation on Dark-Mantled Sooty Albatross and Atlantic Yellow-Nosed Albatross Chicks at Gough Island." *Antarctic Science* 25, no. 6 (2013): 763–766.

Dalrymple, G. Brent. "The Age of the Earth in the Twentieth Century: A Problem (Mostly) Solved." *Geological Society, London, Special Publications* 190, no. 1 (2001): 205–221.

Darwin, Charles R. *Charles Darwin and the Voyage of the Beagle.* Edited by Nora Barlow. London: Pilot Press, 1945.

———. *Darwin's Ornithological Notes.* Edited with an introduction, notes, and appendix by Nora Barlow. London: British Museum of Natural History, 1963.

———. *The Descent of Man, and Selection in Relation to Sex,* 2nd ed. London: John Murray, 1874.

———. *Journal of Researches into the Natural History and Geology of the Countries Visited During the Voyage of H.M.S. Beagle Round the World, Under the Command of Capt. Fitz Roy, R.N.* 2d edition. London: John Murray, 1845.

———. *On the Origin of Species by Means of Natural Selection, or The Preservation of Fa-*

voured *Races in the Struggle for Life*. 2nd ed. London: John Murray, 1860.

Dendis, William. "Black Vultures, Formerly a Southern Bird, Now a Regular Sight in the Hudson Valley." *hv1,* July 28, 2017, https://www.hudsonvalleyone.com.

de Vries, Tjitte, Juan Black, C. Solís, and C. Hernández. "Historia natural del Curiquingue (Phalcoboenus carunculatus) en los páramos del Antisana y Cotopaxi del Ecuador." Ediciones de la Universidad Católica de Quito, Ecuador (1983): 1–83.

de Waal, Frans. *Are We Smart Enough to Know How Smart Animals Are?* New York: W. W. Norton, 2016.

Donovan, Michael P., Ari Iglesias, Peter Wilf, Conrad C. Labandeira, and N. Rubén Cúneo. "Rapid Recovery of Patagonian Plant-Insect Associations After the End-Cretaceous Extinction." *Nature Ecology & Evolution* 1, no. 1 (2016): 1–5.

Ducey, James E. "Fossil Birds of the Nebraska Region." *Transactions of the Nebraska Academy of Sciences* 19 (1992): 83–96.

Dumbacher, John P., and Barbara West. "Collecting Galápagos and the Pacific: How Rollo Howard Beck Shaped Our Understanding of Evolution." *Proceedings of the California Academy of Sciences* 61, no. 2 (2010): 211.

Duncan, Richard P., Alison G. Boyer, and Tim M. Blackburn. "Magnitude and Variation of Prehistoric Bird Extinctions in the Pacific." *Proceedings of the National Academy of Sciences* 110, no. 16 (2013): 6436–6441.

Ekman, Jan, and Per G.P. Ericson. "Out of Gondwanaland: The Evolutionary History of Cooperative Breeding and Social Behaviour Among Crows, Magpies, Jays and Allies." *Proceedings of the Royal Society B: Biological Sciences* 273, no. 1590 (2006): 1117–1125.

Epstein, Jacob. *Let There Be Sculpture.* New York: G. P. Putnam's Sons, 1940.

Ericson, Per G. P., Les Christidis, Alan Cooper, Martin Irestedt, Jennifer Jackson, Ulf S. Johansson, and Janette A. Norman. "A Gondwanan Origin of Passerine Birds Supported by DNA Sequences of the Endemic New Zealand Wrens." *Proceedings of the Royal Society of London. Series B: Biological Sciences* 269, no. 1488 (2002): 235–241.

Fariña, Richard A., Sergio F. Vizcaíno, and Gerry De Iuliis. *Megafauna: Giant Beasts of Pleistocene South America.* Bloomington: Indiana University Press, 2013.

Figueroa, R., and A. Ricardo. "El rapaz olvidado — ¿Por qué hay tan pocos estudios sobre la historia natural y ecología básica del tiuque (*Milvago chimango*) en Chile?" *Boletín Chileno de Ornitología* 21, no. 1–2 (2015): 103–118.

Flannery, Tim. *The Eternal Frontier: An Ecological History of North America and Its Peoples.* New York: Grove Press, 2002.

Flores, Carlos. *Les lliçons de Gaudí.* Translated by Glòria Bohigas. Barcelona: Empúries, 2002.

Flores, Marcelo. "Invasive Species Are Killing Off Rapa Nui's Native Marine Birds," *MoeVarua,* October 5, 2016, https://www.moevarua.com.

Fonkén, M. S. Maldonado. "An Introduction to the *Bofedales* of the Peruvian High Andes." *Mires and Peat* 15, no. 5 (2014).

Frank, Heinrich Theodor, L. D. Oliveira, Fabrício Nazzari Vicroski, Rogério Breier, N. G. Pasqualon, T. Araújo, F. S. C. Buchmann et al. "The Complex History of a Sandstone-Hosted Cave in the State of Santa Catarina, Brazil." *Espeleo-Tema* 23, no. 2 (2012): 87–101.

Fuchs, Jérôme, Jeff A. Johnson, and David P. Mindell. "Molecular Systematics of the Caracaras and Allies (Falconidae: Polyborinae) Inferred from Mitochondrial and Nuclear Sequence Data." *Ibis* 154, no. 3 (2012): 520–532.

———. "Rapid Diversification of Falcons (Aves: Falconidae) Due to Expansion of Open Habitats in the Late Miocene." *Mo-*

lecular *Phylogenetics and Evolution* 82 (2015): 166–182.

Funston, Gregory F., Philip J. Currie, David A. Eberth, Michael J. Ryan, Tsogtbaatar Chinzorig, Demchig Badamgarav, and Nicholas R. Longrich. "The First Oviraptorosaur (Dinosauria: Theropoda) Bonebed: Evidence of Gregarious Behaviour in a Maniraptoran Theropod." *Scientific Reports* 6 (2016): 35782.

Garcilaso de la Vega. *Comentarios Reales Que Tratan Del Origen De Los Yncas, Reyes Que Fueron Del Peru, De Su Idolatria, Leyes, Y Govierno en paz y en guerra: de sus vidas y conquistas, y de todo lo que fue aquel Imperio y su Republica, antes que los Españoles pasaran a el.* Lisbon: Pedro Crasbeeck, 1609.

Goeldi, Emil. "Ornithological Results of an Expedition up the Capim River, State of Pará, with Critical Remarks on the Cracidae of Lower Amazonia." *Ibis* (1903): 472–500.

Goin, Francisco J., Agustín G. Martinelli, Sergio Soto-Acuña, Emma C. Vieytes, Leslie M. E. Manríquez, Roy A. Fernández, Juan Pablo Pino, Cristine Trevisan, Jonatan Kaluza, Marcelo A. Reguero, Marcelo Leppe, Héctor Ortiz, David Rubilar-Rogers, and Alexander O. Vargas. "First Mesozoic Mammal from Chile: the Southernmost Record of a Late Cretaceous Gondwanatherian." *Boletín del Museo Nacional de Historia Natural, Chile* 69, no. 1 (2020): 5–31.

Golgowski, Nina. "See It: Entomologist Films Terrifying Encounter with Giant Yellow Jacket Nest — as Tall as a Man." *New York Daily News,* June 24, 2013, https://www.ny dailynews.com.

González Block, Miguel A., "The *Iztaccuauhtli* and the Mexican Eagle: *Cuauhtli* or Golden Eagle?" *Mexican Archaeology* no. 70 (2012): 60–65.

Gould, John. "Observations on the Raptorial Birds in Mr. Darwin's Collection, with Characters of the New Species." In *Proceedings of the Zoological Society of London,* vol. 5 (1837): 9–11.

Grayson, Donald. *The Great Basin: A Natural Prehistory.* Berkeley: University of California Press, 2011.

Gunderman, Richard. "Bees Are the Second Most Lethal Animals in America." *Quartz,* August 21, 2015, https://www.quartz.com.

Hammond, David S., Valéry Gond, Benoît De Thoisy, Pierre-Michel Forget, and Bart P. E. DeDijn. "Causes and Consequences of a Tropical Forest Gold Rush in the Guiana Shield, South America." *AMBIO: A Journal of the Human Environment* 36, no. 8 (2007): 661–670.

Harrington, Katie J., and Keith L. Bildstein. "Predation of Southern Red Octopus (*Enteroctopus megalocyathus*) by Striated Caracaras (*Phalcoboenus australis*) in the Falkland Islands." *Journal of Raptor Research* 53, no. 2 (2019): 220–22.

Heinrich, Bernd. *Mind of the Raven.* New York: HarperCollins, 1999.

Hill, Len, and Emma Wood. *Penguin Millionaire: The Story of Birdland.* Newton Abbot, England: David & Charles, 1976.

Holldöbler, Bert, and Edward O. Wilson. *The Ants.* Cambridge, MA: Harvard University Press, 1990.

Hoorn, Carina, F. P. Wesselingh, H. Ter Steege, M. A. Bermudez, A. Mora, J. Sevink, Isabel Sanmartín, et al. "Amazonia Through Time: Andean Uplift, Climate Change, Landscape Evolution, and Biodiversity." *Science* 330, no. 6006 (2010): 927–931.

Horton, Helena. "Rare Bird of Prey Escapes from Dartmoor Zoo — Nine Months after a Lynx Broke Out of Its Enclosure." *Telegraph,* March 29, 2017, https://www.telegraph.co.uk.

Housse, P. R. "El tiuque cordillerano (*Phalcoboenus megalopterus*) (Meyen)." *Revista Chilena de Historia Natural* 41 (1938): 131–134.

Hu, Dongyu, Julia A. Clarke, Chad M. Eliason, Rui Qiu, Quanguo Li, Matthew D. Shawkey, Cuilin Zhao, Liliana D'Alba, Jinkai Jiang, and Xing Xu. "A Bony-Crested Jurassic Dinosaur with Evidence of Iridescent Plumage Highlights Complexity in Early Paravian Evolution." *Nature Communications* 9, no. 1 (2018): 1–12.

Hudson, William Henry. *Birds and Man.* New York: Alfred A. Knopf, 1923.

———. *Birds in London.* London: Longmans, Green and Company, 1898.

———. *Birds of La Plata.* 2 vols. New York: E. P. Dutton, 1920.

———. *The Book of a Naturalist.* New York: George H. Doran, 1919.

———. *Far Away and Long Ago: A History of My Early Life.* New York: E. P. Dutton, 1918.

———. *Green Mansions: A Romance of the Tropical Forest.* New York: Alfred A. Knopf, 1916.

———. *A Hind in Richmond Park.* The Collected Works of W. H. Hudson. London: J. M. Dent, 1923.

———. *Idle Days in Patagonia.* London: Chapman and Hall, 1893.

———. *The Land's End: A Naturalist's Impressions in West Cornwall.* The Collected Works of W. H. Hudson. London: J. M. Dent, 1923.

———. *Men, Books and Birds: Letters to a Friend.* London: E. Nash & Grayson, 1925.

————. *The Naturalist in La Plata.* London: Chapman and Hall, 1892.

Hulton, Nicholas R. J., R. S. Purves, R. D. McCulloch, David E. Sugden, and Michael J. Bentley. "The Last Glacial Maximum and Deglaciation in Southern South America." *Quaternary Science Reviews* 21, no. 1–3 (2002): 233–241.

Humboldt, Alexander von, and Aimé Bonpland. *Personal Narrative of Travels to the Equinoctial Regions of America During the Years 1799–1804.* London: George Rutledge and Sons, 1895.

International Union for Conservation of Nature. *The IUCN Red List of Threatened Species.* May 2020, https://www.iucnredlist .org.

James, Matthew J. *Collecting Evolution: The Galápagos Expedition That Vindicated Darwin.* Oxford: Oxford University Press, 2019.

Jaramillo, Carlos, Ingrid Romero, Carlos D'Apolito, German Bayona, Edward Duarte, Stephen Louwye, Jaime Escobar, et al. "Miocene Flooding Events of Western Amazonia." *Science Advances* 3, no. 5 (2017): e1601693.

Jefferies, Richard. *The Story of My Heart: My Autobiography.* London: Longmans, Green and Co., 1901.

Johnson, A. W. "The Giant Coot *Fulica gigantea* Eydoux and Souleyet." *Bulletin of* the *British Ornithologists' Club* 84 (1964): 170–172.

Johnson, A. W., F. Behn, and W. R. Millie. "The South American Flamingos." *Condor* 60, no. 5 (1958): 289–299.

Johnson, Alfred William, and J. D. Goodall. "Birds of Chile and Adjacent Regions of Argentina, Bolivia, and Peru." N.p.: Platt Establecimientos Gráficos, 1965.

Jones, Jason. "Cooperative Foraging in the Mountain Caracara in Peru." *Wilson Bulletin* (1999): 437–439.

Jones, Washington, Andrés Rinderknecht, Rafael Migotto, and R. Ernesto Blanco. "Body Mass Estimations and Paleobiological Inferences on a New Species of Large Caracara (Aves, Falconidae) from the Late Pleistocene of Uruguay." *Journal of Paleontology* 87, no. 1 (2013): 151–158.

Jones, Washington W., Marcos M. Cenizo, Federico L. Agnolin, Andrés Rinderknecht, and R. Ernesto Blanco. "The Largest Known Falconid." *Neues Jahrbuch für Geologie und Paläontologie-Abhandlungen* 277, no. 3 (2015): 361–372.

Karlson, Peter, and Martin Lüscher. " 'Pheromones': A New Term for a Class of Biologically Active Substances." *Nature* 183, no. 4653 (1959): 55–56.

Keitt, Bradford, Steve Junak, Luciana Luna Mendoza, and A. Aguirre. "The Restoration of Guadalupe Island." *Fremontia* 33, no. 4 (2005): 20–25.

Kernahan, Coulson. "W. H. Hudson as I Knew Him." *The Nature Lover,* May 1934.

Kjær, Kurt H., Nicolaj K. Larsen, Tobias Binder, Anders A. Bjørk, Olaf Eisen, Mark A. Fahnestock, Svend Funder, et al. "A Large Impact Crater Beneath Hiawatha Glacier in Northwest Greenland." *Science Advances* 4, no. 11 (2018).

Kracht, Matthew. *A Field Guide to Dumb Birds of North America.* San Francisco: Chronicle Books, 2019.

Krauss, Clifford. "The $20 Billion Question for Guyana." *New York Times,* July 20, 2018.

Kricher, John. *The New Neotropical Companion.* Princeton, NJ: Princeton University Press, 2017.

Kristan III, William B., William I. Boarman, and John J. Crayon. "Diet Composition of Common Ravens across the Urban-Wildland Interface of the West Mojave Desert." *Wildlife Society Bulletin* 32, no. 1 (2004): 244–253.

Ksepka, D. T., T. A. Stidham, and T. E. Williamson. "Early Paleocene Landbird Supports Rapid Phylogenetic and Morphological Diversification of Crown Birds after the K-Pg Mass Extinction." *Proceedings of the National Academy of Sciences* 114, no. 30

(2017): 8047–8052.

Kundu, Samit, Carl G. Jones, Robert P. Prys-Jones, and Jim J. Groombridge. "The Evolution of the Indian Ocean Parrots (Psittaciformes): Extinction, Adaptive Radiation and Eustacy." *Molecular Phylogenetics and Evolution* 62, no. 1 (2012): 296–305.

Laybourne, Roxie C. "Collision Between a Vulture and an Aircraft at an Altitude of 37,000 Feet." *Wilson Bulletin* 86, no. 4 (1974): 461–462.

Legendre, Lucas A., David Rubilar-Rogers, Grace M. Musser, Sarah N. Davis, Rodrigo A. Otero, Alexander O. Vargas, and Julia A. Clarke. "A Giant Soft-Shelled Egg from the Late Cretaceous of Antarctica." *Nature* 583, no. 7816 (2020): 411–414.

Lendvai, Ádám Z., Veronika Bókony, Frédéric Angelier, Olivier Chastel, and Daniel Sol. "Do Smart Birds Stress Less? An Interspecific Relationship between Brain Size and Corticosterone Levels." *Proceedings of the Royal Society B: Biological Sciences* 280, no. 1770 (2013): 20131734.

Levy, Sharon. "Rise of the Coyote: The New Top Dog." *Nature,* May 16, 2012, https://www.nature.com.

Lewis, Daniel. *The Feathery Tribe: Robert Ridgway and the Modern Study of Birds.* New Haven, CT: Yale University Press, 2012.

Li, Quanguo, Ke-Qin Gao, Qingjin Meng,

Julia A. Clarke, Matthew D. Shawkey, Liliana D'Alba, Rui Pei, Mick Ellison, Mark A. Norell, and Jakob Vinther. "Reconstruction of *Microraptor* and the Evolution of Iridescent Plumage." *Science* 335, no. 6073 (2012): 1215–1219.

Lindo, John, Randall Haas, Courtney Hofman, Mario Apata, Mauricio Moraga, Ricardo A. Verdugo, James T. Watson, et al. "The Genetic Prehistory of the Andean Highlands 7000 Years BP through European Contact." *Science Advances* 4, no. 11 (2018): eaau4921.

Livermore, Roy, Claus-Dieter Hillenbrand, Mike Meredith, and Graeme Eagles. "Drake Passage and Cenozoic Climate: An Open and Shut Case?" *Geochemistry, Geophysics, Geosystems* 8, no. 1 (2007).

Longrich, Nicholas R., Tim Tokaryk, and Daniel J. Field. "Mass Extinction of Birds at the Cretaceous-Paleogene (K-Pg) Boundary." *Proceedings of the National Academy of Sciences* 108, no. 37 (2011): 15253–15257.

López, Alejandro, and Sixto Giménez Benítez. "The Milky Way and Its Structuring Functions in the Worldview of the Mocoví of Gran Chaco." *Archaeologia Baltica* 10 (2008): 21–24.

Lyons, S. Kathleen, Felisa A. Smith, and James H. Brown. "Of Mice, Mastodons and

Men: Human-Mediated Extinctions on Four Continents." *Evolutionary Ecology Research* 6, no. 3 (2004): 339–358.

Mann, Charles C. *1491: New Revelations of the Americas before Columbus.* New York: Alfred A. Knopf, 2005.

Manríquez, Leslie M. E., Ernesto L. C. Lavina, Roy A. Fernández, Cristine Trevisan, and Marcelo A. Leppe. "Campanian-Maastrichtian and Eocene Stratigraphic Architecture, Facies Analysis, and Paleoenvironmental Evolution of the Northern Magallanes Basin (Chilean Patagonia)." *Journal of South American Earth Sciences* 93 (2019): 102–118.

Marín, Manuel, Alejandro Kusch, David Oehler, and Scott Drieschman. "Distribution, Breeding and Status of the Striated Caracara *Phalcoboenus australis* (Gmelin, 1788) in Southern Chile." *Anales del Instituto de la Patagonia* 34 (2006): 65–74.

Marzluff, John, and Tony Angell. *Gifts of the Crow: How Perception, Emotion, and Thought Allow Smart Birds to Behave Like Humans.* New York: Simon and Schuster, 2013.

Matthiessen, Peter. *The Snow Leopard.* New York: Viking Press, 1978.

McCann, Sean. "Red-Throated Caracaras Are Way Cool because . . ." Lecture at Beaty Biodiversity Museum, February 18, 2014, https://www.youtube.com.

McCann, Sean, Onour Moeri, Tanya Jones, Sean O'Donnell, and Gerhard Gries. "Nesting and Nest-Provisioning of the Red-Throated Caracara (*Ibycter americanus*) in Central French Guiana." *Journal of Raptor Research* 44, no. 3 (2010): 236–240.

McCann, Sean, Onour Moeri, Tanya Jones, Catherine Scott, Grigori Khaskin, Regine Gries, Sean O'Donnell, and Gerhard Gries. "Strike Fast, Strike Hard: The Red-Throated Caracara Exploits Absconding Behavior of Social Wasps During Nest Predation." *PloS One* 8, no. 12 (2013).

McCann, Sean, C. Scott, T. Jones, O. Moeri, S. O'Donnell, and G. Gries. "Red-Throated Caracara, a Falconid Raptor, Rivals Predatory Impact of Army Ants on Social Wasps." *Insectes sociaux* 62, no. 1 (2015): 101–108.

McGowan, Ed. "Special Sighting: A Crested Caracara at Bear Mountain." *New York State Parks* (blog), February 13, 2015, https://nystateparks.blog.

McGregor, Phlis. "Nova Scotia Birdwatchers Delighted by Visits from Rare Birds." CBC News, October 15, 2015, https://www.cbc.ca.

McIntyre, Sarah R. N., Charles H. Lineweaver, Colin P. Groves, and Aditya Chopra. "Global Biogeography Since Pangaea." *Proceedings of the Royal Society B: Biological Sciences* 284, no. 1856 (2017):

20170716.

McLennan, William. "Exclusive: Bird of Prey Escapes London Zoo and Flies to Park in Kilburn." *Camden New Journal,* January 18, 2018, https://www.camdennewjournal.com.

Mearns, Barbara, and Richard Mearns. *The Bird Collectors.* Cambridge, MA: Academic Press, 1998.

Metcalf, Jessica L., Chris Turney, Ross Barnett, Fabiana Martin, Sarah C. Bray, Julia T. Vilstrup, Ludovic Orlando, et al. "Synergistic Roles of Climate Warming and Human Occupation in Patagonian Megafaunal Extinctions during the Last Deglaciation." *Science Advances* 2, no. 6 (2016): e1501682.

Métraux, Alfred. *Myths and Tales of the Matako Indians (the Gran Chaco, Argentina).* Gothenburg, Sweden: Gothenburg Ethnographical Museum, 1939.

———. *Myths of the Toba and Pilaga Indians of the Gran Chaco.* Philadelphia: American Folklore Society, 1946.

Moreno-Bernal, Jorge W. "Size and Paleoecology of Giant Miocene South American Crocodiles (Archosauria: Crocodylia)." *Journal of Vertebrate Paleontology* 27, no. 3 (2007).

Morrison, Joan L. "Crested Caracara," in *The Birds of North America,* no. 249. Edited by A. Poole and F. Gill. Philadelphia: Academy of Natural Sciences, and Washington, DC: American Ornithologists' Union, 2006.

Morrison, Joan L., J. Abrams, M. Deyrup, T. Eisner, and M. McMillian. "Noxious Menu: Chemically Protected Insects in the Diet of the Crested Caracara." *Southeastern Naturalist* 6, no. 1 (2007): 1–14.

Naish, Darren. "Obscure Fossil Mammals of Island South America: Thomashuxleya and the Other Isotemnids." *Scientific American* online, July 21, 2012, https://www.scientific american.com.

Navarro-Sigüenza, Adolfo G., Hernán Vázquez-Miranda, Germán Hernández-Alonso, Erick A. García-Trejo, and Luis A. Sánchez-González. "Complex Biogeographic Scenarios Revealed in the Diversification of the Largest Woodpecker Radiation in the New World." *Molecular Phylogenetics and Evolution* 112 (2017): 53–67.

Neruda, Pablo. *Art of Birds.* Translated by Jack Schmitt. Austin: University of Texas Press, 1985.

Newton, Ian. *Speciation and Biogeography of Birds.* New York: Elsevier Science, 2003.

Ni, X., D. L. Gebo, M. Dagosto, J. Meng, P. Tafforeau, J. J. Flynn, K. C. Beard. "The Oldest Known Primate Skeleton and Early Haplorrhine Evolution." *Nature* 498

(2013): 60–64.

Nilsson, Maria A., Gennady Churakov, Mirjam Sommer, Ngoc Van Tran, Anja Zemann, Jürgen Brosius, and Jürgen Schmitz. "Tracking Marsupial Evolution Using Archaic Genomic Retroposon Insertions." *PLoS Biology* 8, no. 7 (2010).

Nores, Manuel. "The Implications of Tertiary and Quaternary Sea Level Rise Events for Avian Distribution Patterns in the Lowlands of Northern South America." *Global Ecology and Biogeography* 13, no. 2 (2004): 149–161.

O'Donnell, Sean, and Robert L. Jeanne. "The Nest as Fortress: Defensive Behavior of Polybia Emaciata, a Mud-Nesting Eusocial Wasp." *Journal of Insect Science* 2, no. 1 (2002).

Olson, Storrs L. "A New Species of Large, Terrestrial Caracara from Holocene Deposits in Southern Jamaica (Aves: Falconidae)." *Journal of Raptor Research* 42, no. 4 (2008): 265–272.

———. "A New Species of *Milvago* from Hispaniola, with Notes on Other Fossil Caracaras from the West Indies (Aves: Falconidae)." *Proceedings of the Biological Society of Washington* 88:33 (1976): 355–366.

Park, Madison, Dayu Zhang, and Elizabeth Lindau. "Deadly Giant Hornets Kill 42 People in China." CNN, October 4, 2013, https://www.cnn.com.

Payne, John R. *W. H. Hudson: A Bibliography.* Folkestone, England: Dawson, 1977.

Pearson, T. Gilbert. "Caracara, the Mexican Eagle." *Art World* 3, no. 3 (1917): 264.

Pepperberg, Irene. *Alex & Me: How a Scientist and a Parrot Discovered a Hidden World of Animal Intelligence — and Formed a Deep Bond in the Process.* New York: HarperCollins, 2009.

Perkins, Sid. "Why the Amazon Flows Backward." *Science,* July 15, 2014, https://www.sciencemag.org.

Peteya, Jennifer A., Julia A. Clarke, Quanguo Li, Ke-Qin Gao, and Matthew D. Shawkey. "The Plumage and Colouration of an Enantiornithine Bird from the Early Cretaceous of China." *Palaeontology* 60, no. 1 (2017): 55–71.

Posth, Cosimo, Nathan Nakatsuka, Iosif Lazaridis, Pontus Skoglund, Swapan Mallick, Thiseas C. Lamnidis, Nadin Rohland, et al. "Reconstructing the Deep Population History of Central and South America." *Cell* 175, no. 5 (2018): 1185–1197.

Potier, Simon, Francesco Bonadonna, Almut Kelber, and Olivier Duriez. "Visual Acuity in an Opportunistic Raptor, the Chimango Caracara (*Milvago chimango*)." *Physiology & Behavior* 157 (2016): 125–128.

Potier, Simon, Olivier Duriez, Aurélie

Célérier, Jean-Louis Liegeois, and Francesco Bonadonna. "Sight or Smell: Which Senses Do Scavenging Raptors Use to Find Food?" *Animal Cognition* 22, no. 1 (2019): 49–59.

Prado, José L., Cayetana Martínez-Maza, and María T. Alberdi. "Megafauna Extinction in South America: A New Chronology for the Argentine Pampas." *Palaeogeography, Palaeoclimatology, Palaeoecology* 425 (2015): 41–49.

Prum, Richard O., Jacob S. Berv, Alex Dornburg, Daniel J. Field, Jeffrey P. Townsend, Emily Moriarty Lemmon, and Alan R. Lemmon. "A Comprehensive Phylogeny of Birds (Aves) Using Targeted Next-Generation DNA Sequencing." *Nature* 526, no. 7574 (2015): 569–573.

Pyle, R. L., and P. Pyle. *The Birds of the Hawaiian Islands: Occurrence, History, Distribution, and Status,* version 2, January 1, 2017. Honolulu: Bernice P. Bishop Museum. http://hbs.bishopmuseum.org.

Quammen, David. *The Song of the Dodo: Island Biogeography in an Age of Extinctions.* New York: Scribner, 1996.

Raleigh, Walter. *The Discovery of the Large, Rich, and Beautiful Empire of Guiana, with a Relation of the Great and Golden City of Manoa (Which the Spaniards Call El Dorado), Etc., Performed in the Year 1595 by Sir W.*

Ralegh, Knt., Captain of Her Majesty's Guard, Lord Warden of the Stannaries, and Her Highness's Lieutenant-General of the County of Cornwall, vol. 3. London: Hakluyt Society, 1848.

Rexer-Huber, Kalinka, Graham C. Parker, Micky Reeves, Andrew J. Stanworth, and Richard J. Cuthbert. "Winter Ecology of House Mice and the Prospects for Their Eradication from Steeple Jason (Falkland Islands)." *Polar Biology* 36, no. 12 (2013): 1791–1797.

Riede, Tobias, Chad M. Eliason, Edward H. Miller, Franz Goller, and Julia A. Clarke. "Coos, Booms, and Hoots: The Evolution of Closed-Mouth Vocal Behavior in Birds." *Evolution* 70, no. 8 (2016): 1734–1746.

Rignot, Eric, Jérémie Mouginot, Bernd Scheuchl, Michiel van den Broeke, Melchior J. van Wessem, and Mathieu Morlighem. "Four Decades of Antarctic Ice Sheet Mass Balance from 1979–2017." *Proceedings of the National Academy of Sciences* 116, no. 4 (2019): 1095–1103.

Roberts, Morley. *W. H. Hudson: A Portrait.* New York: E. P. Dutton, 1924.

Rojas Carranza, Alberth, and Nicole Anderson. "First Record of Consumption of Peach Palm Fruits (*Bactris gasipaes*) by the Crested Caracara (*Caracara cheriway*) in Costa Rica." *Spizaetus* 28 (2019): 2–8.

Ross, Kenneth G., and Robert W. Matthews, eds. *The Social Biology of Wasps.* Ithaca, NY: Cornell University Press, 2018.

Ross, William Stewart. *Roses and Rue: Being Random Notes and Sketches.* London: W. Stewart & Company, 1890.

Roth, Kenneth M. *Annihilating Difference: The Anthropology of Genocide.* Berkeley: University of California Press, 2002.

San Diego Natural History Museum website. "Isla Guadalupe Expedition (2000)." https://www.sdnhm.org.

Schulte, Peter, Laia Alegret, Ignacio Arenillas, José A. Arz, Penny J. Barton, Paul R. Bown, Timothy J. Bralower, et al. "The Chicxulub Asteroid Impact and Mass Extinction at the Cretaceous-Paleogene Boundary." *Science* 327, no. 5970 (2010): 1214–1218.

Scott, Charles T. "New Evidence of American Indian Riddles." *Journal of American Folklore* 76, no. 301 (1963): 236–241.

Scott, Robert F. *Tragedy and Triumph: The Journals of Captain R.F. Scott's Last Polar Expedition.* [Facsimile reprint of 1913 publication.] London: Konecky & Konecky, 1993.

Sheehan, Michael J., and Elizabeth A. Tibbetts. "Specialized Face Learning Is Associated with Individual Recognition in Paper Wasps." *Science* 334, no. 6060 (2011):

1272–1275.

Sick, Helmut. *Birds in Brazil.* Princeton, NJ: Princeton University Press, 1993.

Simpson, George Gaylord. *Splendid Isolation: The Curious History of South American Mammals.* New Haven, CT: Yale University Press, 1980.

Skutch, A. F. "The Scourge of the Wasps." *Animal Kingdom* 62 (1959): 8–13.

Slater, Graham J., Olaf Thalmann, Jennifer A. Leonard, Rena M. Schweizer, Klaus-Peter Koepfli, John P. Pollinger, Nicolas J. Rawlence, Jeremy J. Austin, Alan Cooper, and Robert K. Wayne. "Evolutionary History of the Falklands Wolf." *Current Biology* 19, no. 20 (2009): R937–R938.

Smith, R. I. Lewis, and Peter A. Prince. "The Natural History of Beauchêne Island." *Biological Journal of the Linnean Society* 24, no. 3 (1985): 233–283.

Snell-Rood, Emilie C., and Naomi Wick. "Anthropogenic Environments Exert Variable Selection on Cranial Capacity in Mammals." *Proceedings of the Royal Society B: Biological Sciences* 280, no. 1769 (2013): 20131384.

Society of Vertebrate Paleontology. "Ice Age Era Bones Recovered from Underwater Caves in Mexico." *ScienceDaily,* August 24, 2017, https://www.sciencedaily.com.

Soibelzon, Leopoldo H., and Blaine W. Schubert. "The Largest Known Bear, *Arctotherium angustidens,* from the Early Pleistocene Pampean Region of Argentina: With a Discussion of Size and Diet Trends in Bears." *Journal of Paleontology* 85, no. 1 (2011): 69–75.

Solaro, Claudina, and José Hernán Sarasola. "Nest-Spacing, Not Human Presence, Influences the Breeding of Chimango Caracaras (*Milvago chimango*) in a Peri-urban Reserve." *Emu* 115, no. 1 (2015): 72–75.

Somavilla, Alexandre, Itanna Oliveira Fernandes, Marcio Luiz de Oliveira, and Orlando Tobias Silveira. "Association Among Wasps' Colonies, Ants and Birds in Central Amazonia." *Biota Neotropica* 13, no. 2 (2013): 308–313.

Sonnentag, Peter J., and Robert L. Jeanne. "Initiation of Absconding-Swarm Emigration in the Social Wasp *Polybia occidentalis.*" *Journal of Insect Science* 9, no. 1 (2009).

Starrfelt, Jostein, and Lee Hsiang Liow. "How Many Dinosaur Species Were There? Fossil Bias and True Richness Estimated Using a Poisson Sampling Model (TRiPS)." *bioRxiv* 25940 (2015): 1–26.

Steadman, David W., Richard Franz, Gary S. Morgan, Nancy A. Albury, Brian Kakuk, Kenneth Broad, Shelley E. Franz, et al. "Exceptionally Well Preserved Late Quaternary Plant and Vertebrate Fossils from a Blue Hole on Abaco, the Bahamas." *Proceedings of the National Academy of Sciences* 104, no. 50 (2007): 19897–19902.

Steadman, David W., Paul S. Martin, Ross D. E. MacPhee, A. J. T. Jull, H. Gregory McDonald, Charles A. Woods, Manuel Iturralde-Vinent, and Gregory W. L. Hodgins. "Asynchronous Extinction of Late Quaternary Sloths on Continents and Islands." *Proceedings of the National Academy of Sciences* 102, no. 33 (2005): 11763–11768.

Steele, Paul Richard, and Catherine J. Allen. *Handbook of Inca Mythology.* Santa Barbara, CA: ABC-CLIO, 2004.

Suárez, William, and Storrs L. Olson. "A New Species of Caracara (*Milvago*) from Quaternary Asphalt Deposits in Cuba, with Notes on New Material of *Caracara creightoni* Brodkorb (Aves: Falconidae)." *Proceedings of the Biological Society of Washington* 116:2 (2003): 301–307.

Suzuki, Shunryu. *Zen Mind, Beginner's Mind: Informal Talks on Zen Meditation and Practice.* 40th anniversary edition. Boston: Shambhala, 2010.

Swick, Nate. "The Top 10: Craziest ABA Area Vagrants of 2016." *ABA Blog,* February 16, 2017, https://www.blog.aba.org.

Tavares, Erika Sendra, Allan J. Baker, Sérgio

Luiz Pereira, and Cristina Yumi Miyaki. "Phylogenetic Relationships and Historical Biogeography of Neotropical Parrots (Psittaciformes: Psittacidae: Arini) Inferred from Mitochondrial and Nuclear DNA Sequences." *Systematic Biology* 55, no. 3 (2006): 454–470.

Thiollay, Jean-Marc. "Foraging, Home Range Use and Social Behaviour of a Group-Living Rainforest Raptor, the Red-Throated Caracara *Daptrius americanus.*" *Ibis* 133, no. 4 (1991): 382–393.

Tomalin, Ruth. *W. H. Hudson: A Biography.* London: Faber and Faber, 1982.

Turner, Alan H., Peter J. Makovicky, and Mark A. Norell. "Feather Quill Knobs in the Dinosaur *Velociraptor.*" *Science* 317, no. 5845 (2007): 1721.

Twain, Mark. *The Adventures of Huckleberry Finn.* New York: Collier, 1884.

Valderrama, Ximena, John G. Robinson, Athula B. Attygalle, and Thomas Eisner. "Seasonal Anointment with Millipedes in a Wild Primate: A Chemical Defense Against Insects?" *Journal of Chemical Ecology* 26, no. 12 (2000): 2781–2790.

Van Den Ende, Conrad, Lloyd T. White, and Peter C. van Welzen. "The Existence and Break-Up of the Antarctic Land Bridge as Indicated by Both Amphi-Pacific Distributions and Tectonics." *Gondwana Research* 44 (2017): 219–227.

Vuilleumier, François. "Generic Relations and Speciation Patterns in the Caracaras (Aves: Falconidae)." *Breviora* 355 (1970): 1–29.

Wallace, Alfred Russel. "A Remarkable Book on the Habits of Animals." *Nature* 45 (1892): 553–556.

Watson, Traci. "Dinosaur Trio Roosted Together Like Birds." *Nature,* August 25, 2017, https://www.nature.com.

Waugh, Evelyn. *A Handful of Dust.* London: Chapman and Hall, 1934.

Weir, Jason T., Eldredge Bermingham, and Dolph Schluter. "The Great American Biotic Interchange in Birds." *Proceedings of the National Academy of Sciences* 106, no. 51 (2009): 21737–21742.

Weldon, Paul J., Jeffrey R. Aldrich, Jerome A. Klun, James E. Oliver, and Mustapha Debboun. "Benzoquinones from Millipedes Deter Mosquitoes and Elicit Self-Anointing in Capuchin Monkeys (*Cebus* spp.)." *Naturwissenschaften* 90, no. 7 (2003): 301–304.

Whittaker, Andrew. "Nesting Records of the Genus *Daptrius* (Falconidae) from the Brazilian Amazon, with the First Documented Nest of the Black Caracara." *Ararajuba* 4, no. 2 (1996): 107–109.

———. "A New Species of Forest Falcon (Falconidae: Micrastur) from Southeastern Amazonia and the Atlantic Rainforests of

Brazil." *Wilson Journal of Ornithology* 114, no. 4 (2002): 421–445.

Wolfe, Roger. "Interview with Rollo Beck Biographer Matt James." *Monterey Seabirding* (blog), Surfbirds, April 11, 2016, http://www.surfbirds.com.

Woolf, Virginia. *The Letters of Virginia Woolf: Volume Two, 1912–1922.* Edited by Nigel Nicolson and Joanne Trautmann. Boston: Mariner Books, 1978.

———. "Mr. Hudson's Childhood." *Times Literary Supplement,* September 26, 1918.

ABOUT THE AUTHOR

In 1997, **Jonathan Meiburg** received a Thomas J. Watson Fellowship to spend a year in remote communities around the world, a journey that sparked his enduring fascination with islands, birds, and the deep history of our planet. Since then he's written reviews, features, and interviews for print and online publications, including *The Believer,* the *Talkhouse Podcast,* and *The Appendix,* on subjects ranging from a hidden exhibit hall at the American Museum of Natural History to the last long-form interview with author Peter Matthiessen. But he's best known as the leader of the band Shearwater, whose albums and performances have been praised by NPR, *The New York Times, The Guardian,* and *Pitchfork.* He lives in central Texas.

The employees of Thorndike Press hope you have enjoyed this Large Print book. All our Thorndike, Wheeler, and Kennebec Large Print titles are designed for easy reading, and all our books are made to last. Other Thorndike Press Large Print books are available at your library, through selected bookstores, or directly from us.

For information about titles, please call:
(800) 223-1244

or visit our website at:
gale.com/thorndike

To share your comments, please write:
Publisher
Thorndike Press
10 Water St., Suite 310
Waterville, ME 04901